A LESSER SPECIES OF HOMICIDE

Dr Kerry King is an Adjunct Research Fellow with Griffith Criminology Institute, Griffith University, Queensland. Her work is interdisciplinary, drawing on law, criminology, socio-legal and historical studies. Kerry was awarded her PhD at the University of Western Australia in 2015. She subsequently won the Margaret Medcalf Award for excellence in referencing and research. *A Lesser Species of Homicide: Death, Drivers and the Law* is her first book.

A LESSER SPECIES OF HOMICIDE

DEATH, DRIVERS AND THE LAW

KERRY KING

First published in 2020 by
UWA Publishing
Crawley, Western Australia 6009
www.uwap.uwa.edu.au

UWAP is an imprint of UWA Publishing,
a division of The University of Western Australia.

This book is copyright. Apart from any fair dealing for the purpose of private study, research, criticism or review, as permitted under the *Copyright Act 1968*, no part may be reproduced by any process without written permission. Enquiries should be made to the publisher.

Copyright © Kerry King 2020

The moral right of the author has been asserted.

ISBN: 978-1-76080-002-4

 A catalogue record for this book is available from the National Library of Australia

Cover design by Alissa Dinallo
Cover image by iStock
Typeset in Bembo by Lasertype
Printed by Lightning Source

 Publication of this book has been assisted by a grant from the Western Australian History Foundation

 uwapublishing

CONTENTS

Table of Cases   vii

Table of Legislation   x

A Note on Sources   xiii

Song Permissions   xiv

Acknowledgements   xv

Introduction   1
Law, 'accidents' and the 'road toll'

Chapter One   17
Manslaughter and negligent driving causing death, 1946–1974
Increasing the scope of liability, conflating the test of negligence

Chapter Two   41
An overview of Supreme Court trials, 1946–1974
Indictments, verdicts and trends in sentencing

Chapter Three   51
Supreme Court trials, 1946–1974
Key emerging themes

Chapter Four   73
One for the road, 1946–1974
Drinking, driving and criminal negligence

CONTENTS

Chapter Five   109
Killing them softly, 1946–1974
The deaths of pedestrians and cyclists

Chapter Six   129
Dangerous driving causing death and the *Road Traffic Act 1974*
Freeing the Crown from the bonds of negligence?

Chapter Seven   161
Reconsidering *Laporte v R* and the maximum imposable penalty,
1970–2004

Chapter Eight   203
Jess' law, 2004
The 0.15% deeming provision, the causative nexus and
aggravated dangerous driving causing death

Chapter Nine   223
After Jess: Reflecting the value of human life?
'Ordinary' versus aggravated dangerous driving causing death

Chapter Ten   239
A new offence – careless driving causing death – and another law
for another girl – Charlotte's law

Conclusion   263
A lesser species of homicide

Appendices   275

   Table A1: Supreme Court indictments, 1946–1974:   278
   Cases of interest with sampled files marked

   Table A2: Convictions and sentences, 1946–1974:   328
   Vehicular manslaughter and negligent driving causing death

   Table A3: Supreme Court indictments, 1975–1981:   351
   Cases of interest with sampled files marked

Notes   361

Select Bibliography   427

Index   443

TABLE OF CASES

(Non-archival, non-restricted access)

Cases appealed to the High Court and Federal Court are listed under the originating jurisdiction. Unreported, restricted access cases held in archives are listed under the State Records Office of Western Australia in the Select Bibliography. Cases drawn from media reports feature in the Notes.

AUSTRALIA

Australian Capital Territory
Crawley v The Queen (1981) 55 FLR 463, (1981) 36 ALR 241

New South Wales
Evans v Sharman [1973] NSWSC, 135 NSW 39, 10 December 1973
Jiminez v R (1992) 173 CLR 572
McBride v R (1966) 115 CLR 44
R v Jurisic (1998) 45 NSWLR 209, (1998) 101 A Crim R 259
R v Wilkins (1988) 38 A Crim R 445
Veen v The Queen (No 1) (1979) 143 CLR 458
Veen v The Queen (No 2) (1988) 164 CLR 465

Queensland
R v Calder; ex parte Attorney General [1987] 1 Qd R 348, (1986) 22 A Crim R 62
R v Warner [1980] Qd R 207
R v Watson [1960] Qd R 332

South Australia
Kroon v The Queen (1990) 55 SASR 476, (1990) 52 A Crim R 15
R v Coventry (1938) 59 CLR 633
R v Snewin (1997) 190 LSJS 487, (1997) 25 MVR 553

TABLE OF CASES

Victoria
King v The Queen (2012) 245 CLR 588
Nydam v The Queen [1977] VR 430

Western Australia
Ainsworth v D (A Child) (1992) 7 WAR 102
Barron v Western Australia (2010) 55 MVR 123
Blair v Semple (1989) 10 MVR 75
Brown v Western Australia (2011) 207 A Crim R 533
Callaghan v R (1952) 87 CLR 115
Campbell v The Queen (1980) 2 A Crim R 157
Clinch v The Queen [1999] WASCA 57
D'Amico v The Queen (2000) 33 MVR 148
Devine v Western Australia (2010) 202 A Crim R 1, (2010) 55 MVR 486
Drage v The Queen (1989) 44 A Crim R 352
English v The Queen (1995) 82 A Crim R 586
Eves v Western Australia (2008) 49 MVR 259
Farmer v Western Australia [2007] WASCA 219
Hodgson v Thomson (1985) 2 MVR 272
Kaighin v The Queen (1990) 1 WAR 390
Kay v The Queen (2004) 147 A Crim R 401, (2004) 42 MVR 130
Kitson v R (1987) 5 MVR 228
Koltasz v The Queen [2003] WASCA 38
Laporte v R [1970] WAR 87
McKenna v The Queen (1992) 7 WAR 455
Mitchell v The Queen (1986) 4 MVR 347
Moore v The Queen (1995) 15 WAR 87
Nickisson v The Queen [1963] WAR 114
Parsons v The Queen (2000) 32 MVR 319
Penny v Western Australia (2006) 33 WAR 48
Phillips v Carbone (No 2) (1992) 10 WAR 169
Punch v The Queen (1993) 9 WAR 486
R v Browne (1985) 2 MVR 135
R v Campbell [No. 2] (1981) 6 A Crim R 208
R v Krakouer (2003) 30 SR (WA) 186
R v Stebbings (1990) 4 WAR 538
R v Street (1986) 4 MVR 156
Smith v The Queen [1976] WAR 97
Taylor v Western Australia (2007) 177 A Crim R 81, (2007) 48 MVR 562
The Queen v S (No 2) (A CHILD) (1992) 7 WAR 434
Western Australia v Butler [2009] WASCA 110

Western Australia v Gibbs (2009) 192 A Crim R 399
Western Australia v Mitchell [2008] WASC 114
Western Australia v Tittums [2018] WASCA 23
White v The Queen (2003) 39 MVR 157
Wicks v The Queen (1989) 3 WAR 372
Wood v The Queen (2002) 130 A Crim R 518

UNITED KINGDOM

Andrews v Director of Public Prosecutions [1937] AC 576
Hill v Baxter (1958) 1 QB 277
R v Bateman (1925) 19 Cr App R 8
R v Cascoe [1970] 2 All ER 833
R v Evans [1963] 1 QB 412
R v Guilfoyle [1973] 2 All ER 844
R v McBride [1962] 2 QB 167
R v Spurge [1961] 2 QB 205
R v Thorpe [1972] 1 WLR 342

TABLE OF LEGISLATION

STATUTES – AUSTRALIA

Australian Capital Territory
Crimes Act 1900

New South Wales
Crimes Act 1900
Crimes (Dangerous Driving Offences) Amendment Act 1994

Northern Territory
Criminal Code Act 1983

Queensland
Criminal Code Act 1899
Criminal Law Amendment Act (No 2) 1982

South Australia
Criminal Law Consolidation Act 1935

Tasmania
Criminal Code Act 1924

Victoria
Crimes Act 1958
Motor Car (Driving Offence) Act 1965

TABLE OF LEGISLATION

Western Australia
Acts Amendment (Road Traffic) Act 1974
Child Welfare Act, 1947
Coroners Act, 1920
Coroners Act 1996
Crime (Serious and Repeat Offenders) Sentencing Act 1992
Criminal Code Act, 1902
Criminal Code Act Compilation Act, 1913
Criminal Code Amendment Act, 1945
Criminal Code Amendment Act, 1972
Criminal Code Amendment Act, (No. 2), 1956
Criminal Code Amendment Act (No. 3), 1977
Criminal Law Amendment Act 1988
Criminal Law Amendment Act 1992
Criminal Law Amendment (Homicide) Act 2008
District Court of Western Australia Act, 1969
Interpretation Act 1984
Justices Act, 1902
Manslaughter Legislation Amendment Act 2011
Offenders Probation and Parole Act, 1963
Prisons Act 1981
Road Traffic Act 1974
Road Traffic Amendment Act (No. 4) 1981
Road Traffic Amendment (Dangerous Driving) Act 2004
Road Traffic Amendment (Driving Offences) Act 2018
Road Traffic Amendment (Random Breath Tests) Act 1988
Road Traffic (Authorisation to Drive) Act 2008
Road Traffic Legislation Amendment Act 2016
Sentencing Act 1995
Sentencing Administration Act 1995 (WA)
Sentencing (Consequential Provisions Act) 1995
Sentencing Legislation Amendment and Repeal Act 2003
Traffic Act, 1919
Traffic Act Amendment Act, 1930
Traffic Act Amendment Act (No. 2), 1968
Traffic Act Amendment Act (No. 3), 1965
Traffic Act Amendment Act (No. 4), 1957

TABLE OF LEGISLATION

SUBSIDIARY LEGISLATION – WESTERN AUSTRALIA

Blood Alcohol Test Regulations, 1958
Blood Sampling and Analysis Regulations, 1966
Breath Analysis Regulations, 1966

OTHER LEGISLATION

Road Traffic Act, 1956 (UK)
Road Transport Act 1930 (UK)
Transport Act 1962 (NZ)

A NOTE ON SOURCES

The State Records Office of Western Australia holds Supreme Court case files which date up until the early 1980s. Case files are restricted for seventy-five years from the date of prosecution and are not available for public viewing. Permission to use restricted access files was granted subject to the protection of individuals' identities. Throughout this book, where court participants were acting in a *professional* capacity, their identities are revealed. In order to protect the identities of defendants, the deceased and other court participants, prosecutions are referred to using the initials of the defendant in order of first, middle and last name, followed by the year of trial, in the standard format of a case name, ie, *R v K.K.* (1973). Pseudonyms are employed throughout the text, not only to uphold the human dimension of the stories, but also for ease of narration.

The Supreme Court's conditions of access inadvertently give rise to what appears to be an anomaly. From the mid-1970s, the book turns its attention to reported cases and newspapers, publicly available documents in which people's names are published and can therefore be cited. The net result is that, bar a handful of cases, from the mid-1970s until 2018, individuals' identities are revealed. Supreme Court cases dating from the mid-1940s to the early 1970s, arguably less sensitive given the time that has elapsed, are conversely subject to privacy restrictions.

Lastly, as part of the metrication process, Australia converted speed limits from miles to kilometres per hour in 1974. Notwithstanding, some cases that came before the courts after this date still tabled evidence and testimony in imperial units of speed.

SONG PERMISSIONS

The author gratefully acknowledges permission to reprint lyrics from the following songs and publishers:

Cars written by Gary Numan © 2018 Gary Numan USA Universe (BMI) All rights reserved. Used by permission. International copyright secured.

Driving Wheels – J. Barnes/D. Roberts/J. Cain © 1987 EMI Music Publishing Australia Pty Limited (ABN 83 000 040 951). Locked Bag 7300, Darlinghurst, NSW 1300. Australia. International copyright secured. All rights reserved. Used by permission.

Driving Wheels – Words and Music by Jonathan Cain, Jimmy Barnes and David Roberts © 1988 Frisco Kid Music (ASCAP) and Chappell & Co. Inc. (ASCAP). All rights on behalf of itself and Frisco Kid Music administered by Chappell & Co. Inc. All rights reserved. Used by permission of Alfred Music.

ACKNOWLEDGEMENTS

Over the course of the last decade I have been the beneficiary of much guidance, encouragement and support, for which I am truly grateful.

First of all, my thanks to the Western Australian History Foundation for supporting the publication of this book. So too, the Women's Service Guild of Western Australia lent much needed financial support during the course of the initial research.

I am more grateful to Associate Professor Lenore Layman than any tribute I could ever conjure. My thanks too, to Professor Rob Stuart for his tireless support through some very choppy waters.

On choppy waters, without Mr Peter Jordan, Dr Noel Murphy and Dr David Holthouse I simply could not have managed. My sincerest gratitude. I am particularly grateful to Peter for providing me with a quiet place to work at the end of this journey and his enormous generosity.

To the staff at the State Records Office of Western Australia (SROWA), thank you for being so accommodating and helpful. To the former Principal Registrar of the Supreme Court of Western Australia, Mr Frederick Chapman, thank you for granting access to Supreme Court records held by SROWA. Without your permission, the first three decades of this book would not have been possible. I also thank Dr Conole for his assistance with police records and Pam Phelan of the Battye Library for her assistance with newspapers. I too thank Gabrielle Knowles, former Chief Crime Reporter of the *West Australian* newspaper.

To friends and colleagues who supported me throughout this long journey and/or brightened its duration, some for the whole nine yards, some for segments, I thank you – Robin France, Anne Brake, Ron Davidson, Stephen Beesley, Anita Field, Hannah King, Jean and Charlie Mason,

ACKNOWLEDGEMENTS

Philip Nikulinsky, Chris Owen and Lisa Wright. I too thank Professor Mark Finnane of Griffith University for his quiet brand of encouragement.

Much gratitude to Terri-ann White, Kelly Somers, Kate Pickard, Ella Hurt and Charlotte Guest of UWA Publishing for taking on a book about death and bringing it to life. Thanks also to Katie Connolly.

And now to the gushy stuff. To my beloved, Juke Maish – without your grace, support, humour, tenderness and culinary skills this book would not have materialised. I know you will understand the entirety of what I mean when I say to you, *olim periculum nunc salus*. And also, our inappropriately anthropomorphised fur child. Little black rose, you know not, but you provided a much needed antidote to my solitude.

Finally this. While the so-called 'road toll' obviously represents lives prematurely lost, critical to this book are those who *did not* suffer the toll of a road, but the toll of a driver. They were not killed by 'accident', or by an agent of bitumen, but by the negligent acts or omissions of others.

I dedicate this book to those people and their surviving loved ones.

Introduction

Law, 'accidents' and the 'road toll'

A chance interaction with one Western Australian police officer was a pivotal moment that, in conjunction with a sequence of events, culminated in the research that led to this book. In December 2003, in the course of an interview with Senior Constable Andrew Ward, I casually remarked, 'but it was an accident'. Senior Constable Ward gently, but firmly corrected me – 'there ain't no such thing as an accident. Someone or something is always at fault'. His observation struck a resounding chord. No such thing as an accident? Until that instant I was not aware of how wedded I was to the notion, even when I *knew* someone or something was at fault. I could not recall the point at which I had taken my accident vows.

I began to reflect on the changes in driving culture in my lifetime. In the 1970s and '80s, at least in *my* 1970s and '80s, it was common for men to drive home drunk after a night at a dinner party, their wives in the passenger seat, their children sleeping in the back in their pyjamas. The primary goal was to get home without being caught by police. It was a treat to sit on my father's lap as a child, a treat frowned upon by my mother, and steer the car while Dad managed the gears and brakes. Despite all the warnings, when my friends and I obtained our licences it was common to speed and, sometimes, drink and drive. The Victorian Transport Accident Commission's inaugural 1989 campaign slogan, which later went national – 'If you drink and drive you're a bloody idiot' – inspired a counter slogan of bravado and machismo. Campaign stickers on cars and a boyfriend's share house fridge were doctored with a telling disclaimer – 'If you drink then drive you're a bloody idiot, But if you make it home you're a bloody legend!'[1] In the goal of making it home, the harm one might do along the way did not register. The distortion of the campaign message gained such popularity that, thirty years later, it is still possible to buy merchandise that bears the doctored slogan.

Once we got our licences we sang along in our cars, wind in our hair, stereos blaring, perhaps going a little too fast. The Triffids' 'Wide Open Road' was a singalong, driving favourite.[2] Another song emblematic of love lost, loneliness and the road, Cold Chisel's 'Flame Trees', assumed anthemic proportions.[3] Our driving songs were not only about broken hearts. The big blue sky, the open road, and the unfettered freedom the vehicle ostensibly offered loomed large in our national psyche, particularly in the Australian masculine psyche. The late Bon Scott could still be heard roaring his vision, 'Highway to Hell', over the radio.[4] Perhaps if you were an AC/DC devotee you might have also sung along to a more melancholy, bluesy Bon repeatedly crooning that he was going to 'Ride On'[5] as a means to deal with his loneliness and self-destructive behaviour.

Songs from other lands that shared our great love affair with the highway and the vehicle also featured in our driving mix cassette tapes. Predictably, we sang along to themes of lust and love – the call of 'Radar Love' could compel a man to drive all night.[6] Driving was also love gone wrong – The Cars' ballad 'Drive' famously exemplified the theme.[7] It was also a ticket to

INTRODUCTION

existential freedom and escape, surrendering fully to the inevitable, whether that be ecstatic joy, the unknown, death or suicide – The Smiths' 'There is a Light That Never Goes Out' was rewound and played again.[8] On self-annihilation, Kiss' 'Detroit Rock City' hit the theme right on the head.[9] The song told the tale of a speeding, heedless drunk driver, on his way to a gig at midnight, music blaring, doing 95 mph. The protagonist died in a collision with an oncoming truck. While the song might have been held as a cautionary tale, its parable was long lost in its rock-anthem popularity. As in Australia, other recurrent dominant driving themes prevailed.

Like our parents, we too sang along to Steppenwolf's 'Born to be Wild'[10] – not the strongest road safety message. From a handful of random overseas examples, many that graced our nostalgic cassette tapes – ZZ Top's 'Arrested for Driving While Blind', Sammy Hagar's 'I Can't Drive 55', Eagles' 'Take it Easy', Metallica's 'Fuel', Jackson Browne's 'Running on Empty', The Doobie Brothers' 'Rockin' Down the Highway', Van Halen's 'Panama', Meat Loaf's 'Bat Out of Hell' and Mötley Crüe's 'Kickstart My Heart' – it was clear that, right across the spectrum, driving was entwined with a particular kind of masculine freedom, in addition to rebellion, risk and, often, sex.[11] Women were sometimes invited along for the ride, but it was often difficult to separate the woman from the machinery or the action of driving it. Sexual intercourse and reckless, fast driving became figuratively interchangeable – Deep Purple's 'Highway Star', Led Zeppelin's 'Trampled Underfoot' and Prince's 'Little Red Corvette' being prime examples.[12] On the other hand, some men professed their love for their car above any romantic or sexual relationship, Queen's 'I'm in Love with My Car' being a standout example.[13] Driving was also firmly bound with the quest for emancipation. More than fifteen years after its release, we too sang along to Springsteen's 'Born to Run',[14] a young man's entreaty to his girlfriend to escape a town in decline and a future devoid of hope. Liberation, autonomy, desire and the promise of enduring love were all enmeshed with the vehicle, at once instrument of both freedom and death. In the 1970s, vehicular metaphors seemed to be a preoccupation of Springsteen's, with 'Thunder Road' and 'Racing in the Street' reiterating the theme of men's quest for freedom via the open road.[15] Like the majority of cases brought before the courts, these were all principally masculine narratives.

Back on Australian shores, songs of male emancipation poured forth from our radios. In the late 1980s, Jimmy Barnes, like countless others, would offer up the quintessential working class hero's quest for freedom in *Freight Train Heart's* 'Driving Wheels', a song capitalising on the archetypal Australian male, the solitude of the road and, in this instance, his truck.[16] For Barnes' handsome, muscular young truckie, it was the 'rhythm of the highway, as he rolls on down, and city lights as they fade from sight', which 'drives the man behind the driving wheels'. Country music played on the radio and his engine roared 'like a shooting star across a desert sky'. Apparently, if the truckie had a home, it was 'out on the blue horizon', because 'heaven only knows, there's still a rebel in his soul'.[17] Said rebellious truck driver also left motel rooms and broken hearts behind in favour of the highway. As much as I might have fantasised as a teenager, I was not leaving any broken hearts behind, particularly in a truck with a 'Rage with a Raunchy Lady sticker' on the rear window, a sticker I trust many West Australian readers will recall. I was more your 'Magic Happens' sticker kind of girl, with beach shells and feathers spread across the dashboard of my first car, a Mini. As a teenager, I regret to confess, I did like to put my foot down. In that respect, it was altogether possible that I too could have left a trail of broken hearts behind, albeit of an altogether different variety.

Many years later, when I had shed the magic and the Mini, I could not shed Senior Constable Ward's observation. In contrast to the highway anthems, I began to consider the dark side of the motor vehicle, the human cost and 'accidents'. It was not that the costs had failed to cross my mind before, it was just that I had probably considered the so-called 'road toll' part of what Roger

Browning once called 'a low grade war that nobody cares much for',[18] had I considered it at all. I had certainly not given much thought to 'accidents' as a form of crime. Statistics and road safety campaigns seemed to breed apathy and detachment. After that chance interaction with Senior Constable Ward, I became alert to issues that were seemingly ubiquitous but, in spite of the relentless efforts of road safety campaigners, I had failed to see them. Irrespective of the fact that I drove every day, the issues apparently had little, if anything, to do with me. I had failed to absorb the unwitting truth of Gary Numan's synthesised, metallic, catchy assertion that 'nothing seems right in cars'.[19] Indeed, nothing did. I noted our driving passions and culture on one hand and, on the other, roadsides littered with memorials to the dead.

I can only liken the revelation to the purchase of a new car. Once you set your heart on a particular model, suddenly that model seems to be everywhere. After that interaction with Senior Constable Ward, the issues seemed to be everywhere I turned. They were front-page news. People brought before the courts on driving-causing-death and manslaughter charges; stricken, bereaved loved ones outraged by sentences; 'road toll' statistics published after every Easter long weekend and Christmas; booze buses, random breath tests, double-demerit points on public holidays; and everywhere the persistent use of the term 'accident'. It was a term frequently accompanied by 'tragedy'. It was *tragic* that a young man killed his girlfriend or his mates. When I began this research back in 2008, the term *crime* was often speciously absent.

According to bereaved loved ones, the law was an ass, a veritable donkey, a criticism which reverberates across the research of grassroots organisations, psychology and public health scholarship. A grievance recurrent across that literature, a grievance that appears to have no regard for national borders, is that surviving loved ones are invariably deeply dismayed by what they perceive to be lenient penalties and the simultaneous socio-legal characterisation of the offence that precipitated their loved one's death as something less than criminal.[20] I wondered, in the nexus between law and society, was this alleged donkey up against some peculiar difficulties.

In its *Faces behind the figures*, the World Health Organization (WHO), in conjunction with the Association for Safe International Road Travel (ASIRT), drew attention to these perceived injustices.[21] Contributors expressed anger about high rates of acquittal and paltry sentences. Closer to home, one of Lauren Breen's interviewees, a West Australian victim support worker, noted that families felt 'aggrieved' by sentencing outcomes. Surviving loved ones claimed that those convicted of other forms of homicide 'would almost certainly and invariably suffer a penalty of imprisonment', but in the case of road crashes, non-custodial sentences were common.[22] In 1995, the European Federation of Road Traffic Victims observed that the foremost frustration of survey respondents concerned criminal proceedings – 89 per cent of families of those killed claimed justice was not done. A further 75 per cent said that charges were unfair, meaning minor.[23]

More than twenty years later, newspapers continue to report the same grievance. A double-paged spread in the *West Australian* in late March 2017 saw Wayne Pemberton initially call for a minimum ten-year custodial term under the banner of a proposed 'Charlotte's law'. His daughter Charlotte was killed in 2015.[24] The speeding driver responsible for Charlotte's death was given a head sentence of four years and three months, with a non-parole period of just over two years. He was not licensed to drive a motorbike.[25] Wayne and Jackie Pemberton were 'gutted' that the State would not appeal against the sentence.[26] Premier Mark McGowan and Police Minister Michelle Roberts told the media the sentence was 'completely out of kilter' with community expectations.[27] It was *not*, however, out of kilter with sentencing trends. By contrast, the Tasmanian Sentencing Advisory Council recently described the public's response to perceived lenient penalties as 'punitive', and indicated that such misguided responses were linked with 'myths and misconceptions about crime and justice'.[28] To put the public's apparently misguided, punitive response in perspective, the community were outraged when 24-year-old Sarah Paino was killed by a 16-year-old male. He was driving a stolen vehicle at speeds of up to 110 km/h with his headlights off in downtown, inner city Hobart. He ran a red light. Some time before the crash, he had been involved in a high-speed police chase. Paramedics were able to keep Sarah alive long enough to deliver her baby. She left behind two children and a husband. The driver was sentenced to five years' imprisonment. Public outrage turned around the fact that he was made eligible for parole after two-and-a-half years.[29] The Sentencing Advisory Council claimed that public disquiet about sentences for drivers was indicative of a misplaced expectation that the punishment should reflect the tragedy of the loss of human life, rather than the culpability of the conduct. Arguably, in the instance of Sarah Paino's death, the level of fault in the manner of the driving was particularly high.

Notwithstanding, weren't loved ones typically aggrieved by sentences, or, in the case of 'road deaths', did they have a legitimate point? When a death was occasioned by the use of a motor vehicle, *was* it treated as a much lesser species of homicide? On the face of it, it appeared so. Vehicular homicide seemed to be a species apart. Bar the most aberrant circumstances, typically involving a stolen vehicle, a high-speed chase, and a drunken, disqualified driver on methamphetamines, the whole issue seemed to suffer the characterisation of not being *real* crime or *real* violence, albeit of the unintended or recklessly indifferent variety. The not *real* crime characterisation has, in fact, a long history dating back to the early twentieth century.[30] Clearly, this was a form of unlawful killing slow to capture the public's imagination, unlike murders, serial killings and even one-punch deaths, never mind the greater social costs involved. Vehicular homicide seemed to be just part of the banal, daily parade. However, in the time that has elapsed since Senior Constable Ward's remarks, its status as a crime appears to have increased.

Given the changes in driving culture in my own lifetime, I began to wonder how the law had evolved to deal with deaths occasioned by the use of motor vehicles, when judgments about risk and culpable conduct by their very nature must hinge on society's shifting perceptions of the *quality* of that conduct. If the very small snapshots of evidence from other jurisdictions dating as far back as the early twentieth century were accurate, regarding want of prosecution of drivers, the staggering over-representation of vulnerable road users in fatality statistics, high rates of acquittal and egregious sentences,[31] were these isolated examples or were they indicative of a more entrenched, systemic phenomena? Were the claims of living in a 'nanny state', driver vilification and punitive prosecution valid,[32] or was it the case that drivers had been treated with 'reckless leniency'?[33] There was no diachronic study available to answer my questions.

To date, no longitudinal research has been undertaken on legal responses to deaths occasioned by the use of motor vehicles in Australia. While some of the secondary literature includes small snapshots of prosecution outcomes, there has been, as Australian commentators have noted, a dearth of investigation concerning the prosecution of deaths on the road over time.[34] In fact, regarding the frequent assertion that driving-causing-death offences were introduced because juries were reluctant to convict drivers of manslaughter, both the Law Reform Commission of Victoria and legal scholar Douglas Brown have noted that the proposition has never been empirically tested; a deficit that this book addresses.[35] Legal practitioner texts tend to dispassionately cover driving-causing-death and manslaughter charges in a handful of pages.[36] Various law reform commissions and sentencing advisory bodies have made some small contributions to the field.[37] Equally, analogous diachronic studies do not appear to have been undertaken in other countries – curious given the subject's daily relevance to all road users and the number of people killed to date.

Almost every book that touches on the motor vehicle includes a set of sobering fatality statistics. This is no exception. Yet, fatalities are often quickly abandoned following the introductory remarks or, alternatively, their repetition leads to what Cooter and Luckin called a 'statistical normalization' of the carnage.[38] Dismantling that normalisation, particularly with respect to questions of criminal liability, has not been a significant aspect of discourse surrounding the motor vehicle, particularly historico-legal discourse. This book addresses that neglect.

Between 1925, when Australian authorities first began collating national fatality statistics, and the year 2000, official reports indicate that nearly 200,000 people died, or were killed on Australian roads.[39] By the end of 2018, more than 25,000 people had joined that bleak figure.[40] The addition of fatality statistics from the car's introduction to Australia in 1896,[41] were the numbers available, would elevate the official figures appreciably.[42] Furthermore, there were considerable problems with the under-reporting of fatalities in the mid-twentieth century, cause for complaint by Commonwealth statisticians.[43] Of additional indication that the figures do not adequately represent the number of deaths, Northern Territory fatalities were not included in national statistics prior to 1962.[44] Moreover, the numbers represent only those who died within thirty days of the crash. Those who died after the thirtieth day have been excluded from the death count.[45]

Worldwide, the extent of the carnage is alarming. In 1997, Nicholas Faith estimated that 25 million people had been killed since the first British fatality in 1896.[46] The World Health Organization described Faith's estimate as conservative.[47] In 2004, WHO estimated global fatalities at 1.2 million people per year,[48] and by 2018 that estimate had jumped to 1.35 million.[49] Based on these collective figures, upwards of 50 million people have died or been *killed* on the roads. Globally, 'road traffic injuries', as WHO terms them, are the *leading* cause of death for 5–29 year olds and the eighth leading cause of death across all age groups.[50] Almost 60 per cent of those fatally injured are aged between fifteen and forty-four.[51] On average, pedestrians, cyclists and motorcyclists represent around 50 per cent of all deaths.[52] Males are overly represented in fatality statistics, at approximately 77 per cent.[53] They also dominate in terms of those brought before the courts.

Vehicular homicide is predominantly a male crime, although women are now joining the ranks in increasing numbers. WHO anticipated that worldwide, by 2030, 'road traffic injury' will be the fifth leading cause of death.[54]

While statistics play a crucial role in attempts to capture and monitor trends, the enormous amount of quantitative data does not reflect the emotional toll on victims, their families and loved ones.[55] As early as 1935, American freelance writer Joseph Furnas noted that the trouble with the aggregate expression of 'road deaths' was detachment – 'figures exclude the pain and horror of savage mutilation – which means they leave out the point'.[56] He compassionately observed that 'each shattered man, woman or child' who made up the tally of last year's fatalities died a very 'personal death'.[57] Furnas' observation is a recurrent one. In his reflections on the difficulties involved in making effective road safety campaigns that might penetrate the hearts and minds of the driving public, Australian advertising executive and media personality Todd Sampson accurately noted in 2008, 'when one person dies it's a tragedy, but if thousands die it just becomes statistics'.[58]

Statistics have their downsides. Not only does the aggregate statistical representation of deaths on the road tend to breed indifference, it also shuts down important questions. Linguistic subterfuges such as 'road death' and 'road toll' homogenise all deaths on the road as equal based on a shared highway and vehicle. That equivalence is not typically applied to other deaths where criminal liability might be at stake. Critically, many decedents represented in the 'road toll' are not tolls of the road at all – they are in fact the toll of drivers. In many instances, they are also victims of crime. The point is, not all deaths on the road are the same. On the roads, *some* people endanger and kill others. Questions of causation, agency and liability are three of homogeny's foremost casualties. As Robert Davis rightly emphasised, people feel it important to distinguish between 'those hurting' from 'those who get hurt'.[59] Tellingly, according to the 1946 Commonwealth Year book, the year in which this book's trial analyses commences, ninety Australian deaths were reported as 'homicides', whereas 1,206 were classified as 'automobile accidents'.[60] In cases where an individual is at fault for another's death, the distinction between the two categories is one to be questioned.

It follows too that the 'road toll' also obscures human agency. The widespread use of phrases such as 'road traffic death', as though the road and traffic collectively precipitate mortality, is another mechanism by which human agency is obscured. The Victorian Transport Accident Commission's compelling campaign, 'Pictures of You', challenged the persistent use of such phrases. Significantly, rather than use actors, the television advertisement featured bereaved loved ones.[61] During the course of the piece, two short messages were flashed against a black background, made poignant by an almost thirty-second interval of close-up shots of individuals, some crying. The first statement – 'Speeding drivers are the biggest killers on our roads' – was followed by an interval of visible sorrow and the corollary – 'This is why you're photographed when you speed'. Identical language underscored the message at the conclusion, where twelve photographs of decedents were consecutively shown with their name, age and year they were 'killed'. Some legal scholars eschew characterisations of the conduct as 'killing', preferring to describe drivers as 'causers of death'.[62] To some degree, 'causer of death' devalues perceptions of the harm on the grounds that the harm was unintended, a long-term impediment to vehicular homicide's status as a crime. Drivers may not *intend* to harm anyone in particular, but often demonstrate callous indifference to all other road users and the possible, and often likely, consequences of their conduct.

In Australia, vehicular manslaughter sits at the bottom of the fault hierarchy of intention, knowledge and recklessness, as criminal negligence. Intention's stronghold on the apex of criminality is generally considered uncontroversial. Yet, reckless indifference to the lives and safety of others, particularly when in charge of a dangerous object in a public thoroughfare, arguably represents a challenge to received notions of blameworthiness. David Luria has argued that the prosecution of some drivers for 'depraved heart' murder in the United States,[63] or murder based in subjective knowledge of danger, is appropriate in that recklessness demonstrates such disregard for human life as to be on a par with murder. Although malice may not be intentional, it might be implied by unmitigated indifference.[64] Stanley Yeo observed that recklessness' status as more culpable than negligence is regarded in some quarters as controversial, simplistic and an untenable 'adherence to a subjectivist theory of fault'.[65] In 1991, the Law Reform Commission of Victoria suggested that, for the most part, drivers should be charged with reckless murder and involuntary manslaughter, rather than alternative, lesser offences such as culpable driving.[66] Apart from Germany, where drivers engaged in illegal drag-racing have been found guilty of murder, such arguments have fallen on deaf ears.[67] In Australia, 'alternative' driving-causing-death offences dominate the prosecution landscape.

Historically, that the fatal consequences were unintended had a tremendous impact in shoring up vehicular homicide's disputed status as a real and very serious crime, the residual notion of 'accident' presenting its own peculiar set of difficulties. In 1946, Western Australia's Royal Automobile Club (RAC) endeavoured to re-educate its members that, 'accidents don't happen, they are caused'.[68] In 1960, Professor Lewis told the Commonwealth Senate Select Committee of Inquiry into Road Safety that 'civilised society had never really faced the problem of road injury and fatality and deplored the use of the word "accident" with its connotation of inevitability'.[69] From the 1970s, there were widespread calls from the medical profession to abandon the term altogether and growing recognition of its dubious implications.[70] Thankfully, 'accident' has increasingly fallen out of use in investigatory contexts. In 1994, the Western Australian Police unit responsible for investigating fatal crashes was renamed 'Major Crash Investigation',[71] in contrast to the once 'Fatal Accident Squad' and the 'Major Accident Inquiry Section'. In 2004, almost half a century after Professor

Lewis' frustrated observations, the World Health Organization declared a preference for the word 'crash' in that it denoted amenability to investigation and corrective, preventative action.[72] Notwithstanding, the notion of the 'accident' still holds some currency — the idiom has been almost unshakeable.

The cultural neutralisation of crashes as 'accidents' displaces causation and prevention in favour of random inexplicability, absolving drivers as victims of chance rather than, in some instances, perpetrators of varying degrees of fault. 'Accident' implies the absence of foreseeable risk, situating deaths as the result of bad luck, in turn neutralising human agency. Far from being neutral or fixed, the characterisation 'accident' is 'historically contingent',[73] bound by shifting socio-legal judgments about what constitutes risk, causation and liability. Over time, the enduring notion of the 'accident' presented a significant hurdle for prosecutors who were at pains to displace the belief that, simply because the consequence was unintended, did not mean it was neither foreseeable nor culpable. Court participants grappled with the point at which they would be persuaded from the belief that to err is human, and shift to grade that error criminal.

Public health scholars and psychologists have complained that 'road deaths' have been primarily treated as a legal issue rather than a public health issue,[74] a complaint which seems to be without substance. Arguably, for the most part, 'road deaths' have been characterised as a *road safety* issue. Yet, deaths on the road cannot be solely rationalised as a preventative safety matter requiring better funding, better research, better roads and better cars. It is a 'seductive' proposition that deaths can be circumvented by design, while simultaneously circumnavigating drivers' core values and behaviours.[75] As Ball-Rokeach and others have similarly noted, the best-engineered transport system cannot achieve its full potential if existing socio-cultural forces function to the contrary. Neither can the policing of traffic offences if 'the informal driving subculture' works to 'undermine formal driving rules and regulations'.[76] Importantly, 90 to 95 per cent of crashes are attributed to human error.⁷⁷ This book examines *degrees* of human error, the construction of offences to target those degrees, and traces the points and extent to which, over time, the judiciary and community have labelled those degrees culpable.

It is perplexing too that said critics complain of undue emphasis on legal responses. Simultaneously they bemoan the fact that unsatisfactory investigative processes and legal outcomes have the adverse effect of diminishing society's perception of the seriousness of vehicular homicide, devalue the lives of people killed, and compound the minimisation of the public health emergency that injuries and fatalities represent.⁷⁸ If, in fact, unsatisfactory legal outcomes are further augmenting the minimisation of the crisis, then exploring how and why these outcomes occur is imperative.

In contemporary scholarship, the longstanding not *real* crime impediment continues to be observed. Dr Claire Corbett of Brunel Law School noted that serious traffic offences are rarely conceptualised as 'real' crime, or offenders 'real' criminals.⁷⁹ Corbett observed many barriers to criminal status, including the normalisation of risk-taking and correlations to constructions of masculinity, difficulties around intentional harm versus indifference, and neoliberal ideology that fortifies car culture and society's dependence on the motor vehicle, while simultaneously buttressing the minimisation of 'traffic' offences.⁸⁰ For the most part, Corbett noted, deaths on the road have been positioned as a 'traffic' problem, rather than a *crime* problem.⁸¹ University of Leicester's Professor of Law, Sally Kyd (formerly Cunningham and Kyd-Cunningham) has complained of the neglect of car or traffic crime by legal scholars. Both Kyd and Corbett partly attribute this neglect to the flawed, yet pervasive idea that crimes involving vehicles are not *real* criminal offences, but rather are positioned as 'quasi crime', and are thus perceived less worthy of attention.⁸² Such landmark studies that have emerged from the UK tend to focus on a spectrum of offences including speeding, drink-drinking, driving while under disqualification and vehicle theft, where homicide charges are but one of many chapters. The scholarship is primarily concerned with the law as it stands at present.[83] This book complements that scholarship by examining the law's response to deaths occasioned by the use of motor vehicles over more than seventy years, right up to the present, and distinguishes itself in that alleged unlawful killings are its primary focus.

While this is a West Australian story, it is also a story of national and international import. As this book explores matters germane worldwide, its significance is far greater than its geography. The analysis has been limited to Western Australia, not only because of the sheer volume of cases involved, but because driving-causing-death offences vary subtly across Australia and internationally, although, where relevant, cross-jurisdictional observations are made. This book explores the way in which the Western Australian legislature, police, prosecutors and courts responded to deaths occasioned by the use of motor vehicles between 1946 and 2018. It concerns itself only with cases that have come before the courts. It is clear that, until most recently, a driver's conduct had to be *particularly* serious in order to be charged, although what constitutes *serious* has dramatically evolved over time. The year 1946 is taken as the starting point as a moment of major legislative change and 2018 heralded yet another. Much transpired in between.

The nexus of 'road death' and criminal liability has been a neglected subject, a subject that demands investigation as the principal site where socio-legal questions of causation, agency and liability are determined. As Davis once noted, legal discourse is the space where 'society articulates its assumptions about what kind of behaviour is permissible, and why, in the road environment'.[84] Accordingly, this book examines the development, construction and application of vehicular homicide offences over time, paying close attention to parliamentary debates, the emerging case law, judicial reasoning, verdicts and sentences, individual cases and the lives of the people contained therein. Given that the bereaved report that their loved ones' deaths and their grief are subject to a unique form of socio-legal minimisation, one hopes that in the process of examining prosecution outcomes and paying attention to the lives of the people affected, the living are in part supported by valuing the dead,[85] albeit belatedly. The inclusion of individual stories in this book aims to retrieve lived experience from the margins of the 'road toll's' homogeny. Still, the purpose is not simply to lament all lives lost, injuries sustained and hearts broken, although compassion does underpin the investigation. Importantly, this book does not hold that all deaths on the road should be the subject of criminal censure, although too few have been. Such a position would be punitive.

Importantly, this is not a book about the motor vehicle. It is not a book about road safety. Plenty of those have been written. It is an historico-legal study of responses to deaths *occasioned* by the use of motor vehicles. It explores how our weddedness to the machine, to speed, to constructions of masculinity, to drinking and driving, and to the notion of 'accident' intersected with the legal concepts of intention, negligence, dangerousness and, most recently, carelessness, to affect judgments about drivers' conduct. It provides a revealing, if not alarming, forensic examination of trends in sentencing over a seventy-year period. Criminal charges, if laid, are the locus where the core tensions of 'death' versus 'killing' converge. They are the contest between the 'toll of the road' versus 'toll of the driver', and 'accident' versus causation. This investigation goes beyond the repeated contention that the law is an ass – an altogether insufficient explanation – to examine the law in practice.

Chapter One

Manslaughter and negligent driving causing death, 1946–1974

Increasing the scope of liability, conflating the test of negligence

In Western Australia (WA), negligence was the first benchmark employed to determine whether a driver could be convicted for the death of another road user. It remained the yardstick until the introduction of the *Road Traffic Act* in 1974. However, whether on a charge of manslaughter or the alternative offence, negligent driving causing death, what constituted negligence was far from straightforward. This was not only because of the complexity around what constituted 'reasonable' driving conduct. It was compounded by the judgment of the High Court of Australia in *Callaghan v R* in 1952, which in effect rendered the difference between the two offences moot.[1]

In the mid-1940s, more than forty years after the first car was unloaded at Western Australia's port of Fremantle, the WA Parliament introduced a new, intermediate homicide offence under the *Criminal Code Act Compilation Act*, 1913 ('the Criminal Code'/'the Code') to target drivers.[2] Deaths occasioned by the use of motor vehicles had long presented difficulties for prosecutors. Prior to 1946, drivers could be charged only with manslaughter.

If, on the evidence, a charge could not be made out, or the prosecution anticipated a conviction unlikely, a raft of minor charges were often brought in lieu under the State's *Traffic Act, 1919* ('the Traffic Act').[3] In 1945 the Parliament passed an amendment to the Code, introducing a new offence, commonly referred to as negligent driving causing death or s 291A, and sometimes, erroneously, as dangerous or reckless driving causing death. South Australia had introduced an alternative offence to vehicular manslaughter some eighteen years prior. The Northern Territory introduced an alternative offence in 1940 and Queensland in 1943. Victoria and New South Wales notably lagged behind.[4]

Introduced as a private member's Bill, the amendments took effect as of 30 January 1946. November 1945, the month of the Bill's introduction, was a low point, with 289 reported crashes and ten fatalities in the Perth metropolitan area alone,[5] significant numbers for a small city. There were 106 reported fatalities in WA in 1946; ninety-three males and thirteen females.[6] While 106 people were killed or died, only three people were brought before the Supreme Court.[7] Deaths on the road far outnumbered prosecutions.

At the time of the introduction of the new offence, manslaughter attracted a maximum term of life imprisonment. The advent of negligent driving causing death increased the scope of culpable fault behind the wheel and provided prosecutors with an alternative offence, ostensibly easier to prove. It also gave juries the option of delivering an alternative verdict with a markedly lower penalty.[8] The Shadow Attorney General, Ross McDonald, claimed that the amendment would empower the courts to deal with a mounting social problem. The intention of the legislature was to enable a jury to bring in a verdict of either manslaughter or s 291A, according to the seriousness of the conduct. The new offence was not designed to exclude a charge of manslaughter. It was intended to provide a mechanism to ensure that drivers who killed were 'adequately punished'.[9] Adequate punishment was not borne out by trial outcomes over the following decades.

MANSLAUGHTER AND NEGLIGENT DRIVING CAUSING DEATH

On the face of it, the motivation for the introduction of s 291A was simple – juries were apparently reluctant to convict drivers charged with manslaughter. Exposure to a maximum possible sentence of life imprisonment, a term never remotely approached, was seen as a severe punishment for an unintended killing and thus drivers were escaping punishment under the existing provisions.[10] MP Hubert Parker noted that, in his professional experience at the Crown Law Department, juries would not convict drivers unless their conduct was most severe.[11] However, serious conduct was invariably insufficient to secure a conviction. Drivers were getting off 'scot-free', because, in the absence of a lesser charge, there was no available mechanism whereby they could be held to account.[12] The amendments would net drivers who were otherwise slipping through the cracks in the criminal law. But, beyond the laudable attempt to provide a mechanism to prosecute those whose negligent acts or omissions had caused a death, but whose conduct fell short of criminal negligence, something curious had occurred – deaths occasioned by the use of motor vehicles were set apart. This was not exclusive to Western Australia. A wave of driving-causing-death offences were introduced across common law countries between the 1940s and the 1960s. However, the construction of s 291A and its interpretation by the High Court of Australia led to an inimitable situation.

Numerous commentators, in Australia and overseas, have upheld the reasoning that driving-causing-death offences were introduced because of juries' reluctance to label drivers 'manslayers'[13] and rather to commiserate with them. It is a view that has been repeated time and again as an unshakeable fact.[14] This apparent historical phenomenon of juror reluctance and concomitant empathy has been most frequently described as a matter of 'there but for the grace of God go I'. According to 'grace of God' logic, jurors would struggle to identify with an alleged murderer, armed robber or sex offender, but they readily related to the 'poor unfortunate driver' in the dock, the seeming victim of a chance event, 'accident' or tragic twist of fate. Indeed, some judges went as far as to caution jurors against sympathetic impulses. In 1965 Justice Negus warned – 'I do impress upon you though, that you must consider all the evidence fairly, and reach a true verdict, and particularly do not allow your verdict to be influenced by the possibility that the same thing may happen to you some day'.[15]

To date, there has been a lack of evidence to support the claim that driving-causing-death offences were introduced because of juries' reluctance to find drivers guilty of manslaughter.[16] Crown Law Department correspondence dated between the early 1930s and 1945 points to a disproportionate number of not guilty verdicts and reluctance to pursue prosecutions because of the high rate of acquittals.[17] Recent data made available lends weight to the impressions gleaned from that correspondence. Between 1915 and 1944, of 144 people prosecuted for vehicular manslaughter in Western Australia, there were only thirty convictions.[18] Yet, the explanation typically offered for this apparent trend, 'there but for the grace of God', is an oversimplification.

Prior to and following the introduction of negligent driving causing death, verdicts cannot be adequately explained by the simple contention that, across the board, jurors put their driverly bias ahead of any other consideration. An array of complex factors goes unrecognised in that simple account. There was significant alarm and, in some quarters, hysteria about the mounting carnage in the mid to late twentieth century. In response, safety organisations and education programmes were established right around the country, indeed right across the world. Published by the State's Royal Automobile Club (RAC), 'An open letter to a hit and run driver' cautioned that it would be impossible to escape one's memory or conscience, there being no excuse for cowardice.[19] The WA Citizens' Road Safety Association ordered the community to 'STOP accepting our Road Toll as inevitable'.[20] One campaign posed a more ominous warning – 'You are culpable…If you cause deaths, the blood, the curse of Cain is on your head'.[21] The Australian Road Safety Council employed an unambiguous strategy – 'AFTER SUNDOWN SLOW DOWN: DEATH IS SO PERMANENT'.[22] The Minister for Police and the Police Commissioner were inundated with letters from the public, offering suggestions on how to end the bloodshed and advocating severe punishments for those responsible.[23]

The West Australian National Safety Council took a direct approach, erecting a laconic neon warning on top of the Barracks Arch in Perth – 'TAKE IT EASY. SPEED KILLS'.[24] In the late 1950s, the Safety Council and the R & I Bank erected a massive obelisk-shaped neon beacon on top of the R & I Bank in Perth that burnt blue every time a person died on WA roads. In 1964, the light was changed so that the beacon shone a hopeful green on fatality-free days and a portentous red when a road user died. The colour change was accompanied by a new slogan – 'Don't let the BEACON burn RED'.[25] In the Supreme Court, defendants' representatives tried to downplay the beacon's ominous message, suggesting that jurors should put it out of their minds because the 'build up in atmosphere against road fatalities' might affect their capacity to assess the evidence objectively.[26] Concern about the 'road toll' was so grave in some quarters that consideration was given to putting the military on the roads as special constables.[27] Community anxiety and campaign messages seem at odds with the trend towards absolving drivers.

Then again, target audiences are often slow to assimilate campaign messages. In the late 1960s, the WA Police Commissioner described the difficulty in affecting change in drivers' attitudes as trying to 'awaken the motoring public to a responsibility which at present appears non-existent'.[28] Research on drivers' attitudes demonstrates that they have consistently tended to think that road safety messages are intended for someone other than themselves. Participants who took part in the 1979 Australian pilot study for the Cronin campaign expressed concern about 'idiots' on the road, while simultaneously admitting that they often drove whilst drunk, conduct which they ironically failed to deem as either idiotic or a source of potential harm.[29] In the 1980s, Terry's Australian research revealed that drivers believed that road safety messages were intended for 'all the other mugs on the road'.[30] In the 1990s, Davis noted that drivers tend to judge themselves as more capable and more skilled than others.[31] Little has changed. More recently, Corbett's findings in the UK indicate that such attitudes remain remarkably persistent – bad drivers are 'other drivers'.[32] Given the enduring trend towards blaming others, it is interesting that verdicts between the mid-1940s and the mid-1970s, explored in the following chapters, do not reflect a sense of transposed censure.

While 'the grace of God' likely had some impact on verdicts, what constituted a crime as opposed to an 'accident' was a greater sticking point. When drivers *were* found guilty, juries often recommended mercy, even in cases involving very high degrees of negligent conduct. Judges too sympathised with the weight of responsibility defendants might bear for unintentionally causing the death of another person, although that sympathy declined as the twentieth century wore on. The prevalence of deaths occasioned by the use of motor vehicles and the fact that drivers came from all walks of life presented a challenge to conventional notions of crime as deviant, atypical and predominantly working class.

Judges also grappled with vehicular homicide's status in the hierarchy of criminality. In the mid-1970s, when Australia's 'road toll' reached an all time high, Justice Jones diminished its criminal status, while simultaneously emphasising its gravity.

> Manslaughter in these circumstances (which is usually called "vehicle manslaughter") is a crime which is constituted by conduct which is not considered in the ordinary sense criminal conduct (in the same sense that crimes such as rape and robbery are criminal conduct). Nevertheless, in its effects, of course it is as serious as they are.[33]

The problem too had other dimensions. An allied issue lay in the community's indifference to, or partial acceptance of, risk-taking behaviours that were a major factor in crash causation, most particularly drinking and driving. From the mid-twentieth century, road safety campaigns tried to impress upon drivers that drinking and driving would result in crashes, injury and death as a matter of statistical probability. Community attitudes were slow to shift.

A constellation of competing values influenced verdicts and the penalties judges imposed. The car had fast become a symbol of social standing and concurrent utility – a liberating form of mobility bound in social aspirations. Masculinity, drink-driving, speed and risk-taking were for many synonymous and normative. Crashes were frequently framed as the tragic consequence of the impetuosity of youth, rather than unlawful conduct. Non-motorised road users were increasingly marginalised by the vehicle's mounting hegemony. The science of crash causation was only gradually gaining currency. Medicos and scientists struggled to gain community acceptance that alcohol consumption impaired driving ability. The community was slow to relinquish the notion of the 'accident'. Verdicts bore a relationship to this mosaic of factors. Court participants struggled to define which driving behaviours they would label *criminal* and those they considered 'accidental', careless or the consequence of youthful foolishness. In *R v F.F.* (1963) the Crown noted the importance of societal standards when deliberating on degrees of negligence – 'you are the community and it is for you to say what you think is the degree of negligence which you think you would call "gross" and susceptible of punishment'.[34]

The absence of intention made it difficult to secure convictions. Drivers had not set out to hurt anyone. It was not that jurors were unfamiliar with 'accidents'; they had certainly seen workplace injuries and deaths. Unlike other forms of homicide, court participants' assessment of drivers' conduct was compounded by the fact that they were part of the burgeoning transport system in which those deaths occurred. Never before had such a specific species of alleged unlawful killing dominated courtrooms and demanded that juries consider 'accident' causation and, in turn, their own daily behaviour.

Notwithstanding that the defence of 'accident' was not open on a charge of involuntary vehicular manslaughter[35] and intention was neither an element of manslaughter or s 291A, barristers would nonetheless argue that the fatal consequence was unintended. While the defence of accident was not available for offences based in criminal negligence, other defences were open to drivers, including sudden emergency, automatism, and mistake of fact, although most had limited applicability to the circumstances surrounding crashes. Although the defence of accident was not open legally, it remained the default cultural position. Crashes were cast as 'accidental', tragic, unintended and inexplicable – they could happen to anyone.

The introduction of s 291A in 1946 added a new species to the existing suite of homicide offences under the Code, but attracted a much lower five-year penalty and required, initially, a lesser degree of negligence than manslaughter.[36] Precisely what might constitute that degree was left undefined by the Parliament, an oversight that the High Court was called upon to address some six years later. There were and remain two species of manslaughter under WA's criminal law, intentional and unintentional. Unintentional or involuntary manslaughter is that where the mental elements of murder, and historically, wilful murder, are absent. Broadly, this species can be divided into two groups: 1) deliberate acts where the defendant intended to do some harm, but not the degree of harm necessary, for instance, to be classified as murder; and 2) cases where the death was caused by negligent act or omission, including deaths occasioned by the use of motor vehicles.[37] In Australian courts, criminally negligent manslaughter has generally been determined by an objective test. The accused does not have to have formed an appreciation of risk and proceeded irrespective; that is, recklessly. The fault element of the offence is a failure to comply with a prescribed standard of conduct.[38] The defendant's state of mind is not at issue. An accused's subjective belief about the manner of their driving or the degree of risk taken, or otherwise, is not relevant to the inquiry. A conviction of vehicular manslaughter obviously requires not only that a person died, but that the negligent conduct of the defendant was the substantive cause of death. However, the conduct that caused the death had to be, and remains, *so* unlawful as to constitute *criminal* negligence.[39] Whether an act or omission can be held to be criminally negligent firstly depends on whether there has been a breach of duty. That breach forms the basis of liability.[40] Since its inception, the Code prescribed a series of duties. Particular to drivers is the duty of persons in charge of dangerous things.

> It is the duty of every person who has in his charge or under his control anything, whether living or inanimate, and whether moving or stationary, of such a nature that, in the absence of care or precaution in its use or management, the life, safety, or health of any person may be endangered, to use reasonable care and take reasonable precautions to avoid such danger; and he is held to have caused any consequences which result to the life or health of any person by reason of any omission to perform that duty.[41]

The duty of persons in charge of dangerous things was part of the Code since its inception. It was not a species introduced to manage the tragic human consequences of motoring. The duty established by s 266 is to use *reasonable care* and take *reasonable precautions*. Thus, in order to establish manslaughter by negligence the defendant must have *failed* to use reasonable care and take reasonable precautions.[42] However, the degree of that failure must be so significant as to be *criminal*.[43] A conviction requires that the defendant demonstrated a very high degree of negligent conduct, a degree often described as gross, callous, criminal and, sometimes, reckless. The consequences of the failure or breach of duty must have been reasonably foreseeable, rather than remote or distant. Negligence is based in what a person should have reasonably anticipated and ought to have done.[44] However, and importantly, what constitutes foreseeable risk and danger has, by necessity, a corresponding relationship to contemporaneous and shifting understandings about what constitutes an 'accident'.

In Australian courts, criminal negligence is typically determined by an objective test, once referred to as the 'reasonable man test', now the 'reasonable person'.[45] In terms of its application to vehicular manslaughter, the purpose of the test is to determine whether a driver's conduct fell short of what a *reasonable person* or ordinary prudent driver would do in the same circumstances. The reasonable person is purportedly an impartial benchmark – he or she supposedly behaves in accordance with accepted community standards. Not surprisingly, many have described the 'reasonable person' as 'mythical'.[46] In cases involving motor vehicles, jurors were required to assess drivers' conduct in light of how a *reasonable* person might drive. Historically, drink-driving and other commonplace risk-taking behaviours rendered the yardstick of the ordinary prudent driver particularly problematic, given that conduct, particularly for young men, seemed almost normative in the mid to late twentieth century. Gender imbalances in the ratio of female to male drivers also undermined the benchmark's impartiality and its ostensible reflection of *reasonable* community standards. Women's exclusion from jury duty no doubt had a further impact on reasonableness' impartiality.

Exactly what constituted criminal negligence became something of a stumbling block for jurors. In 1964 Justice Hale tried to explain that the distinction between civil and criminal negligence boiled down to a matter of degree.

> [N]obody can say in advance just where simple negligence merges into criminal negligence, but once you understand the distinction, that criminal negligence involves something in the nature of recklessness, then it is for you, the members of the jury, to say whether, in this case, the accused's conduct crossed the border.[47]

In order to be *criminally* negligent, the manner of the accused's driving must have fallen *far below* community standards and have been such that any *reasonable* person would recognise it as 'likely to expose another to the risk of death or serious injury'.[48] The breach of duty had to be far greater than that which would ordinarily give rise to matters of civil liability and compensation. Importantly, in the context of driving, negligence is neither fixed nor absolute. It is contingent on context. Driving 40 km/h in excess of the speed limit on a country road might not be held to be criminally negligent, but exceeding the speed limit by 20 km/h in the immediate vicinity of a kindergarten might be.

Lord Hewart's explanation in *R v Bateman* in 1925 thereafter set the benchmark:

> In explaining to juries the test which they should apply to determine whether the negligence, in the particular case, amounted or did not amount to a crime, judges have used many epithets, such as "culpable", "criminal", "gross", "wicked", "clear", "complete". But, whatever epithet be used and whether an epithet be used or not, in order to establish criminal liability the facts must be such that, in the opinion of the jury, the negligence of the accused went beyond a mere matter of compensation between subjects and showed such disregard for the life and safety of others as to amount to a crime against the State and conduct deserving punishment.[49]

Underneath this simple overview lies some complexity around 'recklessness'. As stated, in Australia criminally negligent manslaughter has its basis in a breach of a duty of care. There is no subjective fault element. While an accused might be guilty of common parlance 'reckless behaviour', in that they wilfully took a risk, the prosecution is not required to prove recklessness as a subjective state of mind. There is no onus to establish that the accused foresaw an adverse consequence or formed an awareness of risk,[50] but *wilfully* continued with a course of action, indifferent to or disregarding the consequences.[51] Recklessness typically requires proof that the defendant chose a course of action and was aware of the risk, meaning the defendant had advertence to the risk,[52] although it may be imputed objectively. In the case of vehicular manslaughter, the benchmark of criminal negligence is met as long as the court is satisfied that a 'reasonable person would have been aware of the harmful conduct and could reasonably be expected to have taken certain measures to avoid those consequences'.[53]

Australian authorities have long favoured the objective test approach to criminal negligence, notwithstanding a handful of judgments by the Victorian courts.[54] On those decisions, some have argued it needless and unnecessary for Australian judges to distort the objective assessment of criminal negligence with the subjective mental element of recklessness.[55] Recklessness arguably has no place in an Australian vehicular manslaughter trial. Still, decades of trial records demonstrate that West Australian barristers and judges repeatedly counselled juries that, in order to convict, the Crown had to prove that the driver was reckless.[56] As the cases unfolded between 1946 and 1974, the term 'reckless' was repeatedly employed in trials. The conflation of negligence with recklessness may have led jurors to believe that wilful risk-taking was requisite, which was not the case. This emphasis arguably affected trial outcomes.

The use of the term 'reckless' in West Australian courts stemmed from the adoption of the Bateman test in *Andrews v Director of Public Prosecutions* in 1937.[57] Explaining the degree of negligence required to constitute *criminal negligence*, Lord Atkin took the matter one step further than Bateman's benchmark of 'culpable, criminal, gross, wicked, clear [and] complete' to include the term reckless.[58]

> Simple lack of care such as will constitute civil liability is not enough. For purposes of the criminal law there are degrees of negligence, and a very high degree of negligence is required to be proved before the felony is established. Probably of all the epithets that can be applied "reckless" most nearly covers the case.[59]

Western Australian judges routinely employed the *Bateman* test when directing juries to the degree of negligence required to sustain a charge, and some utilised the Atkin model. Many seemed to stop deliberately short of the use of the term reckless, likely because they were aware that it might complicate deliberations. Douglas Brown noted that the UK's House of Lords held it appropriate that recklessness be employed in its popular sense and that no confusion would arise from its use.[60] In discussing Australian cases, both Yeo and Wells have argued against that position. Wells claimed that the terms have been erroneously 'conflated', in turn confusing a subjective state of mind with an objective assessment of a breach of a duty of care.[61] Yeo concurred, describing the interchange of the terms 'nonsense'. He further argued that negligence should be regarded as an 'objectively based fault', distinct from subjective recklessness.[62] These criticisms readily apply to mid to late twentieth century West Australian cases.

From another vantage point, the employ of the term 'reckless' in efforts to characterise the quality of the conduct were explicable. Prosecutors were *at pains* to convince juries to relinquish the notion of 'accident' and, in order to do so, they frequently employed 'reckless' as a powerful, provocative term of persuasion. The term was also utilised by judges to underline serious aggravating circumstances. However, the employ of the adjective arguably superimposed a state of mind on an offence that did not require proof of wilfulness or advertence to risk. The emphasis on recklessness compounded the view that only *utterly* exceptional conduct was culpable, despite that the very nature, weight and speed of the machine, in addition to the proximity of other road users, demanded a very high duty of care. The emphasis on recklessness facilitated a socio-legal characterisation of everything other as 'accidental'.

Pleas to amend the criminal law had been voiced as far back as 1934. That drivers continued to evade conviction had troubled prosecutors for decades and the Crown Law Department lobbied extensively over an eleven-year period to effect change.[63] After more than a decade of intermittent consideration, by 1946 Western Australia had a new homicide offence, by penalty the lowest in the Code's hierarchy, to prosecute drivers who killed other road users. Injury on the roads escaped the Parliament's attention. It was almost another thirty years before legislators turned their attention to drivers who caused serious injuries. Although much of the impetus to amend the criminal law came from the Crown Law Department, after 1952 the Crown lost interest in charging defendants with the alternative offence. The High Court's decision in *Callaghan v R* gave the Crown cause to abandon the offence altogether and, instead, to continue charging drivers with manslaughter.

Coming into effect in January 1946, negligent driving causing death, s 291A, was defined as follows:

> Any person who has in his charge or under his control any vehicle and fails to use reasonable care and take reasonable precautions in the use and management of such vehicle whereby death is caused to another person is guilty of a crime and liable to imprisonment with hard labour for five years.

While the offence was based in failing to 'use reasonable care' and 'take reasonable precautions', there was some discrepancy between its definition and the margin notes. The margin notes of the amending Act labelled the section 'reckless or dangerous driving'. The phrase 'causing death' was speciously absent. As a result, the offence was often incorrectly referred to as dangerous or reckless driving causing death, though some judges remained true to the letter of the law, referring to it only as negligent driving causing death. Importantly, and like manslaughter, s 291A did not actually require a person to be physically driving to fall within its compass. In that sense, the phrase 'driving causing death' seemed to distort the issue even further – a vehicle simply had to be under a person's charge or control. While in Australia margin notes are not considered part of statutes, the use of the terms 'dangerous' and 'reckless' were nonetheless problematic. Their interchange added a further layer of confusion to an already complex area.

At the time of the introduction of s 291A, the offence of dangerous driving was already in place under the UK's 1930 *Road Transport Act*.[64] Dangerous driving had also been adopted in some Australian jurisdictions in line with the UK. The *Road Transport Act* rolled dangerous and reckless driving into the same section. They were, however, distinct in that dangerousness was defined as driving a motor vehicle at a speed or in a manner dangerous to the public, having regard to the *circumstances*, including the nature, condition and use of the road, the amount of traffic present at the time, or that which might reasonably be expected.[65] Thus, the use of the phrase 'dangerous driving' in Western Australia, which was operational and dissimilarly defined elsewhere, for what was in fact negligent driving, added a further layer of confusion. The Crown Law Department took a keen interest in the construction of driving-causing-death offences in other jurisdictions, so it was not the case that it was unaware of these potential tensions when the amendments were drafted.[66]

In addition to the confusion associated with the interchange of 'reckless', 'dangerous' and 'negligence', a far more considerable issue emerged. The s 291A offence was defined in the same terms as the duty of persons in charge of dangerous things. So, by definition, the question before a jury in *both* a manslaughter and s 291A case was whether the driver failed to use *reasonable care* and take *reasonable precautions*. Eventually, the coexistence of two provisions under the Code, defined in the same terms, yet with considerably divergent maximum penalties – one life imprisonment and the other five years – precipitated an appeal to the High Court.

The facts that emerged in the first instance judgment in *R v Callaghan* (1952) were that, on the evening of 19 April that same year, 25-year-old John was driving his motorbike along Stirling Highway towards Perth. Some distance ahead, Hilary and Wallace, an elderly couple, were on their way to a show at the Windsor Picture Theatre. Their son had just dropped them off on the opposite side of the road. Before crossing the road, Hilary noticed the headlight of a motorcycle, which she believed was at a sufficient distance for her and her husband to cross the road safely. She told the Coroner that the motorcycle 'must have been going at a terrific speed to have caught us'.[67] Samuel, an eyewitness, said the bike 'roared past' him. He estimated its speed at 60 mph (96.56 km/h). The speed limit on Stirling Highway was 35 mph (56.32 km/h). Constable Fenton, who was travelling in a police car, stated that Callaghan passed his car at significant speed in heavy traffic and crossed the double white lines at about 60 to 65 mph (96.56 to 104.60 km/h).[68] Constable Hannaby, who was travelling with Fenton, stated that he saw Callaghan cross the double white lines and strike the two pedestrians.[69] The motorbike skidded on its side in a shower of sparks.[70] If Callaghan had kept his initial course, Samuel claimed, he would not have struck the couple. He was adamant that Callaghan hit the pedestrians whilst driving in the wrong lane.[71] The testimony of the witnesses was consistent.[72]

The collision happened at 7.20 pm. Wallace was carried 50 feet from the point of impact and died later that night in Royal Perth Hospital.[73] His wife survived him, but suffered serious injuries.[74] Leo Wood, Callaghan's barrister, creatively suggested that Wallace had contributed to his own death because he had failed to cross at a pedestrian crosswalk. There were none in the vicinity. In July 1952, Coroner Rodriguez committed John Callaghan to stand trial.[75] He was charged with manslaughter, but found guilty of negligent driving causing death. Sentenced to two years' imprisonment with hard labour, he was released on bail pending an appeal to the Western Australian Court of Criminal Appeal.

The character report produced by police observed that Callaghan was a heavy drinker who kept company with 'habitual drinkers'. Previously employed by a transport business, he was dismissed after one week for driving recklessly, although the rest of his employment history appeared without incident. Callaghan had a history of offending, including several counts of stealing, escaping custody, driving under the influence, two counts of unlawfully assuming control of a vehicle, speeding, unlicensed driving and failure to insure vehicles. He had been imprisoned twice and was disqualified for drink-driving for three months in August 1951, eight months prior to the incident in which Wallace was killed. He was fined for speeding only two months before Wallace's death.[76]

While there were several grounds to the appeal, the most significant was the contention that the first instance judge had misdirected the jury on the degree of negligence required for a conviction under s 291A. Justice Walker had instructed the jury that, if they were satisfied that Callaghan was to *some* degree negligent, they must take that issue one step further and *grade* his degree of negligence. Accordingly, if there was a lack of care, but not a *gross* lack of care, the appropriate verdict would be negligent driving causing death. If there was a gross lack of care, then the appropriate verdict would be manslaughter. On the jury's retirement, the defence raised an objection. The defence noted that the wording of the duty of persons in charge of dangerous things under s 266 of the Code was 'exactly the same' as that under s 291A and requested that Walker redirect the jury on the matter.[77] The petition fell on deaf ears. In effect, the defence was contending that, if the duty was the same, it would follow that the standard of negligence must equally be. The WA Court of Criminal Appeal did not agree. It ordered that the appeal be dismissed on all grounds, upholding the conviction.[78] Callaghan took his case to the High Court.

In *Callaghan v R* in 1952, the question before the High Court was whether a conviction under s 291A of Western Australia's Criminal Code in effect required only a civil standard of negligence.[79] The Court observed Justice Walker's directions that, in order to be found guilty of manslaughter, the degree of negligence would have to be very grave indeed. Affirming the test in *Bateman*, the defendant would have to demonstrate such a disregard for the life and safety of others as to amount to a crime against the State. The Court noted Walker's direction that, if Callaghan's negligence was something less than that, the jury might find him guilty under s 291A. Consistent with the intent of the legislature, Walker's direction pointed to an intermediate species of negligence. The problem was, however, such a species did not exist. One was either negligent insofar as to give rise to civil liability, or so grossly negligent as to attract the admonition of the criminal law. The net effect of Walker's directions, were they not overturned, would be that a conviction under s 291A would require no greater degree of negligence than that which would give rise to matters of civil liability.[80]

Concurring with Callaghan's counsel, the High Court noted that an inspection of s 266 and s 291A revealed the sections, in their 'critical words', to be identical. The Justices reasoned that it would seem to inevitably follow that the standard of duty required for each offence must also be the same.[81] While the Bench noted that the expression 'use reasonable care and take reasonable precautions' tended to reflect a civil standard of negligence,[82] the Justices reasoned that the phrase had to be regarded in its context – the Criminal Code – a statute dealing with 'crimes involving grave moral guilt'. Accordingly, the degree of negligence had to be criminal.[83] Callaghan's sentence and conviction were quashed.[84]

Other than some general observations made by the WA Law Reform Commission in 1970, there has been no evidence unearthed to date about the impact of the High Court's judgment from 1952 until the repeal of s 291A in 1974.[85] However, this comprehensive survey of unreported cases reveals that *Callaghan v R* presented major difficulties for all court participants and had a profound effect on the State's approach to prosecutions. While the Parliament had introduced a lesser offence to increase the scope of liability and criminalise a broader spectrum of fault, what occurred, post-*Callaghan*, was a narrowing or fixing of the scope. Unlike in any other jurisdiction in Australia, New Zealand or the UK, where jurors had a genuine option between two offences, one more serious than the other, West Australian jurors were left with a perplexing choice. After the High Court's decision, vehicular manslaughter and negligent driving causing death were to all intents and purposes the same, yet, illogically, one attracted a maximum term of life imprisonment and the other five years.

The judiciary wrestled with the logic of the situation. Following the High Court's decision the state of the law was, in effect, that there were two offences indistinguishable save for their respective sentences. In a 1961 case, Justice Virtue told a jury –

> Well, I regret to say, Mr Foreman, and members of the jury that I am unable to offer you much assistance there, because I really don't know the answers myself. However, the legislature has laid down the duty in those terms to constitute two different grounds, and the same standard as I mentioned to you previously – that is, the failure to use reasonable care and take reasonable precautions must amount to a reckless and careless disregard for the life and safety of others – applies to this crime was well as to the other. The only suggestion I can make and the only rational and logical ground of distinction that I can see is that the crime of manslaughter is possibly more serious – should be reserved for more serious breaches of that nature than the other – and there it is – that's what the law lays down and that's what you've got to work out for yourselves.[86]

Justice Virtue voiced a similar view in 1965. He apologised that he could not assist the jury with the fact that the offences were in essence the same, but he emphasised that manslaughter should be regarded as the more serious.[87] Seven years later he made similar directions, two years before s 291A was repealed. His comments demonstrate the problems associated with applying the High Court's judgment.

> I am afraid it is very difficult for me to give an answer to that question because the legislature in its wisdom has really given us no indication as to wherein the difference lies. All I suppose

can be said to you is that manslaughter is a form of homicide and unlawful homicide is of course one of the most seriously regarded crimes under the law, so that probably a conviction for manslaughter should be reserved for something which was the gravest possible type of negligence — manslaughter in other words is a more serious crime than the other, and it is a matter for you to decide between them.[88]

Virtue's contention that manslaughter should be reserved for the most serious breaches of conduct was likewise proposed by Justice Negus in 1963.[89] However, his logic was hotly contested by the defence and the prosecution conceded the accuracy of the challenge.[90] The idea that manslaughter should apply only in cases involving more serious conduct was arguably erroneous given the standard of negligence required for both offences was, post-*Callaghan*, the same, and importantly the provisions were, in terms of their construction and elements, virtually identical. Justice Negus directed the jury that, while the degree of negligence for manslaughter and s 291A were exactly the same, in delivering a verdict of one or the other, they might decide the question of a possible maximum penalty of life imprisonment versus five years on the basis of *feelings*.

> It's my feeling that it's a question of culpability. If you feel that he is culpable enough to be held guilty of manslaughter then you find him guilty of manslaughter; if you feel he is not that culpable then you find him guilty of negligent driving causing death.[91]

The defence countered that Negus was in effect applying s 291A as it stood prior to the High Court's decision, in that a lesser degree of culpability would lead to the alternative, lesser offence.[92] Negus responded that, to his mind, a lesser degree of culpability was different to a lesser degree of negligence. The defence argued that the upshot of Negus' direction would be that the 'standard of negligence may be slightly lesser in the case of s 291A than for manslaughter'.⁹³ Negus conceded that he was quite prepared to redirect the jury. Hatfield contested his proposed approach.

> Negus, J: I'm quite prepared to make it clear, subject to anything Mr Dodd has to say. The standard of negligence is the same but the standard of culpability may justify the lower verdict.
> Mr Hatfield: Your Honour, this is what I had in mind. The jury should be told that if he is not guilty of the degree of negligence amounting to manslaughter then the verdict must be Not Guilty. If he is guilty of that negligence which warrants manslaughter, then they can either find him Guilty of Manslaughter or 291A.⁹⁴

Justice Negus confessed that *Callaghan* had given him a great 'deal of trouble'. While the jury deliberated, he insisted it was 'high time something was done about making clear what was intended by Parliament when they passed Section 291A'.⁹⁵ Hatfield sympathised, noting that *Callaghan* gave every judge the same difficulty.⁹⁶ Negus persisted in the vein that culpability would assist the jury to determine whether a defendant might be guilty of manslaughter or negligent driving causing death. Both the defence and the prosecution opposed his position.⁹⁷

> Negus, J: Very well. It really amounts to this then: If they find him guilty of sufficient negligence as to amount to manslaughter then they consider whether they will find him guilty of manslaughter or negligent driving causing death. In what circumstances do they find him guilty of negligent driving causing death? The only answer I can give myself is if they think him less culpable.
> Mr Dodd: I'm afraid, sir, that would then offend against the High Court's view of [Negus interrupts]
> Negus, J: I don't know that it does, but if you agree with Mr Hatfield on it, well then.
> Mr Dodd: I'm afraid that's my difficulty, sir. I think it has often been put, and I think it's the only distinction one can draw, is that one, as to penalty, is a more serious offence than the other…

Well, judges have found themselves in such difficulty they have in general terms indicated that is the only distinction between the two offences, without going into particulars. I think that's almost a common occurrence in this court.[98]

Callaghan had an immediate and long-term impact on the Crown's approach to prosecutions. Of all defendants that came before the Supreme Court between 1946 and 1974, only fifteen were charged at first instance under s 291A, and eleven of those were before 1952.[99] Those fifteen cases stand against an estimated 304 charges of vehicular manslaughter. After 1952, in all bar four instances, the Crown preferred a charge of manslaughter.[100] Chief Crown Prosecutor Dixon later explained that, as the degree of negligence required for both offences was identical, the Crown left the matter to juries to decide.[101] In essence, the Crown's position was that, if the jury could find the defendant guilty under s 291A, then they could equally find him guilty of manslaughter, and for that reason they should find the defendant guilty of the higher charge and leave the matter to the judge to reflect in sentencing.[102]

In 1970, following criticisms raised by the Chief Justice, the Law Reform Commission of WA was asked to investigate the matter.[103] The Commission's initial working paper suggested that the Crown was 'abdicating its responsibility' and should exercise its discretion and differentiate between less and more serious cases.[104] The Commission also turned its attention to whether the law should be reformulated altogether, proposing a number of changes. One alarming suggestion involved *precluding* a charge of manslaughter if a death was caused by the use or mismanagement of a vehicle, so that a driver could *only* be charged with a lesser offence — a further dilution of the crime's seriousness. There was some concession offered, with the Commission proposing to increase the maximum term of imprisonment from five to seven years,[105] bringing the penalty in line with Victoria.[106] The Commission also entertained the idea of repealing the offence and substituting culpable driving causing death.[107] Consideration was similarly given to repealing s 291A and replacing it with dangerous driving causing death, although there were concerns that it might not resolve the existing difficulties.[108] On balance, the Commission's preferred approach was to make minor drafting amendments to s 291A and, in substance, the offence remained intact until 1974.[109] Only four years after the Commission rejected dangerous driving causing death, it was introduced under s 59(1) of the 1974 *Road Traffic Act*, replacing what had become the problematic s 291A provision.

Between the introduction of negligent driving causing death in 1946 and its abolition in 1974, almost 6,500 people died on Western Australian roads.[110] Strikingly, of those people who died or were killed, only an estimated 319 defendants were charged. Across Australia, fatality rates did not begin to appreciably decline until the end of the 1970s. Western Australia's annual toll peaked at 358 in 1973.[111] As historian Jennifer Clark observed, 1945 to 1970 marked a very bleak period in Australian motoring history.[112] It also marked a very difficult period in the courts.

Chapter Two

An overview of Supreme Court trials, 1946–1974

Indictments, verdicts and trends in sentencing

Until 1974 the Supreme Court had primary jurisdiction over homicide offences, notwithstanding some minor disclaimers raised below. Consequently, the Court's records in effect represent the totality of West Australian prosecutions between 1946 and 1974. The fact that virtually all drivers were brought before the Supreme Court and those records survive facilitates a longitudinal analysis of trial outcomes, the first undertaken anywhere to date. Unreported cases and, in this instance, restricted access indictment files, are of enormous value – a considerable body of law lies hidden within those files. After 1974, jurisdiction over deaths occasioned by the use of motor vehicles devolved for the most part to the lower courts. Later chapters therefore turn their attention to other sources. Notwithstanding the Supreme Court's primary authority over homicide offences, some brief observations on the District and Children's Courts follow, in addition to the role of the Coroner, before providing an introductory overview of indictments, verdicts and trends in sentencing.

On juvenile offenders, there was no indication that vehicular homicide cases were brought before the Children's Court between the mid-1940s and the late 1960s.[1] By the early 1970s, it appeared that some proceedings were initiated in the Children's Court, where defendants were committed to stand trial in the Supreme Court.[2] While a person charged with a homicide offence who was a child pursuant to the State's 1947 *Child Welfare Act* could come under the jurisdiction of the Children's Court, there was little evidence that this authority was exercised. As an alternative, it appears that juvenile offenders who occasioned a death by the use of a motor vehicle were not charged with the death, but rather with a raft of offences under WA's 1919 *Traffic Act*[3] – a homicide charge was difficult enough to sustain against an adult. Prosecutions for taking a vehicle without consent, speeding, and driving without a licence appeared to be common substitutes. This approach mirrored the trend of laying multiple charges against adults when a homicide charge could not be sustained.[4] Accordingly, juvenile offenders do not feature in the following chapters. They are returned to in Chapters Seven and Eight when the conduct of young, unlicensed drivers and community outrage became critical factors in the trend towards higher penalties in the late twentieth and early twenty-first centuries.

The District Court too warrants mention. Following the establishment of the District Court in 1969, s 291A matters fell within the District Court's purview. Manslaughter remained the exclusive province of the Supreme Court, as the District Court had no authority to hear cases where the maximum custodial penalty was greater than fourteen years.[5] While technically, s 291A cases fell within the District Court's jurisdiction, it is unlikely that drivers were charged and brought before the Court between 1969 and the offence's repeal in 1974. Only one exception was discovered that contested the presumption that the District Court's jurisdiction over s 291A went unexercised.[6] Following the High Court's judgment in *Callaghan v R* in 1952,[7] in all bar four cases, the Crown was resolute in its policy of charging drivers with manslaughter. The advent of an intermediate jurisdiction would have been unlikely to alter that steely resolve. The contention that the number of s 291A charges brought before the District Court was negligible is not possible to substantiate unequivocally. The District Court's registers cannot be searched by means of offence.

Between the mid-1940s and the early 1960s, cases were generally first heard at inquest, and, in the majority of matters, it was the Coroner who laid the indictment.[8] The pattern of inquest followed by coronial indictment was initially customary. In the 1940s and 1950s, this typically took the form of a full inquest, while across the entire period all decedents were subject to post-mortem.[9] As those killed in motor vehicle collisions died sudden, violent and unnatural deaths, the Coroner was required to investigate the *cause* of those deaths. Want of coronial indictment did not denote a lack of coronial conviction. In some instances, the Coroner left the formality of the indictment to the Crown. While it is not possible to determine how many times the Crown declined to proceed on coronial indictments, with well over 100 manslaughter nolle prosequis identified, a considerable degree of coronial advocacy seems apparent. The power to indict, a power subsequently repealed, gave coroners, particularly Perth City Coroner 'Pat' Rodriguez, the means to influence attitudes regarding what constituted an 'accident', and to shape public debate. In that respect, Rodriguez was a significant force for change. Given 'accident' or 'misadventure' were possible findings, his approach appeared to demonstrate a concerted attempt to dismantle 'accidents', both as a coronial finding and a default socio-cultural assumption, emphasising instead agency, causation and liability.

Coronial indictments declined dramatically in the early 1960s. The shift to Crown indictments coincided with the establishment of the Fatality and Motor Squad within the Criminal Investigation Branch of the WA Police in 1963 and the death of Coroner Rodriguez in February 1964.[10] The Squad was established to reduce deaths caused by 'intoxicated, reckless or negligent' drivers, and to improve the quality and standard of evidence put before the Supreme Court to 'combat the frequent dismissal of charges of manslaughter'.[11] The fact that the Coroner appeared to take primary responsibility for laying charges until the early 1960s might indicate that WA police were less enthusiastic about prosecuting drivers. This was not the case. Police officers assumed joint responsibility for investigations from the outset, working alongside the Coroner's office.[12] However, the practice does raise the question – if the case was likely to result in a charge, why were drivers not charged without delay? Conceivably, the Crown waited for the Coroner to rule out the finding of 'accident' before embarking on bringing a matter to trial. *Accident* was a commonplace presumption that had to be thoroughly put to bed before negligence could be contemplated.

There were 403 cases of interest identified between the years 1946 and 1974, detailed in Table A1 of the Appendices. Cases were of interest on three grounds – defendants were charged with negligent driving causing death, manslaughter, or unlawful killing.[13] If a defendant was convicted of either of the latter two, it was not always possible to verify whether the charge involved a vehicle; however, it was usually obvious in that sentencing remarks tended to include notations on licence disqualification. For defendants acquitted, it was impossible to determine whether the case involved a vehicle. For that reason, every manslaughter and unlawful killing case was recorded with one exception – where the entries provided some indication that a case was initially a murder or wilful murder charge, cases were not chronicled. Of the 403 cases identified, 150 case files were examined in detail, representing more than a third of the total. Of those 150 files sampled, 120 involved a vehicle. Table A2 of the Appendices lists all defendants found guilty of vehicular manslaughter and negligent driving causing death between 1946 and 1974 and the sentences imposed. Sadly, of the 120 vehicle cases sampled, there were 139 fatalities. In addition to single fatalities, there were sixteen double fatalities[14] and one case that involved the deaths of four people.[15]

When a case involved multiple fatalities, defendants were prosecuted for only one death. Jurors ordinarily were not made aware that more than one person had been killed or died. It was not a deficit of evidence that determined the policy. If there was sufficient evidence to convict on one count, there was enough to convict on two or more. Rather, it seemed that consensus was that punishment for one death was sufficient, particularly as those deaths arose out of a single course of conduct. In Western Australia and Queensland, this approach was born out of a narrow interpretation of s 16 of the States' respective Codes, which prohibited punishing a person twice for the same act or omission,[16] although the case law does demonstrate a lack of accord on the issue.[17] The provision was included to reflect the common law prohibition against being retried for a like offence following acquittal, or being twice convicted when the elements of one offence corresponded to two or more offences. Prior to the 1990s, there was a sense that s 16 of the Code might also prohibit punishment for multiple harms that arose out of one transaction. Punishing an offender for more than one fatality would be to multiply the punishment for the conduct element of the offence – a single instance of criminally negligent or dangerous driving. This interpretation came under increasing challenge in the late 1980s and subsequent amendment in the mid-1990s.[18] The pattern of prosecuting and sentencing for only one decedent in multiple fatality cases was later firmly redressed by s 11(3) of the *Sentencing Act 1995* (WA).

Of the 403 cases of interest, only fifteen people were charged under s 291A at first instance.[19] The remaining 388 cases were manslaughter indictments. The sample revealed that, of those 388 manslaughter cases, almost 80 per cent, or approximately 304 cases, involved a vehicle. Of all homicide offences brought before the Supreme Court, those involving motor vehicles dominated the Court's calendar. Of the total 319 drivers charged – fifteen under s 291A and an estimated 304 charged with vehicular manslaughter – 174 people were convicted in the period, representing a greater than 50 per cent rate of conviction. Of those 174 people, *only* twenty drivers were found guilty of manslaughter. Thus, of an estimated 304 drivers charged with manslaughter, all male, just over 6 per cent were found guilty of that charge. Seven of the manslaughter verdicts were handed down between 1970 and 1974 when the nation's 'road toll' was at its peak.[20] By contrast, 154 defendants were found guilty of, or pleaded guilty to, negligent driving causing death. The exceptionally low rate of conviction for manslaughter in contrast with s 291A demonstrates that legislators and lobbyists of the 1930s and 1940s were correct in their instinct that a less damning title would positively alter the inordinate acquittal rate.[21]

Following the High Court's decision in *Callaghan v R* in 1952, the situation in Western Australia was unprecedented. In other jurisdictions, jurors had a choice between dangerous or culpable driving causing death and manslaughter, and thus a genuine alternative between the gravitas of manslaughter and a lesser offence. Post *Callaghan* and up until 1974, West Australian jurors had one option – criminal negligence – albeit under the banner of two offences with widely disparate custodial terms. Most interestingly, once West Australians had the option of a less damning label but an *equal* standard of negligence, they were willing to find more than half of the defendants guilty. Juries were content, in effect, to find drivers *criminally* negligent, but were unwilling to expose drivers to the penalty for manslaughter. In all but twenty instances, jurors steadfastly resisted the characterisation of manslaughter and the degree of culpability it signified. This new evidence offers a nuanced challenge to 'there but for the grace of God' reasoning. West Australian jurors were *more* than prepared to find drivers guilty of the degree of gross negligence required for a conviction of manslaughter but, overwhelmingly, they were unwilling to attach the characterisation and label normally applicable to that conduct.

While a conviction rate of just over 50 per cent might point to a considerable degree of censure, sentences were another matter. The terms imposed were greatly at odds with the anxiety and rhetoric about road deaths in the period, including *judicial* rhetoric. By way of comparison, across the period, twenty-two cases were identified in which defendants were convicted of non-vehicular manslaughter.[22] Fights between friends and spouses outnumbered all other circumstances and, like deaths on the road, intoxication was often a factor. Sentences for non-vehicular manslaughter varied from a fine, probation or bond, to imprisonment for six months and up to eight years. In addition to an eight-year term, of the longer custodial sentences there was one of seven years, four of five years, one of four years, and two of three; far in excess of sentences handed down to drivers. Putting to one side the five non-custodial sentences, the average term of imprisonment for the remaining seventeen cases was three-and-a-half years. By contrast, of the twenty males convicted of vehicular manslaughter, four received a non-custodial penalty.[23] Of the remaining sixteen, the lowest terms of imprisonment were also for six months. The maximum term of imprisonment imposed for vehicular manslaughter between 1946 and 1974 was four years, compared with eight for non-vehicular. Across the *entire* period, only two drivers were sentenced to four years.[24] One of those sentences was reduced to two years on appeal, with a minimum term of nine months.[25] The other driver's non-parole period was set at eighteen months.[26]

Importantly, the sentences imposed were not indicative of time actually served. Until 1981, an offender was generally entitled to a one-quarter remission on his or her sentence upon entering prison. While historically, the prospect of remission was contingent on good behaviour, by the mid-twentieth century it had become virtually automatic.[27] Thus, the sentences recorded should be considered 'head sentences'. The gap between the term imposed by the courts and time served further widened following the introduction of parole in 1963.[28] Offenders became eligible for parole at the expiry of a minimum term, were a minimum term set. Where the term of imprisonment was greater than one year, judges were generally required to set a minimum, non-parole period.[29] Judges had discretion to decline setting a minimum term owing to the serious nature of the offence and the character and background of the offender. Custodial terms later decreased under the 1981 *Prisons Act* to one third of the head sentence.[30]

The average head sentence for vehicular manslaughter was 2.15 years as against 3.5 for all other manslaughter cases. The fact that other forms of manslaughter attracted, on average, a third longer term of imprisonment, and sentences were up to four years and as high as eight, underscores the perception that vehicular cases were regarded as a lesser species of crime. Importantly, these were not cases of carelessness or inattention. These were very serious instances of gross negligence. If, as Friedman once noted, behind every legal decision remains a 'more powerful, more basic social judgment',[31] the inherent judgment was that gross negligence while in charge of a vehicle was a lesser species of manslaughter. It was less culpable to drive a potentially lethal machine, recklessly, at speed, or while intoxicated, and inadvertently kill *anyone*, than it was to strike an individual while drunk and unintentionally kill them. The machinery of the vehicle seemed to hermetically insulate drivers from the perception of immediacy and violence associated with a fist, as did the fact that the conduct was not directed at any person in particular. Rather, *anyone and everyone* in the driver's path was exposed to the danger.

Further analysis of maximum sentences in vehicular cases reveals that the second tier of penalty below the twice-imposed maximum of four years was fixed at three. A head sentence of three years was imposed in only ten instances.[32] Cases that attracted three-year terms typically involved high levels of intoxication and speed. Of the ten three-year sentences, there were three hit and runs.[33] Of the ten cases, four were convictions of manslaughter and the remainder were s 291A. On the next tier down, two-year terms of imprisonment were imposed in twenty-six instances.[34] Thus, the aggregate of upper-end terms of imprisonment reveals that, across the entire period, of 174 people convicted, only thirty-eight were imprisoned for two or more years. When custodial terms were imposed, non-parole periods were often short. By contrast, in the same period, unlawfully assuming control of a vehicle, or what one might in common parlance understand as stealing, attracted sentences between one and five years, with two years' imprisonment being a common penalty.[35] It was equally culpable, if not more, to steal a car than it was to kill someone while driving one.

In January 1969, following 337 deaths on WA roads the previous year, the government asked the community for suggestions on how to end the bloodshed.[36] By April the government was inundated, with more than 4,000 letters received.[37] One writer predicted that, if something 'radical and drastic' was not done, 'the hazards of road transport will become nearly as great as a full-scale war'.[38] In correspondence with various officials, the public consistently described the situation as appalling, horrific and shocking.[39] Given these sentiments, the road safety campaigns of the period, and the maximum penalties authorised by the legislature, sentences seemed remarkably low. After the High Court's decision in 1952, all convicted defendants were found guilty of *criminal* negligence, a very serious finding, yet bonds, probation, fines, and licence disqualification in lieu of imprisonment were common. Of the 174 defendants convicted across the period, approximately 25 per cent received a non-custodial penalty.[40] By the mid-1960s, a head sentence of twelve to eighteen months for very serious conduct in circumstances of aggravation became routine. Below that threshold, penalties seemed almost token. In 1973 one driver was treated with particular leniency, sentenced to probation and a driver 'refresher course' on a manslaughter conviction.[41] Fines later became customary under the 1974 *Road Traffic Act*.

Chapter Three

Supreme Court trials, 1946–1974

Key emerging themes

In order for a case to proceed to trial, a driver's degree of alleged negligence had to be particularly high. Of the 120 vehicle cases sampled, less than a handful could remotely be categorised as instances of momentary inattention.[1] Aggravating circumstances were typically requisite for an indictment; however, they were not sufficient to secure a conviction. While the Crown repeatedly argued that criminal negligence was contingent on context and, given the quantum of risk the mismanagement of a vehicle posed, the onus was on drivers to act with a very high duty of care, conduct that fell at the mid to lower end of the spectrum of fault did not make it to trial. Unless there was a montage of observed, extrinsically 'reckless' behaviour leading up to the crash, it was near on impossible to secure a guilty verdict.

Prosecutors were tireless in their attempts to impress upon juries that a wide range of conduct should be deemed negligent, rather than reserve that characterisation for the most aberrant driving. The Crown made every effort to broaden conceptions of the scope of what might constitute criminal negligence in a vehicle, emphasising that the failure to modify one's driving in accordance with the changing road conditions was also a serious species of fault. Prosecutors were resolute in their determination to displace the notion of 'accident' with foreseeable risk, although 'accident' was a residual category not easily supplanted. Misfortune and the impetuosity of youth had a stronghold on the minds of court participants. As cases brought before the Supreme Court typically involved circumstances of aggravation, the benchmark of the *reasonable*, ordinary prudent driver seemed to be a yardstick set particularly low.

According to defendant's representatives, crashes were caused by anything other than their clients' conduct. Despite numerous signposts warning of upcoming bends and the need to reduce speed, apparently unexpected changes in the camber of roads were frequently to blame.[2] Nature was cast as the engineer of disaster in the shape of blinding sunlight, rain and trees.[3] 'She' literally 'conspired' to make 'cars collide'.[4] Random seizures and blackouts were also proffered as causative explanations.[5] Some claimed they suffered memory loss, despite no evidence of amnesia or traumatic brain injury.[6] 'I don't remember' was a very common rebuttal.[7] Tyres were also held to be culprits, even when there was no evidence to substantiate a blowout.[8] Coughing fits featured too.[9] Despite all evidence to the contrary, some defendants stridently maintained that they were not driving the vehicle, but rather the deceased was.[10] Alternatively, they simply could not remember *who* had been driving.[11] Such suggestions were often enough to cast a shadow of doubt over the prosecution's case. Defendants' representatives portrayed crashes as inexplicable. A freak 'accident' might happen to anyone, which surely the jury could understand; they were, after all, drivers too. There was, as Mr Hatfield QC argued in defence of one client, 'no such thing as a perfect driver'.[12]

A conviction typically demanded an observed sequence of overtly reckless conduct. Where cases turned around a failure to modify the manner of the driving in accordance with the circumstances, acquittals were guaranteed. Such a failure was not considered grave enough to warrant censure and the families of deceased vulnerable road users bore the brunt of that view. Even conduct that fell at the upper end of the spectrum of fault was no guarantee of conviction. Notwithstanding that the combination of alcohol, speed and serious risk-taking were generally perceived as aggravating factors that would incite the censure of judges and juries or, as Justice Virtue said in 1966, 'make us harden our hearts',[13] the court invariably exercised leniency when sentencing those offenders, particularly when they were young men.

Not only was the discord between the very serious nature of the crimes and the sentences imposed apparent, there was a conspicuous disconnect between judges' sentencing remarks and the penalties they handed down. On a conviction of manslaughter, drivers were liable to twenty years' imprisonment and, under s 291A, five. Drawing attention to the magnitude of human suffering, the violence and the mounting toll, judges increasingly held that exemplary punishment and retribution were necessary. In 1954, Chief Justice Dwyer noted that there were 'more people killed by motor cars than war' and it was *necessary* to impose a term of imprisonment to discourage such conduct.[14] In one case, Justice Negus referred to the imprisonment of a 'decent man' as a cautionary 'sacrifice' for the 'common good'.[15]

Yet the gap between judicial censure and penalty was considerable. For example, in 1956, 18-year-old Lance failed to stop after hitting 15-year-old pedestrian, Bianca.[16] He did not report the collision, and initially denied hitting Bianca when confronted with a sample of fabric from her clothing, which had been affixed to the undercarriage of his van.[17] In fact, after hitting her, Lance returned home, unloaded his vehicle, and then went out for a game of snooker.[18] Immediately after the point of impact, when his passenger stressed that he ought to stop, the only concession Lance offered was to say, 'I hope she's all right'.[19] Bianca was not 'all right'. She died at the scene in the arms of her 16-year-old girlfriend from a fractured skull and brain injury.[20] The jury found Lance guilty under s 291A and recommended mercy on account of his youth. Justice Jackson vehemently described Lance's actions as a 'wanton and reckless disregard for the safety of others'.[21] He sentenced him to twelve months in prison. Lance was entitled to a three-month discount on that term.

Similarly, in 1959 Justice Jackson forcefully described Frank's conduct as 'one of the worst offences of this kind I have ever seen'. Frank hit 11-year-old Karen in broad daylight. She was on a pedestrian crossing in East Fremantle, crossing the road with her mother and sister.[22] Frank did not attempt to brake or stop. Witnesses stated that they had clearly seen three females on the pedestrian crossing and several cars were stationary, waiting for the family to pass.[23] There was apparently nothing to obstruct Frank's view.[24] Frank had difficulty writing his name and address at the police station. He failed his sobriety test.[25] Karen was admitted to Fremantle Hospital with a brain injury and a fractured tibia, fibula, pelvis and skull. Despite immobilisation of her leg, a tracheotomy, and the assistance of a resuscitator, she died a week later on 8 November 1958. At no point did she regain consciousness.[26] Frank was found guilty of manslaughter. Of one of the worst cases he had apparently *ever* seen, Justice Jackson sentenced Frank to eighteen months' imprisonment, pre-remission discount.

While the language of misfortune and unintended consequence was favoured by defendants' representatives over foreseeable risk and danger, increasingly not all judges were content to accept such characterisations. In *R v D.A.W.* in 1965, Justice Virtue retorted – 'These people who go on long car trips and dope themselves up at the beginning – it is a bad show, is it not – really? It is just asking for trouble'.[27] Barrister Walsh agreed that it was a 'bad show', although he argued that his client's conduct, despite a significant consumption of alcohol before and during the journey, was a distinctly lesser species of crime. In fact, it was a *tragedy* that might happen to anyone.

> [I]t was an unpremeditated crime. It is not like someone who deliberately goes out to break and enter a place, knowing full well

that they are committing a crime; or deliberately commits some sort of other crime. This is a tragic sort of crime which could happen to any family in the community, and in view of the serious injuries he did receive, that alone is substantially heavy punishment...He will bear the marks of this accident for the rest of his life.[28]

With regard to age and gender, vehicular homicide was a young man's offence. Between 1946 and 1974, only two women were prosecuted. Both were found guilty under s 291A and neither was imprisoned.[29] It was possible to determine the defendant's age in eighty-six of the 120 sampled vehicular cases. Almost 50 per cent of those drivers were 25 years or under. They were typically characterised as being of good character. The offences they committed were cast as one-off, inexplicable deviations from their usual standard of conduct.

For instance, in *R v B.J.M.* (1960), a character reference described Benjamin hitting a pedestrian, fleeing the scene and subsequently reporting his car stolen to evade detection as being 'dictated by a departure from his normal state of mind'.[30] Even when drivers were convicted, human agency remained suspiciously absent or peculiarly inverted. Cars continued to 'leave' the road, vehicles got 'out of control' and became 'unmanageable',[31] and 'there was no satisfactory answer for why the car behaved the way it did'.[32] Even when actively pursuing prosecutions, police officers were not immune from this peculiar reversal of agency. In cases involving pedestrians and cyclists, descriptions such as 'the deceased struck the vehicle' and the 'man struck the radiator with his head' were not uncommon.[33]

When offenders were twenty-five or older, they were denied the refuge of youthful impetuosity and the mitigation of age as a factor in sentencing. Irrespective of age, a fleeting and momentary departure from one's usual character was a common explanation for 'reckless' conduct, even when defendants had an extensive history of offending and seemed to be 'accidents' waiting to happen. As the decades wore on, the Crown increasingly argued that a good character mattered not; the total disregard for the safety of other road users and the indiscriminate danger posed by negligent driving was the critical issue. It was a position that judges slowly adopted. Given the alarming, mounting rate of the carnage, prosecutors argued for exemplary punishment and general deterrence. That judges were obliged to exercise leniency towards generation after generation of young men, the principal group of offenders, concurrently led to a pattern of sentencing that reinforced the view that the offence was a much lesser species of unlawful killing.

Normative understandings of criminality were also at variance with the ubiquity of the offence, as was the fact that defendants came from all walks of life. The net result was that those who came from difficult socio-economic circumstances were more readily classified as the *worst* kind of driving offender and others, the more affluent, diligent or socially promising, who supposedly found themselves in the dock because of misfortune and inexperience, were characterised as the least. In sentencing submissions, barristers argued for the lives and futures of their young clients, paying scant attention to the lives they had taken. They pleaded that to sentence young men to prison, young men on the threshold of life, would be 'straining justice too far'.[34] By the late twentieth century, youth's status as a mitigating factor would come under sustained attack.

Judges too grappled with the age of the defendants brought before them. In 1966 Justice Virtue explained that the consideration of an appropriate sentence had exercised his mind a great deal and it was distressing to see a young man in such a predicament.[35] As the period unfolded, judicial sympathy for 'good characters' declined, although notably no judge went as far as to say that engaging in criminally negligent conduct while in charge of a dangerous object *might* be indicative of a *bad character*. Unlike other forms of crime, driving conduct was separate and distinct from every other aspect of one's character. In the late 1960s, 'good characters' increasingly became subject to exemplary punishment. Judges began to draw greater attention to the quality and *consequences* of the conduct. In 1969 Justice Virtue stated –

> I can really regard you as a person of previously good character in every respect, but of course the unfortunate fact is that people of good character do commit this type of offence, and with the ever-increasing road toll we just have to do something about it and that is all there is to it, and we cannot treat any case with leniency, however good a man's character is.[36]

Likewise, three years prior Justice Jackson stated that –

> It is of course relevant to take into consideration your good character and the fact that you accepted responsibility for this tragedy without hesitation or quibbling. But unfortunately the fact remains that in most cases of these offences, the persons responsible (and they are often young men) come before this Court with previous good character; and yet the appalling loss of life on the roads due to reckless driving is so serious these days that it is essential in my view that cases where recklessness is shown resulting in the loss of another human being's life should be visited with substantial penalties. If the courts adopted the view that because a driver was previously of good character he should not be penalised, it would certainly not do anything by way of a deterrent to others and that is one of the principal functions which we are bound to bear in mind when imposing sentence. No doubt, this is a tragedy for you but of course it is an even greater tragedy for the young girl and her family and those are the things that must be remembered at this time.[37]

There was a tendency to punish drivers by imposing a short term of imprisonment or a non-custodial term in conjunction with a substantial period of licence disqualification. For example, in *R v J.W.K.* (1948) the jury found Jack guilty of manslaughter. Justice Wolff imposed a sentence of twelve months' imprisonment with permanent licence disqualification. He noted that 'but for' the disqualification the term of imprisonment would have been much longer.[38] In *R v H.A.H.* (1950), Henry was released on bond, despite the fact that his conduct was considered so serious that he was declared unfit to hold a licence for life.[39] In *R v L.G.W.* (1958), 25-year-old Lionel was found guilty of manslaughter and released on bond on account of his youth. He too was disqualified from holding a licence for life, the judge describing his driving as 'a wanton disregard of the rights of other people and their personal safety'.[40] Terms of disqualification varied widely across the period, from a matter of months to a number of years. At the upper end of the spectrum, fifteen people were disqualified for ten years and three men were disqualified indefinitely.[41] There were two cases of twelve years and one of fifteen.[42] It was initially against the law for a judge to disqualify a driver for more than three years.[43] By the early 1960s, fines in lieu of imprisonment became increasingly routine pursuant to the 1902 *Justices Act*.[44]

Disqualification was a two-pronged approach. In theory, it protected other road users from danger and punished the offender by depriving them of their 'right' to drive. Quite unlike any other form of unlawful killing, penalties were often weighed towards dispossessing men of their 'right' to hold a licence as a principal course of action. As a *primary* form of punishment that could scarcely be policed or enforced, disqualification was arguably a meaningless penalty when many defendants were already disqualified when they killed another road user. In one case, the defendant had been convicted twelve times for driving without a licence, but continued to drive irrespective.[45] Indisputably, licence disqualification was necessary and became mandatory in 1956.[46] However, as a principal form of punishment, disqualification underscored harm occasioned by the use of motor vehicles as a species apart.

Despite having killed one or more people, it was unusual for a driver to be permanently disqualified. Opposition to permanent disqualification persisted well into the twenty-first century, much to the increasing outrage of the community. Of the 174 convictions between 1946 and 1974, permanent disqualification was imposed in only nine instances.[47] Barrister and legal scholar Douglas Brown later declared that, 'in the absence of unusual circumstances it is wrong in principle to disqualify a motorist from driving for life. A person should be allowed some hope of driving in the future'.[48] Brown did not clarify what might constitute 'unusual circumstances', but an analogy might explicate the absurdity of the position. People who work in the financial sector and steal from their employer are not allowed to resume control of bank accounts, schoolteachers who sexually abuse students are not allowed back in the classroom, and those who grossly breach professional codes of conduct risk losing their registration and their careers. Yet driving was somehow different. Driving seemed to be an inalienable right. Those who demonstrated *grossly* negligent conduct, and in the course of that conduct killed, were almost always given another chance, even when they had an extensive history of offending.

The extent of many defendants' records demonstrated that they were recidivist 'traffic' offenders who had repeatedly come to the attention of the courts before the final, fatal collision. For example, in 1972, 23-year-old William had been separately convicted of driving a stolen Holden Monaro at the time of the crash, a fact not disclosed to the jury, and was sentenced to two years' imprisonment on that charge.[49] He had previously been imprisoned for stealing cars. Convicted of negligent driving causing death, he was sentenced to three years' imprisonment, with eligibility for parole after two, concurrent with his penalty for stealing the car. Were he released on parole it would in effect render the additional penalty for causing the death nil. He was witnessed driving erratically over a 1.5-mile distance before the crash, at speeds estimated between 55 and 75 mph (88.51 and 120.70 km/h). With a blood alcohol concentration estimated at up to 0.164%, William was significantly intoxicated.[50] A 16-year-old boy, who was a passenger in his father's Volkswagen, died at the scene opposite Fremantle Hospital whilst receiving mouth-to-mouth resuscitation.⁵¹ He suffered extensive injuries.⁵² William had been previously charged with no fewer than twelve traffic offences, including four counts of speeding, wilfully misleading a traffic inspector, careless driving, tailgating, driving under the influence, driving without a licence, and stealing a car, in addition to twenty-nine 'criminal' offences.⁵³

In *R v M.A.J.* (1974) the defendant had been formerly convicted for driving without a licence or whilst disqualified at least eight times in eleven years.⁵⁴ In fact, 34-year-old Malcolm had never actually held a licence. For these offences, he was disqualified for three to six-month periods, inconsequential punishments given that he continued to drive regardless. He had also been convicted of drink-driving and driving under the influence, offences explored in the next chapter.⁵⁵ His record was not unusual. Of the incident that brought him before the Supreme Court, Malcolm had been drinking heavily over several days prior to the crash and was travelling at a speed of 65 to 70 mph (104.6 to 112.7 km/h) at the time of the offence.⁵⁶ He braked to avoid hitting another car, causing his vehicle to somersault through the air. The car flipped several times before finally ending up in a ditch on the opposite side of the road. Malcolm claimed that his dead friend was the driver. He asked his surviving passengers to lie to the police.⁵⁷ He was sentenced to two years' imprisonment with a non-parole period of nine months.

As a penalty, disqualification was additionally flawed because of the ease with which it might be overturned. Applications for extraordinary licences were granted, even in cases involving multiple fatalities where the offender had an extensive record. There were seven cases identified in the sample where a convicted driver applied for an extraordinary licence and five of those were successful.⁵⁸ For example, in 1964 Julian killed two of his friends.⁵⁹ At 4.00 am on Albany Highway, he attempted to pass a friend's car on a bend at high speed. He was on the wrong side of the road.⁶⁰ There was some suggestion in trial that he was trying to goad his friend into a race. There was a side-on collision between the two vehicles, following which Julian hit a tree. His car was reduced to a wreck.[61] His passengers died at the scene.[62] They were both 20 years old.[63] Julian was prosecuted on one count of manslaughter and a nolle prosequi was entered on the other count.[64] He was found guilty under s 291A. Justice Jackson sentenced him to eighteen months' imprisonment on account of his youth and good character, with a non-parole period of six months. He was disqualified from driving for ten years.[65]

Three-and-a-half years later, Julian's solicitors submitted a notice of motion to vary the suspension and disqualification in order to secure an extraordinary licence. Julian was apparently experiencing some inconvenience. He was having to use public transport to get to and from work and could not carry out tests on vehicles whilst there. Julian's application was approved.[66]

In *R v A.M.B.* (1970), Arnold was fined $1,000 for killing his passenger and was disqualified from driving for seven years. Two years later, he too applied for an extraordinary licence. His application was also successful.[67] Judges may have been partially responsible for encouraging defendants not to fear licence disqualification. In *R v E.J.V.* (1969), Justice Jackson told Evan that, on suspending his licence for seven years and sentencing him to three years in prison, if his only avenue of employment post-release was to return to truck driving, then his solicitor would be able to advise as to the procedure of acquiring an extraordinary licence.[68]

Justice Burt took issue with the granting of extraordinary licences. In *R v S.H.* (1965), Samuel was sentenced to two years' imprisonment and disqualified for eight. Three years later, he acquired an extraordinary licence to drive between 6.00 am and 6.00 pm, Monday to Saturday. In 1971, he applied to have his suspension and extraordinary licence status lifted altogether. His application was refused.[69] Justice Burt criticised the practice of issuing extraordinary licences. Rather he thought the

> disqualification of a driver from driving is an important ingredient in the punishment of persons who offend against traffic laws and

again emphasising I am speaking for myself, I always regard it as being part of the punishment and, as I say, an important part. That being so a person who comes to the court for an order that the disqualification be removed or varied must, in my opinion, make out a strong case to obtain such an order. It is not to be thought: Wait a couple of years, make an application to the court and the suspension will be removed as of course. At least, that would not be the result if the application were brought before me.[70]

Of the 120 vehicle cases sampled, only five involved the deaths of family members. When drivers killed relatives, charges were rarely laid. In two of the cases, the decedents were brothers of the accused.[71] One case involved a daughter and in the remaining two, the victims were spouses.[72] In both the brother and daughter cases, the defendants were acquitted. In the case of the wives, both defendants were found guilty and one was sentenced to four years' imprisonment, a penalty imposed only twice in the period.[73] His non-parole period was set at eighteen months.[74]

Intoxication was an aggravating factor in both matters. One of the men had been drinking all afternoon. Justice Negus said that he took into consideration the man's kindness towards his wife and the fact that he had 'suffered a great loss by her tragic death'.[75] He was drunk and driving on the wrong side of the road for some distance before he collided head-on with another vehicle, killing his wife and seriously injuring the occupants of the other vehicle.[76] In some jurisdictions it was a matter of policy to treat drivers who killed family members with leniency, an approach based in notions of natural punishment. In 2007, the UK Crown Prosecution Service amended its guidelines, conceding that, until then, it had been procedure to exercise leniency on the basis that the person had already suffered 'enormous personal loss' and it would be 'oppressive and insensitive' to prosecute.[77] No such official policy could be identified in Western Australia; however, that only five cases were discovered would suggest that a similar approach was adopted in the mid to late twentieth century. In a 1964 case in which the defendant killed his wife, Mr Wallwork submitted that his client was already suffering 'a terrible punishment' and 'I feel your Honour might think that he has been more than adequately punished so far'. He asked him 'to extend what leniency you can to him in view of the loss he has suffered'.[78] It was a loss self-imposed.

Leniency was also evident when drivers killed a passenger. Of the 120 cases sampled, twenty-nine involved the deaths of passengers who were also friends.[79] Of those cases, twenty-one involved high levels of intoxication, and extreme speed was a factor in sixteen instances. Many involved a combination of the two. Racing and 'hooning', or what defence barristers liked to euphemistically call 'skylarking' or 'tomfoolery' were a feature of many.[80] Of the twenty-nine people prosecuted for killing a friend, fourteen were acquitted. There were thirteen s 291A[81] convictions and two of manslaughter.[82]

Of the fifteen guilty verdicts in cases involving passengers, the sentences proved most interesting. The jury recommended mercy in four instances.[83] Eight drivers received a non-custodial penalty, mostly of good behaviour bonds. Only seven drivers were sentenced to jail. With only one exception, penalties were higher when a driver killed a stranger as opposed to someone they knew.[84] This was a significant finding in that drivers arguably owed a very high duty of care to passengers in their charge. When drivers killed friends and family members, the circumstances were typically described as 'tragic', a characterisation which persisted well into the twenty-first century. If the person killed was the occupant of another vehicle whom the defendant did not know, the characterisation shifted more readily from tragic to unlawful. *Propinquity*, by friendship or blood, diminished *culpability*. While the maximum imposable penalty was five years under s 291A and life imprisonment for manslaughter, head sentences where a driver was convicted of killing a friend were as follows – three months, nine months, fifteen months, seventeen months, two of eighteen months and one of two years – well below the highest tiers of three and four years. Indisputably, when men killed their friends they were subject to much lesser penalties.

In 1958, friends Elliot, Warren and Duncan were travelling from Fremantle to Mandurah. Elliot was driving. According to Elliot, before embarking they had several drinks and stopped for more over the course of their journey. Late that morning they visited the Plympton Hotel in East Fremantle. They each drank three middies of beer and two glasses of muscat. Note, beer measurements vary across Australia. In WA, a middy is 285 mLs. Around noon, Elliot, Warren and Duncan visited the Freemason's Hotel in Fremantle and had another middy and two muscats each. Just before 1 o'clock they departed for Mandurah and stopped en route at the Naval Base Hotel for another beer and two more muscats.[85] Less than an hour later, a passenger travelling in a car ahead of the men heard a terrible screeching sound and, on looking out the rear window, saw a car catapulting through the air. She described a man being hurled from the airborne vehicle, fly past the car she was travelling in, and fall to the ground.[86] That man was Warren. He died at the scene.[87] It was estimated that the car rolled six times after it landed. Miraculously Duncan survived. Despite the testimony of Constable Westwood of Pinjarra who stated that, in his opinion, Elliot – 'did not appear to have been affected by alcohol by any great extent; he was coherent in his speech and he spoke reasonably well'[88] – Justice Wolff observed that the circumstances were *most serious*. Given the amount of alcohol consumed, Wolff stated that Elliot *should not* have been driving. However, Elliot maintained that he was a 'seasoned drinker' who could consume 'a considerable quantity of liquor' with little or no effect.[89] The fact that he was on the wrong side of the road when he lost control of the vehicle suggested otherwise. Justice Wolff declared that the escalating 'road toll' and the 'wanton way drivers of motor vehicles behave' necessitated exemplary punishment.[90] Elliot was found guilty under s 291A. According to Justice Wolff, it was *not only* the killing of his friend that was at issue, but the *extreme* danger to which he had subjected *every other* road user.⁹¹ He sentenced 42-year-old Elliot to three months' imprisonment.

In 1956, 18-year-old Bradley was also found guilty under s 291A. The jury recommended mercy on account of his youth. Bradley was not of legal drinking age and alcohol was an aggravating factor in the mosaic of circumstances surrounding his case.⁹² Driving his Morris Minor at speed, Bradley failed to take a bend and veered off the road for a distance of about 170 feet, where he finally hit a tree. The tree was uprooted by the force of impact. One-and-a-half miles before the crash scene, Bradley overtook another vehicle, colliding with it side-on. He did not stop.⁹³ Bradley's friend, 18-year-old Gary, was killed in the final collision. He was thrown from the car. Gary's head was crushed by the force of impact.⁹⁴ Bradley was released on bond.

When a passenger was killed and the surviving passengers were friends of the driver, they tended to band together, claiming they had been asleep and therefore could offer no observations on the manner of the driving.⁹⁵ On the rare occasion where a surviving friend testified against a driver, stating that they had repeatedly asked him to slow down and/or let them out of the vehicle, that evidence was slated as being motivated by monetary gain for injuries sustained.⁹⁶ When the passenger was female, her testimony was derided by the defence as hysterical, evidence of undue nervousness and anxiety,⁹⁷ and a curious female inability to estimate speed, a common characterisation of female witnesses.⁹⁸ Apparently, surviving passengers were greatly exaggerating if they testified to excessive speeds, erratic driving conduct and fear.

The central problem with the hostile or reluctant, slumbering passenger was, without a witness to the manner of the driving, crashes were readily characterised as inexplicable 'accidents', irrespective of the weight of incriminating circumstantial evidence. As if coached, passengers regularly testified that, prior to falling asleep their friend's driving was no cause for concern. In *R v G.C.B.* (1970), Paul, Graham and Adrian were travelling along the Great Northern Highway to Perth. Graham was driving. At the scene of the crash, his Holden Monaro was discovered on its roof. In its path, there was a trail of broken and bent signposts, mowed-down vegetation, and gouge marks of 159 feet. The vehicle travelled a further 150 feet from the cessation of the gouge marks before coming to a standstill.[99] Paul claimed that he fell asleep at Carnamah and woke when the car hit the signposts. According to Paul, there was no previous cause for concern. Prior to the crash, Graham's driving was apparently unremarkable.[100] Crown Prosecutor Dodd retorted that it was very interesting that no one could testify about the manner of the driving because everyone, including the deceased, was *supposedly* asleep.[101] Constable McDonald described what he saw on arrival at the scene – 'I saw a male person in the rear of the vehicle and there was blood and body matter on the lining of the vehicle. There was blood. There was body matter...a lot of body matter'.[102] The blood and body matter belonged to Adrian. He died from a comminuted, compound fracture of the skull.[103]

On that grim note, post-mortem reports provided painstaking details of the injuries victims sustained and causes of death. Despite some claims that discussing injuries is akin to a 'pornography of violence',[104] details of injuries are included throughout the course of this book. The nature and degree of injury is categorically relevant to questions of culpability. While vehicle design and engineering are contributing factors, the severity and type of injury may also speak to the degree of fault. The inclusion of injuries also redresses the violence that the phrase 'road toll' disguises and the neglect of the personal tragedies behind the 'toll'. Such descriptions give 'road toll' statistics a human dimension, albeit a graphic, disturbing one. The view that the nature of injury is relevant to the discussion is not unique. American Professor of Law, Andrew McClurg, provided a detailed, emotional account of the circumstances surrounding his fiancée Kody's incineration in a crash, in the context of a broader, scholarly discussion regarding wrongful death damages.[105] The impulse to lay bare the level of injury and trauma is also common to grief and bereavement literature.

Fractured skulls were common in post-mortem reports. Emergency procedures carried out in attempts to save lives, such as tracheotomy and amputation, were also evident. Disembowelment featured heavily and severed limbs were frequent. Broken and fractured vertebrae, brains protruding from skulls, ruptured spleens, bowels and aortas, lungs and abdominal cavities filled with blood, people drowned in their own bodily fluid – all were commonplace. In Neil's case, all that remained of his body following the explosion of the vehicle were fragments of his dentures and teeth, included in a tiny envelope in the criminal case file marked 'Exhibit E'.[106] One man suffered the trauma of being run over by a bus, which left tread marks on his face and neck.[107] His left arm was also partially severed and his right leg was amputated in hospital where he died the following day.[108] Dawn, a young trainee nurse, died on the Kwinana Freeway. In the course of the collision, she was impaled by a fence post, which travelled through the car, penetrated her left shoulder, traversed through her lung and out of her back.[109]

Nineteen-year-old Daniel was riding his bicycle in Claremont when he was killed, hit head-on by a driver who attempted to overtake two motorcyclists in the oncoming lane. Daniel suffered extensive injuries. The right side of his face was completely torn away and some of his brain tissue was hanging outside of his skull cavity. There was very little remaining tissue – most of Daniel's brain was splattered across the road.[110] Tracey's post-mortem recorded her heart as grossly ruptured and completely detached from its major vessels. Her boyfriend Adam suffered a fracture of the first cervical vertebrae causing 'gross mobility' of his head and a completely severed spinal cord. His brother was driving.[111] Colin was killed on the Great Eastern Highway, Burracoppin. He died of asphyxiation. Following a crash with an oncoming truck, the cab of his prime mover was overturned. It was found upside down at the scene. In effect, Colin was strangled by his own steering wheel.[112] Ted hitched a ride from York on the back of a motorcycle.[113] Hit by a car, he was discovered in the bush at the scene of the crash, about 3 yards from the road.[114] His abdomen was 'slashed open'.[115] The post-mortem detailed a massive traverse wound from which his lower abdominal wall and bowel protruded, in addition to a crushed left leg. He bled to death at the scene.[116] The driver of the motorbike was also killed.[117]

After the car in which she was travelling was hit from behind, Adele managed to crawl out of the wreck. She was found standing on the roadside, screaming and ablaze. Witnesses tried to extinguish the flames.[118] Her husband described the scene.

> The front of the car finished up facing the island and it was burning fiercely. It rested on its roof. I tried to get out. I crawled through where the windscreen had been. This had shattered. I saw my wife standing next to the car screaming. She was aflame. I tried to carry her away from the car. A Police Officer came on the scene and helped me put my wife on the side of the road. I got some clothes off her. The remainder of the clothes were burning. She was in great pain and screaming. I put my jacket over her face to extinguish the flames. The Police Officer also put a jacket over her.[119]

Adele suffered burns to approximately 80 per cent of her body. She died in Royal Perth Hospital four hours later.[120]

There were very few materials discovered in the Court's records that provided a means to address what Lauren Breen aptly called the 'silenced voices'[121] of road trauma. In fact, it was not until the late 1980s that the deceased and bereaved began to assume some prominence as victims of crime in the media. Given a prosecution is between the State, or historically the Crown, and the defendant, it was not surprising that very little evidence was discovered, particularly in a period pre-dating victim impact statements, although a few small traces were found. Mortuary forms offered a small glimmer. Friends and family members were called to morgues to identify loved ones, were they sufficiently intact to be viewed, and the identification of the body forms often survived. The form required signatories to indicate the nature of their relationship with the deceased and the length of time they had known them. Customarily, family members, particularly parents and children, wrote a simple, but on every reading, poignant phrase – 'I have known her all my life'.

Friends and family members were often involved in and witnessed crashes. Their testimonies allow a glimpse into their distress. On the evening of 16 March 1946, Sarah visited the North Fremantle Town Hall to attend the picture theatre with her husband. On leaving, they discovered a crowd of people milling around outside. A man had been hit by a car and was lying injured on the road.[122] Sarah stated –

> My husband and I being qualified first aiders went to see if we could be of any assistance…I had taken the man's pulse; after which I heard a noise to the south…I stood up upon hearing the noise…I saw a pair of very dazzling head lights approaching in the centre of the road, people crossing the Highway from the Town Hall stopped suddenly making room for this approaching vehicle to pass. These lights appeared to be approaching at a terrific pace. I called out "Look out, here comes a car, and it is not going to stop, run Bill." The next thing I heard was a terrific thud and saw my husband in the air. I screamed and ran after the car which was veering from the centre of the Highway towards the west side of the Highway and stopped near the Salvation Army Church. I saw my husband lying in the gutter on the west side of the highway between Barton's Garage and the Salvation Army Church. I was then taken away from the scene…There was a light above the picture hall…I saw the car hit my husband…He was dressed in a dark cardigan with a white shirt…The car came over on the wrong side of the road.[123]

Two mothers testified that their sons were but 200 yards from home when they were killed – so close but so far.[124] Such glimpses were rare in the materials.

By contrast, socio-legal tensions around vehicular homicide's status as a crime and, correspondingly, decedents' status as legitimate victims were embedded in the correspondence addressed to the Court. One defendant had driven his car up on two wheels, around a corner, into the oncoming lane of traffic, killing an 18-year-old woman who was out for a Sunday drive with her friends.[125] She died from a dislocated neck and haemorrhaging due to the laceration of her lungs.[126] The driver's mother claimed that 'nobody could wish for a more perfect son'.[127] Referees defended young men, claiming they had always been 'gentlemanly'.[128] They were good sportsmen on and off the field.[129] They were honest, fair, obedient and of good temperament.[130] They came from good homes.[131] Character references described their family backgrounds – 'his mother is a very good churchwoman lady and capable mother'.[132] His parents have 'stirling qualities'.[133] Wives wrote to judges explaining that their husbands had been good fathers and providers. Almost all writers avoided mention of the conduct or incident which had brought their son, husband, employee or pupil before the court, although one parish priest noted of a hit-and-run drink-driver, a 26-year-old school teacher who made a false report that his car had been stolen –

> The accident that has brought this young boy into this unfortunate position is most regrettable but I think the moral strain he endured for the past few months is almost adequate punishment for any fault he may have committed.'[134]

One wife pleaded to the judge, 'give me my husband back'. Her children woke in the middle of the night, crying for their father.[135] Wives drew attention to the financial hardship they would suffer during their husband's incarceration.[136] Even when a husband had killed a child and had an extensive history of offending, in one instance twenty-four separate traffic convictions, wives spoke of the traumatic impact *his* punishment would have on *their* children.[137] No mention was made of the traumatic impact on the victim's family. Parents claimed that incarcerating their son was a double punishment; young men were simultaneously losing their freedom and livelihoods, forcing their wives and children into welfare dependency. By contrast, recognition of the suffering of the bereaved was absent in the correspondence. One father asked that the judge take his son's finances and 'sad and sorry circumstances' into consideration.[138] In the characterisations of good husband, good son, good father, and promising young man, all understandable attempts to influence sentences, responsibility for the death was conveniently circumnavigated.

There was one single, poignant and powerful counterbalance to this correspondence, which went to the very heart of vehicular homicide's contested status as a crime. A bereaved mother voiced her anguish and indignation. In a letter to Justice Jackson in 1956, she rejected the term 'accident' in favour of what she held to be a more precise description – 'killing'. Confounded and devastated, she argued that her daughter's death and her family's loss were being overshadowed by a misplaced emphasis on mercy and youth.

Your Honour,

In publicity relating to the case arising out of the killing of my daughter, much has been made of claims for sympathy for the accused, Larson, and pleas for mercy on his behalf. There has been no published mention of any sympathy for me or my son. The press report stated that the killer cried in court, but it is noteworthy, too, that it was stated in evidence by him that after killing Bianca he went to play snooker. Did he worry at all?

At the same moment, I was only half alive at home and my son tragically broken down. Now my home is virtually destroyed and I intend abandoning it and living in rooms. I lost my husband 16 years ago when my daughter was three months old and my son four years. I somehow raised them through war in Europe, through bombings and burnings. I brought them to Australia (land of tomorrow, I was told)…Our daughter and sister was our very soul. We were naturalized Australian citizens, settled here.

I donated to Australia two healthy, bright and smart children – not lunatics as that killer Larson is. Larson's expression "there are some sheilas" proves clearly that he saw the girls and my daughter wore a bright red pullover.

If Christians, like myself, justify this horrible killing, what is there left to believe in? I write in this way because so much was made of the family life of Larson. It seems fitting to me that you should know something of the family life of the victim. I hope you will forgive me if I find it difficult to attach more importance to mercy in this case than I do to justice.[139]

Following the decision of the High Court in *Callaghan* in 1952, in all cases the critical issue was whether the nature of the driving constituted a breach of duty sufficient to be characterised as *criminally negligent*. Across the period, the Crown went to great lengths to persuade jurors that a broad spectrum of conduct fulfilled that criterion. Despite those relentless efforts, what emerged from trials was that, in order to secure a conviction, the case had to involve a prolonged sequence of overt and observed erratic behaviour, and, ideally, circumstances of aggravation, including excessive speed and high levels of intoxication. When it came to the question of what constituted using *reasonable care* and taking *reasonable precautions*, intoxication was particularly contentious.

Chapter Four

One for the road, 1946–1974

Drinking, driving and criminal negligence

In the mid to late twentieth century, the lethal combination of two popular pastimes, drinking and driving, posed a significant challenge to the community's understandings of what constituted culpable conduct, as did the mounting evidence of alcohol's detrimental impact on motor skills and reaction times. Despite that evidence, intention remained a significant impediment to convictions – while drunk drivers may have engaged in merriment, celebration, or commiseration, they had not set out to kill anyone. Persuading jurors that the fatal consequences of drinking and driving were not bad luck, but rather a corollary of risk-taking that increased with every single drink was an arduous task. That task was insurmountable when a defendant managed to drive, *seemingly* without incident, up until the point of impact.

In the absence of an overt sequence of erratic conduct, acquittals were virtually guaranteed. Even when drivers were heavily intoxicated and witnesses observed irregular driving, acquittals were common. According to defendant's representatives, their clients were *not* affected by alcohol and were able to handle their liquor. It was simply that they did not see the stop sign, the bend in the road, or the pedestrian on the zebra crossing. Their clients were *not* aware that they were driving down the wrong side of the road. The 'accident' was *not* due to the effects of intoxication. The science of blood alcohol concentration and its hard won advent into statutory law would begin to counter these seemingly inexplicable collisions.

A driver's level of intoxication was not the principal issue at stake in a prosecution. Defendants were not on trial for being under the influence – a point that their representatives adamantly and repeatedly made.

> Just to mention the word drink in relation to a motor car – that follows necessarily that the person is guilty of criminal negligence; just to mention it. All I ask you to do is look at the matter in relation to it. Look at the evidence as to the manner in which the motor vehicle was being driven…He is not charged with drunken driving. You are not here today to determine whether he is guilty of drunken driving; he is not charged with it. He is charged with Manslaughter and I ask you to look at the facts carefully.[1]

Intoxication was a dominant feature of cases brought before the Supreme Court. It was an unambiguous factor in sixty-two of the 120 vehicular cases sampled. It was also an aspect of many other indictments, although the degree of intoxication in those matters was somewhat ambiguous or, alternatively, the evidence suggested that the amount consumed, whether by the driver or the deceased, was less likely to be a factor in crash causation. By the late 1960s, intoxication became something of a prerequisite for an indictment to proceed. However, the sentences imposed underscored the view that drivers' frequent indifference to the risk they posed to *all* road users was held as substantially less blameworthy than other forms of unintentional manslaughter, including those involving drunkenness. Blame was a difficult label to affix when drinking and driving was to some degree socially acceptable.

ONE FOR THE ROAD, 1946–1974

Barrister Walsh's assertion of 1965, that the simple mention of the word 'drink' would cause people to throw up their arms in horror was not borne out by the evidence.[2] That drink-driving was a common feature of cases might have signalled that the Crown believed intoxication lent itself to a greater likelihood of conviction, but where intoxication was at issue, almost as many defendants were acquitted as found guilty. Of the sixty-two indictments where drunkenness was *unambiguously* at issue, there were thirty-five convictions. When found guilty, juries were often enormously compassionate towards drivers who killed while heavily under the influence. In *R v J.C.* (1949) for example, a 19-year-old male admitted to having consumed at least twenty drinks.[3] He hit a cyclist on Canning Highway directly from behind.[4] The driver claimed that he did not see him.[5] The tail light of the cyclist's bike was still burning when police arrived.[6] The driver was so drunk that as soon as he was locked in a police cell, he fell asleep.[7] While the jury found him guilty of manslaughter, it recommended mercy. He received a head sentence of fifteen months' imprisonment.

The early to mid-twentieth century was characterised by momentous advances in research on alcohol and its impact on driving ability. The mounting carnage provided a compelling impetus for investigation. Worldwide, researchers generated extensive data about alcohol's impact on cognitive and motor skills. Closer to home, the persuasive autopsy data collected over a quarter of a century by Perth District Medical Officer, Dr Alva Thomas Pearson, provided compelling evidence for legislators.[8] Advances in research on alcohol's effects developed alongside methods of determining blood alcohol concentration levels. Research into ethanol had begun as far back as the early 1910s and, come the 1930s, it was a burgeoning field.[9] By the time experts came together at the first international conference on alcohol and road traffic in Stockholm in 1950, research was well advanced.[10] While Australian historian Graeme Davison claimed that, by the mid-1950s authorities were moving away from 'legalistic' approaches to 'car safety' in favour of medicalising the problem,[11] in the case of alcohol, in the 1950s medicine actually became law's chief corroborator. Spearheaded by the medical community, the period was characterised by major legislative change worldwide.[12] Rather than a decline in legal responses, the number of driving offences multiplied and became increasingly precise. In Western Australia, blood alcohol and breath testing were introduced in the late 1950s and 1960s respectively, and subsidiary regulations were continually revised to close loopholes that artful defence barristers managed to slip through, time and again.

While medicos in the frontline of the carnage around the country lobbied for harsher penalties, road safety campaigns were slow to shift from 'letting courtesy reign' to more 'hard-hitting' messages about the lethal consequences of drinking and driving.[13] It was not that drivers continued to drink and drive because they were unaware of alcohol's effects – the information was published in print media from the late 1940s.[14] In the 1950s, newspapers began to run articles on the correlation between the amount of alcohol consumed, the likelihood of being involved in, or responsible for, a crash, and the legal consequences which might follow.[15] In the 1930s, medicos and allied scientists had established that impairment was demonstrable at 0.02% and patent at 0.05%, a position widely accepted across the medical and scientific community by the early 1960s. However, unlike alcohol, cautions took some time to absorb.

It was difficult to position drinking and driving as a serious offence when it was socially routine. Professor Lovibond, Head of Psychology at the University of New South Wales later observed that it was 'nonsense to say, "If you drive, don't drink and if you drink, don't drive"' because 'drinking and driving were inseparable'.[16] Notwithstanding, there was a high degree of anxiety about drinking and driving in some parts of the community. The WA Police Commissioner and Minister for Police were inundated with correspondence from concerned citizens, advocating the introduction of severe penalties.[17] The WA branch of the Royal Automobile Club (RAC), peak body for drivers, advised its members that the only safe approach was total abstinence – 'If you drink, don't drive'.[18] Members were cautioned that 'Drinking, then driving not only wrecks cars, but often puts drivers behind different bars'.[19] The RAC declared that the drunken driver, over-confident and unable to properly control his vehicle, was the public's number one enemy.[20] It admonished its members that there was absolutely 'no excuse' for drinking and driving as it invited disaster, dulled reactions and clouded judgment. The RAC warned that 'no driver' had the 'right to wilfully imperil the lives and well-being' of others.[21] The force of these warnings seemed somewhat diluted when positioned alongside beer advertisements.[22] Members were simultaneously advised of the RAC's free legal service, whereby those charged with traffic offences could obtain free advice from RAC solicitors and legal representation in metropolitan courts.[23]

Politicians were quick to condemn drinking drivers in Parliament, although they were reluctant to address their constituents in the same terms.[24] Instead, they issued moderate cautions, asking the community to drink and drive with *care*, rather than abstain. On the evening news in the mid-1970s, Minister for Transport, Traffic, Police and Safety, Ray O'Connor, appealed to the public to take care over the Easter long weekend. He asked 'people who are having a little to drink', to 'drive a little slower'.[25] Addressing younger motorists, he noted that while *they* might believe that alcohol improved their dexterity, they should be careful – 'watch yourselves as far as speed and drink are concerned. Try to stay with us in this particular regard'.[26] 'Trying to stay with us' was a gentle warning given annual fatalities on WA roads were at their peak, and, according to Australian research in the period, intoxication was a factor in at least 50 per cent of cases.[27] The disjuncture between science and prevailing community attitudes was also manifest in the courts. In 1973 Justice Wallace described the belief that one should not drink and drive as a *bias* – 'If some of you firmly believe that one should not drink and drive, then put that bias out of your mind for the moment and treat the evidence as impartially as you are humanly capable of treating it'.[28] By contrast, medicos often adopted macabre imagery and moralising language to sheet the message home. At the Henry Windsor lecture in 1972, Dr Grayton Brown claimed that the 'age-old vice of alcohol excess' had raised 'itself from its rightful position in the gutter' and spread 'its frothing blood over the bitumen'.[29] Such temperance reproach tactics were unlikely to affect the driving conduct of young men.

Despite the fact that data corroborating the devastating consequences of drinking and driving was well established in public discourse, drivers were slow to modify their behaviour. In a period pre-dating random breath testing, where police had to have *just cause* to test drivers, the conviction rate was high. In 1960, of 233 people charged with driving under the influence in Perth, 215 were convicted.[30] By 1969, of 1,509 tests conducted there were 1,404 convictions.[31] In 1975, of 5,311 persons breath tested in the Perth metropolitan area alone, there were 4,769 convictions.[32]

Intoxication was not an element of criminal negligence, but was a possible explanation for overt or flagrant displays of traffic law violation, such as speeding, running stop signs or driving on the wrong side of the road. Importantly, drinking and driving was not a failure to use *reasonable care* and take *reasonable precautions*. It was not a breach of the duty of persons in charge of dangerous things. Accordingly, judges would distinguish criminal negligence from drink-driving in their closing directions to juries. Justice Hale's explanation was characteristic.

> Now, you have just heard some discussion on the question of the drink the accused man had taken at the social party which he and his friends had been attending. You must remember, when considering this aspect of the matter, that the accused is not charged with drunken driving. That is, the offence commonly called drunken driving, and in truth the consumption of alcohol is not, in itself, an element of this indictment at all. Quite obviously a man may be guilty of reckless driving when he is completely sober, and it is equally obvious that although he may have

taken quite a bit of drink he is not necessarily guilty of reckless driving. But intoxication may be relevant in such a charge as the present one. It can in some circumstances provide a very possible explanation – sometimes even a probable explanation – of what actually happened. Whether or not it is of any real relevance will depend both on the nature of the accident and on the amount of alcohol which the driver appears to have consumed, but I would again emphasise, that the fact that a man has been drinking does not in itself prove that he was driving recklessly.[33]

Unless the driving demonstrated a *gross* failure to use reasonable care and take reasonable precautions from the point of view of the bystander, prosecutors had little hope of securing a conviction. Juries were repeatedly directed that drivers who had a considerable amount to drink might in fact drive quite cautiously and carefully, and teetotallers might drive 'recklessly'. Just because a driver was drunk did not mean that he was responsible for the death.

When intoxicated drivers *appeared* to be driving normally, in a straight line, and ran directly into a vehicle, pedestrian or cyclist without braking or swerving, convictions were very difficult to secure. Guilty verdicts demonstrated a preference towards a manner of driving whereby the vehicle was, colloquially speaking, all over the road. A conviction typically called for a demonstrable, extensive and extrinsic departure from the standard of reasonable care – a 'sustained course of reckless conduct'[34] – although the Crown would often argue, in the absence of an eyewitness, that the conduct was self-evident from the crash scene. For prosecutors, cars reduced to unrecognisable wrecks, shop fronts demolished by the impact of vehicles, trees uprooted by the force of impact, and skid and gouge marks that traversed extensive distances were incriminating circumstantial evidence pointing to gross negligence. Driving while taking reasonable care and using reasonable precautions would be unlikely to produce such extraordinary damage.

In *R v C.P.M.* (1974), the prosecution contended that the very nature of the crash supported a conviction. The defendant veered off Albany Highway. His car ended up on its roof in Arthur River.[35] One passenger was thrown through the windscreen. He was found face down in shallow water and was alive for a short time before he drowned.[36] The driver and other passenger managed to crawl out of the upturned car.[37] They were distraught at the scene, frantically screaming their friend's name.[38] The driver's blood alcohol concentration was 0.232%. Forensic pathologist Dr Pocock gave evidence that, at that percentage, the defendant would have been 'seriously affected' and 'grossly impaired in all his faculties, particularly in his ability to drive a motor vehicle'.[39] According to the defendant, his blood alcohol level had absolutely nothing to do with his car veering off the road.[40] The defendant's driving was not observed by any witness, other than the surviving passenger. The driver was acquitted.

When a prosecution involved the death of a passenger who was a friend of the driver and had also been drinking, judges often attributed partial responsibility to the deceased on the basis of assumption of risk.[41] Defendants charged with the death of an intoxicated friend, who together had been involved in some 'tomfoolery', were regularly acquitted.[42] If convicted, they received very lenient penalties, including probation and bond.[43] For example, in 1970, friends Wayne and Ray attended a livestock sale in Merredin.[44] After the sale's conclusion, they visited the Commercial Hotel and drank about twelve middies of beer each.[45] On return to Kellerberrin later that evening, Wayne crashed the car. Ray died from a fractured skull.[46] In sentencing Wayne, Justice Neville apportioned blame to Ray, suggesting that, by drinking a considerable amount and knowing that *someone* would have to drive, he was perhaps 'equally' at fault.[47] He sentenced Wayne to five years' probation and declared him ineligible to hold a driver's licence for the same period.

Judges' sentencing remarks often revealed an inherent bias towards intoxicated passengers, whereby their inebriation somehow diminished the driver's culpability. Holding passengers responsible was at odds with the principle that the driver owed a duty of care to other road users, including his passengers. Once a driver assumed responsibility of the dangerous object, it was he who was duty bound. While there was no legal basis in which a passenger could be held accountable for a driver's conduct,[48] passengers were often held *morally* responsible in that they had been drinking, willingly travelled in the vehicle and, by inference, consented to the circumstances of their death. As such, a kind of socio-cultural contributory negligence was attributed to the deceased. By drinking and consenting to travelling in the car, irrespective of their limited capacity to give informed consent, they too had created the danger and simultaneously condoned the risk. This redistribution of blame and responsibility was disturbing in all cases, but particularly when surviving passengers testified that they had asked the driver to stop the car and let them out. In circumstances obviously impossible to know, where peer pressure may have prevented passengers from asking the driver to modify their conduct, blaming them for their own deaths would seem to be especially callous.

Until the late 1950s, whether a driver was 'under the influence' was measured by the imprecise and generous standard of 'incapable'. What constituted being 'under the influence' shed its ambiguity in 1957, when West Australian legislators defined it as having a blood alcohol concentration of 0.15% or more.[49] In 1930, in line with the UK, the definition of driving under the influence – 'any person who is apparently under the influence of intoxicating liquor', was replaced with 'under the influence of drink or drugs to such an extent as to be incapable of having proper control of the vehicle'.[50] The problem with the terminology was that, in the minds of the public, the term 'incapable' implied a very high level of intoxication.[51] Without a scientific benchmark, interpretations of capability were extremely subjective and defendants' representatives seized upon this to discredit expert witnesses. Witnesses, particularly medicos and police, forcefully contested attempts to discredit their expertise, arguing they had more than ample professional experience to determine whether a driver was drunk. The notion of 'incapable' rather lent itself to the idea that unless a driver was, colloquially speaking, 'rolling drunk', 'pissed', 'three sheets to the wind', 'hammered', 'plastered', 'blotto' or 'shit-faced', he was not unfit to drive.

Prior to blood alcohol testing becoming a matter of law in 1957, whether a driver was 'under the influence' to the extent of being 'incapable' was determined by a sobriety test, a physical examination devised to provide proof of a driver's sobriety or otherwise. Results were not conclusive, but might form part of the mosaic of evidence. In Western Australia, sobriety tests were carried out well into the 1970s, although their use was limited in homicide investigations after the late 1950s.[52] Defence barristers were often contemptuous of the probity of the test and those that conducted them, challenging police officers in the witness box – 'it would only be your word against his, wouldn't it, as to whether he was affected by liquor?'[53] The Crown sought to corroborate test results by adducing eyewitness testimony as to the driver's appearance and demeanour following a crash, which, if sufficiently persuasive, might warrant a conviction for driving under the influence, but would not of itself justify a conviction for the death. Were the driver not transferred to hospital, police would escort the driver to the nearest station to undertake a sobriety test in the presence of a senior officer. A sobriety test consisted of walking a chalk line, heel-to-toe, for 12 to 15 feet; standing on one leg and raising the other knee; writing one's name and address; and a spiral test, which involved an officer drawing a spiral and the driver tracing the outline of the spiral in a different coloured pen. Unlike in Victoria, questions regarding the time and the requirement to repeat the phrase 'six thick candlesticks' were not part of West Australian test procedures.[54]

At a crash scene in 1946, Gareth told the attending physician, Dr Bladen, that he had consumed approximately fourteen beers over the course of the day and had nothing to eat whatsoever.

Bladen noted the smell of alcohol on Gareth and that he was 'somewhat under the influence'.[55] Gareth also told Constable Petterson that he had consumed fourteen drinks.[56] Paramedic James Cameron described Gareth staggering, swaying slightly on his feet and, to a limited degree, slurring his words.[57] On the fact that he had smashed his truck into the rear of a stationary car, Gareth claimed that he heard a bump and did not remember anything else.[58] Constable Lawson also attended the scene. He said that Gareth's speech was slurred, his gait unsteady and his eyes 'red, rimmed and dilated'.[59]

At Central Police Station, in the presence of Constables Lawson and Petterson, Sergeant Chambers conducted a sobriety test. Chambers asked Gareth whether he had recently suffered from any illness, a routine question to identify underlying medical conditions that might be responsible for a similar appearance of confusion and disorientation. Constable Lawson described Gareth's attempt at walking the chalk line – 'He took 1 step and staggered across the room away from the line. He made a second attempt but after taking 1 step again lost his balance'.[60] Sergeant Chambers then asked Gareth to place his hands at his side, draw his right leg up and then place it down, and follow the procedure with his left leg.[61] Constable Lawson said that he lifted one leg about a foot and 3 inches off the ground, lost his balance and staggered to the side. He made two further attempts but failed. When Gareth was asked to write his name on a piece of paper, Constable Lawson noted that he made several botched attempts.[62] Prosecuted for manslaughter, Gareth was found guilty under s 291A. He killed 18-year-old Jim, who had stolen a car. The car had broken down on the side of the road and Jim and his friend Randell were parked on the verge, trying to get it started.[63] Jim suffered an extensive fracture of the skull, an intracranial haemorrhage and gross cerebral lacerations.[64] Gareth was released on bond.

The fact that, by 1957, blood alcohol testing had become a matter of law, albeit on a voluntary basis, was cast in some quarters as an infringement on civil liberties. Even some road safety campaigners were opposed to testing. Opponents argued that tests would violate the rights of drivers and contravene their common law right to avert self-incrimination.[65] The dead had no such immunity. Conducted at post-mortem, their test results were tabled as evidence from the early 1950s, irrespective that they were often passengers and, as such, their blood alcohol concentration was immaterial. Their test results did, however, seem to hold a kind of moral currency, even when they were paying customers. In 1951, a 23-year-old woman who was a passenger in a taxi was killed instantly when the driver, according to his own testimony, took a bend on a suburban street at a speed of 75 mph (120.70 km/h) and crashed.[66] At the time of death, her blood alcohol concentration was 0.17%. Perth District Medical Officer, Dr Pearson, and laboratory analyst, Dr Benjamin Southern, were cross-examined as to her degree of inebriation, as though her intoxication had a bearing on the defendant's conduct.[67] When a passenger was intoxicated it was difficult for the prosecution to secure their status as a legitimate victim and, as a corollary, the defendant's status as an offender.

Barristers attempted to reframe sobriety test results and witness testimony of intoxication as symptoms of shock, concussive injury and, occasionally, spontaneous seizure. As Lewis and Hirsh observed in 1964, a skilful barrister could always cast doubt by suggesting that the presentation of the accused might be due to an array of conditions.[68] It was often claimed that a defendant's appearance was due to a transient, mild traumatic brain injury and this strategy was sometimes successful. For instance, in 1956 Dr Colyner attended a crash scene and assisted Jeffrey to hospital. Jeffrey had suffered some minor injuries. Dr Colyner testified that Jeffrey smelt strongly of alcohol and was so unsteady in his gait that he was definitely under the influence. Under cross-examination at inquest, Colyner did concede that Jeffrey may have suffered a blow sufficient to cause a partial concussion. He maintained, however, that Jeffrey's presentation was primarily symptomatic of intoxication rather than shock. When pressed, Colyner held that shock might have been a partial and minor aspect of Jeffrey's presentation and appearance, but his unsteadiness of gait was due to intoxication. Colyner stated that the odour of alcohol was so strong he had to have the sunroof open en route to the hospital. As to why a sobriety test was not conducted, Dr Colyner stated that he was not requested to conduct a test by police and, in any case, it was unnecessary as Jeffrey was wholly incapable of passing one at any rate. Addressing the Coroner directly, Colyner declared his willingness to testify should the Crown press charges for driving under the influence.[69] Jeffrey was later acquitted of manslaughter.

Mr Wallwork was less successful in his attempts to resituate his client's presentation. In 1964 Karl was driving along Gugeri Street, Claremont, with his mother-in-law, her husband and nephew. Visibility was good and the weather dry. Karl testified that an Austin A40 drove directly towards him in his lane, hitting his vehicle head-on.[70] According to Karl, the vehicle did not alter its course, nor brake prior to impact.[71] Estimates of Vernon's speed, the driver of the Austin, varied between 45 and 55 mph (72.42 and 88.51 km/h) in a 30 mph zone (48.28 km/h).[72] The Austin was completely smashed in and, notwithstanding the car's comparatively diminutive build, it pushed the 1957 Holden, a considerably larger vehicle, backwards from the point of impact some 30 feet, where it was precariously close to plummeting down an embankment.[73]

All occupants of the Holden were taken to hospital, sustaining injuries severe enough to warrant stays of up to five months.[74] Vernon's wife was critically injured and later died following a cardiac arrest.[75] Doctors who attended Vernon described him as appearing inebriated, suffering from alcoholism and smelling strongly of liquor.[76] Observations of being dazed, amnesic, aggressive and possibly concussed were also made. Vernon reportedly oscillated between aggression and confusion in his manner and speech at the crash scene and immediately thereafter at hospital.[77] Earlier that day, he had visited the Fremantle Club for drinks with some friends in the morning and returned home at about 2.30 pm for lunch. His passengers reported that they visited another club after lunch, from around 3.30 pm to 7.30 pm.[78]

The defence challenged the expertise of Drs Benjamin, Bolton, Pearson and Marum. Mr Wallwork cross-examined Dr Pearson as to whether it was consistent with contemporary medical expertise that it was at times difficult to determine whether a man was suffering from concussion, shock or intoxication. Pearson replied that it was 'a very difficult question to answer'. Wallwork rephrased – 'I will put it to you another way doctor. Are the symptoms very similar?' Pearson conceded that they were. Wallwork laboured the point. He asked whether Dr Pearson might be inclined to dispute a citation from the tenth edition of Taylor's *Principles of Practice of Medical Jurisprudence*, where it stated that 'alcohol and other intoxicants may cause effects which on occasion may be diagnosed only with difficulty from the symptoms produced by injury. Conditions of shock or concussion are often attributed to drunkenness'. Dr Pearson reluctantly stated that he agreed with the passage.[79]

The doctors who treated Vernon in hospital resisted Wallwork's attempts to characterise his client's presentation as something other than intoxication. Dr Benjamin *insisted* that Vernon was affected by alcohol, although agreed he might have also been suffering a mild concussion.[80] Dr Marum testified that Vernon's breath smelt strongly of alcohol and he believed that it was the *major* factor in his presentation, concussion playing a much lesser role.[81] He noted that, by the following morning, Vernon's confusion and disorientation had completely resolved – a rapid recovery indicating that his behaviour was due to the effects of intoxication rather than a transient, mild traumatic brain injury.[82] Benjamin contested Wallwork's suggestion that Vernon was concussed, testifying that a flushed face was neither a symptom of concussion nor shock, but of intoxication. Wallwork asked whether he could state that with certainty – 'You can't say with certainty that his flushed face was due to alcohol? – I would have thought it was. – You would have thought it was, but you can't say that with certainty? – I can't think of any other cause that I could have put it down to'.[83]

Vernon was convicted of manslaughter and remanded for sentencing. Twelve days after the verdict, a letter from Dr Fletcher to Justice Negus revealed that the defence were fully aware that Vernon's intoxication was the principal cause of the crash, despite forcefully contesting that proposition at every opportunity in trial. Dr Fletcher advised that he had examined Vernon in prison. He noted that he had two previous convictions for drunkenness and, as a sad twist of fate, his wife had encouraged him to seek help through Alcoholics Anonymous. Dr Fletcher wrote that, contrary to Vernon's trial testimony and claims to sobriety, 'his steady drinking during the week, combined with his continuous drinking throughout the weekend' had 'produced a deterioration' and it was 'during such a bout that he failed to control his car', so killing his wife. He advised that Vernon had 'some insight into his alcoholic problem' and suggested treatment.[84] Justice Negus adopted Fletcher's suggestions, recommending that the last twelve months of his eighteen-month term be served in a rehabilitation centre.[85] Notably Vernon's 'insight' and candour occurred on the eve of his sentencing hearing, well after his opportunity to plead guilty.

Medical experts countered claims regarding the significance of a defendant's alcohol tolerance in relation to their habituation, height and weight, arguing that once a certain blood alcohol concentration was reached, impairment would be experienced in all cases. Defendants' representatives were apt to counter that, despite very high levels of consumption, their clients were habituated drinkers and, as such, they were unaffected by alcohol. Their clients were more than capable of drinking and driving. Drink-driving ability was bound in notions of masculinity – 'real men' could hold their liquor and get themselves and their 'mates' home.[86] The following exchange between the Crown Prosecutor Dodd and the defendant in *R v D.A.W.* (1965) was characteristic of men's claims that they had not, in fact, had too much to drink.

[Mr Dodd commencing]: Did you have a glass of beer at Moora?
I had a glass of beer at New Norcia.
So you had two brandies and a glass of beer?
Yes.

By the way, are you normally a brandy drinker?
No.
Do you usually drink beer?
Yes.
Why were you drinking brandy on this occasion?
I don't know. I just didn't want to have a beer.
So by the time you had left New Norcia, from what you say, you would have had five or six brandies and a middy of beer?
Yes.
I think you have heard evidence given that on the way you bought a couple of chickens and they were eaten and two bottles of beer were passed around and drunk on the way to Bindoon?
I can remember eating the chickens but I don't remember anything else.
That again is highly dangerous [approaching a bend], is it not, at 60 m.p.h. or thereabouts?
Yes.
You would agree that if you were drinking from a bottle going along driving, it would be highly dangerous too, as far as your control of the car was concerned?
Yes.
You said Detective Martin's evidence was correct at this interview. Where did you drink this wine you told him about?
Just after I left New Norcia I had a mouthful of wine.
From the bottle?
Yes.
I suppose mixing brandy, beer and wine would affect you rather more than if you were just drinking the one drink – beer or brandy?
Not necessarily.
You don't think it would affect you?
No.
You have never drunk brandy before?
I have drunk it before, yes.
But not in any quantity?

Not in any quantity.
If you had 10 brandies, I suppose, do you think that would affect your driving?
I don't think so.
I notice you told the Detective "I wouldn't have had more than half a dozen. I didn't drink much at all".
Yes.
That is what you thought of half a dozen, was it?
Yes.
It wasn't too much for you to drink?
Not too much.
Do you think the same thing about 10 brandies?
I think the same thing, yes.
What would you think if you had ten brandies and a middy of beer and some (say a quarter of a bottle of beer as you drove along) wine? Do you think that would have affected your driving, or your ability to drive?
Not over the time, I don't think.
You don't think it would – between 7.00 and 10.30?
I don't think so.
Do you think you would have driven quite normally and quite responsibly, do you?
Yes.[87]

Trial testimonies also demonstrated the degree to which attitudes towards drinking and driving have changed considerably. Between the mid-1940s and 1960s, many drivers freely testified that they drove with a drink in hand or held between the thighs and that they discarded empty bottles out the window. Some defendants explained that the bottle collection in the footwell of the back seat was the refuse of their daily couple of beers at lunch and a couple more on the nightly journey home. One defendant claimed he did so because he was concerned about being fined for littering; his anxiety about being fined for drinking and driving was demonstrably less.[88]

Defendants often reported driving after excessive alcohol consumption as a matter of routine. For example in 1961, Ronan recounted what he called his 'West Coast pub crawl'. By his own admission, he first went to the Oxford Hotel and had a middy of beer. He then drove to the Claremont Hotel and had another. Following that he drove to the Captain Stirling where he had two more. He then went to the Nedlands Hotel where he consumed a further two middies, the Continental where he had two more and, lastly, the Scarborough Hotel where he drank five.[89] Shortly after leaving, he hit a 56-year-old pedestrian. The man was pronounced dead on arrival at Royal Perth Hospital.[90] Constable MacGregor described Ronan swaying by the roadside with red eyes, a glazed appearance and his trousers undone.[91] He apparently kept overbalancing and had to sit down. The stretcher-bearers carrying the injured man were forced to walk around Ronan – he could not orientate himself out of the way.[92] Ronan pleaded guilty in exchange for the manslaughter charge being downgraded. He was one of thirty-four drivers who entered a guilty plea.

Mr Hatfield, Ronan's barrister, appealed to Chief Justice Wolff that his client was a young man, just turned twenty-five, who had a solid work history and a promising career in the Royal Australian Air Force.[93] Hatfield called on a Member of Parliament to provide a character reference, in addition to Ronan's father and a well-known Anglican minister. The parliamentarian stated that he had known the family for three decades and that Ronan had come from a good home.[94] The clergyman told the Court that Ronan would help at church and take part in Christmas plays.[95] Hatfield petitioned the Chief Justice that, were he to imprison Ronan, he would lose his job.[96] Chief Justice Wolff stated that he had serious misgivings about the Crown accepting a plea for the alternative, lesser offence given the degree of negligent conduct involved. He was also 'greatly troubled' about whether to imprison Ronan. Notwithstanding Wolff's serious misgivings about the plea bargaining given the very serious nature of the case, he limited Ronan's punishment to a fine of £350 on the grounds of his youth and good character.[97]

Rory was similarly candid about the amount of alcohol he had consumed. In 1971, 17-year-old Rory visited the Balmoral Hotel at 10.45 am. According to his testimony, he drank beer and green ginger wine. At 2.00 pm, he left to visit a bar in Victoria Park. Over the following hour, he drank several more beers and green ginger wine, before collecting a car and driving down to the riverside. There he and two friends shared eighteen bottles of beer. Rory then drove to the Hurlingham Hotel where he had several Bacardi rums and more green ginger wine.[98] Just before 7.30 pm, he left the Hurlingham to visit his girlfriend and killed a 47-year-old woman and her 16-year-old daughter on the way.[99] Rory's driving was so erratic and alarming that other drivers veered off the road to avoid him.[100] He was travelling at speed in a straight line on the wrong side of the road when he collided with the other vehicle. He did not attempt to correct his course, brake or swerve, hitting the car head-on.[101] Before he fled the crash scene on foot,[102] his face covered in blood, Rory told a witness – 'It wasn't me lady. I've never driven a car in my life'.[103]

In trial, Crown Prosecutor Davies claimed that there was nothing more Rory could have possibly done to display greater reckless disregard, other than perhaps hanging his 'head out of the driver's window yelling out, "I don't care what happens to you"'.[104] The damage to the victims' car was so extensive that the roof had to be cut open in order to extract the bodies.[105] At seventeen, Rory already had an extensive record, with fourteen criminal convictions.[106] He had additionally been nine times convicted of unlawfully driving a motor vehicle and twice for driving without a licence.[107] Rory's barrister claimed that his client was 'too young to be discarded with no hope'.[108] Convicted for one count of manslaughter, Rory was sentenced to three years' imprisonment, with a non-parole period of just nine months.

While a few intoxicated drivers collapsed in tears at crash scenes and readily admitted fault, others were decidedly hostile.

According to the attending officers in *R v C.J.F.* (1967), 18-year-old Callum disparagingly described the cyclist he had just run down as that 'joker lying on the footpath'.[109] He refused to give his name and address, calling Constable Smith a 'copper bastard' who could 'get fucked'.[110] In any event, he told Sergeant Connolly that he was 'fucked' if he knew his name anyway.[111] At Central Station, he broadcast his sentiments widely, allegedly declaring that police officers were all 'fucking copper bastards' who 'sit round the heaters all fucking day'.[112] On being informed that he would be required to submit to a blood test, Callum promptly told Constable Smith to 'get fucked you long skinny copper cunt'.[113] He claimed that he was not intoxicated. Constable Matthews said that Callum's use of 'abusive language' was relentless.[114] On asking whether he might be allowed to 'have a piss', Callum offered to 'piss on the fucking floor'.[115] He refused to balance on one leg for the purposes of a sobriety test, maintaining that he had no part in the incident – 'that fucking bastard on his bike had no light. I was not driving. I was in someone else's car'.[116] In another case where the driver had a blood alcohol content of 0.163% at the time of the crash in which his friend was killed, he asserted that traffic inspectors were all 'standover bastards' who were hell bent on victimising him and his friends.[117] Inebriated drivers often cast themselves as happenstance victims of overzealous police and negligent pedestrians and cyclists.

It was also common for defendants and their passengers to describe stopping for drinks throughout the course of a long journey as unremarkable. For example in 1951, Oscar, a friend and passenger of Brian, described the trip home. Leaving at 11.00 am, they stopped at a hotel in Maylands for drinks, and then continued on to Midland Junction where they stopped for three more drinks. An hour-and-a-half later, the party stopped at Bakers Hill and had a further five or six beers. They arrived in Northam at about 3.30 pm where they visited the Commercial Hotel and had a further three drinks and bought some pies to eat on the way.[118] They later stopped at a pub in Goomalling, about

40 kilometres north-east of Northam. The bartender on duty would later describe Brian as appearing affected by liquor and talking in a loud voice.[119] Constable Wass who attended the crash scene had also seen Brian prior to the collision. Wass knew Brian. He claimed that Brian was uncharacteristically loud and animated, that his enunciation was inconsistent with his usual manner of speaking, and that he staggered when walking and swayed when attempting to stand still.[120] Less than an hour later, Brian crashed into another vehicle on the crest of a hill. A man and his son in the oncoming car were killed.[121]

There was some suggestion that the driver of the other car had consumed two 'glasses' of beer.[122] In Western Australia, a glass of beer measures 200 mLs. The Crown led evidence that established that Brian was on the wrong side of the road when he hit the oncoming vehicle, but the jury found him not guilty. Where cases involved a collision between two vehicles in which both drivers had consumed alcohol, juries were disinclined to convict, even when the deceased's consumption was negligible.[123] This occurred in circumstances when it was clear that a driver hit another vehicle because he was driving over the white lines and into the opposite lane of oncoming traffic. It also occurred in cases where the deceased driver had a substantial blood alcohol concentration but appeared not to be at fault for the collision as he was hit by another driver who was travelling in the wrong lane.[124] Alcohol consumption was enough to cast doubt over a deceased's status as a victim, but was insufficient to establish a driver's guilt.

The amendments of 1957 which introduced the offence of 'driving under the influence', and tied the definition of under the influence to a blood alcohol concentration of 0.15%, signalled the decline of the sobriety test. From then on, drivers with a blood alcohol concentration of 0.15% or more were technically *incapable* of controlling a vehicle. The subsidiary regulations prescribed an elaborate testing methodology.[125] The introduction of the 0.15% offence did, however, fail to have the impact on prosecutions one might have anticipated. In addition, the test remained voluntary. During the same period, voluntary blood alcohol tests were available in England and the USA, while testing was already compulsory in some parts of Europe.[126] While the introduction of blood alcohol testing gave the prosecution the *possibility* of putting concrete evidence before a jury, it did not automatically result in the admissibility of test results or convictions. A finding of criminal negligence typically required a sequential and overt departure from what a 'reasonable driver' might do. A reasonable driver might drink and drive, have a blood alcohol concentration of 0.15% or more, but *appear* to be adequately managing the vehicle from the point of view of a bystander; a sticking point that led to radical amendments to the *Road Traffic Act* in 2004.

Despite that, as of 1957, at 0.15% a driver was incapable of driving, and between 0.05% to 0.14% intoxication was a matter for consideration in trial, the prescribed range was out of step with contemporaneous medical expertise. In 1938, Dr Selesnick had argued that 0.15%, the level deemed 'incapable' in some parts of the United States, and in WA in 1957, was set far too high.[127] Internationally, medicos were advocating that 0.05% was the absolute highest blood alcohol concentration that could be endorsed for the safety of other road users and that the effects of alcohol were statistically significant at concentration levels below 0.05%.[128] At the First International Symposium on Accident and Traffic Medicine in Rome in 1963, it was unanimously resolved that under *no* circumstances should a blood alcohol concentration in excess of 0.05% be acceptable.[129] The 1963 Victorian Royal Commission into the Sale, Supply, Disposal or Consumption of Liquor held that driving with a blood alcohol concentration in excess of 0.05% was selfish, anti-social and irresponsible.[130] The resolutions of the International Symposium and the Victorian Royal Commission were borne out by the Grand Rapids study of 1964, then the most extensive epidemiological study conducted worldwide.[131] It canvassed almost 6,000 drivers involved in a crash against a substantial control group. The study correlated increased risk of crash involvement with blood alcohol concentrations, persuasively demonstrating that the probability of crash involvement increased exponentially at 0.08% and over.[132] At 0.15%, the probability of *causing* an 'accident' was estimated at more than twenty-five times as likely as that of a sober driver.[133] The results of the survey demonstrated increased risk at levels as low as 0.04%. Crash involvement increased dramatically as blood alcohol concentrations approached 0.05%.[134]

Of course, some of the benefits that the 1957 amendments might have yielded would depend on whether the driver consented to giving a blood sample. In the early 1960s, interest groups began writing in earnest to the government, lobbying for the introduction of mandatory testing.[135] The Commissioner of Police responded that the introduction of a compulsory regime was controversial. He claimed that, as there were ongoing disputes as to the accuracy of the science, a science that was in fact well established, he was disinclined to introduce compulsory testing.[136]

Breath tests were introduced in Western Australia in 1965, alongside mandatory breath and blood testing in limited circumstances.[137] The following year extensive regulations were introduced for breath analysis and procedures, in addition to a systematic revision of the existing blood alcohol regulations.[138] Breathalysers were advantageous in that they made an immediate reading possible, as opposed to waiting several days for a result. The amendments ostensibly signalled the end to a driver's right to decline a test in certain circumstances,[139] although drivers still refused. Where a person had suffered a fatal injury, or an injury that required immediate medical attention, and the police had *grounds* to believe that a driver occasioned or was the proximate cause of injury and was *affected* by alcohol to the extent of *impairment*, an officer could *require* the driver to submit to a preliminary breath test.[140] In addition, where a driver required immediate medical attention and was incapable of undertaking a breath test or breath analysis equipment was not available, a blood sample could be compulsorily taken in hospital, although there were significant tensions between prosecutors and police when medicos refused to administer tests and hospital administrators backed their staff.[141]

In 1968, drink-driving laws came under further review. The Director of the Public Health Laboratories, heads of department and senior surgeons of Royal Perth Hospital, and academics of the University of Western Australia wrote to the Minister for Transport, demanding legislative change and harsher penalties. The signatories stated that, in WA, over one-third of 'dead drivers' were 'frankly drunk'. They noted that legislative efforts to date had had no effect on fatality rates, which continued to escalate unabated. Signatories informed the Minister that, of *all* admissions to Royal Perth Hospital, 12 per cent were road crash victims. In line with international consensus, they contended that the two skills most critical for driving – perception and judgment – were impaired at 0.05% and dangerously suppressed at 0.08%. Accordingly, they argued that the law should be amended to make 0.08% an offence in line with the UK's amendments of 1967.[142]

Commonly referred to as drink-driving, the 0.08% offence was introduced in 1968.[143] Importantly, the introduction of the offence did not establish a 0.08% blood alcohol concentration as a measure of incapability, but rather as a strict liability offence. It was not until 1992 that driving with a blood alcohol concentration equal to or exceeding 0.05% and below 0.08% became an offence in Western Australia.[144] By international standards, bar the USA,[145] WA was slow to legislate. Czechoslovakia introduced 0.03% as proof of impairment in the mid-twentieth century,[146] Norway introduced an offence of 0.05% in 1936, and in 1957, Sweden lowered the threshold from 0.08% to 0.05%.[147] Victoria was the first Australian state to adopt 0.05% in 1965.[148]

The *Traffic Act* was further amended in 1968 to give police greater powers. Under the amendments, if an officer had *grounds* to believe that a driver was involved in an incident occasioning injury or damage to property, or had committed any offence under the Act of which driving was an element and 'had alcohol in his body', the officer could *require* the driver to submit to a preliminary roadside screening test, also known as an alcotest.[149] The purpose of the test was to determine if any further action was required, although *random* breath testing was not introduced in WA until 1988.[150] If preliminary results indicated a driver's blood alcohol concentration was in excess of the prescribed level, the driver was required to submit to a further, more sophisticated breath analysis or blood test.[151] Notwithstanding, drivers could and did refuse. Aspects of the 1968 amendments were poorly drafted, which created significant obstacles.[152]

Under the blood alcohol test regulations, results were calculated back to the *time of the incident* on the basis that concentration levels rose at 0.016% per hour for the first two hours after the last drink, and then fell at the same rate for a further two hours.[153] Tests had to be conducted within four hours of the incident.[154] The fact that the exact time of the last drink was critical to an accurate calculation of a driver's blood alcohol concentration provided enormous scope for distorting and disputing test results. When in dispute, that scope gave the defence a diversionary avalanche of mathematical and scientific minutiae to raise doubt and confusion in the minds of the jury. Barristers were particularly keen to revisit defendants' initial statements as to the time of their last drink in order to skew test results in their favour. Despite the fact that this represented an implicit admission that their client had initially lied to police, counsel pursued the issue in order that test results might be revised downwards or, at minimum, called into question. Another common tactic was to prolong the cross-examination of laboratory analysts to dampen the impact of their testimony by obfuscating the test results in a morass of detail. Mr Wood's drawn out cross-examination of Harry Kretchmar in 1970 was characteristic.

[Mr Wood commencing]: This shows, does it not, that the actual alcohol level in the sample she was analysing was .178 per cent?
Correct.
Well, at 0.178 per cent, as they say. That was the actual content, was it?

That is the actual content of the sample as received by the analyst. That would be the level of alcohol in the blood of the person from whom the sample was taken?
That's correct; yes.
I think the certificate is based on the fact that at the time of the taking of the sample and the date was 1.52 a.m. on the 3rd March 1970. Is that right?
That's right, yes.
The calculation that the accused's alcohol level at what it called the "time of the occurrence", which we know was the accident time, which was 0.193, is based on two facts is it not?
It is based on the two facts of the two times involved; that is, the time at which the accident happened and the time at which the last drink was taken.
Now, those facts respectively: The time of the accident was 11.05 p.m. – that is, before midnight – prior to when the test was taken; and the time of the last drink was at 10.00 p.m. Is that right?
Yes.
I notice, looking at para.4 of this certificate, Exhibit "E", that there is a clause in there – a printed clause – with an answer put in – in, "alleged time of last drink" and there is the answer in that certificate about "10 p.m." Is that right?
Yes.
Could you make a calculation of what the alcohol level of the person would have been at 11.5 p.m. [sic] if the time of the last drink had been 11 p.m. – five minutes before the accident?
The last drink was had at 11 p.m.?
Yes, five minutes before the occurrence of the accident. Could you calculate that for us?
0.163. If the last drink were at 11 o'clock since the blood alcohol concentration rises for two hours, the maximum concentration in the blood will be at 1 o'clock. The event took place at 11.05 so from 11.05 until 1 the blood is increasing in alcohol concentration. That means that it is going up for 115 minutes isn't it? 11.05 to 12 is 55 minutes and from 12 until 1 is 60. 60 and 55 makes 115. From

1 until 1.52 – that is after 2 hours – it is falling, so it is falling for 52 minutes. The difference between 52 and 115 I make 63, so it is actually a net rise of 63 minutes. It rises .016 in 60 minutes, so it is near enough to .017. You've got to subtract that from the actual concentration found in the sample which would bring it down to 0.163. It rises .016 in 60 minutes, so that is near enough to .017 and you have to subtract that from the actual concentration found in the sample, to bring it down to 0.163.

So you are saying, in effect, that if the accused had had his last drink of alcohol about five minutes before the accident his alcohol level at the accident time (or "the time of the occurrence", as it is called) would be 0.163 per cent. Is that right?

That's right.

I think in the course of your explanation you said there is a rise in the alcohol level for two hours after the time of the last drink. Is that right?

Yes.

And I take it that is due to the fact that it takes time, once the drink has passed into the body through the mouth for the alcohol to be ingested into the bloodstream. Is that right?

Yes. That is right.

Then this process of ingestion goes on for a couple of hours does it?

Yes.

Two hours; then it reverses and starts to diminish?

Yes.

If a person had had his last drink at 11.00 p.m. and was involved in an accident not long after (and he was under the influence of alcohol at the time of the accident) would you expect him to show symptoms of being under the influence of alcohol?

[Justice Neville] He is not an expert on that, I don't think.

All right, sir. I think that is all I wanted to ask Mr Kretchmar.[155]

Defendants' representatives continued to argue that crashes were inexplicable, even when test results revealed blood alcohol levels well in excess of the 'incapable' threshold, pointing to a plausible explanation for a driver's loss of control. Without an eyewitness to support the allegation, or where a passenger was a reluctant or hostile witness, guilty verdicts were virtually impossible to secure. While the Crown occasionally managed to convince the jury that the manner of the driving could be deduced from the crash scene, the defence argued that, as no one had witnessed the manner of the driving, the driver could not be held responsible.

In *R v G.C.B.* (1970), Graham claimed he could not recall anything about the crash in his initial statement to police. Graham, Paul and Adrian were travelling home from a holiday. Graham recalled that he had two beers at Northampton, half a glass of beer at Dongara and a cup of rum at Mingenew or Three Springs. He also told Constable Gibson that he had bought a bottle of rum and consumed some during the course of the journey. At the hospital, he told Constable Gibson he could not remember what happened.[156] Immediately prior to the scene of the crash there was a reduce speed sign, a further sign to indicate an upcoming intersection and an additional sign warning of an approaching bend.[157] Graham's surviving passenger claimed he was asleep at the time of the crash.[158] There were no other witnesses.

The Crown highlighted the inconsistencies between Graham's testimony in trial and his initial statement. On speed, the Crown noted that, if the party *had* left Geraldton at 6.30 pm and the crash occurred at Walebing at 11.00 pm, and they stopped for two-and-a-half hours along the way, there were only two remaining hours to travel 208 miles (334.74 km). Therefore, Graham must have been travelling at a speed greater than 50 to 60 mph, which he claimed.[159] In his initial statement, Graham maintained that he did not remember anything, other than what he had had to drink, contrary to his position in trial where he claimed that he *did* remember the events but had seen only one of the road signs, was not speeding and simply overshot the bend.[160] He had thought that the road continued straight ahead, became confused, and hit the gravel.[161] However, the gouge and tyre marks at the scene commenced well into the bend of the road.[162] On reflection, it seemed that Graham had time to consider an alternative explanation. Prosecutor Davies was particularly interested in the point at which the defendant abruptly ceased his disclosure at the hospital and refused to sign his statement.

> [Mr Davies commencing]: What does the next part say? "I don't remember anything else until I was brought to the hospital. I don't know what time I was brought to the hospital." That does not agree with what you are saying today, does it?
> That is why I didn't sign it then.
> That is why you did not sign it?
> That's right. I didn't want to tell the constable what happened in case I ended up like I am now – in court being prosecuted. I never thought I would be in an unlawful killing charge. I didn't like the consequences, so I declined from signing.
> Well you told the constable you couldn't remember?
> That is what I told him yes.
> So you told the constable all about the earlier drinking?
> Yes.
> But you decided not to tell him any more. The last thing you told him was that you were going along the road having a drink from a bottle of rum. You decided that any more might get you into trouble. Is that right?
> That is not right.
> Why did you tell him "I don't remember"?
> Because I didn't think the amount of alcohol I had had would have affected me as far as a breathalyser or blood count were concerned. I wasn't concerned about that part of it at the time.
> So you do remember?
> I remember all right, sir.[163]

Despite calculations of Graham's blood alcohol concentration being as high as 0.193%, Mr Wood appealed to the jury that *any one of them* who had driven with the 'greatest of care' for decades would appreciate that an occasion might arise when 'for some extraordinary inexplicable reason you just don't see something'.[164] The inexplicable extraordinary reason was, according to the defence, neither alcohol nor speed. There was, according to Mr Wood, no evidence of reckless conduct. The marks on the road indicated that the defendant was in the correct lane and he had simply taken the bend too wide and hit the gravel, losing control.[165] Wood claimed that, other than the car running off the road, there was no evidence to suggest that Graham was not managing the vehicle properly.[166] His surviving passenger maintained that Graham's driving was unremarkable prior to falling asleep.

In closing, the Crown held that the defendant's blood alcohol level, well in excess of the 'incapable' threshold, conclusively proved that Graham would have been unable to drive with reasonable care and caution.[167] Prosecutor Davies argued that the extensive damage to the vegetation, broken and bent signposts, gouge marks in the road, tyre marks of 159 feet, coupled with a further distance of 150 feet before the car finally came to rest, were indicative of a speed much greater than 50 mph,[168] and the combination of speed and intoxication was criminally negligent. The jury found Graham not guilty. Forty-four years later, a blood alcohol concentration of 0.15% or more would *deem* Graham responsible for the death.

Once blood alcohol concentration levels became a matter of law, evidence thereof was subject to relentless dispute. Test results were hotly contested by defence barristers who cried persecution, irrelevance and inaccuracy, arguing that results should be ruled inadmissible as their prejudicial value overshadowed their probative weight. Results were also subject to contest because of conflicting statements regarding the time of the driver's last drink. Drivers seemed acutely aware that they could alter the outcome of test results by providing false statements regarding the time of their last drink, a problem well known to prosecutors and police. Perth barrister Heenan gave away another method of deception when he mentioned in a newspaper interview that, if a driver had one or two 'medicinal' drinks after the crash and before police arrived, it would be impossible to establish his blood alcohol concentration at the time of the collision.[169]

Under the blood alcohol provisions, if a driver's blood alcohol concentration was 0.05% or less at the time of the alleged offence, that was *prima facie* evidence that he or she was *not* under the influence of intoxicating liquor. A reading in excess of 0.05% but less than 0.15% *could* be considered in conjunction with other relevant and admissible evidence, but would not of itself give rise to a presumption that the driver was under the influence.[170] A result of 0.15% or more, calculated back to the time of the alleged offence, was *prima facie* evidence that the driver was under the influence and incapable of driving.[171] Despite the introduction of the 0.08% offence in 1968, by the late 1960s, some judges were interpreting 0.15% as the threshold for admitting evidence. On occasion, blood alcohol concentrations below that threshold were ruled inadmissible.

In *R v A.R.B.* in 1970 for instance, Mr Miller argued that evidence regarding his client's blood alcohol concentration should be ruled out. He claimed that, as 0.15% was the legal presumption of incapability, and below that concentration there was no presumption one way or another, anything under 0.15% was 'redundant' and should not be led as evidence. While he conceded that driving with a concentration of 0.08% was an offence it was, according to Miller, simply that.[172] His client's blood alcohol concentration was 0.091%.[173] While the Crown acknowledged that Justice Burt had recently held a reading under 0.15% inadmissible, it argued that the question of admissibility did not arise from the statute.[174] Justice Wickham resolved the matter on the side of the defence, stating that

> I am not satisfied that the test result is admissible under the statute for purposes other than sub–s (4) of s.32(c), and that being so I would find Dr Hainsworth's evidence being based as it is on the result of the breathalyser test, or at least directed to the effect of

the approximate result of that test to be inadmissible. In any event, having regard to the fact that the defence will be presented on the basis that the accused never at any time saw the deceased, although the evidence of the accused being affected by alcohol may be just relevant, its relevance in my view is minimal and the prejudicial effect of it so outweighs its probative value that I should, in my discretion, exclude…in addition to that, [exclude] all evidence that the accused had consumed any alcohol at any material time including, as I have observed from the depositions, one piece of evidence that his breath smelled of liquor.[175]

The fact that intoxication was not an element of manslaughter or s 291A bolstered attempts to argue against the admissibility of evidence thereof. For example, in *R v G.N.M.* (1969), Justice Virtue absented the jury to consider Mr Singleton's opposition to the evidence. Singleton argued that, as drink-driving offences were distinct from manslaughter, his client's blood alcohol concentration bore no relevance as to whether he was driving in a criminally negligent manner. He protested that its admission would prejudice the jury.[176] The defendant's blood alcohol concentration was estimated between 0.129% and 0.193% at the time of the crash.[177] A precise figure was not possible given conflicting testimony as to the time of his last drink. Crown Prosecutor, Mr Parker, conceded that while the test of negligence did not turn on intoxication, evidence of blood alcohol should be admissible where its probative value was of weight. Parker argued for its inclusion because of the very nature of the crash – the accused was on the wrong side of the road at the point of impact. He fled the scene. The fact that he had consumed a significant amount of alcohol might assist the jury in its consideration of what would appear to be otherwise inexplicable events.[178] Justice Virtue ruled in the Crown's favour.[179]

In another trial that same year, Mr O'Dea similarly moved to have his client's test results excluded.[180] Witnesses described an EJ Holden being driven erratically, veering from one side of the road to the other, at considerable speed.[181] The driver, Evan, had attempted to overtake several cars on the inside gravel verge and tailgated a number of vehicles in the lead up to the crash.[182] According to Constable Barrett, Evan could barely talk or recall his name at the scene of the crash and collapsed to the ground, crying.[183] He had an extensive record, including drunken and reckless driving, four charges of speeding, failure to stop at stop signs and car theft, and he had been suspended from driving on three occasions.[184] In the course of the crash, Evan hit a Morris 1100 from behind. The impact forced the Morris across the opposite lane where it ended up wrapped around a lamp pole. Evan's car was discovered at the scene on its roof.[185] Sharon was driving home after collecting her husband from his nightshift in Kwinana. Her 10-year-old son was in the passenger seat. She died at the scene.[186]

Evan claimed he was trying to overtake Sharon but, as he attempted to do so, she slowed down and suddenly swerved to the right, causing him to inadvertently hit her vehicle. Despite the fact that he was employed as a truck driver, Evan maintained he was unaware that an unbroken white line to the right of the driver's side indicated that overtaking was prohibited.[187] Mr O'Dea argued that the crash was caused by Sharon's distraction – he contended that she and her husband were arguing.[188] Sharon's son and husband's testimonies were apparently of little weight because they were not paying attention to the manner of Sharon's driving.

> One can feel sorry for Mr Bennett and his son. One can get very emotional about these poor unfortunate people, but do they know whether the vehicle slowed or not? Now really do they know? They don't know what hit them, I think would be the correct way of putting it. They were driving calmly along in their car; the boy sitting in the front seat looking at the fireflies (paying no attention to the driving); Mr Bennett sitting quietly in the back (also paying no attention to the driving). How do they know whether the vehicle was slowing down or was not slowing down? They were not paying attention. Why should they know?[189]

The lowest possible calculation of Evan's blood alcohol concentration at the time of the crash was 0.156% and the highest 0.220%.[190] Again, the uncertainty turned around the time of Evan's last drink. His defence argued that the prejudicial impact of the test results outweighed their probative value. Justice Jackson contended of the emerging case law that, if the evidence of consumption of liquor was such that it would have an effect on the manner of the driving then it was admissible. If it was merely to demonstrate that the defendant had had *something* to drink it would not be.[191] When efforts to have laboratory results excluded were unsuccessful, the defence simply rejected their importance in the closing arguments. Accordingly, while Evan conceded that he did drink that evening, he insisted it had not affected his driving ability and he was able to drive quite competently. Mr O'Dea stated that his client was not 'driving carelessly, recklessly, [or] dangerously'.[192] The jury were not convinced. Evan was found guilty under s 291A and sentenced to three years' imprisonment with a minimum non-parole period of twelve months.

In sharp contrast, in 1972 Bailey left a trail of tyre marks of a distance of 234 feet before he hit a tree. He careered off a straight stretch of road.[193] His brother Adam and Adam's girlfriend Tracey were killed in the crash. Justice Wickham ruled the defendant's blood alcohol concentration and expert testimony regarding the effects of that concentration inadmissible on the grounds of irrelevance.[194] Bailey's blood alcohol concentration was calculated between 0.146% and 0.210% owing to variant reports on the time of his last drink. While Wickham noted that the car had left a straight road and hit a tree, he held there was *no* evidence, other than the happening of the 'accident' itself, to suggest that the defendant was failing to act with reasonable care.[195] Irrespective of the weight of international evidence, that impairment was evident at concentrations below 0.05%, Wickham delivered this surprising précis.

> To say therefore statistically, as the result of clinical or other studies, the probability is that a man with a blood alcohol content of that of

the accused could not focus his eyes properly, his sense of judgment of distance and speed would be adversely affected, and that his reaction time would be gravely affected throws no light on the cause of the occurrence in the particular case...I rejected this evidence not because the weight was slight and its form likely to be prejudicial but on the ground that it was not relevant at all... In this particular case the most that Dr. Laurie's evidence could establish or help to establish was that the driving skills of the accused might be impaired. It could not help to establish in what particular respect the skill of the accused failed in a way relevant to the happening. There was nothing to support a Crown case that the accident happened through lack of skill and which could in turn be explained by the accused's alcoholic condition so as to elevate a case of lack of skill to negligence and from there to gross negligence. There were no eye-witnesses to the accident and the accused could remember nothing, and there was simply no connection between the proposed evidence and the central facts in issue...[196]

Bailey was acquitted.

Unless there was a montage of extrinsically 'reckless' observed conduct leading up to a crash, supported by eyewitness testimony, it was difficult to secure a conviction, particularly in instances where drivers had failed to regulate or modify their driving in accordance with the circumstances. As criminal negligence was also contingent on context, the Crown's fundamental position was that, in assuming control of a large, heavy piece of machinery in the propinquity of others, a very high duty of care was required. It was here that prosecutions proved the most difficult.

Chapter Five

Killing them softly, 1946–1974

The deaths of pedestrians and cyclists

While it was difficult to prosecute cases involving collisions between vehicles, or single-vehicle crashes in the absence of an observed sequence of negligent conduct, those involving pedestrians and cyclists proved even more challenging. In addition to exemplifying the mounting hegemony of the car, cases involving vulnerable road users epitomised the difficulties associated with displacing the notion of 'accident'. Where intoxication was an aggravating and contributing factor, the prospect of conviction increased, but only if there was an observed sequence of *exceptionally* bad driving. In the absence of eyewitnesses, responsibility for the 'accident' was readily attributed to the deceased. Where alcohol was not at issue and cases turned around drivers' failure to modify their conduct in accordance with the circumstances, acquittals were virtually guaranteed.

Given their charge of a dangerous object, drivers had, and retain, a duty to keep a proper lookout for pedestrians and cyclists. Notwithstanding that duty, the issue at stake was the point at which court participants were prepared to deem a driver's failure to use reasonable care and take reasonable precautions *criminal*. Cases involving pedestrians and cyclists demonstrated that drivers were given very wide latitude. On the observations of others who have noted, based on snapshots of historical data, that pedestrians and cyclists appeared to be disproportionately represented in fatality statistics, that courts and juries adopted a merciful approach to drivers who killed vulnerable road users, and that few of those cases made it to trial,[1] Western Australian Supreme Court cases were probative. Of 120 cases sampled between 1946 and 1974, thirty-seven involved vulnerable road users.[2] Of those, there were thirteen cyclists and twenty-four pedestrians. Eight of the cases were hit and runs.[3] Of the thirty-seven males brought before the Supreme Court for the deaths of vulnerable road users, twenty-one were acquitted.[4] Of the sixteen convictions, five were pleas, four in exchange for downgrading the charge from manslaughter to s 291A. Of the sixteen men convicted for killing a pedestrian or cyclist, one quarter received a non-custodial penalty. Of the remaining twelve, only one offender received a penalty of more than two years – a hit-and-run driver who mounted a kerb and hit a woman and her child who were walking along the pavement. The woman was killed. Her 8-year-old daughter survived.[5] The driver was sentenced to three years in prison.[6] Most offenders were penalised with a head sentence between six and eighteen months.

Of the eight hit-and-run cases, there were five guilty verdicts. Chronologically, the sentences imposed were as follows – three years' imprisonment, released on bond, twelve months' imprisonment, six months' imprisonment and eighteen months' imprisonment with a non-parole period of five months.[7] Hit-and-run drivers invariably claimed that they simply did not know how their vehicle had become damaged, yet sought to conceal and repair dents and damage overnight, all the while maintaining to investigating officers that they had not been involved in a crash.[8]

Not only was there the matter of killing another road user, there were also the additional and separate charges of failing to render assistance, leaving the scene of a crash, failure to report an 'accident', in addition to other possible charges, including driving under the influence and, sometimes, driving whilst disqualified or unlicensed. However, if a guilty verdict was secured for the death, the additional charges were invariably dropped. Drivers were therefore not charged with or penalised for the additional aspects of their conduct that were considered especially grave. When the victim was a pedestrian or cyclist, the so-called 'callous indifference'[9] of leaving a person to die without help or assistance seemed to have little tangible impact on sentences. The mitigating factor of youth generally outweighed the merciless conduct of hit-and-run offenders.

According to defendants' representatives, the problem was that pedestrians and cyclists were never *visible* enough. It was an effective defence, sufficient to cast doubt over the evidence mounted by the prosecution. Of the twenty-four pedestrian cases,[10] there were only nine convictions.[11] Even when the factual circumstances had all the hallmarks of a particularly serious offence, sentences were remarkably low against that authorised by the legislature. Despite the fact that a driver's conduct may have demonstrated a *gross* failure to use reasonable care and take reasonable precautions, in addition to fleeing the scene, failing to report the crash and very high degrees of intoxication, penalties were egregiously lenient. Verdicts also demonstrated that, in order to be convicted for killing a pedestrian or cyclist, the degree of negligence had to be utterly exceptional.

Despite the fact that hit-and-run 'accidents' were cast socially as an inhumane, abhorrent act of cowardice, there was a conspicuous discord between that public perception, judges' sentencing remarks and the penalties imposed, more so than 'road deaths' in other factual circumstances. For instance, in 1950, Walter hit a 16-year-old cyclist on Adelaide Terrace at 4.30 pm on New Year's Eve.[12] Walter made no attempt to brake. There were no drag or skid marks. He was witnessed travelling on the wrong side of the road well in excess of the speed limit at the time of the crash.[13] Walter failed his sobriety test.[14] His speech was reportedly thick and his eyes bloodshot.[15] Justice Walker's own sentencing notes indicated that Walter was a married man with two children. He noted that Walter was known to be a 'careful driver'. He was apparently devoted to his 'crippled' sister.[16] Walter fled the scene. Charged with manslaughter, he was convicted of the lesser offence of negligent driving causing death at the conclusion of a six-day trial. Justice Walker released him on bond.

In *R v B.J.M.* (1960), Benjamin ran down a 15-year-old boy in Oxford Street, Leederville, dragging the boy and his bicycle along the road for some distance underneath his car.[17] In a calculated attempt to avoid responsibility, he abandoned his car and hailed a taxi to a car park in the city where he told the attendant that his car had been stolen. The attendant disputed Benjamin's claim — it was necessary to surrender a ticket to drive a vehicle out of the parking lot.[18] Benjamin later presented at CIB Perth, with shards of glass on his coat and conspicuously protruding from his pockets. He reported that his vehicle had been stolen.[19] Benjamin was found guilty of manslaughter. Astonishingly, Justice Jackson stated that he *did not* take into account the hit-and-run nature of the offence, *nor* the false report to police on the theft of the vehicle. Instead, he sentenced Benjamin to six months' imprisonment on account of his good character.[20] Benjamin was a 26-year-old schoolteacher.

In *R v N.K.* in 1958, Chief Justice Dwyer severely reprimanded Norman, stating that he had demonstrated 'complete disregard' and 'callous indifference' — 'To leave a woman on the road to die is just about the limit of what you could do in the way of harm by driving a motor car'.[21] Norman had been drinking at the Avon Bridge Hotel for three hours prior to the collision.[22] He claimed that he 'wasn't real drunk', but conceded that he had had 'quite a few'.[23] Norman was thirty-three at the time of the offence. He stated that he felt only a *slight* bump and could not explain how the deceased's groceries, including her eggs, ended up smashed all over his car.[24] Charged with manslaughter, he was found guilty under s 291A. Chief Justice Dwyer stated that the hit-and-run aspect of the offence *demanded* penal treatment.[25] For his 'callous indifference', Norman was sentenced to twelve months' imprisonment, pre-remission discount.

Irrespective of whether it was broad daylight, the driver was drunk, or the pedestrian was on a zebra crossing, defence barristers ingeniously characterised pedestrians and cyclists as architects of their own demise. This was despite the fact that approaches to pedestrian crossings were plainly marked with zigzag lines up to 140 feet prior,[26] in addition to extensive signage. The Crown contended that drivers did not see vulnerable road users because they failed to use reasonable care and take reasonable precautions, keep a proper lookout and modify their driving in accordance with the circumstances and the proximity of vulnerable road users. Despite the Crown's relentless efforts, juries of the 1940s, '50s, '60s and '70s did not consider the failure to modify one's driving conduct in relation to the propinquity of pedestrians and cyclists sufficiently negligent to warrant a conviction. In the hierarchy of road users, drivers reigned supreme.

The question at stake in all cases remained the *manner* of the driving. Unless there was a *demonstrable* sequence of fault from the point of view of a bystander, criminal negligence was impossible to establish. Colin was a case in point. In April 1964, he was working at his tearooms in High Street, Fremantle.[27] At about 3.00 pm that afternoon, he visited the Buffalo Club. He could not recall how many drinks he consumed, but returned to work about an hour later. At around 6.00 pm he shared a bottle of beer with 'the old chap that works out the back' and closed the shop at 9.30 pm, returning to the club where he had six middies in a one-hour period; that is, just over 1.7 litres of beer. Colin had not eaten over the course of the entire day.[28] On his journey home along Canning Highway, Colin struck a 48-year-old man, William, who was thrown into the air by the force of impact.[29] It was a clear night with little traffic. William had just alighted from a bus and, alongside a young woman, was crossing the highway. He later died in Fremantle Hospital from bronchial pneumonia, a gastric haemorrhage and an acquired brain injury.[30]

While the testimonies as to the exact timing varied, Colin left the scene shortly after the crash.[31] Witnesses saw him accelerate up the highway from Bicton back towards Fremantle and recorded his vehicle's registration number.[32] One witness stated that Colin got out of his car, walked over to the man lying in the middle of the road, looked at him, got back in his vehicle and drove away.[33] Colin was apprehended at his home over two-and-a-half hours later by Constables Spears and McAtee.[34] He consented to a blood test and also underwent a sobriety test at Central Station at around 3.00 am.[35] According to Sergeant Harris, on walking the chalk line some four hours after the crash, Colin staggered at his seventh, tenth and twelfth steps.[36] He was equally unsuccessful at balancing, losing his stability upon raising his right leg off the ground.[37] On arriving at Colin's home, Constable Spears described him fumbling at the door handle, walking unsteadily, and falling into the chair nearest the door where he sat, swaying from side to side. Spears also claimed that his speech was so slurred as to be utterly incoherent.[38] Colin claimed that the officers' testimonies regarding his appearance and sobriety were fallacious. Rather, his demeanour was symptomatic of nervousness and concern.[39]

Colin made conflicting statements regarding how much he had had to drink. On Colin's original statement that his last drink was at 5.00 pm, the Crown argued that this was a deliberate lie to cover the fact that he had been drinking until much later. By the end of the trial, there was general agreement that Colin's blood alcohol concentration at the time of the collision was about 0.23%, more than 60 per cent *over* the established level of incapability.[40] Colin claimed that, at the time of the collision, he was quite capable of driving his car and his consumption of alcohol did not in *any way* affect his driving.[41] He initially denied being the driver and told police that his vehicle had been stolen.[42]

At trial, Colin maintained that he left the scene in order to seek help. The fact that he did not stop to get any was, according to his testimony, the product of his confusion.[43] Over the course of his journey home, he was observed by many witnesses, including Detective Sergeant Johnson. Johnson was parked at a service station almost 10 kilometres from the crash scene when he heard a scraping noise and saw an 'old model Holden' drive past. He described the exterior sun visor, ordinarily fitted above the windscreen, hanging down the passenger side of the car and dragging along the kerb.[44] The obvious damage to Colin's car did not deter him from driving it on a conspicuous round trip home, back towards Fremantle, up Stirling Highway, into the city and along the freeway to Como. The car broke down a short distance from home. He walked the remaining distance.

Cross-examined on his initial statement that his car had been stolen, Crown Prosecutor Dodd insisted that Colin was prepared to tell the police 'any lies to escape any possible consequences' and was trying to 'put it over' the officers.[45] Colin maintained that he had intended to get help and lied about the vehicle being stolen because he 'got confused and didn't know what to say'.[46] Yet within minutes of leaving the scene, Colin drove past two police stations. He did not stop to seek assistance.[47] He also explained that his failure to seek help was because he felt he needed to go home and talk to his mother and perhaps a lawyer.[48] The prosecution countered that he did not leave the scene in order to seek assistance and, regardless, witnesses were in the process of telephoning for help. Colin explained his neglect as a symptom of both his confusion and concern.

> [Mr Dodd commencing]: You got confused; nothing had happened to confuse you after the collision, had it?
> I was quite concerned. I saw this chap lying on the ground and [Dodd interrupts]
> What a funny thing to do if you were concerned; you mean you were concerned for his welfare?
> I was; very much so.
> And you dashed off and left him there, as far as you were concerned?
> Yes.

And you drove all these miles in and out of streets before you got home?
Yes.
And even when you got home you had still not made up your mind to admit to your being the driver of the car which struck the man?
No.
You persisted to deny it.
Yes.[49]

Moments before the crash, William alighted from a bus alongside a young female passenger. William and Rowena were not acquainted. Rowena had been out for the evening playing table tennis. She gave evidence that, when she was almost at the kerb's edge of the highway, she began running towards the corner of Yeovil Crescent. According to her testimony, she simply 'felt like running'.[50] In a mood of zest and exuberance, she stated that she often ran out of 'sheer physical enthusiasm'.[51] Rowena said that she heard a sudden swishing sound and, looking backwards, she saw William being hit by the car. She claimed that he was a few yards to the Bicton side of the double white lines, meaning he was more than halfway across the highway. According to Rowena, the car ran directly into William, throwing him into the air. The car then veered right, mounting the footpath on the opposite side of the road.[52] Colin's barrister, Mr Wood, argued that Rowena caused the crash.[53] According to Wood, Colin had suddenly swerved to his right to avoid Rowena because she ran out in front of him.[54] She was running *not* out of youthful exuberance, but rather because she was 'fearful of some part she might have played in this tragedy'. Wood claimed Rowena was desperately trying to extract herself 'from the incident which she had caused'.[55]

According to Mr Wood, the tragic event that happened to his client could have happened to a 'complete tee-totaller who had never had a drink in his life'.[56] Mr Dodd countered that, far from responding to a sudden emergency, Colin had a clear, uninterrupted view for 200 yards and, by his own admission, he had seen both pedestrians from 150 yards away.[57] He had acted like a man with a guilty mind.[58] Dodd noted that William had 'stuck out like a lighthouse on a well lit highway' and yet Colin managed to plough directly into him with violent force.[59] He contended that the very nature of the crash proved that Colin was paying 'absolutely no attention and was being grossly negligent' – had he exercised *any* reasonable care or precaution whatsoever the collision could simply not have occurred.[60] Dodd insisted that Colin's drinking and resultant drowsiness, inattention and inability to cope with an emergency was the only possible explanation as to why he hit William.[61]

Mr Wood characterised his client as an innocent party faced with a terrible predicament – it was a 'fairly human reaction to want to run away from trouble', and any person in that situation would have felt compelled to flee because their story would be derided based on a 'few drinks'.[62] On the manner of the driving, there was no testimony from any eyewitness to suggest that Colin was mismanaging the vehicle prior to the collision. As Wood explained, the question before the jury was *how* the accused drove his car.[63] Colin was observed by many witnesses driving in a straight line in the correct lane prior to the crash.[64] Ronald was driving towards Fremantle on the opposite side of the highway. He testified that he saw the defendant's car travelling at speed and then swerve suddenly. Under cross-examination he said –

> [Mr Wood commencing]: And it was travelling in your direction on the other side of the road?
> Yes. It was travelling towards the Leopold Hotel.
> On its correct side of the road?
> On the correct side.
> Was it travelling in a straight line?
> It seemed to be. I never took any notice of how it was travelling.
> There was nothing to indicate that it wasn't travelling in a normal way, was there? Until this incident happened?
> Yes.[65]

Similarly, under cross-examination Detective Sergeant Johnson, who later saw Colin travelling through Cottesloe, reluctantly agreed that there was nothing to suggest he was mismanaging the vehicle, despite the fact that the sun visor was hanging off the side of the car, dragging along the kerb and making a piercing noise. Colin was not speeding, in the wrong lane or driving erratically.[66] Like almost half of the defendants who were highly intoxicated, Colin was found not guilty. In 2004, forty years after William's death, major amendments to the *Road Traffic Act* would seek to address the problems exemplified by the evidence in Colin's case.

Bias towards pedestrians was also evident in approaches to policing. In 1967, Detective Sergeant Goodman of CIB wrote to the Traffic Branch urging that CIB be notified 'as soon as possible' of cases in which pedestrians crossing roads on marked crosswalks were struck and injured by drivers. Goodman emphasised that, despite the fact that the injuries sustained were often very serious, officers were *failing* to charge drivers for grievous bodily harm or bodily harm, and rather were charging them with very minor traffic offences. Goodman requested that CIB be involved *immediately* so that detectives could attend the scene and assess the evidence with a view to criminal charges.[67]

As with other offences, guilty pleas had a substantial impact on the sentences imposed. For instance, in *R v R.J.F.* (1961) Ronan was driving on the wrong side of the road when he hit a pedestrian. He had had thirteen beers prior to the crash.[68] Ronan entered a guilty plea under s 291A. He was fined £350. By contrast, four years later Layton had had very little sleep. He stayed out all night, returning home around 6.00 am on the day before the crash.[69] At 6.30 am the following morning, Layton was driving along Rockingham Road after another night out when he hit a guidepost on the opposite side of the road and then a jogger.[70] The jogger, Ethan, was apparently highly visible and running against the flow of traffic on the verge.[71] He was regularly seen jogging in the morning. Layton pleaded not guilty. The Crown argued that, as Layton took several hundred feet to stop, the clear inference was that he was not only driving while fatigued, in the wrong lane and perhaps whilst intoxicated, but at a significant speed.[72] Layton was convicted under s 291A and sentenced to twelve months' imprisonment, with a non-parole period of six. Neither Layton nor Ronan had a history of offending.

When the prosecution's case was that a driver had failed to modify their conduct in accordance with the circumstances and the proximity of pedestrians and cyclists, and intoxication was *not* at issue, or was not admitted in evidence, securing a guilty verdict was extremely difficult. Convictions were rare. Such circumstances were readily cast as 'accidents' and misfortune. Trial outcomes in cases involving pedestrian crossings were particularly revealing. For example, just before 10.00 pm on 11 February 1970, Allan dropped off his girlfriend at East Perth railway station.[73] On his return trip home, he overtook his friends, who were travelling in the car ahead, at an estimated speed of 45 to 50 mph (72.42 to 80.47 km/h) in a 30 mph (48.28 km/h) zone.[74] Near the intersection of Brisbane and Beaufort Streets, Allan hit 68-year-old Alistair, a resident of a local invalid home.[75] Alistair was on a pedestrian crossing at the time.[76]

Allan said that he did not see Alistair until just before he hit him, although ahead of Allan, another car had slowed to a near standstill to let Alistair pass and a car travelling in the opposite direction was stationary.[77] Allan claimed that a car in front of him had braked suddenly, forcing him to take evasive action and, in the course of that action, he hit Alistair.[78] The Crown argued that Allan was lying and there was no other car; rather Allan had driven directly into the victim.[79] Photographs from the crash scene showed that the crosswalk was visible from at least 70 yards and there were zigzag lines warning of its approach. Streetlights flooded the area, making the crosswalk highly visible. The Crown argued that Alistair was on the crosswalk for some time. He 'was there for anyone to see who had looked'.[80] Allan had a blood alcohol concentration estimated between 0.91% and 0.131% at the time of the crash,[81] a fact not disclosed to the jury. Justice Wickham ruled the test results inadmissible on the grounds that their relevance was negligible and their potential impact prejudicial.[82] Allan was found not guilty.

In a 1968 case, the Crown again argued that it was the responsibility of the defendant to modify his driving in accordance with the circumstances and that the failure to do so constituted criminal negligence. Intoxication was not at issue. Hayden was driving at about 30 to 35 mph (48.28 to 56.32 km/h), just above the speed limit for the area, on approach to a crosswalk when, he claimed, a child 'suddenly ran out in front of him'.[83] There were zigzag marks on approach to the pedestrian crossing, a 'SCHOOL' traffic sign, and another that read 'CROSSWALK'.[84] White parallel lines on the road marked the crossing and children were milling about and standing on either side of the road waiting to cross.[85] It was reportedly a sunny day and the crosswalk was visible from approximately 200 yards.[86] A car coming from the other direction had stopped to let the children pass.[87] Eight-year-old Jane was on the crosswalk when she was struck. Mr Franklyn examined the defendant.

> [Mr Franklyn commencing] You were still travelling at 35 mph?
> Yes.
> In effect, travelling over a zig-zag sign which is completely visible and apparent, which you know warns you of a crosswalk?
> Yes.
> Past the school sign that is orange with black print which you can give us no reason for not seeing it.
> Yes.
> Then really it comes back to this: You can't tell me why you did not see Di-Pinto's stationary car which would be at the right hand side; you can't tell me why you did not see children of your left side of the road outside of the school, where other witnesses saw them; you can't say why you did not see the zig-zag line or why you did not see the school sign?
> I did see the car, but I can't say whether it was stopped.

Di-Pinto said he was stopped, waiting for these children; then he saw your car coming; then he looked to the right; then there was the impact. You don't recall seeing him stopped at all.
No.[88]

The defence argued that Jane had failed in her *equal* obligation to look where she was going.[89] A 10-year-old witness testified that Jane had stopped for 'a second or so' but she did not see her look to her right or left.[90] Mr Gunning acknowledged that while his client had killed a 'little kiddy', the child had run out in front of his car and, as far as his client was concerned, there was a roadway and he was entitled to proceed across it.[91] Mr Franklyn countered that it was not a case of 'bad luck'; there was no reason why Hayden should not have seen the signs and slowed down.[92] Franklyn argued that, in the circumstances, Hayden's speed was excessive, that children do not appreciate danger in the same way adults do and thus a very high degree of care and caution was required.[93] He noted that other witnesses saw the children milling about, yet Hayden failed to do so. Other drivers had slowed down and indeed stopped to let children cross. Franklyn argued against the notion that a conviction of criminal negligence demanded truly aberrant conduct – 'One is capable of killing a person with a motor vehicle at 35 mph. One is capable of taking insufficient care at 35 mph'.[94] According to the prosecution, having regard to the circumstances, Hayden's conduct was grossly negligent – '"School" implies that there are children about who may not be thinking. You have a dangerous weapon. Be on your guard'.[95] Hayden was found not guilty.

In a case that came to trial in 1966, Max was approaching a train station at about 9.45 am.[96] According to Max, the car in front of him slowed down on approach to the station.[97] The road was flat and marked with zigzag lines over a 140-foot distance prior to the crossing. Max testified that he knew there was a crossing,[98] but *believed* the vehicle in front of him was slowing to drop off a passenger, rather than slowing to allow a pedestrian to cross.

Why he had formed that belief was unclear; the passenger doors of the supposed car in front had not opened. Max's passenger claimed that Max approached the crossing at a speed of 32 to 33 mph (51.49 to 53.11 km/h).[99] With no view of the oncoming traffic or conditions ahead, Max overtook the vehicle ahead. He hit a 49-year-old woman, Wilma, who died the following day in Royal Perth Hospital.[100] The vehicle which had supposedly obscured Max's vision drove off.[101] Neither Max nor his passenger could recall its registration number.[102] Max claimed he had looked, but did not see the woman. Like Jane and Alistair, Wilma was on a crosswalk when she was hit.

In Mr Dodd's words, the Crown's case was that 'no-one with reasonable driving skill in daylight could strike anybody on a crosswalk unless he was being completely and utterly reckless'.[103] He argued that the driver was not paying attention which, given his duty of care under the criminal law, was *grossly* negligent.[104] Mr Wood countered that Max had not seen Wilma because two telegraph poles had obstructed his view.[105] Dodd responded with utter disbelief – 'how could anyone driving and looking miss that woman...How could you miss her if you looked?'[106] Wilma weighed 15 stone, 11 pounds.[107] Dodd asked the jury whether they thought a 9-inch lamp pole could have obstructed a woman of Wilma's size crossing the road.[108] Other drivers had seen her clearly.[109] The Crown argued that Max's speed and failure to keep a proper lookout caused Wilma's death. The defence asked the jury whether they believed there should be a margin for human error.[110] The Crown argued that the degree of precaution required on approach to a pedestrian crossing was 'second nature'[111] – Max's conduct fell far below that of a reasonable driver and was therefore criminal.

In his closing address, Mr Wood stated that the issue was *not* whether Max had knocked down a woman on a pedestrian crossing.[112] That was not in dispute. He argued that there was no law *requiring* a driver to stop at a crossing and, irrespective, the law 'does not punish a person for a momentary lapse, for an error of judgment, for a miscalculation'.[113] He emphasised that there was no element of excessive speed.[114] The Crown's evidence regarding braking distance and speed was, according to the defence, but 'a nigger in the woodpile'.[115] According to Wood, the deceased, Wilma, should be forced to bear some of the responsibility because, in *almost all cases*, deceased pedestrians contributed to the cause of 'accidents'.[116] Accordingly, she was hurrying for the train, was not concentrating, and did not look with the degree of attention that an ordinary person ought to.[117]

Justice Jackson directed the jury that motorists had a duty to employ a very high degree of care and precaution when approaching pedestrian crossings, which were designated for the *sole* purpose of pedestrians' safety. He stated that Max had done the most dangerous thing a driver could do in such circumstances – he had ignored the warnings and overtaken another vehicle at speed, without any vision of what lay ahead.[118] The jury found Max not guilty, but added a revealing rider – 'We find his actions were lacking in caution and, to a degree, negligent, but not to the point of being criminally negligent'.[119]

As stated, of the 120 sampled cases brought to trial, only thirteen decedents were cyclists and interestingly, of those, eight cases were prosecuted before the close of the 1950s.[120] Like pedestrians, cyclists were also readily cast as agents of their own demise. The diminutive number of cases involving cyclists brought to trial suggests that the Crown and police had little confidence in those charges succeeding. Of the thirteen, there were seven convictions, three of manslaughter and four under s 291A.[121] The maximum penalty handed down was eighteen months and the lowest, two suspended sentences.[122] As was the case with pedestrians, the defence claimed that cyclists were *never* visible enough. Bicycles were found at crash scenes mangled under the chassis of vehicles, often beyond recognition. They were sometimes scattered in pieces across the road. On occasion, mangled bike frames were produced as evidence in trial.[123] If a light globe from a bicycle could not be located, or the generator switch was in the 'off' position, doubt was quickly cast over the prosecution's case. There was an expectation that, despite the force of impact, bicycle lights should still be burning brightly when police arrived.

In the early hours of one morning in 1961, Bob was driving past the Polish Club on the corner of Fitzgerald and Charles Streets, Northam.[124] Revellers were milling about the road and footpath.[125] By his own admission, Bob was driving at 35 mph (56.32 km/h).[126] Some claimed his speed was higher.[127] Bob stated that he had consumed 'half a dozen schooners'. In Western Australia, a schooner of beer measures 425 mLs. Bob also shared a bottle of Brandivino with three friends. From 100 yards, he said that he could see people, 4-foot deep into the road, and cars parked bumper to bumper on both sides of the street.[128] It was estimated that between eighty and 100 people attended the Club's dance.[129] Bob stated that he did not reduce his speed at 50 yards. At 20 to 30 yards he claimed that he became aware that people might step out into the road from behind parked cars and so eased his foot off the accelerator, although he stated that he was still travelling at about 35 mph.[130] According to witnesses he was 'going far too fast in the circumstances'.[131] One witness claimed he was travelling at 45 to 55 mph (72.42 to 88.51 km/h). Under cross-examination in the initial proceedings, the defence discredited that testimony on the grounds that the witness was only seventeen and thus had insufficient driving experience to estimate speed.[132]

Bob drifted to the opposite side of the road,[133] apparently to put some distance between his vehicle and the people coming out of the club.[134] He testified that he saw a cyclist riding an unlit bicycle about 15 to 20 feet away. He said that he collided with him because he could not avoid doing so.[135] Witnesses saw a 'dark shape' fall off Bob's car.[136] The Crown contended that Bob had demonstrated utter disregard for the safety of others in the manner of his driving and 'put himself in this position where finally he could not avoid an object – a man on a bicycle, and as a result that man was killed'.[137] The defence inferred that the absence of a light globe on the cycle was not due to the crash, but rather a globe had never been attached.[138] Constable Woodlands noted that bicycle generators only became activated at 4 mph in any case.[139] The generator switch was found in the 'on' position at the crash scene.[140] The Crown argued that, even if the bike were not lit, a careful driver would have seen the cyclist. Bob's headlights cast light for a distance of more than 20 feet.[141] He was found not guilty.

As was the case with pedestrians, when cyclists were killed, very high levels of intoxication were insufficient to secure convictions. According to defendants, it was not their level of intoxication that affected their ability to see a cyclist, but rather the cyclist was not *visible* enough. In 1965, for example, Derrick hit a cyclist on the way home from the Waverley Hotel, just after 10.00 pm. The weather was fine and dry, visibility was good and the road was reportedly well lit, with streetlights at 50-yard intervals.[142] Derrick had been at the hotel since 6.30 pm, where he drank approximately ten middies of beer and several whiskey sours.[143] He had nothing to eat.[144] Seventy-year-old Liam was cycling home from his friend's place. He and his friend regularly ate dinner together and watched television.[145] Liam and his bike were carried approximately 180 feet from the point of impact.[146] The gouge marks and blood on the road indicated, according to the prosecution, a very violent impact and a high degree of speed.[147] Derrick finally brought his car to a standstill 300 feet from the point of the initial collision.[148] The Crown argued that this was no mere 'glancing blow'.[149] There were bloodstains down the entire left side of the car.[150]

Under cross-examination, the attending officers conceded that it was a matter of traffic regulation that bicycles were required to have a rear reflector light.[151] Liam's bicycle had none. Vehicle examiner Constable Tully stated that the bike did have a rear and front light and generator, but the switch of the generator was in the 'off' position when examined.[152] A torch was found at the scene. The defence argued that the torch belonged to Liam and he was carrying it because his generator was not working.[153]

Under cross-examination, Constable Archibald testified that Liam was wearing dark-coloured clothing.[154] The defence doggedly pursued the visibility argument, all the while avoiding the issue of intoxication.

According to the Crown, the only possible conclusion was that, a driver who hits a cyclist, be the cycle lit or otherwise, in an area flooded by streetlights, was paying absolutely no attention to the road.[155] In any case, Mr Dodd noted that the force of impact and the distance travelled from the point of impact could have switched the bike's generator off.[156] Mr Dodd observed that everyone should have sympathy for a driver who hits a cyclist when a bike 'wobbles out' in front of their car. However, in this case, the extensive damage to the vehicle and bicycle, in addition to the distance travelled from the point of impact, demonstrated that the driver had made no attempt to break or stop, but rather hit the cyclist 'fair and square from the rear' at speed.[157] While many people attended the scene, there was no witness to the collision.

Derrick was reportedly very distressed, crying at the scene, a response that readily lent itself to a positive characterisation of him in trial. He told Constable Archibald that he had 'just killed a man' and he 'wished to tell the truth'. At the scene, Derrick repeated, over and over, 'Oh my God, what have I done?'[158] Mr Hatfield led evidence to substantiate that Derrick was a well-dressed man, respectful to the attending officers.[159] He made a calculated closing bid to the jury – 'Now you are all motorists. You know, without my telling you, the menace of an unlit bike in the roadway no matter what the conditions are'.[160] There was, according to Hatfield, no evidence of reckless mismanagement of the vehicle.[161] His client was on the correct side of the road. The fact that his client was extremely drunk had no bearing on his driving or the fact that he did not see Liam. Liam was simply not visible enough. Derrick was acquitted.

On drivers' testimonies, it was as though cyclists were magnetically attracted to their vehicles and inexplicably veered into them. In 1950, Nigel described driving his truck up a hill on Goldfields Road just after 9 o'clock.¹⁶² He claimed he was quite sober when he left the bar just minutes before. This was at some contrast to the statements of witnesses who had seen Nigel that evening.¹⁶³ Nigel had been in the Commercial Hotel since 1 o'clock that afternoon and drank steadily until he left that night.¹⁶⁴ According to the secretary of the local road board who attended the scene, there were no lights burning on Nigel's truck.¹⁶⁵ Constable Vinicombe said the light on the right side was burning dimly, there were no rear or indication lights, and the left hand headlight was disconnected. Furthermore, there was no tread on the truck's tyres. Eamon's cycle was not fitted with any lights.¹⁶⁶ He was cycling in the opposite direction on his way to his night shift at the local railway yard.¹⁶⁷

Nigel stated that he saw Eamon from a distance, travelling in the centre of the road. Nigel claimed that he swerved suddenly to his left about 25 feet before impact because Eamon failed to alter his course. He testified that as he swerved, Eamon swerved too, steering into him.¹⁶⁸ The diagram of the crash scene was open to another version of events. The skid marks on the opposite side of the road suggested that Nigel was driving on the wrong side at the point of impact and, on impact, swerved, dragging Eamon and his bicycle under the chassis across to the left side of the carriageway.¹⁶⁹ Nigel's truck had to be elevated so that Eamon's mangled body and bicycle could be retrieved.¹⁷⁰ His body was caught under the oil sump. His neck was broken.¹⁷¹ Nigel was acquitted. Eamon was buried in an unmarked grave at Dowerin cemetery.¹⁷²

In 1974, barrister Leo Wood's accurate declaration, made some eight years prior, that the law 'does not punish a person for a momentary lapse, for an error of judgment, for a miscalculation'¹⁷³ would come under review. Over the course of the previous three decades, the deaths of pedestrians and cyclists, like so many others, had been invariably characterised as the unfortunate result of a momentary lapse, rather than drivers' failure to use reasonable care and take reasonable precautions and to modify their conduct in accordance with the changing road conditions. It was difficult to secure convictions, even in circumstances of aggravation, and almost pointless to pursue cases that fell at the lower to middle end of the spectrum of fault. Despite the Crown's best efforts, verdicts revealed that, when a vehicle was involved, the benchmark of criminal negligence was set disproportionately high, particularly given the quantum of risk posed by the mismanagement of vehicles. Convictions across the period demonstrated a preference towards an observed and lengthy sequence of 'reckless' and erratic driving. The introduction of dangerous driving causing death in 1974 would seek not only to widen the scope of culpable conduct by introducing a lower threshold of fault, but in theory would hold a greater number of drivers to account for the consequences of momentary inattention and so-called 'lapses in judgement'. The introduction of the new offence had, however, other unintended consequences.

Chapter Six

Dangerous driving causing death and the Road Traffic Act 1974

Freeing the Crown from the bonds of negligence?

In 1974, negligent driving causing death, s 291A of the Criminal Code, was repealed in favour of a new homicide offence, dangerous driving causing death, under s 59(1) of the *Road Traffic Act 1974* ('the *Road Traffic Act*').[1] Only four years prior, the WA Law Reform Commission had rejected a proposal to introduce an analogous offence.[2] Following a lengthy parliamentary debate, almost none of it concerning the prosecution of deaths on the road, the Bill passed in late 1974.[3] Dangerous driving causing death thus replaced negligent driving causing death, which, following the High Court's decision in *Callaghan v R* in 1952,[4] could not deliver on legislator's best intentions. As of 1974, subject to the degree of fault demonstrated by a driver, the majority of prosecutions would now come under the banner of 'traffic'. The Criminal Code was amended to make dangerous driving causing death an alternative offence to manslaughter.[5] A charge of manslaughter was still available if open on the evidence.

The introduction of dangerous driving causing death was but one aspect of a wave of reform, in part motivated by the desire to consolidate all traffic-related matters that had been distributed across a range of statutory implements. Under the *Road Traffic Act*, all 'traffic' matters became incorporated into one single statutory entity. Responsibility for policing 'traffic' became temporarily vested in the newly established Road Traffic Authority, a short-lived experiment that was abandoned in 1981 when the policing of traffic offences reverted to the full control of the WA Police.[6] This short-lived experiment effectively set traffic offences apart from all other forms of crime, an approach a UK Royal Commission previously described as 'objectionable'.[7]

Reducing the carnage and addressing the toll was part of the rhetoric from both sides of Parliament. Despite that rhetoric, the matter of prosecuting drivers who killed was drowned out by parliamentarians' resistance to new measures to target drinking and driving, including the grounds on which police officers could legally test drivers, and increased fines for drink-driving offences.[8] Opponents to the Bill seemed more concerned about the looming possibility of living in a 'police state' and defending drivers' 'civil liberties', than liberty's fatal consequences.[9] After all, parliamentarians were *more than* capable of managing their vehicles with blood alcohol concentrations in excess of 0.08%.[10] Apparently, men would suffer 'embarrassment and humiliation' were they pulled over to supply a blood or breath sample in front of their wives and children.[11] The government countered that, if the same number of citizens were being killed in any other circumstance, people would take to the streets en masse and march in protest.[12] The Opposition warned that the measures would be most unpopular and, if enacted, the Bill's consequences would constitute 'brutality'.[13] The government held its nerve, claiming that it was demonstrating the initiative and courage to save lives.[14]

Superintendent Lee later noted that dangerous driving causing death was introduced to rectify the problems associated with meeting the 'stringent requirements' of proof under the Code.[15] The new offence was designed to free the Crown from 'the bonds of negligence', making it much easier to prosecute and convict drivers.[16] As the previous three decades bore out, the degree of negligence required to sustain a conviction exceeded the factual circumstances in almost 50 per cent of cases. Conduct that fell at the middle to the lower end of the fault spectrum was not brought before the courts. Only cases that fell at the upper end were prosecuted. When a vehicle was involved, the exacting standard required for a conviction of criminal negligence, both legal and social, meant that a great number of drivers evaded prosecution and conviction. In *theory*, the introduction of the new offence meant that it would be easier to secure verdicts as the new provision widened the scope of culpable conduct. There were, however, less desirable consequences. As the Law Reform Commission of Victoria later noted of similar offences, the introduction of another alternative driving-causing-death offence conveyed 'the wrong message to the community'.[17] That the death was brought about by the mismanagement of a vehicle, rather than any other implement or object, somehow warranted a dramatic reduction in penalty. Deaths occasioned by the use of motor vehicles were singled out as a distinct and lesser species of violence and harm. For driving conduct which fell at the very low end of the spectrum of fault, this was entirely appropriate. For conduct at the middle to upper end of the spectrum, this was a regressive step.

Under the new offence, a driver's transgression was not based in criminal negligence, but rather in whether the driving was *dangerous*. The Opposition's Thomas Hartrey, a former barrister, was the only parliamentarian who took issue with the proposed offence.[18] Based on almost four decades' experience with traffic offences in the courts, he warned that he was 'speaking with the anger of a prophet', declaring that the Bill's enactment would portend an era of harsh and punitive measures against drivers.[19] Hartrey argued that a driving-causing-death offence should be included in the *Road Traffic Act* only were it identical to s 291A under the Code. He claimed that s 291A required a high degree of negligence or 'reckless disregard for life and limb',[20] which he emphatically supported,[21] arguing that the new offence should be precisely the same and require an equally high threshold of negligence.[22] It was precisely that threshold that had made it so difficult to secure convictions over the previous three decades.

Despite the existence of comparable offences in other jurisdictions, in Australia and overseas, Hartrey derided the drafting of s 59(1) as 'disastrous'. Implausibly, he protested that even the 'slightest degree of negligence'[23] could result in a conviction for a crime as serious as manslaughter. Hartrey's position was that drivers should be prosecuted *only* if they demonstrated wilful, reckless behaviour. He further argued that the circumstances encompassed by s 59(1) could not reasonably be considered criminal,[24] and he was particularly concerned that carelessness or inattentiveness, which he regarded as legitimately 'accidental', might result in men being unfairly persecuted. Exemplifying his apprehension, he asked his parliamentary colleagues to consider an example.

> For argument's sake, let us suppose a man is driving his wife to a picnic, and someone yells to him from across the road. His attention is distracted, which it should not be because that is careless driving; as a result his wife is killed and he is responsible for the fatal accident. He is then charged with the manslaughter of his own wife. That would be absolutely wrong, and yet that is the correct interpretation of the words used in this provision.[25]

Hartrey's interpretation was not wide of the mark. In *theory*, the new offence made lapses in judgment grounds for prosecution, contingent on the circumstances surrounding the driving, although Hartrey's employ of the offence 'manslaughter' was erroneous. His hypothetical scenario fell well short of the breach of duty required for manslaughter, his claims being misrepresentative, if not histrionic. Hartrey claimed that the degree of negligence required to sustain a conviction under s 291A amounted to recklessness and an 'I don't give a damn attitude',[26] spurious given that wilful conduct or a driver's subjective belief regarding his or her driving was immaterial. In fact, Hartrey speciously claimed that a conviction under the Code required an element or degree of recklessness or guilty conscience, despite the fact that Australian courts had long treated criminal negligence whilst in charge of a vehicle as a matter for objective assessment, a fact Hartrey would have been fully aware of given his long legal career. Of the new provision, he was surprisingly concerned that, if the *manner of the driving* could be said to have *caused* the death, the driver could be found guilty.[27]

Hartrey took further issue with s 59(1) on the basis that it encompassed the threat of danger to 'any person', rather than 'the public'.[28] He objected to the prospect of an inattentive, distracted driver being prosecuted for killing a passenger.[29] It was a targeted criticism – the inclusion of 'any person' within the section was intended to extend the definition of those endangered to include a driver's passengers. Under dangerous driving simpliciter, West Australian courts had previously held that driving in a manner dangerous 'to the public' applied only to those outside the vehicle.[30] Hartrey's reasoning gave the impression that he sought to exclude passengers from the censure that s 59(1) might afford. Minister for Transport, Traffic, Police and Road Safety, Ray O'Connor, described Hartrey's position as 'weak in the extreme'.[31] He noted that the section was designed to encompass people within *and* outside the vehicle, because they were equally vulnerable to 'being killed'.[32] Despite Hartrey's objections, s 59(1) was passed as follows and remained substantially intact until 2004.

> Any person who causes the death of or grievous bodily harm to another person by driving a motor vehicle in a manner (which expression includes speed) that is, having regard to all the circumstances of the case, dangerous to the public or to any person commits an indictable offence which may, at the election of the person charged, be dealt with summarily.

Chief Justice Jackson later noted that the language of s 59(1) sat 'in marked contrast' to s 291A of the Code. The new offence was *not* expressed in 'terms of negligence'.[33] Unlike s 291A or manslaughter, dangerous driving causing death was not based in a failure to use reasonable care and take reasonable precautions, but rather in driving a vehicle in a manner, which was, having regard to the circumstances, *dangerous*. The core of the offence lay in the manner of the driving. The driving had to be such that, it would be dangerous to the public or, indeed, any person. Chief Justice Jackson noted that the intent of the legislature was to *exclude* negligence as an element of the offence.[34]

The new provision rolled two types of harm – injury and death – into one offence. Under s 59(2)(b), a driver caused the death or harm whether they did so directly or indirectly. A driver could be held responsible for a death that occurred up to a year and one day after a crash.[35] Foreshadowing claims of contributory negligence, it was immaterial that the death or harm might have been avoided by proper precaution on the part of someone other than the driver.[36] Like other homicide offences, where a person received medical treatment and subsequently died, either as a result of the initial harm or the treatment, subject to the treatment being proper and applied in good faith, the driver would be held to have caused the death.[37]

The mechanical condition of the vehicle also fell within the ambit of the new offence.[38] Driving could be dangerous if a vehicle's unroadworthy condition was the primary cause of a crash and the driver had, *or should have had*, knowledge of its defectiveness. A driver could proffer a defence that the crash was due to a mechanical defect, such as brake failure, of which he or she had no knowledge – a defence of sudden emergency was open on a charge under s 59(1).[39] A bee, a frequent hypothetical example, which suddenly flew into the cab of a car causing enormous distraction and distress to the driver, might also constitute grounds for a sudden emergency defence or involuntariness.[40] Sudden illness, such as a heart attack, might similarly support the defence. The defence of accident was excluded.

A defence based on mistake of fact was also open, although in practical terms it would be very difficult to establish.[41] Under mistake of fact, or honest and reasonable mistake, a driver had to have been acting in accordance with a mistaken belief as to the material circumstances. However, the mistake had to be one a reasonable person might make – it had to be *honestly* held and *reasonably* based. For example, the defence might argue that the accused honestly believed that he or she did not realise they were driving the wrong way up a one-way street. Under all circumstances, the mistaken belief would pose a question as to whether that belief was reasonable.[42] A defence of emergency might also be coupled with honest and reasonable mistake. For example, a driver might claim that he or she drove at high speed (sudden emergency) because they *believed* they were being chased by another driver who posed a physical threat, when in fact they were not under chase (mistake of fact). On the first limb alone, sudden emergency, it would be unlikely that there was sufficient evidence to substantiate that the driver was speeding because he or she was fleeing in terror, but coupled with mistake of fact, that is, that the accused *honestly* believed there was a threat, the two combined might support a defence.[43]

An accused might also raise a defence of involuntariness or automatism, in that he or she was not *consciously* in control of the vehicle and therefore could not be said to be 'driving' as such.[44] Involuntariness might be put forward in the event where there was no warning of sleep's onset, or in an automatistic state, such as a seizure. In terms of falling asleep, the key consideration is the period prior to the onset of sleep. As per *Kroon v The Queen* in 1990 and the High Court in *Jiminez v R* in 1992, if a driver knew or *ought* to have realised that there was a substantial risk of falling asleep, yet continued to drive, he or she may be said to have been driving dangerously.[45] In the mid to late twentieth century, sleep and blackouts were a common excuse and 'one of the first refuges of a guilty conscience'.[46]

Despite judicial assertions that the *manner of the driving*, a phrase central to the case law, was what distinguished s 59(1) from vehicular manslaughter, this seemed more a matter of semantics than practice. Decades of trial transcripts demonstrated that the *manner of driving* was also central to judges' directions to juries in determining criminal negligence. Repeatedly they emphasised that the *manner* of the driving had to have *caused* the death and this continued after the advent of the *Road Traffic Act*.[47] Historically, the emphasis on the *manner* of the driving was partially born out of the need to emphasise to juries that the task before them was to assess, 'objectively', the degree of negligence demonstrated by the driver. The principle, that the *manner* of the driving distinguished dangerous driving causing death from criminally negligent manslaughter was somewhat nebulous, although the driving had to be objectively, and of itself, *dangerous* rather than fail the benchmark of the *reasonable* person or 'ordinary' prudent driver.

The introduction of dangerous driving causing death in 1974 was marked by what seemed to be a rather unusual prosecution and penalty regime for something as significant as causing the death of another person. A defendant could elect to have his or her case heard summarily, absent a jury – an alternative criticised in the course of the Bill's passage. Penalties became contingent on the jurisdiction in which a case was heard.[48] Thomas Hartrey was opposed to summary judgment on the grounds that a charge of dangerous driving causing death was so serious he would not risk having the matter decided solely by a magistrate.[49] Strangely, there were no objections on the grounds of leniency. Yet if convicted summarily, an offender was liable to significantly lower penalties. Summary judgment remained in place for almost forty years following the introduction of the *Road Traffic Act*.[50] Until the introduction of careless driving causing death in 2016, dangerous driving causing death was the only homicide offence to which summary judgment had ever applied.

The construction of s 59(1) favoured fines over custodial penalties. Where possible, drivers who killed were to be fined rather than imprisoned. The legislature preferenced fines over custodial sentences, not only by giving them priority, but also by increasing the maximum imposable monetary penalties.[51]

DANGEROUS DRIVING CAUSING DEATH

On summary conviction, the maximum fine was initially set at $2,000 or up to eighteen months' imprisonment.[52] If convicted on indictment, drivers were liable to a fine of up to $5,000 or up to four years' imprisonment.[53] In 1976, the Assistant Commissioner of Police said there was 'considerable merit' in increasing the penalties, which he regarded as far too lenient. The Commissioner cautioned, however, that heftier fines might encourage more defendants to take their chances at trial.[54]

There was no revision of custodial penalties for the next thirty years, with the exception of cases involving stolen vehicles. As of 1992, defendants who were driving a stolen vehicle at the time of the crash would be liable to a maximum term of imprisonment of twenty years on indictment.[55] The only other substantive amendment was the increase of maximum imposable fines, although fines failed to keep abreast of inflation. By 1991, for example, the fine for dangerous driving causing death on summary judgment had doubled to only $4,000.[56] The maximum fine on indictment doubled to $10,000.[57] By mid-2004, the maximum imposable fine on indictment was set at $20,000 and $8,000 on summary conviction,[58] sums never imposed in either instance. Bar stolen vehicles, the maximum terms of imprisonment on indictment and summary judgment set in 1974 remained in place for the next three decades.

Notwithstanding that, following the High Court in *Callaghan v R*, the first alternative driving-causing-death offence was based in criminal negligence and the second in dangerousness, custodial penalties for alternative driving-causing-death offences decreased between the mid-1940s and the late 1980s. Fines became routine. Summary judgment was central to this trend. As a charge of dangerous driving causing death did not exclude cases at the upper end of the spectrum of fault, the decline in custodial terms and the increase in fines signified a further minimisation of the seriousness of the crime. The maximum four-year term under s 59(1) was one year less than the maximum penalty imposable under s 291A, and drastically lower than the maximum term of life imprisonment for manslaughter. By comparison, in the same year that dangerous driving causing death was introduced, the maximum custodial term for causing grievous bodily harm in circumstances absent a vehicle was set at seven years.[59] On at least one occasion, the Crown pursued this discrepancy, charging a driver with two counts of grievous bodily harm under s 297 of the Code, rather than injury under the *Road Traffic Act*. It was an effective tactic – the driver was sentenced to three years' imprisonment, with a minimum term of eighteen months, a penalty far in excess of that typically imposed for dangerous driving causing death. The sentence was upheld on appeal.[60]

The WA Law Reform Commission gave some consideration to summary judgment in 1970, recommending an increase in the number of indictable offences open to expedited procedures. Increasing the scope of summary judgments would, according to the Commission, reduce costs, redistribute work more appropriately between the courts, and be an expedient, efficient way to deal with more prevalent, less serious offences. While the Commission recommended that the scope of summary offences should increase to include, for example, breaking and entering a non-residential premise, gross indecency, bringing stolen property into the State and forgery, driving-causing-death offences were notably absent from the list. Notwithstanding, s 59(1) was enacted on the basis that prosecutions could, in the Commission's terms, be resolved quickly and with 'less publicity'.[61] In 1978 the *Road Traffic Act* was amended so that, irrespective of whether a defendant elected to have the matter dealt with summarily, if the court was of the opinion that the case should be prosecuted on indictment, it could commit the defendant to stand trial.[62] The amendments also made it possible for a summary jurisdiction to refer a convicted defendant to a higher court if the factual circumstances of the case were so serious that the court held its sentencing powers to be inadequate.[63] Summary judgment also provided a further option. As an alternative to dangerous driving causing death, defendants could instead be convicted of careless or dangerous driving simpliciter, which in both instances would attract a maximum fine of $200 in the mid-1970s.[64] This provided a mechanism to impose a penalty when the causative nexus between the driving and the death could not be readily established.

As an alternative offence to manslaughter, segregated from all other forms of homicide in its statutory context, specific to driving, and with a lenient penalty regime, the operation of dangerous driving causing death gave further weight to the impression that causing a death by the mismanagement of a vehicle was far less consequential than all other forms of involuntary homicide. The emphasis on fines and the option of summary judgment further underscored that interpretation. While it was entirely reasonable not to put a defendant to full trial when the level of fault demonstrated in the manner of their driving was *particularly* low, rarely were those cases brought before the courts. Summary judgment was routinely utilised in cases where conduct fell at the upper end of the spectrum of fault, fault that traversed the bounds of criminal negligence. The employ of dangerous driving causing death to prosecute conduct which was to all intents and purposes *criminally negligent*, but had become, overnight, *dangerous*, was counterproductive to the objective of elevating the seriousness of the mismanagement of vehicles in the hearts and minds of the driving public.

Comparable offences were not included in traffic legislation in other Australian jurisdictions. Like offences were included within criminal statutes, although at least one jurisdiction initially categorised the same offence as a misdemeanour.[65] As was the approach with the UK's *Road Traffic Act 1956* and New Zealand's *Transport Act* of 1962, situating the offence within WA's *Road Traffic Act* generated the impression that the wrongdoing was a matter of 'traffic' rather than individual criminal conduct. Then again, the High Court's decision in *Callaghan v R* would have likely rendered any attempt to insert another driving-causing-death offence into the Code vulnerable to challenge.

On dangerous driving causing death's statutory context, the WA Law Reform Commission's 2006 homicide issues paper is of particular interest. Amongst other things, the Commission requested submissions on whether the offence should be retained under the *Road Traffic Act* or abolished altogether.[66] Respondents advanced various arguments for retaining the offence. The Department of Public Prosecutions submitted that, as the charge encompassed lesser degrees of fault than manslaughter, it was a necessary mechanism to address a broader spectrum of culpable conduct. For more serious cases, the Department noted that a charge of manslaughter could be laid for 'grossly negligent driving' where open on the evidence.[67]

The Law Society of Western Australia, peak body for barristers and solicitors, also made a submission in favour of retaining the offence, startling though it was. Echoing the pro-motoring arguments of the mid-twentieth century, when critics argued that driving offences were not *real* crimes, nor offenders *real* criminals,[68] the Law Society held that, as people charged with the offence were generally 'law abiding citizens' who had come to the attention of the courts *solely* because of the manner of their driving, they should be charged with the lesser offence. Like the West Australian Criminal Lawyers' Association, the Law Society claimed that, as offenders were typically of good character and did not have criminal records, it was appropriate that dangerous driving causing death be kept peripheral to the Code.[69] The Society's position lends itself to an appraisal of the Code as a statute reserved for *real* criminals who commit offences as diverse as trespassing, common assault, stealing, receiving stolen property, falsely acknowledging deeds and obstructing railways. Conversely, typically law-abiding drivers who happened to kill other road users by means of their dangerous conduct should be protected from the debasing compass of the Criminal Code. Deaths occasioned by the misuse of motor vehicles appeared to be a species *sui generis*. In the Law Society's account, an individual's driving conduct seemed divorced from questions of crime and character; driving was a species apart. Yet the conduct of those who caused the death of another person in all other circumstances would automatically be appraised via the definitive lens of criminality, the Criminal Code. In any event, defendants' records frequently contradicted the Society's assertions – offenders often had extensive criminal records.

It was not long before dangerous driving causing death came under appeal in the courts. The decision in *Smith v The Queen* in 1976 was the first time the WA Court of Criminal Appeal had the opportunity to consider dangerous driving causing death under the new *Road Traffic Act*.[70] The Court's judgment was regarded as the authority for the next fourteen years and was largely adopted in the next precedent.[71] The facts of the case were that, prior to the collision, the appellant, Smith, was 'steadily' drinking for over two hours at Wundowie Golf Club.[72] On leaving the club and rounding a bend in the road, he collided with an oncoming vehicle. Its two occupants, a married couple, were killed.[73] His appearance following the collision was consistent with being affected by alcohol.[74] The Crown's case was that Smith caused the crash because he was driving on the wrong side of the road. While the defence did not refute that contention, they maintained that Smith was 'dazzled' by the headlights of the oncoming car.[75] Smith was found guilty on one count of dangerous driving causing death in the District Court and sentenced to twelve months' imprisonment. He appealed both the conviction and sentence.[76]

Grounds for appeal included the admissibility of evidence regarding alcohol consumption.[77] The appellant court held that, if the evidence regarding alcohol consumed *prior to the crash* tended to show that the defendant was affected by alcohol *at the time of the crash*, then that evidence was admissible and probative.[78] Notwithstanding, the most significant ground of appeal in *Smith* was the contention that the first instance judge had failed to direct the jury that *criminal negligence* was an element of dangerous driving causing death.[79]

While Smith's appeal was dismissed, Chief Justice Jackson and Justices Lavan and Wickham took the opportunity to elucidate the scope of the new offence, with Jackson delivering the judgment. As dangerous driving, in addition to that which resulted in death, was already in effect in other jurisdictions both in Australia and overseas, and the former was an offence under Western Australia's repealed *Traffic Act*, the Court had ample precedent to draw upon.[80] As per the High Court in *McBride v R* in 1966, the WA Court of Criminal Appeal distinguished dangerous driving causing death from criminally negligent manslaughter.[81] Chief Justice Jackson emphasised that negligence was *not* an element of dangerous driving – a driver could be said to be *dangerous* without being negligent.[82] Consistent with the existing authorities, the appellant court held that dangerous driving was not based in a breach of duty of care.[83] Whether driving could be said to be dangerous depended on the manner of the driving, the circumstances in which that driving took place, or whether the two combined posed a risk. The failure to keep a proper lookout when there was no one about and no traffic in the vicinity could not be said to be dangerous. The context in which the driving occurred was critical to the determination of fault. In order to be dangerous, the driving had to be 'in reality and not speculatively, potentially dangerous to others'.[84] Following Chief Justice Barwick in *McBride v R*, a piece of driving might be intrinsically dangerous in *all* circumstances or *because* of the specific nature of the circumstances.[85] The proximity of other road users, the context in which the driving occurred, and the manner of the driving were the crucial factors.

According to the judgment in *Smith*, dangerous driving had to be 'objectively' determined by reference to an external standard.[86] Like *criminal* negligence, the notion of a fixed external standard problematically implied some social consensus about what constituted dangerous conduct. The driver's state of mind and/or subjective belief regarding the quality of their driving was, and remains, immaterial. The WA Court of Criminal Appeal followed the High Court's judgment in *R v Coventry* in 1938 –

> indifference to consequences is not an essential element either of driving in a culpably negligent manner, or of driving at a speed which is dangerous to the public, or in a manner which is dangerous

to the public. The driver may have honestly believed that he was driving very carefully, and yet may be guilty of driving in a manner which is dangerous to the public. The jury is to determine, not whether the accused was in fact, as a matter of psychology, indifferent or not to the public safety, but whether he has driven in a manner which was dangerous to the public. The standard is an objective standard, "impersonal and universal, fixed in relation to the safety of other users of the highway".[87]

A driver's appreciation or realisation of the danger he or she posed had no bearing on the inquiry.[88] Importantly, the offence required something greater than a departure from an ordinary standard of caution and care. In order to be dangerous, the driving had to demonstrate a 'serious breach' of 'proper conduct'.[89] The 'objective quality'[90] of the driving would be best determined from the point of view of a bystander. For that reason, cases involving drivers who were under the influence and *appeared* to be managing the vehicle until the crash instant would still remain tremendously difficult to prosecute. Chief Justice Jackson advised that, in order to assess the driving, juries should 'place themselves, in their mind's eye, at the scene of the accident'.[91]

For some, the question of whether the driving was dangerous was a circular one – a death resulted, ergo the driving was dangerous. Despite his extensive experience as a lawyer, Thomas Hartrey adamantly supported this interpretation when he complained that the wording of the new offence was patently 'stupid'. At odds with some of his other objections, he retorted – 'Why should it be so worded? If a person has killed someone, there is no doubt that whatever he did was dangerous to that person – highly dangerous! So, that is complete stupidity'.[92] Hartrey was mistaken. As the High Court held in *McBride*, a conclusion of dangerousness could not be derived from resultant damage or consequence.[93] As such, it was erroneous to presume that the driving was dangerous because a death occurred. While the damage *might* afford evidence of the manner of the driving, the result could not be said to mirror the *quality* of the driving.[94] Dangerousness cannot be imputed simply because a collision occurred. Neither can the lack of a crash or fatal consequence negate that a driver's actions may have been very dangerous indeed. The fundamental issue is the degree of fault demonstrated in the manner of the driving. Importantly, in order for the offence to be established, the driver had to be 'in breach of the section' at the instant of the crash.[95] To substantiate a charge, that breach would be decisive at the point of impact; however, driving dangerously sometime prior and in the lead up to the collision might be sufficiently contemporaneous to connect the conduct and the result.[96] The manner of the driving had to have *caused* the death.

The appellant court in *Smith* also applied Justice Atkinson in *R v Evans* of 1963. Citing *Evans*, Chief Justice Jackson held that, if a jury believed, having regard to the circumstances, the manner of driving was dangerous to other road users, then 'on the issue of guilt' it did not matter whether a driver was 'deliberately reckless, careless, momentarily inattentive or even doing his incompetent best'.[97] The application of *Evans* in *Smith* not only confirmed that the driver's perception was immaterial, it further signalled that the spectrum of fault had widened. It was now theoretically possible that a moment's inattention, or that which might ordinarily be understood as careless driving, could be elevated to dangerous, subject to the context in which it occurred. By comparison, manslaughter excluded momentary inattentiveness or misjudgement, requiring a flagrant display of *grossly* negligent conduct, a bar that had been set particularly high by West Australian juries. The possibility that careless driving could theoretically be elevated to dangerous driving causing death, contingent on circumstance, was a significant departure from previous years when verdicts demonstrated a preference towards an *extensive* sequence of overt negligence to meet the benchmark for the alternative offence.

One of the most concerning aspects of the introduction of dangerous driving causing death was that, *in practice*, it further diminished the gravity of the harm by diluting the nomenclature of the conduct. What might once have been appositely labelled *criminal negligence*, was readily diluted to 'dangerous'. Undercharging, plea bargaining and the desire to secure convictions meant that very serious factual circumstances began to come before the courts under s 59(1). The factual circumstances of matters brought before the lower courts over the following decades bears out that dangerous driving causing death became a catch-all for a broad spectrum of conduct, most particularly wilful, blatant risk-taking and reckless indifference. Furthermore, in the Supreme Court, where drivers were charged with manslaughter, juries continued to prefer the alternative, lesser offence.

For example, in March 1976, a 40-year-old married couple were driving along Marmion Avenue at 9.45 pm when their vehicle was struck head-on by another car. They were both killed. Another passenger survived. According to the CIB report, David Humble was travelling at approximately 80 to 85 mph (128.7 to 136.8 km/h) on approach to a bend, where he lost control of his vehicle and careered into the oncoming lane. He was racing Colin Parker. Humble and Parker were pitting their cars against one another. They agreed to race at a party earlier that evening and had set markers out on the road.[98] Both were charged under the unlawful common purpose provisions of the Code.[99] Humble had a blood alcohol concentration between 0.123% and 0.127%.[100] The jury found the co-accused not guilty of manslaughter. They were instead each found guilty of *one* count of dangerous driving causing death. It remains difficult to comprehend why premeditated racing in a public thoroughfare at a significant speed, in the wrong lane and in the immediate proximity of other road users whilst intoxicated was not of sufficient gravitas to warrant a conviction of manslaughter.

Likewise, in November 1979 Geoffrey Campbell was driving through Balga, a built-up area, at around 8.00 pm, at a speed of approximately 115 km/h in a 60 km/h zone, when he collided with another vehicle.[101] He had a blood alcohol concentration between 0.094% and 0.117%.[102] The Crown Prosecutor described the violent force of the collision in which Campbell's car 'drop-kicked' the small white Hillman Hunter sedan almost 2.5 metres in the air and 30 metres backwards from the point of impact.[103] The driver and passenger were killed instantly. Campbell had a history of traffic offending, including licence suspensions and drink-driving offences.[104] He was brought before the Supreme Court in September 1980 on one count of manslaughter, but was convicted of the alternative offence. Campbell appealed his conviction on the grounds that the trial judge misdirected the jury by failing to address the issue of causation; that is, whether the manner of his driving *caused* the death.[105] He served one month of his sentence before his conviction was quashed and a retrial ordered. At retrial, Campbell was again found guilty of dangerous driving causing death. He received a head sentence of twelve months' imprisonment with a minimum term of two months, a sentence appealed by the Crown. He was released after serving his minimum term.[106]

At the upper end of the spectrum of fault, the distinction between s 59(1) and manslaughter was, and remains, unclear. In 1970 the WA Law Reform Commission forewarned that, in all circumstances, the difference between the two offences would not be trouble-free for trained legal professionals, much less jurors.[107] While dangerous driving required something in the order of a 'serious breach',[108] that breach was theoretically less than that which would support a charge of manslaughter. When defendants were charged with manslaughter, juries were required to distinguish between the two offences. They often struggled to do so.

Rhiannon and Sarah were a case in point. In 1976, the two young women were moving into a flat together. They travelled back and forth from Belmont to Glendalough, moving their possessions over the course of the day.[109] While stationary at the traffic lights at the intersection of Epsom Avenue and Great Eastern Highway, they were hit directly from behind by a white Holden utility vehicle. Rhiannon was pulled from the car and died on the side of the road following attempts to resuscitate.[110] Prior to the crash, several witnesses saw a white Holden utility vehicle travelling at speeds estimated at up to 100 km/h in a 60 km/h zone, weaving in and out of traffic and colliding with other vehicles.[111] John's driving was apparently of such concern that several drivers pulled off the road in order to avoid a collision. Prior to the crash, John's passenger, Simon, was seen hanging out of the car window, trying to touch other vehicles and pedestrians. Witnesses reported John and Simon 'skylarking', yelling and shouting.[112]

At the time of the crash, John's blood alcohol concentration was 0.262%,[113] a level of intoxication compounded by medication. Following a car crash the previous year, he had experienced transitory episodes of blurred vision and unsteadiness, caused by damage to his inner ear, resulting in problems with his balance.[114] John was prescribed Stemetil by a neurologist at Royal Perth Hospital and was instructed to take half a tablet, three times a day, slowly increasing to a full dosage. Dr Keith Grainger advised the Supreme Court that John was instructed not to drive for at least a fortnight until established on the therapeutic regime, and he was warned that, if combined with alcohol, the medication would have additional side effects and would markedly affect his judgment.[115] John had reported that, prior to taking the medication, his sense of disorientation was so severe that, on occasion, it had caused him to steer his car in a straight line when attempting to turn a corner.[116]

Despite testimony from many eyewitnesses that John's driving was highly erratic, the defence claimed that there was insufficient evidence to support a charge of manslaughter. In fact, at the commencement of proceedings, John's barrister, Mr Wood, attempted to have those testimonies ruled out on the grounds that there was no certainty that the car observed in the lead up to the crash was John's, nor that he was driving it.[117] Wood claimed the prejudicial value of those testimonies would be both 'dangerous' and 'disastrous'.[118] Conveniently putting to one side his client's blood alcohol concentration, Mr Wood suggested that, as John was under the influence of medication at the time of the crash, the collision occurred independently of his will. He was therefore not responsible for his actions.[119]

At the end of the trial and after extensive deliberations, the jury sought further clarification. Despite Justice Jones' comprehensive directions, the jury foreman asked whether Jones might again explain the difference between criminal negligence and dangerous driving causing death.[120] Justice Jones emphasised that criminal negligence was the more serious of the two offences, proof of which required driving in such a 'grossly careless manner' as to be 'outrageous' and 'amount to a crime against everybody'.[121] On the difference between the two offences, it was 'a matter of degree'.[122] If the jury came to the conclusion that the defendant drove his car in a manner which was, having regard to the circumstances, dangerous to the public or indeed any person, then the offence was constituted. On the difficulty in distinguishing between the two offences, he remarked that the difference might not be very significant.[123] Yet comparison of the respective penalties demonstrated something entirely different, with a manslaughter conviction attracting a maximum custodial term of life imprisonment and dangerous driving causing death four years. Justice Jones explained that, while the jury might find the driver's conduct dangerous and 'very serious', they might 'not feel it is so serious as to be criminal negligence'.[124] Advising the jury that he could not assist them any further, he stated that it was a matter for them to decide just how negligent they considered the driving to be.[125] Jones observed that, while the task before the jury was not an intellectually demanding matter, it was still of considerable difficulty in respect to the *social judgment* they were required to make.[126] The jury's social judgment was that John was guilty of manslaughter. Justice Jones sentenced him to five years' imprisonment, until then an *unprecedented* penalty in the history of sentencing. John's non-parole period was set at seventeen months. He was disqualified from holding a licence for seven years.

Confusion about the distinction between dangerous driving causing death and manslaughter was not limited to jurors. It was also a source of confusion for police and magistrates. Fifteen months after the introduction of the offence, Jean Edwards was killed when she was travelling in a vehicle driven by Colin Pyer.[127] Pyer made a right-hand turn directly across an oncoming lane of traffic, colliding with another car.[128] He stated in interview that he was not the driver.[129] Witnesses identified him as the driver.[130] Pyer had a blood alcohol concentration of 0.246% at the time of the crash.[131] Due to appear on charges of driving without a licence, driving under the influence, providing false and misleading information and careless driving, Pyer did not appear before the court and a warrant was issued for his arrest.[132] He was not charged with Edwards' death. A coronial inquest later found that Pyer had *caused* Edwards' death.[133] Almost a year-and-a-half after Jean Edwards was killed, Crown Prosecutor Murray provided advice to WA Police, noting that there was sufficient evidence to charge Pyer with dangerous driving causing death.[134] Superintendent Pages-Oliver advised the Assistant Commissioner of Traffic that he could not understand why Pyer was charged with the lesser offence of careless driving in the first place.[135]

Confusion or resistance to the increased scope of culpable conduct afforded by dangerous driving causing death was not restricted to the police. On 1 February 1976, Gary White was driving with a blood alcohol concentration between 0.08% and 0.111%.[136] Failing to negotiate a right-hand bend, he lost control of his car, veering to the incorrect side of the road where he collided with a tree and a 6-year-old pedestrian, Kathleen Craggs, who was wheeling her bicycle home.[137] Due to its momentum and speed, White's vehicle continued its trajectory after striking Kathleen and hit another tree.[138] It was a clear summer's day. A witness described the incident.

> This Holden car then hit the west kerb and it then went up over the kerb off the roadway onto the verge and still kept going south on Atkinson Street, this car was going pretty fast as it was going along the side of the road on the sand, but I could not say exactly

what speed. I would say that this car would have been travelling at…I reckon [it] was about 50 to 60 mph. This car was bouncing around and swaying around a lot from side to side and up and down in the air as it went along…she [the deceased] was not on the road at any time and was running when I saw her, as though she was trying to get away from the Holden car that was then heading straight towards her at a fast speed. The next thing I saw was that when the girl was about 10-12 feet off the roadway on the verge, she was hit on the right side…There were no other kids on the road. The only child around at the time was the little girl who got hit and she was well and truly off the road when the car came around the bend.[139]

White was found guilty of dangerous driving causing death in the District Court and fined $350. The police file was referred to District Coroner Forrest.[140] Forrest responded – 'having perused your file I consider that the facts disclose and warrant a finding of ACCIDENTAL DEATH, but as the matter has been adequately litigated, I do not propose to hold an Inquest'.[141] The currency of 'accident' had clearly endured.

While the WA Court of Criminal Appeal in *Smith* fully explicated the scope of the new offence, some members of the police and judiciary seemed slow to grasp its compass, resulting in insufficient charges being laid and cases being dismissed. While momentary inattention and doing one's 'incompetent best' fell within the scope of the charge, some remained of the view that such conduct was legitimately accidental. For example, in March 1976, Robert Wilson was a passenger in a sedan driven by George Walker.[142] Travelling through an intersection, Walker's car was struck by a car driven by Carmella Flemming. She entered the intersection against a stop sign. She did not slow down on approach. Flemming was charged with dangerous driving causing death. She pleaded not guilty.

Magistrate McGuigan dismissed the charge against Flemming on the basis that there was no evidence to support the Crown's case.

DANGEROUS DRIVING CAUSING DEATH

According to McGuigan, the failure to stop at a stop sign was an ordinary daily prospect for which no party should be held responsible.

> Every driver knows that it is on the cards at an intersection even one protected by lights or a stop sign that there is a good chance that some vehicle is going to overlook the stop lights or sign. In civil cases it seems to be a fairly standard approach on intersection matters that neither party is held to be blameless. Driving through a stop sign is regarded as being one of the ordinary contingencies of the road. Dangerous driving usually incorporates an element of speed but there was no evidence of speed…I cannot see that in law it is a prima facie case of dangerous driving. There but for the grace of God goes nearly every driver on the road.[143]

The investigating officers were horrified. Former Senior Inspector Pages-Oliver of the Prosecuting Branch advised his superiors that, with respect, 'his worship was wrong'.[144] Alarm sounded from higher office. The Premier, Sir Charles Court, added his voice to the concerns. 'Rather surprised', he wrote to the Attorney General and the Commissioner of Police. The Premier disapprovingly noted that the Magistrate was 'virtually saying' that, if a driver ran a stop sign, all he or she had to say was that they did not see the sign and 'plead that it is one of the traffic hazards that the unfortunate victim has to suffer'.[145] Pressure eventually led to Flemming being brought before the District Court on a charge of dangerous driving causing death in October 1976. She pleaded guilty and was fined $500.

Defendant's representatives also seemed reluctant or unwilling to accept the scope of the judgment in *Smith*, in particular, that an instance of inattention might be elevated to dangerousness, contingent on the circumstances surrounding the driving. In December 1977, 20-year-old Malcolm Hewison was killed. He was a passenger in a vehicle. His friend, 17-year-old Brett Bond was driving at a significant speed when, on an approach to a bend, he took his attention from the road to speak to a passenger in the back seat and crashed into an electricity pole. He was brought before the East Perth Children's Court on a charge of dangerous driving causing death.[146] Mr Bonamelli submitted that his client had committed no offence. If his conduct were to be characterised at all, at the very most it might be classed as 'no more than careless driving'.[147] The Magistrate disagreed.

> In my opinion, for a driver to completely withdraw his attention from the road while proceeding at a speed, not of itself dangerous, but one of which the vehicle was moving an appreciable distance in a very short time, when approaching a bend with a pole in the near vicinity and a car close ahead is manifestly dangerous to the criteria laid down by McBride – v – the Queen…and Smith – v – R. As far back as 1938 it was held in R – v – Coventry that a momentary lapse of attention if it resulted in danger to the public was not outside the prohibition against dangerous driving and much the same was said in R – v – Gosney 1971…The defendant is convicted as charged.[148]

Bond was found guilty of dangerous driving causing death and fined $250.

Despite the lenient penalties imposed, the prosecution of drivers such as Bond and Flemming did herald positive developments. That such cases were being brought before the courts demonstrates that incidents involving lapses in judgment and *transitory* instances of bad driving were being pursued. Prior to the *Road Traffic Act*, it was impossible to prosecute such cases.

Similar to the circumstances in the Flemming case, in 1975, 17-year-old Jeremy Finch also ran a stop sign, killing his passenger, Kevin. The sign was visible for 200 metres, the weather fine and dry. Witnesses testified that Finch did not reduce his speed on approach. He was found guilty of dangerous driving causing death in the District Court and fined $500.[149] Likewise, in September 1977, 17-year-old John Lowndes failed to stop at a stop sign. He crashed into a Mini Moke, causing it to spin around in the opposite direction and roll onto its left side.[150] A 7-year-old boy in the rear of the vehicle was killed.[151] Lowndes pleaded guilty to dangerous driving causing death in the Fremantle Children's Court. He was fined $60. By contrast, the circumstances in Gary White's case, where he hit two trees and mounted a kerb, killing pedestrian Kathleen Craggs, underlined a concerning development.[152] Arguably, White lost control of his vehicle because he had a significant blood alcohol concentration and was travelling at speed on approach to a bend. He received a penalty of $350. Fines were not reserved for cases of momentary inattention.

Michael John Roche was a case in point. On 25 July 1976, 15-year-old Amanda 'May' Nash was riding a bicycle along Bay View Terrace, Mosman Park.[153] Apparently, Amanda was not so much *riding* the bicycle as sitting on the seat and pushing it along with her feet.[154] Accounts differ, but according to the initial statements, her friend Tina was riding behind her.[155] Other accounts suggest that Tina was walking along the verge.[156] Amanda had spent that morning with her horse, Vagabond. Her father recorded a video of her and her beloved horse.[157] It would be the last images he would ever capture of his daughter.

Tina and Amanda were both wearing 'tennis whites'. Witnesses reported them as being 'highly visible'.[158] After hitting Amanda and narrowly missing Tina, Roche fled the scene in his Holden Torana.[159] Roche was celebrating his birthday the day he killed Amanda. He woke at 11 o'clock that morning. By noon, he was ensconced at The Mosman Park, a tavern, with his friends, where he drank four middies of beer between midday and 1 o'clock. He then returned home.[160] Roche later visited a friend's house where he had 'three or four' stubbies, although he conceded it 'could have been more...I could have had up to 6'. The pair returned to the tavern for the evening Sunday session. They arrived at 5.00 pm and Roche left at a quarter to six. In those three quarters of an hour, he drank a further six or seven middies of beer.[161] Ten minutes after he left, Amanda Nash was dead.[162] At Fremantle Police Station the following morning, Roche said he had the radio on full volume when he heard a bang. He could not remember seeing Amanda or hearing her bike scrape along the road.[163] He claimed that he was driving along, 'ran off the road' and thought he 'hit a post or something', but 'just kept on driving'. Attempting to clarify what he believed had occurred, he stated, 'I thought I hit the kerb and side-swiped a post'.[164] On the accuracy of his recollection, he conceded that it was 'all pretty blank' and the incident was 'over in a minute'.[165] The interviewing officer suggested that Roche's intoxication had caused the collision.

> I put it to you that you had too much beer to drink and that, *that* is the reason you hit something?
> It could be the reason. I had a fair amount to drink and I thought I was capable of driving.[166]

Concerns were raised that Roche was not charged with manslaughter.[167] The Assistant Commissioner of Traffic justified the course of action to the Commissioner of Police, explaining that the investigating officers felt that, had Roche been charged with manslaughter, he would have been acquitted. They formed a belief that a lack of evidence regarding the manner of Roche's driving prior to the point of impact, in addition to want of an independent witness, precluded a charge of manslaughter.[168] Yet, evidence to the manner of the driving and witnesses to that driving were equally required to charge him with dangerous driving causing death. Amanda's friend, Tina, witnessed Roche's driving. She positively identified his vehicle and described it swerving all over the road and up the kerb. She did state, however, that he was travelling at a normal speed.[169] Roche was fined $1,000 for dangerous driving causing death, $200 for failing to stop and $100 for failing to report the incident. More than forty years later, there exists a garden dedicated to Amanda's memory at Presbyterian Ladies College, her alma mater.

Michael Solonec also received a fine for what could only be described as grave mismanagement of a vehicle in circumstances of aggravation. At 9.00 pm on 22 October 1977, he was driving along Railway Road, Shenton Park. On approach to a stop sign at the intersection of Railway and Onslow Roads, he was seen driving erratically, speeding and in the wrong lane. Solonec failed to heed the stop sign, colliding head-on with a Fiat sedan and killing 17-year-old Luke Holland. Solonec was reportedly drunk at the scene, although no evidence of blood alcohol concentration was tendered in court.[170] There was some suggestion that he had suffered a blackout as a consequence of using hallucinogens.[171] There were almost twenty witnesses to Solonec's driving. He pleaded guilty to dangerous driving causing death. Solonec was fined $200 and disqualified from driving for seven years.

Christopher Corrigin was also fined. On 21 November 1976, he was driving along Oceanic Drive. He and his three passengers had been at Steve's, a well-known bar in Nedlands. Corrigin had a blood alcohol concentration of 0.170% at the time of the crash. Driving at a speed of approximately 95 km/h, he struck the kerb and veered off the road onto the verge. Swerving back onto the road, he veered into the oncoming lane of traffic, striking the opposite kerb and an electricity pole. His friend Rodney was killed and his two surviving passengers were seriously injured. Corrigin pleaded guilty to dangerous driving causing death and one count of driving under the influence. He was fined $1,000 for Rodney's death and $200 for driving under the influence.[172]

Despite the fact that the degree of fault demonstrated by drivers typically brought before the District and Magistrates Courts was well in excess of momentary inattention, fines remained egregiously low. In 1978, Cooper was aware that there was a serious problem with the brakes of his car. The brakes had to be pumped four to five times before they would engage. His friends had repeatedly warned him not to drive the car in its condition. Cooper failed to stop at a stop sign, killing two women travelling in another car. His blood alcohol concentration at the time of the crash was 0.092%. He pleaded guilty to one count of dangerous driving causing death and a charge of drink-driving. For the latter, he was fined $100. For killing one of the women, he received four years' probation and a community service order. The second charge of dangerous driving causing death was withdrawn.[173]

These penalties were consistent with sentencing trends in the 1970s, trends which continued into the late twentieth century. Referring to the $1,000 fine Michael Roche received for the hit-and-run killing of Amanda Nash, the Assistant Commissioner for Traffic assured the Commissioner of Police that a review of the penalties imposed in other cases demonstrated that 'the penalty in this instance is reasonably consistent' with other cases.[174] He provided a table, reproduced here as Table 1.

Table 1: Penalties applied to charges under s 59, 1975–1976

20 May 1975 Dangerous driving causing death Collie Police Court Summary judgment	$350 fine
20 June 1975 Dangerous driving causing death Bunbury Children's Court	$250 fine
21 July 1975 Dangerous driving causing death District Court	$1,500 fine
8 July 1975 Dangerous driving causing grievous bodily harm District Court	Twelve months' imprisonment, six months minimum term
4 October 1975 Two counts dangerous driving causing grievous bodily harm Fremantle Police Court	$500 per count
24 August 1975 Dangerous driving causing death Supreme Court	Twelve months' imprisonment

DANGEROUS DRIVING CAUSING DEATH

9 October 1975
Dangerous driving causing grievous bodily harm
Summary judgment

$850 fine

9 October 1975
Dangerous driving causing death
District Court Geraldton

Two years' imprisonment,
four month minimum period

19 October 1975
Dangerous driving causing death
York Police Court
Summary judgment

$1,000 fine

23 November 1975
Dangerous driving causing grievous bodily harm
Summary judgment

$350 fine

30 November 1975
Dangerous driving causing death
Summary judgment

Nine months' imprisonment

26 December 1975
Two counts dangerous driving causing death
Supreme Court

Bond

6 January 1976
Dangerous driving causing grievous bodily harm
Summary judgment

Dismissed pursuant to s 669 of
the Code

[No date]
Dangerous driving causing grievous bodily harm
Summary judgment

$400 fine

22 July 1976
Dangerous driving causing death
Roebourne Police Court
Summary judgment

$1,000 fine

18 July 1976
Dangerous driving causing death
Summary judgment

$1,000 fine

Source: letter from the Assistant Commissioner (Traffic) to Commissioner of Police, 11 August 1976

Notably, of the ten cases of dangerous driving causing death, only three drivers were imprisoned. One driver who killed two people was released on bond.

Sentences were somewhat higher in the Supreme Court where defendants were found guilty of dangerous driving causing death as an alternative verdict to manslaughter, although fines remained common. Records of cases brought before the Supreme Court between 1974 and mid-1981 survive in the archives. Sixty-seven defendants were brought before the Supreme Court, detailed in Table A3 of the Appendices. Three cases were joint prosecutions.[175] Of the sixty-seven people, only four were charged under s 59(1).

Of those sixty-seven defendants, forty-two were convicted.[176] Jury preference for the alternative offence to manslaughter clearly remained high with thirty-two defendants convicted of dangerous driving causing death, versus ten found guilty of manslaughter.[177] Of the thirty-two people convicted under s 59(1), sixteen were incarcerated.[178] Of those, eight received head sentences of twelve months or less, with some as low as six. Non-parole periods brought some sentences down to a matter of weeks.[179] Between 1974 and 1981, with only one exception,[180] terms of imprisonment for dangerous driving causing death did not exceed two years in the Supreme Court, half the maximum imposable penalty. In the same period, in all bar two instances, manslaughter convictions attracted terms of imprisonment between eighteen months and five years. In the remaining two cases, both offenders received a fine, one of $750 and the other $1,000 in conjunction with a 200-hour community service order.[181]

Of those defendants found guilty of dangerous driving causing death in the Supreme Court, where cases were theoretically the most serious, some were fined as little as $500, as against the maximum imposable fine of $5,000. Bonds, probation and community service orders were routinely imposed.[182] As Table A3 demonstrates, at least one driver was released on bond for the deaths of two people. Of the twelve people fined in the Supreme Court between 1974 and mid-1981, for either dangerous driving

DANGEROUS DRIVING CAUSING DEATH

causing death or manslaughter, ten were penalised $1,500 or less. One defendant was fined $4,000 on a guilty plea, a comparatively severe penalty.[183]

Fines were imposed in cases with very serious factual circumstances. For example, at around 9.30 pm one night in December 1974, Mark was driving along Scarborough Beach Road after drinking with his wife and friends when he hit a pedestrian who was attempting to cross the road. Mark fled the scene, although he stopped on his way home to inspect the damage to his vehicle. He continued drinking after he returned home, preventing an accurate calculation of his blood alcohol concentration at the time of the crash. He did, however, test over the limit.[184] Witnesses saw Mark's vehicle, a white Holden, speeding and 'behaving erratically' prior to the incident. Others, including a bus driver, saw him hit the pedestrian.[185] There was a distance of 205 feet from the point of impact, where Giovanni's right shoe was found on the road alongside a spray of broken glass, to where his body landed. Crown Prosecutor Mr Overman argued that the distance was indicative of significant speed and force of impact. There was no evidence, Mr Overman said, that Giovanni had wings, at least not prior to his death.[186] The defence countered that Giovanni was the 'author of his own destruction' because he had attempted to cross the road in an unsafe place.[187]

Mark fled the scene with his headlights off. He was followed by the bus driver who recorded his vehicle registration number.[188] While Mark initially told police that he was not involved in the incident, he quickly revised his explanation, saying he thought he had hit a pole.[189] There was no damage to any traffic lights, signs, or poles in the area.[190] Under questioning, Mark was asked *precisely* what he had collided with. He claimed he hit a 'set of lights'.[191] The detective responded frankly – 'There's blood on your car. Lights don't bleed'.[192] Mark was fined $750 on a manslaughter conviction and disqualified from driving for three years. Save for the fines imposed in the lower courts, there appeared to be little uniformity in sentencing.

During the same period, much higher penalties were imposed in cases arguably less serious than causing the death of another person/s. Drug use and possession, for instance, were heavily penalised. Between the mid-1970s and the early 1980s, custodial terms for possession of small quantities of marijuana with intent to sell ranged between twenty months and four years. Penalties for stealing a vehicle also remained custodial, although had dropped to three to six months, as opposed to the one to five-year terms imposed in the 1950s and 1960s. By contrast, when a death was occasioned by dangerous driving, offenders were generally fined.[193]

The mid-1970s heralded portentous changes in the taxonomy and prosecution of 'road death'. The introduction of dangerous driving causing death under the *Road Traffic Act* signalled a widening of the scope of culpable fault and, paradoxically, a simultaneous attenuation in the characterisation of the conduct, both in perception and penalty. In many instances, circumstances that could only be described as criminally negligent had suddenly become *dangerous*. Thereafter, for almost forty years, drivers could elect to have their cases dealt with summarily and, as a result, receive substantial reductions in penalties. In the 1980s, many members of the judiciary began agitating for sentencing reform, arguing that, while the legislature had placed a significant value on human life, judges were not exercising the scope of punishments available to them. In Western Australia, the judiciary was somewhat constrained by precedent, although the relevance of those precedents came under increasing attack. By the early 1990s, the combined effects of judicial activism, the efforts of Crown prosecutors and mounting public pressure began to effect change.

Chapter Seven

Reconsidering *Laporte v R* and the maximum imposable penalty, 1970–2004

R v J.E.W.E. (1976), a case involving the death of a young woman explored in the previous chapter, and *R v A.M.C.* (1979), a case which involved the death of three family members, have significance beyond the traumatic circumstances in which those four people were killed. The five-year sentences imposed in both those matters contradict the position expounded by the West Australian judiciary regarding the maximum penalty ever imposed, from the judgment in *Laporte v R* in 1970,[1] when the sentencing benchmark was first firmly established, until the early 1990s.

There was a prolonged delay between calls for higher penalties and their materialisation. As in decades previous, after the introduction of the *Road Traffic Act* in 1974 judges continued to stress the gravity of dangerous and criminally negligent driving and its devastating impact on the community. Yet, that appraisal was consistently at odds with the sentences imposed. While drivers were imprisoned for killing other road users prior to the introduction of the *Road Traffic Act*, in the late 1970s and 1980s, in accordance with the Act's emphasis on fiscal penalty as a first course of action, fines became commonplace. Not simply reserved for inattention or misjudgement, fines were imposed in circumstances where the conduct could only be described as *grossly* negligent. If, as the High Court of Australia emphasised, the fundamental principle of sentencing is that a sentence should be proportionate to the gravity of the offence,[2] sentences for deaths occasioned by the use of motor vehicles pointed to relative inconsequence.

The benchmark for sentencing drivers in WA was set down in *Laporte v R* in 1970 – a benchmark all but immoveable for more than twenty years, with two overlooked, but important exceptions. The appellant in *Laporte* was convicted of manslaughter and sentenced to four years' imprisonment. He appealed on the grounds that the sentence was manifestly excessive. In their joint judgment, Justices Jackson, Nevile and Lavan correctly reflected that they could not recall a four-year term in a similar case.[3] *Laporte* was in fact the first Western Australian case to attract a term of four years, followed by *R v C.F.C.* in 1973. The Court observed, however, that there had been a four-year sentence imposed in *R v Watson* in Queensland in 1960,[4] an analogous jurisdiction, and cited the Judge's remarks that such a sentence was indicative of a 'particularly bad' course of conduct.[5]

The appellant Court in *Laporte* held that the sentence imposed at first instance by Justice Wickham was, by comparison, severe and halved the term to two years, with a minimum non-parole period of nine months.[6] Although the Court noted that the circumstances of the case were serious, they were not as severe as many others previously tried in Western Australia, which had been subject to much lower penalties. While the decision emphasised that it was not feasible to standardise sentences or set a tariff for vehicular homicide, the Court observed that most cases would tend to fall somewhere along a continuum, subject to the material facts and the offender's antecedents and record.[7] From then on, Western Australian judges followed the dictum of *Laporte v R* (1970) which signalled four years as the *maximum* imposable penalty, reflecting the worst possible conduct. *Laporte* became entrenched as the sentencing benchmark, although reliance on the judgment was somewhat misguided. The yardstick set by *Laporte* had not always been followed.

The first Western Australian test case concerning dangerous driving causing death, *Smith* v *The Queen* of 1976, further entrenched approaches to sentencing.[8] The judgment imported the two-tiered categorisation of dangerous driving from *R v Guilfoyle* of 1973,[9] which held that the offence was generally the result of momentary inattention or misjudgement by a driver with an otherwise good record, or, more seriously, the consequence of selfish disregard, which might include a degree of recklessness. For the inattentive driver, *Guilfoyle* held a fine and disqualification for the minimum statutory period as an appropriate penalty. If a driver had a history of offending, he or she should be prevented from driving for an extended period. For drivers who demonstrated selfish disregard, a custodial sentence with a long period of disqualification was deemed necessary. The court in *Guilfoyle* further reasoned that circumstances of aggravation, including intoxication, would elevate the seriousness of the offence and should attract a higher penalty.[10]

According to the judgment in *Smith*, the appellant's conduct fell within the second *Guilfoyle* category. Despite the defendant's sound driving record, Chief Justice Jackson held that the nature of the conduct was such that a custodial sentence was justifiable, there being nothing to demonstrate that the trial judge had exceeded his discretion. In accordance with the material filed in the appeal, Jackson observed that dangerous driving causing death had tended to attract sentences of three to nine months in Australia and the United Kingdom and thus, under the circumstances, a sentence of twelve months was neither gratuitous nor unreasonable. Based on the evidence filed in support of the appeal, he noted that cases involving intoxication, including manslaughter, had tended to attract sentences of eighteen months to two years.[11] Yet, the material filed incorrectly downplayed previous terms of imprisonment. Historically, cases involving intoxication combined with an observed sequence of negligent conduct had, in some instances, attracted longer terms. Alcohol was an unambiguous feature in seven of the ten cases in which defendants were sentenced to three years' imprisonment between 1946 and 1974.[12] Nonetheless, the classification of conduct as either carelessness or indicative of selfish disregard, the two-tiered *Guilfoyle* approach, remained fundamental to sentencing in the following years. It was an approach later criticised and rejected by members of the West Australian judiciary.[13]

The reliance on the judgment in *Laporte* as the definitive yardstick was in error; an error subsequently entrenched by repetition. Such was the persistence of the oversight that in *Ainsworth v D (A Child)* (1992), Chief Justice Malcolm stated that, until 1992, no vehicular manslaughter case had ever attracted a sentence in excess of four years in Western Australia.[14] It was an observation repeated in other cases, including *The Queen v S (No 2) (A CHILD)* and *McKenna v The Queen*, both in 1992, and in *English v The Queen* in 1995.[15] The claim that four years was the maximum sentence ever imposed was apparently the chief constraint against increasing penalties – judges were hampered by precedent. The assertion was incorrect. At least two cases contradict the claims regarding the four-year maximum penalty, a sentencing myth that persisted until the mid-1990s. Both were tried within less than a decade of *Laporte*.

Contrary to Chief Justice Malcolm's assertion, in *R v J.E.W.E.* (1976) and *R v A.M.C.* (1979) both defendants were convicted of manslaughter and sentenced to five years' imprisonment, the former with a non-parole period of seventeen months and the latter, three years. *R v J.E.W.E.* involved the death of a young female passenger, Rhiannon, who died on the side of the road after the car she was in was hit directly from behind while stationary at a set of traffic lights. *R v A.M.C.* involved the deaths of three people – a married couple and their adult son who were on holiday from South Australia, caravan in tow. The 19-year-old defendant, Andrew, was prosecuted for only one death, then a standard approach to multiple fatalities. At the time of the crash,

Andrew had a blood alcohol concentration of 0.224%.[16] He had been twice previously convicted for driving under the influence, his last offence being two months before the fatal collision, when he was disqualified from driving for two years.[17]

The facts of *R v A.M.C* were that, on 25 September 1978, Andrew took his friend's prime mover without permission. The vehicle was later seen 'weaving from one extreme edge of the road to the other, almost colliding with the guide posts'.[18] A road worker who witnessed Andrew's driving considered contacting the police in order that they might intervene, but regrettably did not.[19] Andrew claimed that, just before the crash, there was a failure in the steering mechanism and the vehicle simply 'bounced' onto the wrong side of the road.[20] The holidaymakers' car was discovered upside down at the scene, banana-shaped and bent in the middle. The caravan was totally demolished.[21] Debris was scattered for some distance along the Esperance–Coolgardie Road. Andrew was found at the scene, trapped inside the cab, pleading to be rescued.[22]

A surviving son visited from South Australia to collect objects recovered from the crash scene and personal effects found on the bodies of his parents and brother. He was the recipient of sundry items, including camping equipment, cameras, a first aid kit, an esky, items of clothing, wallets, touring atlases and his mother's jewellery, including her necklace, replete with lucky charm pendants. A sum of $443.70 found at the crash scene was also involuntarily bequeathed.[23] Justice Lavan said it was difficult to imagine a worse case, declaring Andrew 'a menace on the road'. While he professed his reluctance to send a young man to prison and, despite a glowing reference from the Premier of South Australia, he claimed that the circumstances were such that he had no option but to impose a severe sentence.[24]

First instincts might be that the terms imposed in *R v J.E.W.E.* and *R v A.M.C* were the act of a maverick judge whose decisions were regarded as non-conformist or ill-considered. This was not the case. The cases were separately presided over by Justices Lavan and Jones. Not only was Lavan a senior member of the Court, he sat on the bench in *Laporte*. While not requisite, neither Lavan nor Jones provided any justification as to why he was breaking with the dictum of the State's highest court. While decisions of higher courts regarding sentencing offer guidance, they are not binding authorities, sentencing being a discretionary exercise. Nonetheless, one might dismiss the anomaly by reasoning that subsequent judges were aware of the sentences, but deliberately overlooked them. This is explicitly contradicted by the case law, which is unambiguous in the assertion that *no* driver in Western Australia had ever been sentenced to a term in excess of four years for dangerous driving causing death or manslaughter prior to the early 1990s.

The fact that the sentences in *R v J.E.W.E.* and *R v A.M.C.* escaped the judiciary's attention and the four-year benchmark became legitimated by repetition is, of itself, concerning. Whilst both cases went unreported, they could have been cited as a basis for imposing higher penalties. The sentences in *R v J.E.W.E.* and *R v A.M.C.* had the potential to effect change – a potential lost when terms of imprisonment were erroneously curtailed on the basis of the judgment in *Laporte*. While the difference between four and five years may seem inconsequential, it may have gone some small way towards shifting social attitudes about the seriousness of the offence. Had the trajectory set by those cases been followed, the Crown might have been more expediently relieved from appealing to the judiciary to reflect the gravity of offences in the sentences they handed down over the next twenty years and to exercise the full range of penalties conferred upon them by the legislature.

In the 1980s, the Crown began to launch appeals against sentences. In *Hodgson v Thomson* (1985), for instance, the defendant killed a motorcyclist by failing to give way, turning directly into the path of the rider. He was fined $100.[25] The State appealed on the grounds that the penalty was manifestly inadequate. The appellant court held that a fine of $750 would have been a more appropriate penalty. In *R v Browne* that same year, a driver who killed his brother-in-law when he collided with another vehicle was convicted on indictment for dangerous driving causing death. He was neither fined nor disqualified. The appellant court concurred with the Crown that the trial judge had given undue regard to matters personal to the offender and that the case clearly called for the imposition of a fine and mandatory disqualification. Browne was subsequently fined $1,000.[26] In *R v Street* in 1986, the State was less successful. The driver was sentenced to nine months' imprisonment on one manslaughter conviction in a case where he killed four people. He was disqualified from driving for two years. The Crown appealed against the sentence and the term of disqualification. The defendant appealed against the finding of manslaughter. Surprisingly, Justice Rowland stated that it was difficult to identify *anything* in the case 'which should have excited the attention of the Crown to justify its appeal'. The sentencing aspects of the appeal were dismissed. The term of disqualification was increased to four years.[27]

Frustration regarding lenient penalties had begun to boil over in the courts in the 1970s. In *R v S.K., J.S. & A.L.S.* (1978), a case involving the joint prosecution of three young men racing one another along Old Mandurah Road en route to a drag race at Ravenswood, Crown Prosecutor Davies challenged youth's importance as a mitigating factor in sentencing.[28] While age is, as a rule, a significant mitigating factor, clemency towards young offenders seemed to spawn defeat. The offence was overwhelmingly a young man's crime, yet the courts were required to exercise a greater degree of leniency towards them. Youth's mitigating impact was at cross-purposes with the goal of ostensibly deterring and punishing the principal group of offenders.

The pre-sentence reports in *R v S.K., J.S. & A.L.S* indicated that two of the three co-accused did not feel any sense of responsibility for their friend's death,[29] despite tailgating and overtaking on a narrow road at 80 mph (128.74 km/h) in the lead up to the crash.[30] One witness estimated their speeds to be as high as 100 mph (160.93 km/h).[31] Despite admitting to driving at speed, one defendant insisted that it was an 'accident' and 'no one should be to blame'.³² Another co-accused reportedly demonstrated some remorse and emotional distress regarding his friend's death.³³ His remorse was such that, just over two weeks later, he was convicted of driving with a blood alcohol concentration in excess of 0.15% on a separate, unrelated charge. His subsequent offending was apparently caused by his distress over recent events.³⁴

In the sentencing proceedings, Crown Prosecutor Davies lamented that Western Australia was, like other parts of the country, 'suffering an incredible and increasing carnage'.³⁵ According to Davies, the carnage was the consequence of a variety of circumstances, ranging from 'pure accidents' to deliberate courses of conduct. For Davies, the case fell squarely into the deliberate class – the defendants *knew* their conduct was wrong, yet participated in a course of action that not only demonstrated disregard for the safety of other road users, but their passengers and friends. It was 'miraculous', he said, that no other party was hurt.³⁶ Of the two defendants who were loath to accept any responsibility for their friend's death, both had significant records, including numerous licence disqualifications and fines for careless driving, speeding, failure to stop at stop signs and driving whilst disqualified.³⁷ The judge noted their lack of remorse.³⁸ The other defendant had an acute sense of personal responsibility for the death of his friend and no previous record.³⁹ In light of the annual toll, Davies argued that exemplary punishment and deterrence should be, above all, the principal consideration in sentencing.

> From a community point of view, once you have this conduct, then it must be brought home to others who would think about doing it that they must not, and it will not be brought home to them in any way which results in any leniency once it has occurred. That, I think, highlights the conflict, with respect, your Honour, in this sentencing matter. Of course each of these three young persons does not need anything [sic] to tell him he should not have done it. He would have known had he bothered to think. He does not need now to be rehabilitated. Each of the prisoners would know,

if he sat down, and indeed probably does know, that he must not do it again. It is not the point that, subject to traffic convictions, they have led blameless lives; it is not the point, with respect, in the Crown's submission, that they are good family young men, good workers and so on...What, in the Crown's submission, sentences in this matter must be aimed at, are positively (hopefully it can be done) dissuading others of like inclination to succumb to the temptation to make the decision to simply behave in this way. Deterrence, with respect your Honour, when one is dealing with the deliberate conduct, is paramount and fundamental.[40]

There was mounting agreement with Davies' frustration in other Australian jurisdictions. While the judiciary were often highly critical of drivers' wanton disregard for the safety of other road users, emphasising the need to deter, the penalties they imposed were at odds with their reproaches, and equally out of step with the extent of penalties authorised by parliaments.[41] Sentences are, of course, a sanction of last resort, a long-standing tenet that was given formal effect in WA in 1988 in accord with the Australian Law Reform Commission's recommendations.[42] However, two years later, the measure of *last* resort shifted when the comments made by Sheppard in *Crawley v The Queen* some seven years prior, were adopted by the WA Court of Criminal Appeal, setting a benchmark to re-examine the four-year maximum and transform trends in sentencing.[43]

In *Crawley v The Queen* (1981), an appeal to the Federal Court in the Australian Capital Territory, the driver was convicted of culpable driving causing grievous bodily harm and sentenced to twelve months' imprisonment, with an order that he be released on bond, in addition to a fine. He had driven his car at a significant speed into an intersection and, disregarding a 'Give Way' sign, ploughed into another vehicle. On appeal, the Federal Court held that the first instance judge did not have the discretion to impose a combined penalty. The penalty therefore had to be set aside and an alternative imposed.[44] What was open, rather, was a period of imprisonment of up to three years, a fine of up to $2,000, or another non-custodial penalty.

A substantive factor affecting the matter on appeal was the time that had elapsed since the offence. The offence was committed in April 1977, yet the defendant was not convicted until July two years later. Four years had passed between the incident and the appeal in mid-1981 and, given that delay and the facts of the case being relatively straightforward, Justice Fox believed that remitting the case to the trial judge for re-sentencing would be inappropriate.[45] While the Court set the custodial sentence aside, imposing a fine instead, Justice Fox noted that, despite the defendant's favourable work history and character, public interest was paramount and the courts needed to do what they could 'to keep down the road toll'. While Justices Sheppard and Blackburn concurred with Fox, they additionally argued that the fine imposed on the appellant should be the heaviest the legislation allowed for.[46] Sheppard was reluctant to impose a fine in lieu of imprisonment, favouring incarceration. In discussing his reluctance, he made a persuasive argument that the community's minimisation of road violence demanded redress.

Given the delay between offence and appeal, Blackburn reasoned that sending the appellant to prison would be an undignified 'spectacle', thereby justifying a monetary penalty which might otherwise seem lenient.[47] The maximum imposable fine was $2,000, a penalty set some ten years prior, which Blackburn believed was in desperate need of review. As dangerous and negligent driving was, according to Justice Blackburn, a 'social evil' resulting in great loss of life, it was critical for the courts to give considerable weight to retribution and deterrence.[48] Blackburn observed the trial judge's comments that

> such offences are prevalent and have been a matter of continued and even increasing concern to the courts. In particular courts have made it clear in their treatment of such breaches that anyone who offends in this way may expect that there will be punishment.

This is so even though such offenders quite frequently are upright members of the community, as is the accused here.[49]

However, with Blackburn's only recourse a fine, he considered $2,000 too lenient and, had all other things been equal, declared his preference for a custodial term.[50]

Justice Sheppard agreed. He was likewise concerned about 'social evil', concurring with Blackburn's desire not only to impress upon the appellant the seriousness of his conduct, but to make an example of him.[51] While Sheppard noted that the offence transpired within a matter of seconds, he considered it especially serious, describing the appellant's actions as 'entirely disgraceful'.[52] His assessment was at significant contrast with verdicts of previous decades which required a prolonged sequence of overt mismanagement to secure a conviction. Sheppard described the 'road toll', or as the trial judge disparaged, 'what is described as the toll of the road', as 'one of the most serious social problems' in Australia. He observed that the problem was encountered on a daily basis by the judiciary, whom frequently targeted their remarks at drawing long-overdue social and political attention to the crisis.[53] Sheppard observed his own comments from *Evans v Sharman* as far back as 1973 that, while it was critical to implement and improve engineering safety measures and provide adequate compensation to those injured,

> there is underlying them an assumption that people will continue to drive as they now do. Plaintiffs are injured by human failure, usually negligent driving upon the highway. That is the test which the law presently imposes before liability will arise. From 1960–1969 inclusive 30,000 persons died on Australia's roads. Many more were injured. Thus for each death upon the road there are numbers of injured persons, many maimed and scarred for the rest of their lives. The impact of death and injury is not only disastrous to the victims themselves and their families who are directly affected but is an enormous waste to the community. Unless Australians

as a whole are prepared to come to grips with this problem and change their driving habits, the position will only worsen. Until a licence to drive a motor vehicle comes to be regarded as a privilege rather than a right and until bad driving, even though it may very often be no more than a momentary act of carelessness, comes to be regarded in the community as anti-social conduct deserving of censure rather than indifference or tolerance, or amongst some younger persons, even admiration or amusement, so the problem will remain.[54]

In 1990, 2,331 people were killed on Australian roads and 24,961 people were injured.[55] In *R v Stebbings* that same year, Chief Justice Malcolm and Justice Wallace would endorse Sheppard's comments, thereby setting a precedent for higher penalties in Western Australia. Terms of imprisonment began to increase for manslaughter convictions, although dangerous driving causing death continued to attract fines. In the same period, a new characterisation of offenders began to emerge – 'death drivers'. Despite the damning label, the sentences reported beneath the headlines continued to lag behind calls for higher penalties. In the late 1980s and early 1990s, 'death drivers' were receiving fines between $2,000 and $5,000, with some as low as $600. Not reserved for inattention and momentary misjudgement, fines continued to be imposed in cases involving very serious factual circumstances. Unlike Sean O'Connell's findings in Belfast,[56] in Western Australia 'death driver' was not only employed to mark those who killed whilst driving a stolen vehicle or those who drove recklessly, it was a characterisation applied across a very wide spectrum of conduct and circumstances, including deaths ruled as accidents at inquest. Sensationalist headlines evoked imagery of drivers as grim reapers on wheels. Pressure began to mount in the community.

The practice of fining drivers was attracting renewed criticism. The judgment in *Blair v Semple* in 1989 found a chorus of condemnation.[57] On 28 April 1989, the driver pleaded guilty in the Fremantle Court of Petty Sessions to two counts of dangerous driving causing death. He was fined a total of $3,000 – $1,500 per deceased – in addition to $1,750 for leaving the scene, failing to render assistance and refusing a breath test. He was found hiding in the sand hills near the scene of the crash. Driving on the wrong side of Cockburn Road, Coogee, around 10.00 pm, he collided head-on with an oncoming vehicle, killing two of its occupants – brothers – instantly. A wife of one of the men was a passenger in the vehicle. She survived.[58]

The Crown appealed the sentence on the grounds that the degree of fault demonstrated by the driver was far greater than mere misjudgement, bringing the offence well within the second-tier *Guilfoyle* category. The State contended that the Magistrate had failed to take into account the seriousness of the offence and, rather, there was a need to penalise the offender and make an example of him. According to the grounds of the appeal, the sentence was inadequate because more than one person was killed, the defendant had consumed alcohol prior to the crash, had a history of traffic offending, fled the scene, lied to police and demonstrated a total lack of remorse.[59]

Justice Franklyn held that the Magistrate was not in error, finding the penalty imposed within the range of his discretion.[60] He concurred with the Magistrate that the offender's behaviour was consistent with cowardice rather than a refusal to assist. According to Franklyn, there was no evidence that the driver was speeding or drunk, and he overturned the initial finding that he was significantly affected by alcohol. His refusal to be breathalysed, reports of him smelling of alcohol, or the fact that he was driving on the wrong side of the road would not 'justify a conclusion' that he 'had been drinking to a marked degree'.[61] Interestingly, the Court held that the fact that more than one person was killed *did not* increase the seriousness of the offence, a matter returned to later in this chapter.[62] *Blair v Semple* epitomises the inappropriate employ of dangerous driving causing death in lieu of manslaughter. It is difficult to comprehend why driving on the wrong side of the road, directly into an oncoming vehicle, could be categorised as anything *less* than a gross failure to use reasonable care and take reasonable precautions. 'Dangerous' seems an inadequate description of the conduct. Justice Franklyn held that the facts of the case did not support a characterisation of deliberate recklessness or selfish disregard.[63]

Franklyn's judgment did not go unnoticed. In a letter to the editor of the *West Australian*, Ross Bindon contrasted the driver's conduct and punishment with that of the victims', who were on the correct side of the road and 'sentenced to instant death'.[64] He observed that the driver had previously accrued three speeding convictions, one 0.08% conviction and three convictions for refusing to be breathalysed, pointing to seven lost opportunities to address his behaviour. The publication of the driver's avoidance technique was of particular concern to Bindon, who noted that any 'semi-literate' reader would now be acutely aware that, in the event of being stopped by the police, they could simply refuse a breath test.[65] Refusal might well incur a fine, but would assist in evading jail. This was not a new tactic. It was a common avoidance technique, practised across previous decades. The appeal in *Blair v Semple* was characteristic of the State's continued efforts, in trials and appeals across the mid to late twentieth century, to elevate the seriousness of vehicular homicide offences. In *R v Stebbings* in 1990, that persistence would finally pay off.

The circumstances in *Stebbings* were that, just after midnight on 23 August 1989, the 23-year-old respondent was driving his Holden Commodore along Marmion Avenue. At the intersection of Flinders Avenue he collided with another vehicle, a Honda Prelude sedan, killing its driver and a passenger. A second passenger survived, suffering injuries.[66] At trial it emerged that, approximately 8 kilometres prior and leading up to the crash, the respondent was seen driving at an 'enormous speed', estimated between 180 and 200 km/h in a 70 km/h zone.[67] He pleaded not guilty. He was convicted on two counts of manslaughter and one count of dangerous driving causing grievous bodily harm. The

Honda was 'almost ripped into two parts held together only by the left rocker panel'.[68]

The trial judge described Stebbings as a 'pleasant, clean-cut young man' who came from a good home and whose family appeared to be 'nice people'. On that basis she remarked that he was 'completely different' from like offenders, an impression which weighed heavily in her deliberations. According to psychological reports, Stebbings was profoundly depressed and remorseful, and the trial judge noted that, in addition to any punishment she imposed, he would have to live with his actions for the rest of his life.[69] She did comment that it was not the worst case she had ever seen – Stebbings was not intoxicated, driving on the wrong side of the road or without headlights, or while drinking out of a bottle.[70] She sentenced Stebbings to eighteen months on each count of manslaughter, to be served concurrently, in addition to twelve months for grievous bodily harm, concurrent with the manslaughter terms. The net effect was that, for two convictions of manslaughter and one of grievous bodily harm, Stebbings was given a head sentence of eighteen months, on which he would be entitled to a one-third remission. He was also made eligible for parole. The State appealed on the grounds that the sentence was manifestly inadequate.[71]

Grounds of appeal included the contention that insufficient regard was paid to the fact that the defendant was convicted of manslaughter, rather than dangerous driving causing death. Ground four of the appeal held that the trial judge had given undue attention to matters personal to the respondent and insufficient weight to the fact that two people were killed and another seriously injured. Grounds five and six maintained that drivers *had* to be deterred from posing an unacceptable risk to other road users and that the sentence failed to adequately reflect the community's concerns regarding the devastating consequences of negligent driving.[72] The Court unanimously upheld the appeal.

While Chief Justice Malcolm accepted the assessment of the defendant's character at first instance, he drew heavily on the observations Sheppard made in *Crawley* in 1981, that death and injury on the road were one of the most 'serious social problems facing the Australian community'.[73] In accordance with *Crawley*, he argued that the need for deterrence outweighed the offender's personal antecedents and that it was necessary to impose a sentence commensurate with the seriousness with which the legislature and the community regarded the offence. On the value of *Laporte* in sentencing, he signalled that the judgment should be reconsidered; however, he stopped short on offering any specific guidance, stating that *Stebbings* was not the appropriate forum for a full review.[74]

Justice Wallace offered additional observations on what guidelines, if any, previous decisions might offer. According to Wallace, sentences had to be viewed *not only* in terms of the factual circumstances, but equally in their historical and social context, signalling that past sentences might be outdated in light of the present. As he noted, the principles which emerged from *Laporte* were twenty years old and since 1970, 'community cost and individual suffering' had 'reached a most serious degree'.[75] He too drew heavily on Sheppard's observations in *Crawley*. While Justice Malcolm believed the circumstances of the case to be most serious, he did not consider them the very worst. Nevertheless, he concluded that the actions of the respondent displayed such an irresponsible, reckless disregard for other road users that, irrespective of his youth and good character, the sentence was insufficient.[76] Justices Wallace and Kennedy concurred, stating that the need for general deterrence outweighed the respondent's personal circumstances, including his age and antecedents.[77] The respondent was so distressed that he was in danger of taking his own life.[78]

The appellant Court set the sentence aside and substituted three years for each count of manslaughter and two years for the grievous bodily harm conviction, with all sentences to be served concurrently.[79] The net result was that the respondent received a three-year head sentence for killing two people and seriously injuring another, double his initial penalty. By contrast, ten men were sentenced to three years' imprisonment between 1946 and

1974, although those penalties were for the death of one person.[80] In that regard *Stebbings* demonstrated that, by 1990, things had changed considerably. Defendants *were* being prosecuted and sentenced for multiple fatalities, but received similar penalties to those handed down in previous years for the death of one person. Notably, however, those cases had significant aggravating factors and the defendants, poor antecedents, unlike the respondent in *Stebbings*. While the Court in *Stebbings* was unanimous in its view that the consequences were far from 'accidental', some notions remained firmly entrenched. Discouragingly, Justice Kennedy reiterated the view that the respondent was not 'in the ordinary sense of the word, a criminal'.[81] An avalanche of media and community pressure between 1990 and 1992 would make evident that a particular category of offender would come to be zealously ascribed that label.

The decision in *Stebbings* was a pivotal moment in the history of sentencing, a moment when the judiciary began to challenge the validity of *Laporte*, revising custodial terms upwards and thus elevating perceptions of the seriousness of deaths occasioned by the use of motor vehicles. Deterrence and the violent, needless deaths of other road users began to eclipse youth's stronghold on mitigation, which historically had occasioned substantial discounts in penalties. Internationally, grassroots organisations representing the plight of victims, such as MADD (Mothers Against Drunk Driving), CADD (Campaign Against Drinking and Driving), RID (Remove Intoxicated Drivers) and, later, RoadPeace and Brake, multiplied.[82] While such grassroots activism did not occur in Australia, media attention did begin to turn towards the suffering and plight of victims, both deceased and bereaved. Images of grief-stricken family members, complaining of lenient penalties while holding photographs of loved ones killed by 'death drivers' became more common. Notwithstanding that sensationalism, the trauma and bereavement of unlawful killings occasioned by the use of motor vehicles were slowly being retrieved from the anonymity and homogeneity of the 'road toll'.

While the tide of public opinion had begun to turn, the wave of increasing concern was swiftly hijacked by a focus on a particular type of offender. Unfortunately, not all of the renewed attention to appropriate penalties emerged from a careful reconsideration of what constituted dangerous or grossly negligent conduct while in charge of a motor vehicle. When incidents involved stolen cars, high-speed chases and juvenile offenders, community outrage became amplified; part of the national groundswell of attention to juvenile crime in the early 1990s.[83] Newspaper headlines advocated 'getting tough' on young offenders.[84] Headlines in support of bereaved children implored – 'Thief should have watched my mother die'.[85] The Children's Court of Western Australia came under increasing attack for apparently failing to impose adequate sentences.

In 1991, following a sustained campaign spearheaded by Richard and Margaret Wilson and Perth radio station 6PR's Howard Sattler, that outrage reached fever pitch. The Wilson's son Neville had been killed by a juvenile male who was driving a stolen vehicle.[86] Ads appeared in the *Sunday Times*, promoting a 'Rally for Justice'. 'Fed up' readers were encouraged to 'JOIN IN THE PROTEST TO SUPPORT VICTIMS OF JUVENILE CRIME'.[87] Almost 30,000 people responded to the campaign and Sattler's calls to 'lock them up', gathering outside Parliament House.[88] The rally was primarily motivated by a sense that the community was 'under siege' from juvenile offenders, or more particularly Aboriginal males, who stole cars and goaded police into high-speed chases, whereby 'innocent' people were killed.[89] Every day Sattler took to the airwaves, issuing his stolen vehicle report. Between mid-1990 and February 1992 there were ten deaths involving juveniles and stolen vehicles in Western Australia,[90] compared with a total of 207 deaths in 1991 alone.[91] Nonetheless, juveniles who stole cars and killed other road users received a disproportionate amount of publicity. Sattler described offenders as 'scum' and 'the lowest form of human life'.[92] His listeners phoned in, mirroring his sentiments.[93] Rather than WA being in the midst of a juvenile crime wave, the State was in the heat of a 'media wave' – there was no significant increase in juvenile crime in the period.[94] Following the rally, parliamentarians were 'swamped' by demands for reform.[95]

Criticisms of Sattler, the government's response to the rally and the punitive culture from which it emerged have been extensive.[96] It is not difficult to appreciate why. A documentary of the events, *Demons at Drivetime*, showed Sattler's producer, Ainslie Hodgkinson, scouring through newspapers looking for 'something that's going to make people's blood boil', because 'Howard loves controversy'.[97] It worked. Without any sense of irony, Hodgkinson explained that she was looking for issues that were 'black and white'.[98] On radio, Sattler kept up a relentless campaign. Come the day of the rally, attendees jeered and shouted, holding placards demanding – 'Bring back capital punishment NOW', 'An eye for an eye' and 'Adult crime, Adult time'. 'BRING BACK THE BIRCH' and 'LAW MAKERS GET REAL' were also writ large. Some protesters maintained that the government should save on public expenditure and, as an alternative to imprisonment, expediently 'hang the bastards'[99] – those 'bastards' being juvenile offenders or 'juvies', a term which became synonymous with young Aboriginal males who stole Holden Commodores.[100] The crowd held homemade nooses high in the air, demonstrating their apparent support for capital punishment and simultaneously venting their anger towards Hal Jackson, President of the Children's Court, while victims took the podium and recounted stories of loved ones killed.[101]

Amongst the most prominent cases was that of Perth businessman, Mario Ambrosino, who was killed in a collision involving three under-age males in a stolen vehicle in April 1990. Neville Wilson, a 26-year-old motorcyclist, whose bereaved fiancée spoke at the rally, was killed in June 1991.[102] The 16-year-old who killed him was sentenced to eighteen months' imprisonment on a manslaughter conviction. Police Minister Graham Edwards described the sentence imposed by Hal Jackson as 'pathetically lenient'.¹⁰³ Leigh Houghton, a young mother, was killed two days before the rally on 18 August.¹⁰⁴ Four months later, Margaret Blurton and her 1-year-old son, Shane, were killed on 25 December by a 14-year-old juvenile escapee under police pursuit in a high-speed chase.¹⁰⁵ It was a decisive moment, or as Hal Jackson called it, 'an appalling coincidence of facts'. Margaret was ten weeks' pregnant at the time.¹⁰⁶ The driver had approximately 200 prior convictions.¹⁰⁷

On Saturday 4 January 1992, 12,000 people attended a candlelight vigil outside Parliament House. By Monday morning, the steps of Parliament were a sea of flowers.¹⁰⁸ Ian Taylor, the Acting Premier, announced that the government would introduce new and stricter penalties to target repeat offenders.¹⁰⁹ On 6 January, the daily newspaper favourably reported the Premier's media release that 'rehabilitation of hard core offenders who stole cars and committed violent crimes [would] no longer be the main priority'.¹¹⁰ The government would 'lock them up'.¹¹¹ The Opposition raised the bar further, proposing that any driver who killed while driving a stolen vehicle in a high-speed chase should be charged with felony murder.¹¹²

Parliament was precipitately recalled to deal with a hastily drafted Bill. By 9 March 1992 the *Crime (Serious and Repeat Offenders) Sentencing Act* (WA) was operational. It attracted widespread criticism, not least of all from the Federal Attorney General and the Human Rights Commissioner, on mandatory and indeterminate detention and breaches of Australia's obligations under the International Covenant on Civil and Political Rights, in addition to the United Nations Convention on the Rights of the Child.¹¹³ Repeat and juvenile offenders who had previously committed 'proscribed' or 'violent' offences would automatically be sentenced to eighteen months' imprisonment with no set release date; that is, at eighteen months they would become eligible for review, rather than release.¹¹⁴ If convicted of dangerous driving causing death whilst driving a stolen vehicle, defendants would be liable to a term of imprisonment of up to twenty years, bringing the sentence in line with that for manslaughter and adding sixteen years to the existing statutory maximum.

Though the footage of the rally evinced a decidedly lynch-mob atmosphere, it was also apparent that sensationalist messages garnered most of the attention at the expense of other salient points. Placards imploring 'Remember the Victims' and asking, 'Where is the Justice?' seemed long overdue pleas. While juvenile crime and high-speed chases were the focus of public anger and the government's response, the events of the early 1990s did draw attention to 'road' violence, penalties and the hitherto largely unrecognised truth that the deceased were often, in fact, victims of crime rather than the toll of the roads. Unfortunately, the prospect of any ongoing, meaningful public discourse was hijacked by a retributive, racist backlash. Notwithstanding, during the same period, victims' families and loved ones, including those killed by someone *other than* an under-age Aboriginal male, began to feature in news reports as subjects worthy of compassion.[115] Cautionary tales of the guilt and remorse experienced by drivers who had killed or injured others also began to receive occasional coverage.[116]

While the complex issues around sentencing juvenile offenders are beyond the scope of this book, characterisations of aspects of the 1992 *Crime (Serious and Repeat Offenders) Sentencing Act* as retributive and regressive are well founded. Still, within that critique there has been a simultaneous failure to appreciate other issues. The protests were also part of a long history of reassigning blame and responsibility to a homicidal, driving 'Other'.[117] From the early twentieth century, the constant reinvention of a deviant, driving 'Other' helped facilitate the enduring perception that the problem was 'out there' rather than being much closer to home. The Parliament's response was not only a moment of punitive law making under extreme pressure, but a moment whereby *bad drivers*, which they undoubtedly were, became the almost exclusive province of deviant, under-age, Aboriginal male car thieves. Although there was in fact no juvenile crime wave, the community was arguably *entitled* to be concerned about violent deaths which occurred as a consequence of highly reckless conduct, although proper regard to statistics should have resulted in greater concern about routine, habitual risk-taking, including their own. Nonetheless, victims' families were understandably aggrieved that their loved one's deaths had been routinely treated as a lesser species of violence and harm. On air, Sattler interviewed a bereaved father who argued that sentences should be proportionate to offences and that an eighteen-month sentence for the death of his son was 'not justice whatsoever'.[118] Irrespective of the reputation of the radio host, the father's thoughts on the matter seem entirely reasonable. Yet contrary to the father's appraisal, from the introduction of the *Road Traffic Act* until the early 1990s, eighteen months was not a lenient penalty.

While the *Crime (Serious and Repeat Offenders) Sentencing Act* (WA) became operational in March 1992, the appellant courts had already begun to revise sentences upwards in manslaughter cases on the back of the decision in *Stebbings* before the Parliament intervened. There was a mounting sense that terms of imprisonment were in desperate need of reconsideration. Chief Justice Malcolm argued in *Ainsworth v D (A Child)* (1992), a dangerous driving causing grievous bodily harm case heard under the former provisions, that

> the continued carnage on our roads and the increasing prevalence of dangerous and reckless driving by juveniles and young adult offenders, particularly those making unauthorised use of motor vehicles or driving stolen vehicles, makes it necessary to reconsider the approach to sentencing in these cases where death or injury has resulted.[119]

In *Punch v The Queen* (1993), the Court of Appeal explicitly stated that Chief Justice Malcolm's remarks were equally applicable to manslaughter.[120] By the early 1990s, Western Australian courts had all but dispensed with the *Laporte* benchmark. Decisions of the period followed cases from other Australian jurisdictions where sentences were increased on appeal in order to provide a legitimate basis for revising penalties upwards as part of a national trend. The 1987 appeal in *R v Calder* in Queensland was one such example cited in West Australian courts – a case where a sentence for two counts of dangerous driving causing death was increased from nine months to four years.[121] Justice Derrington put drivers on notice.

> Each offence such as this, inflicts the most serious individual pain and loss, and collectively the large incidence of such violence produces enormous community loss. This is both economic and, if it continues, moral in the brutalising effect of acceptance of such disregard for the lives and safety and rights of others. It is, moreover, a cost that can be avoided...One must avoid the extremes of the emotive response with which these matters are dressed up in media coverage, and must address the problem with calm rationality. That still leads to a recognition of the gravity of the offence, which is mostly unacknowledged by those persons who are irresponsible enough to commit it. They must now be regarded as having had fair warning.[122]

On the back of the judgment in *Stebbings*, the amendments to the *Road Traffic Act* and the introduction of the *Crime (Serious and Repeat Offenders) Sentencing Act*, terms of imprisonment in some Western Australian cases increased dramatically. The judiciary was keen to emphasise its neutrality in the face of accusations of populism and sensationalism. While taking into account community sentiment, judges were adamant that they were not capitulating to public opinion and pressure.[123] Penalties for vehicular manslaughter increased, as did rates of imprisonment across the board, growing from 47 per cent to 57.5 per cent between 1990 and 1997.[124]

The Queen v S (No 2) (A CHILD) in 1992 was a significant moment in the trend towards longer terms of imprisonment in manslaughter cases. The 15-year-old defendant pleaded guilty to manslaughter and seven other related offences, including fleeing the scene, failing to render assistance, failure to report an accident, unlicensed driving and stealing a vehicle. He was sentenced to a total of two years' imprisonment.[125] The Crown appealed on the grounds that the sentence was manifestly inadequate, giving insufficient weight to community protection, deterrence and punishment, and undue emphasis to the defendant's age.[126] The defendant had driven a stolen car at speed on the wrong side of the road, switching the headlights off and on to avoid detection. He was under the influence of alcohol at the time. The police gave pursuit. The boy struck a Volkswagen in the rear at 'considerable force', carrying it 30 to 40 metres from the point of impact. Pieces of the car were strewn over an extensive area and the engine was discovered almost 15 metres from what remained of the body of the vehicle. A female passenger, thrown from the Volkswagen, died at the scene from head trauma.[127] The defendant was initially charged with felony murder, an approach that was also considered in *McKenna v The Queen* that same year.[128] The defendant in *The Queen v S (No 2)* had 120 prior convictions and an extensive history of drug and alcohol abuse.[129] The Supreme Court upheld the Crown's appeal, doubling the boy's effective sentence from two years to four,[130] a significant penalty for a juvenile and, putting aside the two five-year terms previously discussed, only the third case identified in which a Western Australia driver was sentenced to four years' imprisonment.

In his reasons for judgment, Chief Justice Malcolm objected that *Stebbings* had come to be considered the new benchmark for sentencing in vehicular manslaughter cases. He argued that it was inappropriate to standardise terms because of the variety of factual circumstances and factors that might be involved in any individual case. The Court held that the circumstances in *The Queen v S (No 2)* were far more serious than *Stebbings*, Chief Justice Malcolm stating that, 'it must be brought home to those who drive in such a manner that their behaviour cannot be tolerated'.[131] Had the offence been committed by an adult, Malcolm held that a term of six years would have been warranted[132] – a term of imprisonment never before envisaged in Western Australia. Justice Seaman set the bar even higher.

Justice Seaman's reasons, later adopted in *McKenna v The Queen* in 1992, were of particular interest. He acknowledged the difficulty between reconciling public safety with the mitigating factor of youth.[133] He asserted, however, that the critical issue before the Court was the degree of criminal negligence demonstrated by the driver, and emphasised what he believed to be the law's fundamental objective – community protection.[134] On gravity, he declared that there were some circumstances, including the case before him, in which the degree of negligence was so gross as to 'transcend considerations of "accident" and "duty"'.[135] Crucially, Seaman drew a line between past and present approaches to sentencing, and one firmly underneath the widespread perception that deaths occasioned by the use of vehicles were a lesser species of unlawful killing.

> For the purpose of sentencing those offenders it is my opinion that the fact that the unlawful killing is caused by a motor vehicle is incidental and that a consideration of past patterns of sentencing in motor vehicle manslaughter cases is not relevant. It seems to me that the matter for consideration is the degree of criminality of the unlawful killings.[136]

Anticipating the prospect that recent increases in terms of imprisonment might be understood as setting a new maximum, he emphasised that there could be no tariff for vehicular manslaughter as it was an offence which ranged from inadvertence to something approaching murder.[137] Drawing on *Stebbings*, he claimed that the need to deter others was greater than matters personal to the defendant, and in the case before him that was even more germane.[138] Seaman proposed a means to calculate an appropriate sentence – the starting point would be that given to an adult in the same factual circumstances, with a substantial deduction for the defendant's age.¹³⁹ He commenced at ten years, half that of the maximum penalty for manslaughter. For a 15-year-old boy, however, he stated that anything in excess of four years would be 'crushing'.¹⁴⁰

The decision in *McKenna v The Queen* in 1992 exacted an even higher penalty. As in *The Queen v S* where the defendant was initially charged with felony murder, McKenna was also initially charged under the dangerous act or felony murder rule. Under the provision, if a death is caused during the course of an unlawful purpose, a purpose likely to endanger life, a manslaughter charge can be upgraded to murder, despite the absence of intention.¹⁴¹ As the WA Law Reform Commission explained, dangerous act murder 'is treated as equivalent to an intentional killing because the accused has killed a person while committing a serious criminal offence'.¹⁴² However, the felony murder provision cannot be invoked unless there is a distinct and separate unlawful purpose – 'the act which causes the death cannot be the same as the unlawful purpose'.¹⁴³ Accordingly, the unlawful purpose in *McKenna* and *The Queen v S (No 2)* – fleeing the police in a high-speed chase – could not at once constitute the unlawful purpose and criminal negligence.¹⁴⁴ The charges were amended to manslaughter. Justice Rowland's comments in *McKenna* gave some indication that West Australian courts would be unlikely to entertain further the prospect of charging offenders with felony murder in driving-causing-death cases.¹⁴⁵

McKenna was 3.5 years older than the offender in *The Queen v S (No 2)*. As such, and in addition to a raft of aggravating circumstances, he was subject to a higher penalty – eight years' imprisonment on a plea to manslaughter.¹⁴⁶ He had a significant history of traffic offending, including two convictions for reckless driving and one for dangerous driving. Two of those were committed whilst under police pursuit.¹⁴⁷ The grounds of McKenna's appeal were that an eight-year sentence was, in every respect, excessive, and represented a capitulation to public outrage rather than an abidance of sentencing norms.¹⁴⁸ Yet, the circumstances in *McKenna v The Queen* were unprecedented. The case was exceptional. Across the previous fifty years, no other case was discovered with such extreme aggravating circumstances. The majority upheld the sentence on appeal, Justice Rowland dissenting. Rowland believed that the judge had given insufficient weight to the applicant's adolescence, immaturity, and 'absolutely dreadful background', and argued that six-and-a-half years would have been a more appropriate sentence.[149]

The circumstances in *McKenna* were that the defendant stole a car, his second in as many days. He was spotted by police sitting in the vehicle in a car park with a friend.[150] The police signalled to him and he fled. Unable to exit the car park, the exit being obstructed by a vehicle occupied by a woman and her baby, McKenna rammed the woman's car, forcing it into the street. The police gave chase as he sped through the streets of Subiaco. During the course of the pursuit, McKenna ran stop signs and traffic lights at speeds of up to 150 km/h. It was Friday, lunchtime, in a densely populated shopping and residential precinct. At the final, fatal intersection of Hamersley and Rokeby Roads where, at 150 km/h, he drove through a stop sign, McKenna's vehicle became airborne and subsequently collided with another car.[151] After impact, the vehicle continued its trajectory and McKenna hit Adriana Rossi who was riding her bicycle. Thrown a tremendous distance, she was fatally injured. McKenna fled the scene. Under the influence of amphetamines at the time, he had been recently released from prison. At 18.5 years of age, he was already a disqualified driver, with nineteen convictions of driving while disqualified or unlicensed to date.[152] In the course of the police interview McKenna stated that he stole the vehicle because he intended to use it in a high-speed chase if those circumstances prevailed, and he would have 'done his best' to outrun police.[153]

Justice Seaman concurred with the prosecution that the totality of the circumstances combined with McKenna's record demonstrated complete contempt for the law and total disregard for the safety, lives and property of others.[154] Justices Seaman and Ipp held that, as vehicular manslaughter was an offence against public safety, deterrence was of greater importance than the defendant's antecedents.[155] Seaman reiterated his observations in *The Queen v S (No 2)*, including his assertion that the principal consideration was the degree of criminality exhibited, and that the instrument of that criminality, the vehicle, in addition to past sentencing patterns, were irrelevant.[156] Seaman and Ipp concurred that an appropriate starting point for sentencing would be sixteen years and, with a significant discount on the basis of age, a sentence of eight years was not excessive.[157] The *Laporte* four-year maximum was all but buried.

The sentence in *Punch v The Queen* in 1993 exceeded that of *McKenna*. The circumstances of the case were extensive but, in short, Punch was forty-one at the time of the offence and had a significant history of violent offending over three decades, including a previous conviction for manslaughter.[158] He had been incarcerated for most of his life.[159] At the time of the collision, he was under pursuit by another driver who believed that Punch had broken into his home.[160] Intoxicated, Punch reportedly drove at 100 km/h along Nicholson and High Roads and, driving through a red light at 5.00 pm on a weekday, he collided with another car, killing the female driver.[161] At the time, he was on bail for six charges – refusing a breath test, two counts of unauthorised use of a motor vehicle, two counts of driving unlicensed and one count of driving under the influence – facts which weighed heavily against him. He had previously been disqualified from driving for life.[162]

Punch fled the scene. He was later apprehended by police.[163] On the manslaughter conviction, he was sentenced to ten years' imprisonment and denied parole eligibility.[164] He was also sentenced to an additional, cumulative term of two years for other unrelated offences. Punch was entitled to a one-third remission on his sentence upon entering prison. The first instance judgment was appealed on several grounds, including that the sentence exceeded the grounds of discretion.[165] The sentence was upheld, the appellant court observing Justice Ipp's remarks in *The Queen v S (No 2)* that the circumstances demonstrated not only 'wanton disregard', but a 'strong element of premeditation'.[166]

In the course of the appeal, the Court reaffirmed that there could be no set tariff for manslaughter or dangerous driving causing death, given the wide variety of factual circumstances in which those two offences were committed.[167] Seaman's observations in *McKenna* were followed by the Court, Justice Murray agreeing with his remarks that some circumstances *exceeded* the bounds of accident and duty, and the fact that the killing was occasioned by the use of a vehicle rather than any other object was of no relevance.[168] Justice Anderson noted that courts were bound to consider the maximum penalties authorised by the legislature and regard the totality of Punch's offending, the absence of any mitigating factors, and numerous circumstances of aggravation as very grave indeed.[169]

In as much as *Stebbings* set a precedent for imprisoning drivers convicted of manslaughter with otherwise flawless records and good antecedents, the decisions in *The Queen v S (No 2)*, *McKenna* and *Punch* established a benchmark for offenders at the opposite end of the spectrum. *Clinch v The Queen* of 1999 continued this trend.[170] In *Clinch*, the 19-year-old appellant was on parole for convictions of attempted robbery, unlawfully being on premises and two counts of stealing a motor vehicle.[171] In the incident which brought him before the courts yet again, he followed a woman home from a train station and used a rock to smash a glass door to gain entry. She hid in her bedroom screaming.[172] Stealing her purse and car keys, he fled in her car.[173] Significantly affected by alcohol and marijuana, Clinch was observed driving in a dangerous manner. He was pursued by police, with emergency siren activated. As Clinch entered the dual carriageway of Wanneroo Road on the incorrect side, police abandoned the pursuit. Clinch collided with a northbound vehicle, head-on. The driver suffered severe chest injuries and died two hours later.[174] Clinch had previously been disqualified from driving for life and had a long history of stealing vehicles, burglary and violent assault.[175] On a guilty plea, he was sentenced to a total of eight years' imprisonment with no eligibility for parole. For two counts of aggravated burglary and one count of stealing, he was sentenced to twelve months' imprisonment on each charge, each concurrent with one another and with the eight-year term. He appealed against his sentence. His appeal was unsuccessful.[176]

In some rare instances, higher penalties were not the sole preserve of cases involving stolen vehicles. Wilful and deliberately reckless conduct, particularly when the driver was unlicensed, for a time attracted greater penalties than ever before. For example, in *White v The Queen* in 2003, the appellant court described the sentence as 'severe', although not in error, and within the range of discretion.[177] White's representative argued that, unlike *Punch* or *McKenna*, there were no aggravating features typically associated with the upper end of the spectrum of culpability. White was not on parole or bail, he was not driving a stolen vehicle, nor was he engaged in a high-speed chase. He was not under the influence to the extent of being incapable of driving, nor was his vehicle in any way defective.[178] His defence also noted that he had no prior traffic convictions or disqualifications as factors in his favour. Justice Templeman described that as 'something of a cleft stick' – White had never applied for or held a licence, although had ample opportunity to do so at 42 years of age.[179] He had apparently driven on only four or five occasions in his life, limiting his opportunity to receive a traffic conviction, although one of those was to journey over 3,000 kilometres across the Nullarbor from Sydney to Perth.[180] Rather than mitigating, the trial judge described this as evidence of White's 'total disregard for the laws of the road'.[181]

On a night in October 2002 around 11.30 pm, White was driving a borrowed car through the streets of Northam.[182] His speed was estimated at between 60 and 70 km/h in a 50 km/h zone, although it was possibly higher given the tremendous damage to the victims' car.[183] White had a blood alcohol concentration of 0.072% at the time of crash.[184] On approach to an intersection, his passenger warned him of the stop sign, to which White retorted – 'What stop sign?' – and accelerated through the intersection, colliding with another vehicle.[185] The testimony of White's passenger, Mr McGee, was 'damning'.[186] Cheryl and Timothy Smith were killed instantly. They were both thirty-one. The couple were travelling with their two children, Bradley and Christopher. Their sons survived the crash.[187]

In great distress, White ran directly from the scene of the crash to the Northam Police Station where he was immediately taken into custody.[188] He pleaded guilty at the first available opportunity.[189] The judge held that White's driving was not a momentary lapse, but 'dreadful driving, well and truly within the definition of grossly reckless'.[190] As far as he was concerned, White's split-second decision in conjunction with the mosaic of aggravating factors, including speed, consumption of alcohol and the fact that he did not hold a licence, surpassed the threshold for gross negligence. In contrast with cases before the late 1980s, in which charges tended to be brought for only one of the deceased, the judge noted that, while the number of fatalities 'did not automatically increase penalty by that number arithmetically', the fact that the defendant's actions resulted in the death of more than one person was an important consideration.[191] The quantum of harm that resulted from one act was a matter garnering attention in the courts. Notwithstanding his contrition, White was sentenced to ten years' imprisonment on each count of manslaughter, to be served concurrently. He was made eligible for parole.[192] The sentence was upheld on appeal.[193]

Although some terms of imprisonment in the 1990s and early 2000s were, compared with the past sentences, extraordinarily high, putting *White* to one side, sentences of three or more years were generally reserved for recidivists, car thieves and unlicensed or disqualified drivers. For instance, in an appeal against an eighteen-month sentence on a conviction of manslaughter in 1992, the Crown was successful in having a 15-year-old boy's penalty increased to four years' imprisonment on the grounds that he had a long criminal history. He suffered intellectual impairment from years of drug abuse.[194] In the *MacPherson* case, the defendant was an escaped prisoner who, under police pursuit, ran a red light at high speed, killing another driver. He pleaded guilty to manslaughter and was sentenced to seven years' imprisonment.[195] Dominic Indich killed two of his cousins and seriously injured three friends while driving a stolen car in a high-speed police pursuit. He was heavily affected by cannabis. Dominic was 22 years old. He had a criminal record dating back to the age of seven. His licence had been cancelled for life five years before.[196] He pleaded guilty to two counts of dangerous driving causing death and three counts of dangerous driving causing grievous bodily harm. He was sentenced to eight years' imprisonment.[197]

Such penalties were not applied across the board. There were glaring inconsistencies. In the late twentieth century, judges continued to hand down minor penalties for very serious conduct. In most instances, sentences remained comparatively lenient and, in some instances, arguably trivial. For instance, in a 1992 case, a 17-year-old male killed two of his friends while driving at a speed of 160 km/h with a blood alcohol concentration of 0.148%. He was found guilty of manslaughter and sentenced to 150 hours' community service.[198] That same year, another 17-year-old male crashed a stolen Commodore after running a red light at speeds of up to 160 km/h, killing his 13-year-old passenger. He was sentenced in the Children's Court to twenty months' detention on a manslaughter plea.[199] In *Koltasz v The Queen* in 2003, the driver had not slept for twenty-one hours and had a blood alcohol concentration of 0.10%.[200] He fell asleep at the wheel, failed to negotiate a bend, and collided with a concrete power pole, killing two people and grievously injuring another.[201] He had been disqualified from driving for nine months only three days before the crash.[202] While he was sentenced to two-and-a-half years' imprisonment on each count of causing death and twelve months for causing bodily harm, the court ordered that his sentences be served concurrently.

The unprecedented sentences of the 1990s and early 2000s seemed to suggest that perceptions of vehicular homicide's gravity had intensified. The trend was the result of a confluence of factors, including a shift in public perception and renewed attention to 'road deaths', changes in approaches to sentencing in multiple fatality cases, judicial reappraisal, the amendments of 1992 and a period of what some have described as punitive sentencing.[203] What was simultaneously at play was that drivers who could be readily cast – socially and legally – as the criminal archetype were given substantial penalties. Higher penalties for recidivists and car thieves, as against comparatively low penalties for dangerous or criminally negligent conduct absent any other hallmark of criminality, reinforced the perception that vehicular homicide, by definition, had to involve *exceptional* circumstances, abjectly homicidal behaviour and a bad character, rather than a manner of conduct disproportionately lacking while in charge of a dangerous object.

In dangerous driving causing death cases, fines remained commonplace for momentary, albeit fatal inattention and lapses in judgment. Unfortunately, fines were not reserved for cases that fell at the lower end of the fault spectrum. Judges continued to impose fines in circumstances of particular gravity. For example, in 2002, a speeding driver who hit a 13-year-old girl who was crossing the road on her bicycle was fined $5,000 for dangerous driving causing death.[204] Community service orders were *also* utilised in cases where the conduct was well beyond the scope of momentary inattention. In a case where a female driver collided with another vehicle while driving in the wrong lane under the influence of methamphetamines and marijuana, and killed two people, the judge imposed a 200-hour community service order.[205]

In 1996, a 73-year-old woman was killed when two men were driving alongside one another on a single carriageway at 110 km/h, apparently admiring each other's vehicles. They claimed they were not racing. Christopher Hammer's lawyer said his client was 'extremely sorry'. Such was his remorse that he was photographed outside the Central Law Courts 'giving the finger' to the press. Both men pleaded guilty to dangerous driving causing death. Hammer was fined $7,000 and the other driver, Shane Hall, was fined $5,000.[206] In 1996, a 25-year-old man fell asleep at the wheel on Toodyay Road, Midland, killing a couple and their son. His parents, passengers in his vehicle, were both seriously injured. On three counts of dangerous driving causing death and two of causing grievous bodily harm, he was fined $8,000.[207] He was granted an extraordinary licence four months later.[208] In a 1998 case where a truck driver was convicted of two counts of dangerous driving causing death and fined $6,000, widow, Tracey Turner, told the press, 'How do I go home and tell my children that the man who killed their father has walked off scot-free? It just does not seem enough punishment for a man who has killed two innocent people'.[209] Instead of slowing down or stopping on encountering a blinding cloud of gravel dust, he instead drove his prime mover into the oncoming lane of traffic.[210] That same year, the NSW Court of Appeal resolutely held that a non-custodial term for dangerous driving causing death should be an *exception*, as should a custodial term less than three years.[211] According to the NSW Court of Appeal, non-custodial sentences should be reserved for cases of momentary inattention and misjudgement,[212] a decision later noted by Western Australian courts.[213]

The decision in *Stebbings* put paid to the view that a young man with otherwise good antecedents brought before the court on a manslaughter charge should not be incarcerated. In addition to changing approaches to sentencing, there were also indications that what constituted dangerous and negligent conduct had shifted considerably by the early twenty-first century. Fatigue was one such area. In *Wood v The Queen* of 2002, the defendant allegedly fell asleep while driving along the freeway on Easter Monday and, drifting to her left, ran over a man in the emergency lane, killing him.[214] In the twenty-three hours prior to the incident, she had not slept at all, and had slept only five to seven hours over the previous two days. There was no evidence of speed or intoxication.²¹⁵ Wood was a young woman with good antecedents and no record.²¹⁶ Even so, the trial judge noted that one-third of all deaths on the road were fatigue related and, as such, fatigue was no less an issue than intoxication or speed.²¹⁷ Three weeks later, he sentenced her to eighteen months' imprisonment, stating that her conduct fell within the higher Guilfoyle category, demonstrating selfish disregard and a degree of recklessness.²¹⁸ While fatigued drivers had been prosecuted in the past, the decision in *Wood v The Queen* established a standard for imprisoning them.

In line with *Stebbings* twelve years earlier, the judgment in *Wood* demonstrated that young drivers without a record could well be imprisoned. This was a seismic shift. Wood's appeal was unsuccessful, although the majority of the Court acknowledged the case was 'most difficult'.²¹⁹ Justice Wallwork dissented. Even the State conceded that a custodial sentence was not the only alternative.²²⁰ At appeal, Justice Murray concurred with the trial judge that the seriousness of the offence lay in the fact that a person who drives while significantly fatigued deliberately behaves in a manner that reduces their capacity to drive, increasing the risk posed.²²¹ Wood was unrepentant. She claimed she had a sneezing fit, an account not accepted by the court. She apparently had a clear view of the emergency lane for 223 metres and thus ample opportunity to see the deceased. She pleaded not guilty.²²² Interviewed by the local press, her mother adamantly declared that her daughter was 'not a criminal' and to imprison her with *actual* 'criminals' was a crime.²²³ By contrast, fatigue cases of the 1990s, even those involving multiple fatalities, had tended to attract non-custodial terms.²²⁴

Notwithstanding the judgments in *McKenna*, *Punch* and *Clinch*, where the appellant courts consistently upheld sentences of unprecedented length, other appeals were successful. In *D'Amico v The Queen* (2000), the driver was fleeing the scene of an attempted burglary.²²⁵ There were some extenuating circumstances in that her car had been kicked and hit with a bottle by nearby partygoers and a fight had broken out. She had attended the party earlier that evening. Fleeing the attacks, she drove along the street where the party was underway, a very short distance from the scene of the attempted burglary, which had set off an alarm and attracted, from the revellers' point of view, unwanted attention from a security patrol and potentially the police. Partygoers were milling about on the road and verge.[226]

In the course of attempting to flee, she struck Andrew King, Jacqueline Nielson and two other women who were sitting on the kerb. She did not stop to assist. In fact, she reversed her vehicle and inadvertently struck Andrew again in the course of her escape.[227] She later came forward to the police.[228] Reports were that she had driven down the poorly lit street at some speed, tyres squealing, with her headlights off.[229] Accelerating rapidly, she lost control of her vehicle after the windscreen was hit by a projectile object, thrown by a partygoer. The object cracked the windscreen. Ducking for cover, she swerved to the left.[230] She was sentenced to eight years' imprisonment for the manslaughter of Andrew King and two concurrent years for bodily harm to Jacqueline Nielson. Her sentence was reduced to five years on appeal.[231] Justice Ipp noted that, while it was not possible to set a tariff for vehicular manslaughter, previous sentences did offer a guide.[232] As such, the Court ruled that the circumstances of *McKenna*, for instance, were far more serious than *D'Amico*, and thus her conduct did not warrant as severe a penalty.[233]

Sentencing in dangerous driving causing death cases remained problematic, not least of all because conduct that was arguably *grossly negligent* continued to be brought before the courts under s 59(1). This problem was further compounded by the fact that the maximum penalty of four years was a limited scope in which to reflect a very wide spectrum of fault. As judges were required to sentence high-end offences within that scope, the four-year maximum left little room to penalise drivers whose level of fault fell at the middle to the bottom end of the spectrum. The disparity between ordinary cases of dangerous driving causing death against those involving a stolen vehicle under the 1992 amendments, and thus a potential maximum penalty of twenty years, was also the subject of judicial criticism.[234] For the 'ordinary' dangerous driver, the maximum penalty remained fixed at four years.

There were other irregularities to the 1992 amendments. As of 1992, under s 378(2) of the Code, if a person stole a vehicle and drove it recklessly or dangerously, he or she would be liable to a maximum penalty of eight years' imprisonment.[235] In effect, this meant that the reckless or dangerous driver of a stolen car could be imprisoned for twice the length of time as someone who actually killed whilst dangerously driving their own vehicle. Initially the judiciary defended this irregularity. In 2000, Justice Ipp noted in *D'Amico* that, while it might appear that terms of imprisonment for manslaughter were comparatively much lower than those under s 378(2) of the Code, the new offence was a stand-alone measure, designed to target 'premeditated criminal behaviour that endangers the safety and well-being of the general community'.[236] Dangerous driving in one's own car apparently lacked conscious, deliberate action. Nor did it apparently pose the same threat.

Contrary to Ipp's moderate endorsement in *D'Amico*, Justice Wheeler took the opportunity in *Parsons v The Queen* (2000) to voice his opposition. He asserted that, in terms of dangerous driving, the courts' capacity to reflect a wide range of fault, from inattention to 'inexcusable disregard for public safety', was poorly served by the statutory maximum of four years' imprisonment, or eighteen months on summary judgment.[237] Giving weight to mitigating factors without generating a perception of leniency was additionally problematic in such a narrow framework. Justice Wheeler added that the task of sentencing was further complicated by s 378(2) of the Code.[238] While he observed that s 378 offenders typically demonstrated a 'calculated disregard for public safety', he vied that the penalty bore no 'logical relationship' to the offence, given that the same manner of driving was ostensibly 'sixteen times' more serious if the vehicle was stolen, although the threat to public safety was equal.[239] On the matter of dangerous driving causing death in a stolen vehicle attracting a maximum term of twenty years' imprisonment, as opposed to four in all other circumstances, Wheeler claimed the disparity was utterly at odds with community values. While theft was a serious matter, he emphasised that the primary issue was the threat drivers posed to public safety in the *manner* of their driving.[240] According to Wheeler, the appropriate remedy would be to align the *manner of the driving* to the scale of penalties, and allow extenuating factors to be taken into account as circumstances of aggravation in sentencing deliberations.[241]

The longest head sentences handed down between 1970 and 2004 were shared by Darrin Fox on two counts of manslaughter and a grievous bodily harm charge, and Raymond Kay on two counts of dangerous driving causing death, one count of dangerous driving causing grievous bodily harm and one of bodily harm.[242] Both men were sentenced to twelve years' imprisonment. Fox was sentenced in 1999, prior to the *Sentencing Legislation Amendment and Repeal Act 2003* (WA). Under the former *Sentencing Administration Act 1995* (WA) he was entitled to release after serving two-thirds of his sentence, bringing his actual term down to eight years. Kay's conviction in 2004 came after those amendments, with Judge Robert Viol making the one-third discount of four years clear in his sentencing remarks. It was the fifth time Fox had been caught driving under the influence and his sixth conviction for driving while disqualified. At the time of the crash, he was under a lifetime disqualification.[243] His previous convictions involved particularly high blood alcohol concentrations – 0.192%, 0.188%, 0.235% and 0.183%.[244] Fox had a blood alcohol concentration of 0.199% when he killed 17-year-olds Sarah Jane Taylor and Jeffrey Mique Foster at Port Kennedy. He pleaded guilty to two counts of manslaughter and one count of unlawful grievous bodily harm.[245] Crown Prosecutor Lloyd Rayney described the killings as 'the worst of their type'.[246]

On finishing work, Fox consumed three cans of beer. He later arrived at the Port Kennedy Tavern at around 5.30 pm and became involved in a fight. He was refused service at 9.00 pm because he was drunk and was ejected from the tavern at 10.30 pm after urinating on the bar. Following his eviction, Fox drove his Ford Falcon over the garden beds in the car park and into the drive-through bottle shop, where he smashed into another vehicle and abused the driver. He then fled in his car. Over the following twenty-five minutes, he was observed narrowly missing several vehicles. He was witnessed driving at speeds of 90 to 100 km/h on the wrong side of the road and directly into the oncoming traffic on Ennis Avenue.[247] The *West Australian* published a map of his journey – 'The Road to tragedy'.[248] His estranged wife, Kerry, had apparently tried to stop him from drinking and driving for years and, according to newspaper reports, would frequently call police to notify them of her husband's whereabouts.[249] Kerry told reporters that her husband should have been given the maximum imposable penalty.[250] Fox was sentenced to twelve years' imprisonment, his effective term thus being eight years. He was made eligible for parole after six years.

In *Kay v The Queen* (2004) the appellant, Raymond Kay, was convicted on two counts of dangerous driving causing death, one count of grievous bodily harm and one of bodily harm.[251] Judge Robert Viol sentenced Kay, a 60-year-old truck driver, to four years' imprisonment on each count of dangerous driving causing death, three years for the grievous bodily harm charge, and one year for bodily harm. He ordered that all of the sentences be served cumulatively.[252] Under the new *Sentencing Legislation Amendment and Repeal Act 2003*, his total twelve-year sentence was reduced to eight years.[253]

Kay was driving a road train. It was 10.30 pm. On approach to a railway crossing, he hit a stationary car. The force of impact drove the car into the path of an oncoming freight train. The railway crossing lights were flashing.[254] Kay was driving a 9-ton prime mover from Perth to Sydney with 28 tons of freight onboard.[255] It was the third time he had struck the rear of a vehicle while driving a road train.[256] Two of the people in the car were killed and another suffered bodily harm. A passenger on the freight train suffered grievous bodily harm.[257] Notwithstanding the very serious circumstances of the case, one of the most significant aspects was the approach to multiple fatalities. Ground four of Kay's appeal contended that the trial judge had erred in ordering cumulative sentences, as the consequences arose out of a single act or transaction.[258] Ground five held that the judge had demonstrated little regard for the principle of totality in imposing a sentence so 'grossly disproportionate' to the criminality of the defendant's conduct.[259] The judgment of the appellant court in *Kay v The Queen* offered some important guidance on sentencing in multiple fatality cases, which, despite the decision in *Phillips v Carbone (No. 2)* in 1992, appeared to remain contentious.

As far back as 1992, in *Phillips v Carbone* the West Australian Supreme Court ruled that the appellant *was* liable to two counts of dangerous driving causing grievous bodily harm and thus *double* the statutory penalty, notwithstanding that the injuries arose out of the same transaction.[260] The Supreme Court held that the driver was not protected by s 16 of the Code, which prohibited punishing a person twice for the same offence, because the offence was actually twice committed; that is, the causing of bodily harm to *two* individuals.[261] Justice Ipp concluded by providing a helpful summary.

> In my view, s 16 is intended to provide protection to a person who is found guilty of one offence and is then found guilty of another upon substantially the same facts. It is not, in my view, intended to give protection to a person who, by one physical act or omission causes multiple harm to different persons or things. It is not, for example, intended to avail the person who by a single act of depressing a plunger causes an explosion that injures more than one victim. If the phrase "act or omission" is to be construed as meaning the essential elements of the offence, protection may be afforded to the perpetrators of such crimes. That, in my opinion, cannot be the law. There is a fundamental distinction between a single act that contravenes more than one statutory provision, and a single act that harms more than one person.[262]

In *Kay*, Justice Miller likewise noted, in accordance with Chief Justice Lee in *R v Wilkins* of 1988 that, in the case of multiple fatalities and injuries on the road, different considerations might apply.[263] As the NSW Court held in *Wilkins*, just because the maximum penalty for dangerous driving was set at five years, it was an 'extraordinary' suggestion that the penalty be fixed at five years whether the driver killed one person or fifty.[264] Prior to the late 1980s, Western Australian defendants tended to be prosecuted for only one death. Multiple charges were brought before the courts, but once a conviction was secured on one count the Crown declined to prosecute the others. In *Wilkins*, Chief Justice Lee held that, in multiple fatality cases, a penalty that reflected the magnitude and actual consequences of the driver's actions was 'not unjust or unfair' but rather 'wholly in accord with the ordinary principles of justice'.[265] The WA Court of Criminal Appeal followed Lee's approach.[266] In circumstances where the maximum penalty was an insufficient reflection of the quantum of harm, Lee declared that 'the court not only may but ought to impose cumulative sentences'.[267] Miller adopted that reasoning, stating the argument was even more compelling in Western Australia, given the maximum penalty for dangerous driving causing death was far lower than most other Australian jurisdictions.[268]

Justice Miller noted the comments of Justice Templeman in *White v The Queen* that the number of decedents should not multiply the penalty 'arithmetically'.[269] He also stated his preference for the reasoning in *R v Wilkins*, disagreeing with the South Australian Court of Criminal Appeal in *R v Snewin* in 1997, where the judgment held that the appellant could be punished only for a single act, rather than its six consequent deaths.[270] While Miller noted that there had been a recent tendency towards concurrent sentencing in multiple fatality cases in Western Australia, there was nothing to prohibit a cumulative approach in order to reflect the enormity of the crime committed.[271] On the fifth ground of Kay's appeal, that the sentence was 'grossly disproportionate to the gravity' of the offence, Miller stated that he could not recall a case in which an offender was sentenced to twelve years for dangerous driving causing death offences under the old law, when defendants were entitled to a one-third remission discount upon entering prison, resulting in a sentence of eight years.[272] Accordingly, the Court of Appeal quashed Kay's eight-year sentence and substituted a series of penalties totalling six years.[273] The Court overlooked the fact that Darrin Fox received a twelve-year sentence in 1999 under s 59(1) of the *Road Traffic Act*.

In the course of the judgment in *Kay*, Justice Murray reaffirmed Justice Wheeler's observations in *Parsons v The Queen* (2000), describing the existing sentencing provisions as unsatisfactory and inconsistent.[274] According to Murray, the fact that a vehicle was stolen 'was of no particular relevance' and demonstrated nothing of the actual *manner of the driving*.[275] Murray further argued that the summary provisions available under s 59 and the associated lesser penalties compounded the peculiarity of the current framework. He called on Parliament to redress the matter.[276] Justice Miller also observed that the four-year maximum on indictment under the *Road Traffic Act* was 'surprisingly low', particularly against twenty years if the vehicle was stolen.[277] He asserted that it was of little solace to a family that a driver could ordinarily be sentenced to four years, but five times that length of time if he or she stole the car.[278] He too insisted that the disparity between the sentences demanded urgent attention from the Parliament.[279]

Justices Murray and Miller's observations were favourably reported by the State's daily newspaper – 'Death drivers may get more jail'.[280] Attorney General Jim McGinty stated that it was the first time the discrepancies in the law had been brought to his attention and that the penalties clearly needed to be 'upped several times'.[281] His assertion that the matter had only come to his notice was at odds with the fact that a Bill to amend the *Road Traffic Act* was already before Parliament and dangerous driving causing death was under extensive review. Despite considerable opposition, McGinty's Bill passed in late 2004, although the amendments did not entirely accord with the judiciary's petitions.

Chapter Eight

Jess' law, 2004

The 0.15% deeming provision, the causative nexus and aggravated dangerous driving causing death

On the morning of Friday 8 August 2003, 10-year-old Jess Meehan began the day by singing 'Happy Birthday' to her dog, Millie. Later that afternoon she was riding her bicycle home from school when, on crossing Marmion Avenue, she was hit by a Toyota Hilux.[1] She died two days later in hospital. The 19-year-old driver, Mitchell Walsh-McDonald, recorded a blood alcohol concentration of 0.165% at the time of the collision.[2] Jess Meehan's death triggered radical amendments to Western Australia's *Road Traffic Act*, the most substantial changes to dangerous driving causing death since its introduction.

Not only was Walsh-McDonald more than three times over the legal limit at the time of the crash, he was also under suspension and therefore an unlicensed driver.[3] He had been twice convicted of drink-driving offences as a juvenile,[4] and for a third time in the incident in which Jess was killed. The investigating officers formed the view that they could not charge Walsh-McDonald with dangerous driving causing death because, in essence, there was no evidence that he was driving dangerously, or that the manner of his driving *caused* Jess' death.[5] The fact that he was under the influence was not, as West Australian Attorney General Jim McGinty accurately explained, 'determinative' of whether his driving was dangerous.[6] He was not seen speeding and evidence from the crash scene indicated that he attempted to stop before impact.[7] Walsh-McDonald pleaded guilty to driving under the influence and without a licence. He was disqualified from driving for a further two years and fined $1,700.[8] He was not charged with Jess' death. The community was outraged.[9] The Attorney General told the Western Australian Parliament that justice had not been served.[10]

The following year the Attorney General publicly declared that s 59(1) of the *Road Traffic Act* was deficient. In June 2004, less than a year after Jess Meehan was killed, he proposed a raft of amendments to the legislation, the totality of which were to ostensibly ensure that those who killed while under the influence or in other circumstances of aggravation would feel the full force of the law.[11] McGinty's controversial amendments were enacted later that year, coming into effect as of 1 January 2005.[12] In October 2004, the same month the Bill was under review by the Standing Committee on Legislation, Walsh-McDonald was charged with dangerous driving causing death.[13] As the incident occurred prior to the 2004 amendments, he was prosecuted under the former provisions. Walsh-McDonald stood trial in March 2006 and pleaded not guilty.[14] He admitted to drinking eleven full-strength beers over a two to three-hour period before the incident. He claimed that Jess had suddenly darted out in front of his vehicle and he could not avoid hitting her.[15] The jury took ninety minutes to acquit him.[16]

Walsh-McDonald continued to make the headlines long after Jess' death. Between 23 September 2008 and 2 February 2009, he was convicted of drink-driving offences three times. He also recorded three convictions for driving under suspension, in addition to failing to stop and providing a false name to police. Tailed by the media, he was filmed driving illegally by

Channel 7's *Today Tonight*. Former WA Road Safety Council Chairman, Grant Dorrington, described him as a remorseless 'time-bomb' who should be sent to jail.[17] Lack of remorse was not always the case. Jess Meehan's mother described holding Walsh-McDonald's hand as he stood in the dock before the trial, telling him she forgave him. He sobbed openly.[18] Notwithstanding his apparent contrition, in June 2009 Walsh-McDonald was again charged with driving without a licence. He was penalised with a further nine months' disqualification and a $1,500 fine.[19] The sum total of his disqualifications meant that he was not allowed to resume driving until 2013.[20] On the cycle of disqualification and recidivism, and the fact that he had never been imprisoned, Cheryl Meehan later asked – 'What will it take? Does he have to be caught 46 times before they take him off the road for good?'[21] It was a fair question. Given Walsh-McDonald had repeatedly breached disqualification orders and twice been convicted of driving with a blood alcohol concentration in excess of 0.15%, it was within the courts' discretion to imprison him.[22] In 2010, he was *again* brought before the courts on four counts of driving under suspension.[23] He received a suspended jail sentence and a further thirty-six months' disqualification.[24]

Despite having recorded six drink-driving convictions, in 2012 Walsh-McDonald applied for an extraordinary licence.[25] His application was opposed by the Department of Transport. Astonishingly, he was granted an extraordinary licence on a number of conditions, including that he not drink for a period of eight hours prior to driving and that he have a zero blood alcohol concentration at all times whilst driving. On 8 August 2013, ten years to the day that Jess Meehan was killed, Mitchell Walsh-McDonald appeared in the Perth Magistrates Court. He was charged with driving with a blood alcohol concentration of 0.103%, using a mobile phone whilst driving, and two other breaches of his extraordinary licence conditions. He was driving outside his specified permitted hours and was not displaying his extraordinary licence plates.[26] He was fined a total of $2,850. His extraordinary licence was cancelled.[27] Although Walsh-McDonald subsequently changed his name to Mitchell William Donald Walsh, his pattern of offending did not change. In April 2014, he was brought before the courts on yet *another* charge of unlicensed driving.[28] Magistrate Randazzo delivered the news – 'Time is up Mr Walsh'. He sentenced him to nine months in prison.[29]

Walsh seemed to take little heed of Randazzo's candour. On the 29 December 2017 he pleaded guilty to driving under the influence of an illicit drug. In January 2018, he was also charged with, amongst other things, stealing a motor vehicle and attempting to pervert the course of justice. On the 24 January 2018, Walsh's driver's licence was finally cancelled. The following month he was charged with seven other driving-related offences, including a further illicit drug charge and exceeding the speed limit by 45 km/h or more.[30] On 2 March 2018, he was jailed for twelve months for a series of driving and dishonesty offences.[31] In May 2019 Mitchell Walsh was back before the courts for a litany of traffic offences including stealing cars, speeding and seven counts of driving without a licence.[32]

The claim that a review of the case file more than a year after Jess' death apparently led to Walsh-McDonald finally being charged seems a mendacious explanation. Earlier that year, State Counsel briefed members of Parliament that it was not possible to lay charges based on the evidence.[33] The WA Police submitted to the Standing Committee on Legislation that the reason Walsh-McDonald was eventually charged was that, amongst other things, a pharmacologist had provided an expert opinion that, at a blood alcohol concentration of 0.165%, a person would be seriously affected by alcohol, unable to recognise an emergency nor respond to it in a timely manner.[34] Such expert opinion had been common knowledge since at least the mid-twentieth century. The Western Australian benchmark of incapability had been set at 0.15% in 1957, thus the pharmacologist's opinion was hardly a revelation. From the mid-1940s, the Crown pursued prosecutions on the basis that the consumption of alcohol significantly impaired drivers' motor skills (in the physiological sense), vision and spatial perception, and therefore their driving was *intrinsically* negligent. Those attempts were usually unsuccessful. On the WA Police's own submission to the Standing Committee, the history of trial outcomes in dangerous driving causing death cases *did not* support the conviction of intoxicated drivers in the absence of overt demonstrations of explicitly dangerous conduct.[35]

On review, the expert's opinion on Walsh-McDonald's blood alcohol level and its impact on his driving were apparently supported by eyewitness testimony and other forensic evidence. This was at some disparity with the initial view that the manner in which Jess had crossed the road negated the possibility of a charge. That Walsh-McDonald *was* charged more than a year later seemed to bear a stronger correlation to the weight of public and political pressure, rather than new light on the evidence. That he was not charged initially was resituated in the media and by some parliamentarians as the consequence of inadequate police investigation and laziness,[36] rather than an *accurate* reflection of the difficulty in proving that drivers' skills were *intrinsically* flawed at such blood alcohol concentrations, and decades of experience that attempts to secure convictions in like circumstances were generally futile. Nonetheless, McGinty sought to close what he described as a 'massive loophole' in the law, so that drunk drivers, *ipso facto*, became dangerous drivers – presumed liable for deaths unless *they* could prove otherwise.

While public protest fell short of the scenes witnessed in 1991 when an estimated 30,000 people gathered before Parliament House, over a decade later almost 10,000 people signed a petition to amend the law, a petition instigated by Jess' parents, Peter and Cheryl Meehan. Signatories demanded that so-called 'anomalies' in the legislation and leniency in sentencing be addressed.[37] Public opinion seemed heavily in favour of holding drinking drivers who *killed* to account, despite the fact that drink-driving remained a remarkably common offence – 13,300 drivers were found to have blood alcohol concentrations in excess of the legal limit in 2004.[38]

The public backed the Meehan's call for justice and, in support of the petition, headlines encouraged readers to 'Sign up for tougher laws'.[39] The death of a 10-year-old 'innocent' child was a perfect focal point to incite outrage. The campaign was spearheaded by the Meehans with support from within the corridors of Parliament. In a characteristically 'for us or against us' declaration, Peter Meehan told the media that it was a matter of being part of the solution or part of the problem; a position reiterated by Dianne Guise on the floor of the lower House.[40] In the upper House, Peter Foss contemptuously remarked that it would be more accurate to refer to the amendments as 'Jess' mother's law' rather than Jess' law.[41] Rowdy scenes accompanied the Bill's passing. The local press described Jess' parents choking back tears on its passage.[42] With the advent of the *Road Traffic Amendment (Dangerous Driving) Act 2004*, the Attorney General stated that, as of 1 January 2005, 'drunks' would be 'punished quickly and appropriately'.[43]

As Foss' remarks indicate, the amendments were not a matter for universal approval. In addition to the usual anxieties about distracted drivers, 'ordinary mums and dads' and 'grannies' being victimised,[44] the Bill came under fire from the legal fraternity. The Subcommittee appointed to review the Bill received submissions from the Law Society of Western Australia, the Criminal Lawyers' Association of Western Australia and Dr Neil Morgan, then Director of Studies at UWA's Crime Research Centre. Despite the widespread public popularity of retribution, the legal community's criticism that the Bill reversed the onus of proof and abolished causation was given serious attention by the news media. Former West Australian Premier, Peter Dowding, chimed in to the debate, describing the proposed amendments as 'draconian'.[45] The government was accused of populism and posing a threat to civil liberties, the Bill being but one in a raft of tough new laws.[46] WA Law Society President, Ian Weldon, cautioned politicians against engaging in a 'bidding war' to appear tough on crime.[47] Critics argued that the polls were dictating legislative change at the expense of fundamental legal principles.[48]

Heated accusations came thick and fast. The Opposition accused McGinty of using the death of a child to further his career.[49] The President of the Criminal Lawyers' Association, Hylton Quail, who later represented Walsh-McDonald, accused McGinty of making 'populist' proposals to 'buy votes' and the government of knee-jerk reactions.[50] Instructing officer on the Bill, State Counsel George Tannin, countered that the outcry was nothing more than hyperbole and media hysteria.[51]

Such was the concern about the proposed amendments that, before the second reading speech could commence in the upper House, Murray Criddle moved a motion without notice that the Bill be referred to the Standing Committee on Legislation, a move that garnered majority support.[52] In response, the Attorney General declared to the news cameras, a declaration emotively underscored by Jess' parents standing beside him, that the Council's actions verged on 'criminal', a term McGinty repeated on radio, and he was 'absolutely disgusted' that the Opposition and the Greens had effectively killed the Bill.[53] Jess' parents were outraged. Peter Meehan urged parliamentarians to pass the Bill so that his daughter might not have died in vain.[54]

The Leader of the Opposition in the upper House, Norman Moore, was equally disgusted. He argued that the Bill represented a challenge to fundamental legal principles and thus the Legislative Council had an obligation to examine the proposed changes very carefully. Not only was McGinty's response 'populist', Moore said, it was 'absolutely outrageous', 'grossly disrespectful' and utterly 'disgraceful' that he had publicly denounced the Council's referral of the Bill for review as 'criminal', in turn denigrating the Parliament. Moore suggested that the Premier, Dr Geoff Gallop, should take his Attorney General aside and impress upon him his obligation to treat the Parliament and its processes with respect, and that McGinty should apologise for inferring that Members 'support drunken drivers who kill children'.[55] The Greens' Jim Scott held that McGinty's actions were tantamount to 'blackmail' and bullying. He declared not a single member was disinclined to pass the Bill, the Council simply wanted it subjected to proper examination.[56] Ultimately, however, the Greens did not support the amendments, arguing that the reversal of the onus of proof and the abolition of causation set dangerous precedents.[57] Peter Foss claimed that, despite McGinty's training as a lawyer, he was behaving more like a 'cheap publicist', treating 'victims' as political leverage. He was 'sickened', he said, that the government was duping the Meehans to believe that, were the law passed, their child would not have died in vain but for some greater purpose.[58] Member of the upper House, George Cash, accused the Attorney General of advancing his career over Jess' dead body.[59]

Despite McGinty's public assertion that the Opposition was trying to 'kill' the Bill, reference to the entirety of the parliamentary debate demonstrates a great deal of support from all sides of Parliament. There were, however, considerable concerns about whether the amendments to s 59(1) reversed the burden of proof. Members of the Opposition repeatedly and openly declared that they would support the Bill, whilst at the same time expressing their reservations about its broader ramifications.[60] Unlike the scenes in Parliament in 1974, where Opposition members countered that they were more than capable of managing a vehicle after having 'one too many',[61] in 2004 both sides of the House concurred that too many people were dying on the roads as a result of drink-driving. It was a situation that apparently could no longer be tolerated.[62] The Legislative Council referred the Bill to the Standing Committee on Legislation on 24 September 2004. By 27 October, the Committee had sought written submissions, held public and private hearings, and swiftly produced an extensive report. The report raised serious concerns. Its first recommendation cautioned members to be 'fully cognisant' of the Bill's implications.[63] Three members of the Standing Committee vowed they would not support the Bill's passage without substantial amendment. The remaining two dissented.[64]

At the root of the Committee's caution was the causative nexus between the *manner of the driving* and the *death*. For decades, prosecutors had struggled to secure verdicts in cases where drivers were heavily intoxicated and *appeared* to be managing the vehicle, yet inexplicably ploughed into another car, a cyclist or a pedestrian ostensibly because they simply did not see them. Without an observed sequence of overtly flagrant conduct, and even with, intoxicated drivers frequently evaded conviction. This trend continued after the introduction of dangerous driving causing death in 1974, underscored by the judgment in *Smith v The Queen* in 1976, which held that the *manner of the driving* should be assessed from the point of view of an objective bystander.[65]

While the consumption of alcohol was known to cause a dramatic increase in response times and a corresponding decline in motor skills, and the relationship between levels of consumption and crash involvement were well established and publicised, in the absence of other manifest displays of dangerous conduct, medical evidence of intoxication was insufficient to secure a conviction. On this, the government claimed that the law was ambiguous. However, the issue was not so much ambiguity but a high degree of evidential difficulty with which the amendments sought to dispense. What McGinty labelled 'deficiencies', only brought to his attention following the death of Jess Meehan, had long been at issue before her death, and had presented a challenge to prosecutors over the course of the twentieth century. Under what became known as Jess' law, at 0.15% a driver would be deemed incapable of driving and presumed to have occasioned the death, irrespective of whether, from the point of view of a bystander, the driving *appeared* dangerous.

Despite the outcry from the legal fraternity, the substance of the government's Bill had form. The amendments replicated existing provisions of s 52A and s 52AA of the New South Wales *Crimes Act* and mirrored aspects of s 318 of Victoria's *Crimes Act*, whereby driving under the influence to the extent of incapability was deemed to be dangerous or culpable driving.[66] The maximum imposable penalty under the NSW provisions was six years less than that proposed in Western Australia.[67] Notably, dangerous driving in ordinary circumstances attracted a maximum penalty of ten years in New South Wales, considerably higher than Western Australia's four.[68]

The amendments of 2004 abolished s 59(1) and in essence created a new two-way offence. Section 59(1)(b) incorporated the existing definition of dangerous driving which was, and remains, driving in a manner, including speed, that having regard to the circumstances is dangerous to the public or any person. Section 59(1)(a) added a new limb. If a driver was under the influence of drugs or alcohol to such an extent as to be *incapable*, the driver would automatically be charged with occasioning the death. In effect, the new section deemed the driving dangerous and presumed the driver responsible for the death. While the 0.15% benchmark of incapability for blood alcohol already existed under s 63 of the *Road Traffic Act*, its import into s 59 made intoxication a determinant of dangerousness that required no proof that the driving *was* dangerous, save for a blood alcohol test. Drinking and driving to the extent of a 0.15% blood alcohol concentration, in addition to drug-affected driving, was statutorily declared to be intrinsically dangerous. Blood alcohol levels below 0.15% did not fall within the ambit of the provision. In those cases, the manner of the driving would continue to be the determining factor.

Given the weight of the medical evidence and statistical data regarding crash involvement, declaring a piece of driving dangerous at a blood alcohol concentration of 0.15% or more was, in some respects, a piece of statutory commonsense. It was a step which in effect gave formal recognition to a scientific fact. In 2004, Margaret Quirk MLA noted that drivers with a blood alcohol concentration of 0.05% were seven times more likely to be involved in a crash and at 0.15%, the probability of crash involvement multiplied twenty-five times.[69] However, it was not only the deeming provision that concerned critics. There was further cause for concern.

Under the amendments, the prosecution would no longer be required to establish that the dangerous driving, deemed or otherwise, *caused* the death. In all instances, the prosecution would have to establish only that the motor vehicle was driven in a dangerous manner by a person who was involved in an incident occasioning a death.[70] In effect, dangerous driving *causing* death was no more. State Counsel George Tannin, the instructing officer on the Bill, defended the abolition of the causative nexus between the manner of the driving and the death, and the substitution of 'involvement in an incident', because it would save the prosecution from having to go 'through all the rigmarole of proving a causal connection'.[71] Contrary to the position of the High Court in *McBride v R* in 1966, he claimed it was a matter of logic that causation was established if an incident occurred and the offender was driving.[72]

The net result of the amendment would be to relieve the State of the obligation to establish a connection between the manner of the driving and the resultant harm. Rather the prosecution would have to prove that the *incident* occasioned the harm, in which the driver was involved.[73] Being 'involved in an incident' expanded the ambit of the offence. Under the amendments, circumstances in which a driver was not directly involved in the death of another road user, but their driving conduct precipitated a chain of events, such as causing another driver to swerve, were incorporated within the scope of the offence.[74] Former President of the Court of Appeal, Justice Steytler, later confirmed that the reconstruction of s 59(1) and its fundamental alteration of the elements of the offence in effect created a *new* offence.[75] In the course of the debate in the upper House, George Cash argued that the abolition of causation – that is, that the dangerous driving *caused* the death – did away with the fault element of the offence.[76] Others claimed that it rather 'simplified' it.[77] The Standing Committee considered the causation aspects of the Bill most 'unusual' and, despite Tannin's protests, the majority of the Standing Committee believed that it was contrary to the very basis of criminal liability and punishment – a basis grounded in the relationship between the actions of the accused and the consequences of those actions.⁷⁸ Under the amendments, a driver's principal fault was that they were driving while heavily under the influence. It was therefore *presumed* that their driving was dangerous and occasioned the death because they were incapable of managing the vehicle, although the Bill did provide a defence to the charge.

Parliamentarians also raised complaints regarding the Bill's apparent inconsistencies. Sue Walker noted that the amendments should logically go further.⁷⁹ On that front, the Criminal Lawyers' Association agreed.⁸⁰ Under the proposed amendments, the deeming provision did not encompass dangerous driving simpliciter. Only drivers who had blood alcohol concentrations of 0.15% or more, or were heavily affected by drugs and killed or injured were deemed dangerous. For those who *did not* kill or injure, their driving would not be deemed 'dangerous' and would remain subject to the existing criteria. Walker questioned why a driver with a 0.15% blood alcohol concentration who caused death or injury would automatically be deemed dangerous, but a driver who hit the wall of a house, for example, would remain exempt.⁸¹ If the intent of the amendments was to deter drink and drug-affected driving, and limit and punish its fatal consequences, then the logical step would have been to target that conduct across the board. McGinty claimed that the government's objective was to target 'a specific evil',⁸² a claim that rather lent itself to the interpretation that the locus of evil was the death, not the conduct which precipitated that violent and tragic result.

On the matter of increasing penalties, there seemed to be no objections. Aside from the amendments of 1992, which increased the penalty from four years to twenty if the vehicle was stolen,⁸³ the maximum term of imprisonment had been fixed at four years since the offence's introduction in 1974. Compared to other Australian jurisdictions, Western Australia's penalties had remained extraordinarily low. Queensland increased the maximum term of imprisonment for dangerous driving causing death from five years to seven in circumstances of aggravation, specifically intoxication, as early as 1982.⁸⁴ In 1994, NSW increased the maximum penalty from five years to fourteen years' imprisonment in circumstances of aggravation, and ten years in all other circumstances.⁸⁵ In 2004, under South Australian law, drivers who were culpably negligent, reckless or dangerous were liable to ten years' imprisonment for a first offence, and fifteen for a subsequent one,⁸⁶ as though the legislature envisaged that a driver who killed might kill again. Since 1974, four years had remained the statutory maximum for a single fatality under s 59(1) of Western Australia's *Road Traffic Act*, were the vehicle not stolen.

Under the amendments, convicted drivers would be subject to significantly higher penalties if the driver was deemed incapable or the offence was committed in other circumstances of aggravation. If a driver was under the influence to the extent of being incapable, he or she would be liable to a maximum custodial term of twenty years.⁸⁷ Circumstances of aggravation – driving a stolen vehicle, exceeding the designated speed limit by more than 45 km/h or attempting to escape police pursuit – would also render an offender liable to a twenty-year penalty.⁸⁸ In 2018, the WA Labor government would seek to expand the scope of the provisions by reducing the speed limit and by bringing unlicensed drivers within the compass of aggravating circumstances.⁸⁹

The 2004 amendments also targeted drivers' refusal to consent to blood alcohol testing. Drivers who sought to evade punishment by refusing to provide blood or breath samples faced a maximum custodial term of fourteen years.⁹⁰ Surprisingly, summary judgment and its alternative penalty structure was left intact. Cases that fell within the deeming provision or circumstances of aggravation could still be dealt with summarily and thus face a substantially lower penalty.

John Prior appeared before the subcommittee appointed to review the Bill on behalf of the Criminal Lawyers' Association. He warned that the 0.15% deeming provision would flaunt the 'might of the State' against individuals.⁹¹ As Prior noted, the onus would be on the intoxicated driver to provide evidence that he or she was *not* responsible for the death. He argued that, in practical terms, the proposed s 59(1)(a) reversed the onus of proof, so that drivers would have to prove their innocence, rather than the State establish their guilt. Whether the government referred to the section as a presumption of liability, a rebuttal presumption, a reversal of the onus of proof or a deeming provision, Prior claimed the net result was the same – the driver would be deemed to have caused the incident, whether they did so or not.[92] The NSW Court of Criminal Appeal had previously come down on the side of the WA Criminal Lawyers' Association on a comparable section of the NSW's *Crimes Act*, which held that the section transposed the burden of proof.[93] In addition to the available defences under the Code, the amendments afforded drivers an additional defence to the charge. Drivers could counter that death was 'not in any way attributable' to their intoxication or their driving conduct.[94] On 'not in any way attributable', State Counsel George Tannin conceded that discharging the defence would be very difficult, a difficulty he described as entirely deliberate.[95] As the WA Law Reform Commission later noted, 'not in any way attributable' meant that, if the death could be partially attributed to the accused, the defence could not be satisfactorily discharged.[96]

Under attack, the government made 'no apology' for targeting drunk drivers.[97] That was, as member of the upper House Kim Chance noted, 'the whole purpose of the legislation'.[98] The Criminal Lawyers' Association warned that, while the Major Accident Squad was one of the best branches of the WA Police, highly trained and conscientious, the deeming provision might lead to shoddy investigative practices. The Association warned that, if a driver was breathalysed at 0.15% or more at the scene of a crash, police would have all the evidence they needed to secure a conviction and might cease investigating, irrespective of whether the driver's actions *actually* caused the incident. Accordingly, the deeming provision might lead to overworked or 'slack' officers failing to do their job.[99] The Association claimed that accused drivers would be in the inimical position of having to collect the evidence themselves, long after the crash scene had been cleared.[100] George Tannin countered that the application of the law would rely on the common sense of the WA Police and the Department of Public Prosecutions.[101]

Parliamentarians also drew attention to the Bill's perceived excesses and severity. Member for the South West, Paddy Embry, asked how he might possibly explain to his constituents that drinking and driving had now seemingly surpassed the gravity of wilful murder. He observed that those accused of murder remained entitled to a presumption of innocence, but drivers who had a blood alcohol concentration of 0.15% or more were to be presumed guilty.[102] For many legal commentators and parliamentarians, the deeming provision set a troubling, dangerous precedent.[103]

The Criminal Lawyers' Association argued that the provision was 'unnecessary'.[104] Driving under the influence to the extent of incapability was already an offence under s 63 of the *Road Traffic Act*,[105] spokesperson Prior rightly noted, and probative and admissible in a prosecution under s 59(1). He claimed that it was virtually 'axiomatic' that the driver would be imprisoned in cases involving high levels of intoxication;[106] a claim explicitly contradicted by the case law and close examination of decades of unreported cases. Prior contested McGinty's assertion, arguing that there was no difficulty in substantiating causation between the manner of the intoxicated driving and the death,[107] an assertion at odds with the fact that Walsh-McDonald was not charged in the first instance.

On the basis of his experience acting for the Department of Public Prosecutions, Prior claimed that dangerous driving causing death was a charge generally 'easy as pie' to prove because the test of dangerous driving was an objective one.[108] It was, according to Prior, not difficult to secure a conviction.[109] Yet the very nature of the test, where the manner of the driving had to be envisaged from the point of view of a bystander, made dangerousness very difficult to substantiate in cases where intoxication was a factor. Emphasising the fault element of the existing offence – that the driving *caused* the death – Prior argued that the focus should remain on the *quality* of the driving, not its consequence. By contrast, the deeming provision was based in a presumption that, at 0.15% the quality of the driving must be intrinsically flawed. Prior advised the Standing Committee that it should delete the 'superfluous' provision altogether.[110] Parliamentary Counsel provided assurances that there was nothing to fear. Deeming provisions had been employed across many Western Australian statutes. Internal correspondence within Parliamentary Counsel identified eighty statutes that included one or more deeming provisions that reversed the onus of proof.[111]

The Criminal Lawyers' Association called for statistical evidence to support the government's claim that causation was a sticking point in the prosecution of cases involving intoxication.[112] This research can certainly provide some historical evidence to refute Prior's assertions. Between 1946 and 1974, for example, of the sixty-two indictments sampled where drink-driving was unequivocally at issue, twenty-seven cases resulted in acquittals; certainly not an indication of 'easy as pie'.[113] The Association's assertion is difficult to contradict after 1974, not because of its accuracy, but rather because of the difficulties associated with accessing lower court records, the principal jurisdictions between 1974 and 2011. Notwithstanding, circumstances such as those in *Blair v Semple* in 1989 lend support to the government's assertion that the causative nexus remained a sticking point.[114] In *Blair v Semple*, Justice Franklyn held that there was no evidence that the driver was drunk and overturned the initial finding that he was significantly affected by alcohol because he refused to be breathalysed. The fact that he was driving down the wrong side of the road with his headlights off did not 'justify a conclusion' that he 'had been drinking to a marked degree'.[115] While scientific methods of determining blood alcohol concentration superseded sobriety tests during the mid-twentieth century, when that evidence could not be secured, commonsense became the principal casualty.

Some parliamentarians drew attention to cases with similar factual circumstances to the Meehan case, stressing the necessity of the amendments. The McIlveen case was one such example. The driver, Marnie Bishop, had a blood alcohol concentration of 0.171%. She was driving down a dimly lit street when she hit Watson McIlveen.[116] Some of the difficulty turned around the fact that Bishop's passenger repeatedly altered her version of events, finally claiming that she was asleep at the point of impact, thereby denying the prosecution any witness to Bishop's driving. Bishop was not charged with McIlveen's death. She was fined $800 for driving under the influence.[117] Despite being highly intoxicated and running over McIlveen, there was no evidence that she was driving *dangerously*. On behalf of his constituents, former backbencher Mark McGowan wrote to the Department of Public Prosecutions to inquire as to whether Bishop might be charged with a more serious offence. The Department advised that there was no *prima facie* case to support a charge under s 59(1). As McGowan noted in Parliament, what that meant for the McIlveen family was that their son was killed, the woman who killed him was fined $800 for driving under the influence and, as far as the law was concerned, that was the end of the matter.[118]

George Tannin told the Committee that the proposed changes would rectify and remedy the 'evidential deficiencies' which the Walsh-McDonald and McIlveen cases exemplified.[119] He claimed the Bill *did not* reverse the onus of proof, but rather described it as 'deemed proving subject to rebuttal' whereby, if a driver claims that he or she was capable of driving and not dangerous, he or she must prove it.[120] Somewhat semantically, Tannin claimed that, strictly speaking, the deeming provision of incapability was not a reversal of the onus of proof 'because the defence requires the proof of something that is not an element of the offence'.[121] Historicising the reasons for amending the legislation, Tannin correctly observed that there had been nearly four decades of serious campaign efforts warning drivers of the dangers of drinking and driving. He noted that the Bill gave statutory recognition to the fact that, at 0.15%, a level of intoxication that the legislation 'assumes is pretty awful', a driver is a danger to themselves and the community.¹²² It could not be a secret in contemporary society, Tannin argued, that a blood alcohol concentration of 0.15% was dangerous – 'It just cannot be, and if this legislation appears harsh to those people who might risk that, I am really content with that'.¹²³ People who had a couple of glasses of wine after work were not the target, Tannin emphasised, but those who continued to drink to a point where the question of intoxication was entirely unambiguous.¹²⁴ At a blood alcohol concentration of 0.15%, member of the Upper House Ken Travers reasoned, a crash could not be considered an accident, but was rather wilful, intentional behaviour that played 'Russian roulette' with the lives of other road users.¹²⁵ Terry Waldron MLA stated that, what needed to be impressed upon the community, particularly young people, was that people who drive in excess of the limit and kill are in fact 'criminals'.¹²⁶ The deeming provision put an end to the evidential burden that, for more than fifty years, had made it so difficult to secure convictions.

In the course of the debate and in submissions to the Standing Committee, critics of the Bill sought to illustrate the injustices the deeming provision might give rise to with cautionary, hypothetical scenarios. Chief amongst them was the suggestion that drivers might be held responsible for suicides.¹²⁷ In the event that a driver was the unwitting victim of a pedestrian intent on killing themselves, who deliberately ran out in front of a vehicle to effect their own death, and the driver had a 0.15% blood alcohol concentration or more, under the new provision the driver could be deemed to have caused the death. The driver would have recourse to the defence that his or her intoxication in *no way* contributed to the death. Another potential abuse of the provision was posed by the hypothetical in which an entirely sober driver rear-ended another vehicle on the freeway in peak hour, causing a domino of collisions involving, for the sake of discussion, six vehicles.¹²⁸ For the purposes of illustration, the driver whose conduct initiated the chain of events is in car number one. The passenger in car number two is killed and in the sixth car, two persons suffer serious injuries. The driver of the fourth car has a blood alcohol concentration of 0.165%. Under the deeming provision, critics held, the driver of the fourth car could be held liable for the death and injuries because he or she had a blood alcohol concentration of 0.15% or more and was involved in the 'incident'. Another scenario employed to warn of the possible abuse of the provision was that in which a driver with a blood alcohol concentration in excess of 0.15%, who, notwithstanding his or her intoxication, was complying with the road rules. Travelling through an intersection, the intoxicated driver's vehicle is hit by another vehicle which ran a red light.[129] In the event that the driver who ran the red light died, despite the fact that the intoxicated driver did not cause the crash, he or she could be deemed responsible for the death.

So grave were concerns about the amendments and their potential abuse by police and prosecutors, the Legislative Council inserted a clause as a condition of the Bill's passage. Under this condition, the Minister would be obliged to carry out a full review of the amendments' operation after eighteen months had passed. The review was due to be undertaken in mid-2006 and tabled before Parliament as soon as practicable.[130] Despite the amendments' 'dangerous precedent',[131] and the apparent potential for gross injustices, the report has *never* been tabled. Correspondence with the parliamentary library and the offices of Rob Johnson, then Minister for Police and Road Safety, Troy Buswell, then Minister for Transport, Housing and Emergency Services, and former Attorney General, Christian Porter, over a six-month period in 2012 confirmed this oversight. Almost six years after the report was due, it had not even been commenced.[132] In July 2012, the Managing Director of the Department of Transport advised that the author's discovery and correspondence had prompted the government to engage an independent analyst to conduct the review, in addition to commencing joint-agency working group discussions, with thanks for bringing the oversight to the Minister's attention.[133] Almost thirteen years overdue, the report is *still* yet to be tabled before Parliament.

Though in many respects welcome, the 2004 amendments had the added, undesirable effect of further segregating *particularly* serious vehicular cases from all other forms of homicide, thus reinforcing the idea that unlawful killings involving vehicles were a peculiar species apart. The amendments labelled that which was by penalty and, arguably, in many instances, by fault, criminally negligent, as *dangerous*. As such, the new maximum penalty of twenty years sent an unfortunate, unwitting signal. In order for a driver to be significantly penalised for killing another person, the manner of the driving had to be truly aberrant, doing little to underscore the need for the entire community to adopt a degree of care proportionate to the quantum of risk. In many respects, Jess' law targeted *exceptional* conduct and set the bar of *exceptional* very high. Making the maximum penalty for dangerous driving causing death in circumstances of aggravation equal to that of manslaughter seemed to suggest an equivalence in gravitas, but only for the truly homicidal driver or thief, not typically requisite for other forms of unintentional manslaughter. As such, Jess's law inadvertently underscored the notion that the problem was 'out there', rather than being far closer to home.

Chapter Nine

After Jess: Reflecting the value of human life?

'Ordinary' versus aggravated dangerous driving causing death

Jess' law came into force as of 1 January 2005. No longer would the Crown have to establish that the *manner* of the driving *caused* the death, but rather that the vehicle was driven in a dangerous manner by a person who was involved in an incident *occasioning* a death. The media continued to employ the phrase dangerous driving *causing* death, perhaps because the new terminology would only prove unfamiliar to the public. The relevant sections of the *Road Traffic Act* also maintained the previous descriptor, if only in title rather than substance.

From January 2005, prosecutions would fall under s 59(1)(a) of the *Road Traffic Act*, the provision which deemed drivers incapable, or s 59(1)(b), the former construction of dangerous driving, notwithstanding the abolition of causation. In the absence of aggravating circumstances, prosecutions under s 59(1)(b) continued to attract a maximum penalty of four years' imprisonment on indictment. For those dealt with summarily, even in circumstances of aggravation, the maximum custodial penalty was set at eighteen months. By June 2008, that penalty had increased to three years. Fines were maintained as an alternative to a custodial term. Manslaughter was still available if open on the evidence.

Before losing office in 2008, the Labor government took the long overdue step of increasing the maximum penalty for 'ordinary' cases of dangerous driving occasioning death from four years to ten on indictment, a move that Jim McGinty mooted as far back as 2004.[1] In 2011, the Liberal government took the *momentous* step of abolishing summary judgment altogether, a move welcomed by the Royal Automobile Club of Western Australia (RAC), which had campaigned heavily on the issue.[2] Renewed attention was brought to the leniency afforded by summary judgment when, in 2009, a 32-year-old, drug-affected driver, Lee Toplass, drove his car down the wrong side of Kwinana Freeway, killing a 37-year-old woman and injuring her son. McKenzie McGuigan was seen frantically flashing her headlights at the oncoming vehicle moments before impact. Her son was pulled from the burning wreck and suffered severe injuries. The matter was dealt with in the Fremantle Magistrates Court. For one count of occasioning death, one count of bodily harm and driving under the influence of drugs, Toplass received a combined three-year sentence and a fine of $800. He was made eligible for parole after eighteen months and was disqualified from driving for two years. Mick McGuigan, McKenzie's husband, told the media that the family were 'devastated and outraged'.[3] He implored – 'Where's the human decency and the value of human life?'[4] His question was not only the plea of an understandably distressed husband and father. The value of human life as reflected in penalties had continued to trouble many members of the judiciary, even after the introduction of Jess' law.

As of 2011, almost forty years after the advent of the *Road Traffic Act*, in *all* instances, dangerous driving occasioning death would be a matter for indictment in the District Court.[5] On announcing the abolition of summary judgment and the reinstatement of a maximum term of life imprisonment for manslaughter, former West Australian Attorney General Christian Porter made an alarming revelation – of the thirty-four cases of dangerous driving occasioning death brought before the courts over the previous year, only *four* were the subject of indictment.[6] The continued availability of summary judgment limited the impact the 2004 amendments might have otherwise had. Some magistrates remanded offenders to the District Court for sentencing because they felt the maximum penalty available to them was inadequate. Ironically, in some instances, the sentences imposed in the District Court were less than those that could have been imposed by a local magistrate.

Former Attorney General Porter held that the abolition of summary judgment and exposure to higher penalties would mirror community expectations about deaths caused by 'gross recklessness' and the 'enormity of a loss of life'.[7] He stressed that the amendments would give the courts 'the capacity to ensure sentencing practices for manslaughter and dangerous driving causing death better reflect community sentiment', and added that the government would 'closely monitor' how the courts utilised 'their expanded discretion'.[8] The RAC hoped that the amendments would signal the advent of more appropriate penalties, simultaneously ending the distress and disrespect caused to surviving loved ones when serious and horrific circumstances were dealt with summarily.[9] While the abolition of summary judgment was a momentous, overdue step, ending recourse to fines and egregious penalties, the RAC and Porter's aspirations were not entirely realised by the sentences that followed the abolition, nor had they materialised after the introduction of Jess' law.

As former President of the Court of Appeal, Justice Steytler observed, in 2004 the legislature saw fit to equate the maximum sentence for manslaughter with aggravated dangerous driving occasioning death.[10] Equivalence, however, was not always apparent. On 10 May 2007, Damian Gibbs was travelling between 150 and 161 km/h on Tonkin Highway.[11] The speed limit was 100 km/h. Gibbs crashed into the back of a motorbike. Yoke Vance died at the scene. She was dragged 150 metres under the carriage of Gibbs' car. Her husband, Gerald, later died in hospital.[12] Eyewitnesses described Gibbs' driving as 'erratic' and his speed as 'excessive'.[13] The force of impact was so severe that Gerald Vance's motorcycle was embedded in the front of Gibbs car in an upright position.[14] Given the degree of speed involved, Gibbs' offence fell within the aggravating sentencing provisions. He pleaded guilty in the Perth Magistrate's Court. Magistrate Cicchini referred him to a higher court for sentencing.[15] For the total of his offences, Gibbs was sentenced to four-and-a-half years' imprisonment. The State appealed on a number of grounds, including the inadequacy of the sentence.[16]

On review of the relevant authorities, the majority judgment held that the sentences were neither inadequate, individually or in total.[17] Justice Miller disagreed. He held that the sentence was *manifestly inadequate* and that a sentence of five years and three months would more appropriately mark the gravity of the offences, whilst taking into account Gibbs' remorse, guilty plea, antecedents and character.[18] Echoing his former arguments, he stated –

> In my opinion, the provision of a maximum sentence of 20 years imprisonment in cases where death has been occasioned in circumstances of aggravation is an indication that the legislature is truly endeavouring to reflect the value which is to be placed upon human life. Whilst all other sentencing considerations are always relevant, this issue (the value to be placed upon human life) is of particular consideration in cases of motor vehicle manslaughter and dangerous driving occasioning death. It is, in my opinion, something that needs to be reflected in the sentences to be imposed in the present case.[19]

It was an all too familiar observation and one Miller returned to in *Western Australia v Butler*, also in 2009.[20] Butler's case was the first to be brought under s 59(1)(a) since the 2004 amendments. Between 2005 and 2009, the Crown appeared to prefer manslaughter charges in cases involving high levels of intoxication.

In *Western Australia v Mitchell* in 2008, for example, the driver had a blood alcohol concentration of 0.205% and drove down the wrong side of the freeway at night. Rather than utilise s 59(1)(a), Mitchell was charged with manslaughter. On one count of manslaughter, the court imposed a six-year term, with a further cumulative six-month sentence for driving while disqualified, in addition to a raft of concurrent sentences for other charges where he had previously failed to appear before the courts.[21]

Returning to *Western Australia v Butler*, the circumstances were that, on 18 April 2008, 24-year-old Benjamin Butler was driving along a suburban residential street. He accelerated heavily into the oncoming lane to overtake two vehicles on a single carriageway. One of the vehicles ahead of him was attempting to turn right. Butler collided with the car, mounting the kerb. His vehicle then became airborne, whereby it landed in Tania and Jamie Moorby's front garden, then crashed into the brick wall that separated the Moorby's home from their neighbours, colliding into the front porch. The damage to the property was extensive. Tania Moorby was pushing her 11-month-old daughter Grace in a pram through her front garden. She and her daughter were hit. The force of impact threw them into the neighbouring property. Grace's body was found under a pile of bricks.[22] Butler had a blood alcohol concentration in excess of 0.166%, although he had ceased drinking ten to eleven hours prior and had slept in the interim.[23] A fly-in, fly-out mineworker, Butler was on leave and, reportedly, a two-day drinking binge.[24] His blood alcohol concentration brought him within the compass of s 59(1)(a), exposing him to the twenty-year penalty.

Under threat from some angry bystanders, two of which had dragged him to the ground, Butler tried to leave the scene. Pursued, he was detained only 400 metres away.[25] Apparently deeply remorseful, he pleaded guilty without hesitation.[26] In the District Court, Judge Keen sentenced Butler to two years and ten months for dangerous driving occasioning death, and a cumulative sentence of ten months on the bodily harm charge, resulting in a total sentence of three years and eight months' imprisonment. He was made eligible for parole after one year and ten months.[27] The State appealed.

Given the Parliament saw fit to equate aggravated dangerous driving occasioning death with criminally negligent manslaughter, at least in penalty, the sentences imposed warrant comparison. The highest, contemporaneous sentences for manslaughter in the period, such as those in *Penny v Western Australia* in 2006, *Farmer v Western Australia* and *Taylor v Western Australia*, both in 2007, and *Western Australia v Mitchell* in 2008, had ranged between just over five years to eight.[28] As was observed in *Penny*, prior to 2003 manslaughter cases had generally tended to attract terms between two years to six years and eight months.[29] The eight-year penalty imposed in *Penny* for one count of manslaughter was later described as 'an outlier'[30] and higher than any sentence previously imposed. It was, however, equal to the penalty imposed on Darrin Fox in 1999, a case that went unreported, albeit for *two* counts of manslaughter and one count of grievous bodily harm.[31] Of the highest penalties imposed for manslaughter between 2006 and 2008, they were more or less on a par with the sentences in *McKenna v The Queen* (1992), *Punch v The Queen* (1993), *Clinch v The Queen* (1999), the penalty imposed on Darrin Fox in 1999 as per newspaper reports, and *White v The Queen* (2003).[32] After 2008, a number of higher sentences were imposed, such as the eight-and-a-half year sentence in *Brown v Western Australia* in 2011, the eleven-year sentence imposed on Antony Fogarty in 2014,[33] and the nine-year sentence imposed on Brandon Rhys Peterson in 2018.[34] In the *Butler* appeal in 2009, Justice Wheeler gently suggested that the sentences imposed in the most serious cases to date may have been 'somewhat less than the statutory penalty provided by the legislature' and that it might be 'desirable to firm up penalties for offences of this extreme nature'.[35]

Granted, the circumstances in Butler's case were not as excessive. Nonetheless, Crown Prosecutor Ken Bates told the appellant court that the sentences were inadequate because the factual circumstances were 'extremely serious and at the higher end of offending of this type'.[36] Justice Wheeler noted the State's contention that the nature of Butler's driving was 'particularly serious'. It was an assertion, she held, that *could not* be made out.[37] She generously described his speed and attempt to overtake two vehicles whilst accelerating heavily in the oncoming lane as 'foolhardy', and noted that there was no evidence that the driving, prior to that 'relatively brief period', was deficient.[38] Furthermore, she stated that the *real* culpability of drinking and driving lay in *deliberately* going out and consuming alcohol and driving thereafter, which the respondent did not do. She expressed doubt that the public would know that they had a significant blood alcohol concentration long after they had ceased drinking.[39] In agreement with Justice Wheeler, Justice Pullin said that, in the way the expression is ordinarily understood, Butler did not 'drink and drive'.[40] It was as though the offence had taken on an element of premeditation. Butler had consumed a great deal of alcohol, gone to bed, woken, and in the early afternoon of the following day *still* had a very elevated blood alcohol concentration, a level by which one would surely feel some effects. He had not, however, *deliberately* set out to drink and drive.

Justice Miller made a compelling case in his dissenting judgment. He held that, with a blood alcohol concentration of 0.166%, Butler must have known he was incapable of driving, yet, irrespective, he chose to drive and 'did so dangerously'.[41] He characterised the overtaking manoeuvre as dangerous and his speed in a residential area as excessive.[42] On Butler's consumption of alcohol and the time that had elapsed before the collision, he stated –

> In my opinion, it is no answer to this appeal to say that the respondent's culpability was lessened by reason of the fact that he had consumed alcohol on the night/early morning prior to the accident and was in a different position from a person who had gone out drinking and had then driven home whilst affected by alcohol. On any view of it, with a blood alcohol level of 0.166%,

the respondent must have known that he was incapable of getting behind the wheel of a motor vehicle on the day of the accident. His counsel accepted as much when making submissions to the sentencing judge.[43]

Miller noted that the sentencing judge had characterised the circumstances 'towards the higher end of the continuum of low to high' and, as the respondent had demonstrated remorse and had good antecedents, general deterrence was the *key* factor in sentencing.[44] Emphasising the importance of deterrence and retribution, he noted that 2004 amendments were in part 'an endeavour to reflect the value of human life', an aim 'underlined by the tragedy that occurred' in the case of Grace's death.[45] He argued, given the range of sentences previously imposed, the penalties afforded to the courts, and the factual circumstances of Butler's case, the sentence imposed for Grace's death was *manifestly inadequate*. Miller proposed that, for the charge of occasioning death, a four-year term would have been appropriate, in addition to a ten-month cumulative term for the bodily harm charge.[46] Were he not constrained by the judgment in *Western Australia v BLM*, he added, he would have sentenced the respondent to a total term of seven years and three months.[47] Justice Miller retired from the bench later that year.[48]

Following his retirement, Justice Miller might have been encouraged by the sentencing outcomes in a handful of circumstances. Sentences in a small number of dangerous driving occasioning death cases dramatically increased. In *Devine v Western Australia* in 2010, for example, 21-year-old Luke Devine had driven at speeds of up to 220 km/h on a dark country road, despite the desperate pleas of his girlfriend, Casey Anderson. He wanted to see how fast his car would go. In addition to his girlfriend, Devine had two other passengers in his car. Devine lost control of the vehicle and smashed into a power pole.[49] He pleaded not guilty, denying any responsibility.[50] He claimed that the crash was caused by a kangaroo. Fifteen-year-old Hayley Morrison was killed and teenager Garry Press was seriously injured and left with permanent disabilities.[51] Devine had a propensity for speed. The night before the fatal collision, he was driving at speeds of up to 190 km/h. His passenger threatened to 'boot his head in' if he did not slow down.[52] Forebodingly, Devine also told a friend the day before the crash that when he died 'it would be in a car accident and he would be going "flat out"'.[53] Clearly he had failed to appreciate that he might hasten a friend's death rather than his own.

Judge Keen reportedly 'blasted' Devine, stating that it was 'an outrageously bad and dangerous piece of driving...it was driving at a speed which you intended to reach'.[54] He declared that Devine had demonstrated a total disregard for his passengers' safety, and a lack of remorse for the fatal consequences of his 'deliberate' actions.[55] Keen emphasised that

> motor vehicles, when driven in this way, are lethal weapons. People have to understand that they are entrusted with the use of such a vehicle, but against strict requirements as to its use. Those that abuse the use in this fashion must expect to receive severe punishment.[56]

On one count of aggravated dangerous driving occasioning death and one count of dangerous driving occasioning grievous bodily harm, he sentenced Devine to a total of seven years' imprisonment.[57] The sentence was reduced to six years on appeal. Devine was made eligible for parole after four years.[58] Importantly, the reduction of his custodial term was not because the sentence imposed for the death was considered too severe. In fact, the appellant court held that a term of imprisonment of five-and-a-half years for the death was neither unjust nor unreasonable, albeit severe. Rather, it was the accumulation of the sentences which breached the principle of totality and did not 'bear a proper relationship to the overall criminality involved'.[59]

In this history of sentencing and, even with the reduction of the custodial term on appeal, Devine's head sentence was substantial. Prior to 2004, sentences approaching that imposed on

Devine required a *mosaic* of aggravating factors, including driving with a high blood alcohol concentration or while drug-affected, in a stolen vehicle at speed, with a history of traffic offending. In that respect, Devine's sentence demonstrates that, in some limited instances, the 2004 sentencing provisions for circumstances of aggravation were having a considerable impact.

So too, on occasion, was the deeming provision. The sentence in *Barron v Western Australia* in 2010, the highest known sentence imposed for one count of dangerous driving occasioning death under s 59(1)(a) to that date, was *not* disturbed on appeal. In 2007, driving on a straight, dark road, Kevin Barron hit John Donnelly. Donnelly died at the scene. It was four days before Christmas. Donnelly was on the gravel verge, hitchhiking, and apparently visible via Barron's headlights for up to 70 metres prior to the collision.[60] Calculated back to the time of the incident, Barron had a blood alcohol concentration of 0.187%. He pleaded not guilty to dangerous driving occasioning death, but guilty to driving under the influence.[61] He had a history of traffic offending, including five charges of driving whilst unlicensed and three 0.08% convictions.[62] Inconceivably, he had previously been convicted for dangerous driving causing death on two separate occasions. He was first imprisoned for twelve months in 1983 for the death of his brother. He later killed a colleague and received an eighteen-month sentence in 1996.[63] In the case of John Donnelly, a seven-and-a-half-year term was imposed, the appellant court rejecting the claim that his sentence was excessive.[64] Barron's case gives weight to the impression that higher-end sentences have been reserved for those who can be readily cast as the criminal archetype. Nevertheless, his conviction and penalty sit in stark contrast to cases involving pedestrians and cyclists in the late twentieth and very early twenty-first centuries. Without a witness to the *manner of the driving* and the 0.15% deeming provision, the case against Barron would have been very difficult, if not impossible, to mount.

Despite the outcome in *Barron*, the 2004 amendments did not *routinely* bring about higher sentences than ever before. In

AFTER JESS: REFLECTING THE VALUE OF HUMAN LIFE?

fact, there has been a remarkable status quo in 'ordinary' cases of dangerous driving occasioning death and, in many instances, little change where cases feature aggravating circumstances. Had he not retired, Justice Miller might have continued to bemoan that neither criminality nor the value of human life were being adequately reflected in penalties. The term imposed on Melissa Waters in 2013, for example, attracted widespread criticism, sparked a candlelight vigil and the campaign, Pledge for Nate.[65]

The circumstances of the case were that, between 6.30 and 9.30 pm, 35-year-old Waters had been drinking at a club. She left the club around 9.30 pm to drive her husband and daughter home and then returned to purchase alcohol, food and cigarettes. Waters and a group of friends retired to a friend's house. Over the next four hours, Waters continued drinking. Her friends hid her car keys and pleaded with her not to drive. After they fell asleep, Waters found her keys and left.[66]

Driving home, Waters lost control of her vehicle, skidded across two oncoming lanes, mounted a verge, collided with a tree and then drove up an embankment and through a timber fence. She then collided with the double-brick wall of Nate and Kai Dunbar's bedroom. There was no evidence that Waters attempted to brake. The children's room was all but demolished. Eight-month-old Nate was found pinned under the front wheel of Waters' Toyota Hilux inside what remained of his bedroom. His brother witnessed the entire incident. Nate's mother Stacy tried to assist her son's breathing, but could not get her lips over his mouth, such was his position with a tyre pinning him down by the chest and his face pressed hard against the tyre wall. Waters climbed out of the passenger side, over Stacy and Nate, and left the scene. She was found wandering in a nearby street, disorientated. Emergency services and police arrived. They attempted to raise the vehicle with jacks and airbags. Nate did not survive.[67]

At the time of the incident, Waters' blood alcohol concentration was 0.17%, bringing her within the compass of s 59(1)(a). She pleaded guilty to the death and driving under the influence. In her statement to the court, she said that she would 'spend the rest of her life attempting to atone for the pain she has caused'.[68] Sentenced to three years and eight months' imprisonment, she was released after a year and ten months.[69] John Quigley, the Dunbar's local Member, described the sentence as 'hopelessly inadequate'.[70] Nate's mother pointed to what she perceived to be irregularities in the social judgments implicit in penalties. In a contemporaneous case where an accountant was sentenced to seven years for stealing $1.6 million from a client, Stacy Dunbar observed, 'when you have a justice system that puts the value of money higher than that of someone's life, we've got a really, really big problem'.[71]

Like Waters, in 2014 43-year-old Andrew Richmond was also penitent. Unlike Waters, he had previously been convicted for drink-driving on three occasions. Richmond had committed his most recent offence one month before the incident. He was convicted on that charge two days before the fatal collision. Driving an unlicensed vehicle forty-eight hours later, with a blood alcohol concentration of 0.166%, Richmond sped through a red light and crashed into another vehicle, killing two men.[72] He failed to appear in court. A warrant was issued for his arrest.[73] Richmond later stated that he was profoundly remorseful, describing his actions as 'atrocious'.[74] He said that he was disgusted with and ashamed of himself. In a statement read to the court, Richmond said he wished he could give the two men back to their families.[75]

Peter Liebeck and Ben Brown were killed. Danny Woolhead was left with serious injuries. On two counts of aggravated dangerous driving occasioning death, one count of dangerous driving occasioning grievous bodily harm, driving an unlicensed vehicle and driving under the influence, Richmond was sentenced to eight years' imprisonment, with six years non-parole.[76] There were rowdy scenes in the court, with Brown's sister trying to jump the dock in an attempt to attack Richmond. Family members screamed abuse when the sentence was handed down, calling him a 'dog'.[77] One man threatened that he would be waiting for Richmond on his release from prison and another shouted,

AFTER JESS: REFLECTING THE VALUE OF HUMAN LIFE?

'we hope you rot in hell'.[78] Outside the District Court, Peter Liebeck's mother told the media that the sentence was 'a joke' and that the laws must change.[79] Little did she know that, in the history of West Australian sentences, the penalty was far from a joke.

In spite of the efforts of some vocal members of the judiciary and successive governments, sentences in cases that fell short of the aggravating circumstance provisions remained fairly static. Matthew Eves was a case in point. The collision occurred in 2006, before the increase in maximum penalty for ordinary dangerous driving. Eves was towing a large trailer. He was witnessed veering all over the road. His driving was such that other drivers had attempted to get him to pull over.[80] Significantly fatigued and unwell, Eves had not eaten a great deal during the day.[81] He woke at 5.30 am and travelled south to Bunbury at around 6.15 am. He worked all day and around 8.30 pm drove back to Perth. The crash occurred on the Old Coast Road, sometime after 10.30 pm.[82] In the collision between Eves' vehicle, trailer and two oncoming cars, three people were killed.[83] Two men were incinerated in their car.[84] Eves said that he 'heard a bang and saw a vehicle explode behind him', but claimed he 'did not know that a collision had occurred'.[85] According to Eves, he returned to the scene and saw a man standing alight in front of a car, screaming for help and water. He left to seek assistance at the Lake Clifton Roadhouse, but on finding the roadhouse shut, drove to his mother's home, more than 100 kilometres away.[86] The timber frame of Eves' trailer was snapped in half.[87] Witnesses stated that there was no one at the scene matching Eves' description.[88] Eves contacted the police the following morning.[89] He received three cumulative sentences of one year and eight months for each death, a five-year sentence which was reduced on appeal to three years and four months. Justice Miller dissented.[90]

John Hellewell was another case in point. In 2008, 19-year-old P-plater, Hellewell, killed his girlfriend, 16-year-old Ashleigh Purser. Hellewell was racing another driver. He reached speeds of up to 130 km/h on the Mitchell Freeway and lost control of his vehicle, whereby his car spun right across the carriageway into a clump of trees. Hellewell initially entered a plea of not guilty. He claimed that the crash was caused by water on the road.[91] Crown Prosecutor, Mrs Fletcher, noted that Hellewell made 'a very serious and deliberate decision' to drive in the manner he did.[92] Subsequent to the offence in which his girlfriend was killed, he committed two further offences – exceeding the speed limit by more than 20 km/h and a drink-driving offence.[93] With a maximum custodial penalty of three years open to him, Magistrate Bayley referred Hellewell to the District Court so that he might receive a higher sentence. Hellewell was sentenced to sixteen months' imprisonment and made eligible for parole after eight months.[94] Ashleigh's stepfather, Tony Morrissey, described the sentence as 'simply pathetic' and a 'complete slap in the face'.[95] Her mother, Chelsea Morrissey, described it as a 'joke'.[96]

Cory Nepia-Keelan was another case in point. On 27 May 2011, the 23-year-old learner driver had a blood alcohol concentration of 0.107%. Travelling at night at speeds between 80 and 100 km/h in a suburban street with a 50 km/h limit, he lost control of his vehicle, traversing across three driveways and verges before slamming into Luke Beyer's vehicle. Beyer was stationary at an intersection. He had just finished work for the evening and had gone to collect his friends from the cinema. Beyer's parents were later forced to make the devastating decision to turn off their 17-year-old son's life support system. His mother described the point at which she finally began screaming – when her son turned blue.[97] Two of Beyer's passengers suffered minor injuries, as did Nepia-Keelan and his passenger. Nepia-Keelan pleaded guilty to dangerous driving occasioning death, two counts of dangerous driving occasioning bodily harm, drink-driving and contravening his learner's permit.[98] He was reportedly profoundly remorseful and overwhelmed with guilt, with District Court Judge Stavrianou noting that he had lost 20 kilograms since the crash.[99]

In sentencing Nepia-Keelan in February the following year, Judge Stavrianou stated that, drinking and driving was 'one of the most serious social problems causing loss of life' in Australia, and a term of immediate imprisonment had to be imposed to send a message of general deterrence. Nepia-Keelan was sentenced to four years' imprisonment, with a minimum non-parole period of two years. The court issued an order of $1,800 compensation to Luke's parents. He was also fined $750 for drink-driving and $250 for breaching his learner's permit.[100] Outside the court, Luke's mother told the media – 'Basically he's going to serve two years...I'm just shocked that that's the total time that he's going to spend in jail for ending my son's life...The penalties aren't tough enough and it makes me feel that his life wasn't worth anything'.[101]

The circumstances surrounding the death of Kerrie Christensen and the injuries sustained by her husband Rod in October 2012 fell just short of the 0.15% deeming provision. Suzanne McKenzie attended a day at the races with her estranged husband and their two children. The sentencing judge accepted evidence that the separated couple had argued. Suzanne's husband was the designated driver. In the course of an argument on the return journey home, he apparently threatened to drive the family into a ditch in order to kill them. Instead, he stopped the car, got out and left Suzanne stranded on the side of the road. She decided to drive her children home. On leaning into the back of the vehicle to comfort her children, Suzanne McKenzie swerved into the oncoming lane of traffic. McKenzie pleaded guilty to dangerous driving occasioning death, dangerous driving occasioning grievous bodily harm and drink-driving. Rod Christensen was in a coma for weeks and endured months of rehabilitation. McKenzie had a blood alcohol concentration of 0.139%. She was sentenced to two years' imprisonment, but was released on parole in July 2014. She was disqualified from driving for five years.[102]

In May 2015, McKenzie was granted an extraordinary licence. Her application was opposed by the Department of Transport. Under the terms of her licence, she was permitted to drive on weekdays between 7.00 am and 7.00 pm in order to attend work and take her children to school and medical appointments.[103] Shadow

Minister for Police, Road Safety and Crime Prevention, Michelle Roberts, told the media that 'decisions like this have the effect of reducing the severity of a judge's sentence – extraordinary licences should only be granted in extreme circumstances'.[104] Judge John Staude accepted that McKenzie's circumstances were 'extreme'. On a single-parent income, he noted, her costly commute to work involving taxis and public transport was causing 'extreme hardship'.[105] It was 'unduly expensive', 'unduly time-consuming' and 'unduly inconvenient'.[106]

It remains that successive State governments have failed to review the impact of the 2004 amendments. This work goes a long way towards addressing that omission. Despite being due to be tabled in 2006, the review has still not publicly materialised. This seems a remarkable breach of statutory obligation given the matter was brought to the attention of the former Liberal government in 2012. Nonetheless, it is clear that some of the most pessimistic predictions voiced in 2004 have not transpired. Drivers have *not* been subject to punitive sentencing or prosecution. Nor would it seem have they been held liable for circumstances beyond their control by virtue of the incapability provision. Far from punitive, it would seem that, over time, the provisions came to be viewed as inadequate – apparently, too many drivers were still slipping through cracks in the law. In 2016 and 2018, the Parliament would pass further amendments to widen the scope of culpable fault behind the wheel and address dangerous driving causing death's ostensible shortcomings.

Chapter Ten

A new offence – careless driving causing death – and another law for another girl – Charlotte's law

First proposed in 2015, the new careless driving causing death offence was all but buried within a sizeable omnibus Bill that amended four separate pieces of legislation.[1] Comparable offences were already in place in Tasmania, New South Wales, South Australia and the Australian Capital Territory. Queensland followed suit in mid-2018.[2] First tabled in November 2015, the West Australian Bill did not reappear before Parliament until August 2016. From its debut in 2015 to its consideration some nine months later, the Bill's scope and objectives expanded considerably. Nonetheless, it swiftly passed in just over a month. The *Road Traffic Legislation Amendment Act 2016* introduced many commendable initiatives, including compulsory blood testing in cases of death or injury, point-to-point speed cameras and alcohol interlocking devices. Licence disqualification would now commence from the date of release from custody. There remain, however, some aspects of the amendments which already show signs of failing their intended purpose.

As far back as April 2015, the former Minister for Police and Road Safety, Liza Harvey, touted the government's intention to introduce new offences of careless driving causing death, grievous bodily harm and bodily harm.[3] On grounds for reform, she noted that drivers who did not meet the threshold of dangerous driving causing death were charged only with careless driving simpliciter, and faced a maximum penalty of $600. Harvey described this as 'an insult' to bereaved families and loved ones.[4] While a $600 fine may certainly seem derisory, this penalty was not in place to reflect a death, but rather the *conduct* of the driving, that of *carelessness*, not the fatal outcome of which, rightly or wrongly, the driver had been acquitted. Nevertheless, the government sought to rectify 'insults' by increasing the maximum fine for careless driving simpliciter to $1,500, a more appropriate reflection of the quantum of risk, and by introducing careless driving causing death, with a maximum penalty of three years' imprisonment or a fine of up to $36,000.[5] Such custodial terms have rarely been handed down in 'ordinary' cases of dangerous driving occasioning death. Fines of that magnitude have never been imposed.

Careless driving causing death, more accurately careless driving *occasioning* death, sailed through Parliament. Had successive governments carried out their obligation to review the operation of dangerous driving causing death under the 2004 amendments and *table* those findings as required, or review the findings of the operation of careless driving causing death in other jurisdictions, members might have been better equipped to interrogate the government's Bill. The passage of yet another driving-causing-death offence might not have been so smooth. In addition to transparency and statutory obligation, it would seem to be a matter of common sense to review the operation of the *existing* offence, before introducing *yet* another, in part designed to address the apparent failings of the existing provisions. There was, however, little opposition in Parliament.

Nick Goiran and Shadow Attorney General John Quigley, both former barristers, raised concerns, as did Bill Johnston and Rob Johnson, former Minister for Police, Emergency Services and Road Safety under the Liberal government, turned Independent.

Johnson assured his parliamentary colleagues that he felt sorry for anyone who suffered because of the actions of a careless driver, but he opined that sending drivers to prison for up to three years for momentary distraction was 'draconian'.[6] Johnson was not opposed to punishment in some form, but characterised the extent of the penalty regime as the Minister 'trying to sound and be tough'.[7] He rightly observed that cases involving drunk and drug-affected drivers had failed to attract the penalties the government now proposed for the much lesser offence of carelessness.[8] Shadow Attorney General Quigley described the move to imprison a momentarily distracted driver, *not a driver*, he emphasised, who was on the phone or texting, but one who was momentarily distracted without any other evidence of improper conduct, as 'harsh and unusual' and that there was no quality of that conduct which could warrant imprisonment.[9] He labelled the proposed penalty a 'travesty' and a tough-on-crime move.[10]

Labor Member Bill Johnston feared the new offence would have the undesirable upshot of watering down *existing* penalties and verdicts. Directing his concerns to cases involving injury, he observed that it 'seems we are now giving the courts a way out of convicting people for the more serious offence of dangerous driving causing bodily harm'.[11] Johnston's concerns are equally applicable to fatality cases. In response, Minister Harvey claimed that the new offence should *not* be considered an alternative to dangerous driving,[12] odd given the fact that cases which resulted in careless driving convictions because they failed the threshold of dangerous was a stated purpose for the new offence. Even more perplexing, the Minister claimed that, 'once alcohol is involved' the threshold of dangerous driving is generally met,[13] erroneous given that a blood alcohol concentration below 0.15% does not meet the threshold of dangerousness. Minutes later she stated that, if the elements of dangerous driving causing bodily harm were not met and the accused was likely to be acquitted, then the alternative verdict could be considered.[14]

The Liberal Party's own Nick Goiran said that while he supported the majority of the Bill, he wished to 'distance' himself from 'one element'.[15] He was particularly concerned that a person who committed an act of carelessness could be sent to prison. Touching on strong community sentiments, he observed that 'the issue here is that the community will say, "Yes, but someone has died", and because someone has died there has to be a substantial penalty'.[16] While Goiran understood why emotions ran high, he was not convinced that the offence ought to be introduced, nor was he persuaded that a maximum penalty of three years' imprisonment was justified, particularly when the severity of that penalty was 'above and beyond every other Australian jurisdiction' with a comparable offence, an accurate observation.[17] Goiran feared the 'unintended consequences' that careless driving causing death might bring about.[18] Rising to speak to his colleagues well after 9.00 pm on 13 September 2016, he stated that any one of them might be momentarily inattentive on the way home that night and cause a 'freak accident' which could result in imprisonment.[19] In the media that same day, the author warned listeners and readers of unintended consequences of an altogether different variety.[20] Surprisingly, the new offence attracted no other media coverage.

By introducing careless driving occasioning death, the former government sought to target a number of related issues. The offence broadens the scope of liability, netting a greater number of drivers within the compass of culpable fault. Minister Harvey stated that careless driving causing death would bring distracted or inattentive drivers who killed other road users while putting on make-up, changing the radio station, drinking coffee or addressing passengers in the back seat, for example, to account.[21] Yet as far back as the late 1970s, sober drivers who were *not* travelling at speed and momentarily took their attention from the road in order to speak to passengers in the back seat were successfully prosecuted for *dangerous* driving causing death.[22] Granted, these were rare instances, but they have been brought before the courts.

The new offence also provides police and prosecutors with a mechanism to charge drivers whose conduct falls short of shifting socio-legal understandings of what constitutes dangerousness. It also addresses the difficulties of securing a conviction in the absence of an eyewitness or aggravating circumstances. The offence ostensibly provides a safety net to prevent drivers getting off 'scot-free'. While one suspects that the primary motivation was the difficulty of sustaining a charge of dangerous driving occasioning death, this was absent from the public discussion, a discussion overshadowed by rectifying 'insults' to families.

Some of the rationale put forth in favour of the offence seemed inconsistent. In the Bill's second reading speech, Minister Harvey noted that 'the distinction between what is considered driving in a "dangerous" manner and what is considered "careless" driving can be negligible'.[23] Paradoxically, nine months later she said that, 'the gap between dangerous driving causing death and careless driving where a death may have been caused, is significant'.[24] Addressing the Upper House, Attorney General Michael Mischin said that there were 'too many variables to enable specific definitions to be prescribed of what constitutes dangerous or careless driving'.[25] As such, he objected that the determination of the degree of fault was 'left to the discretion of the court[s] to decide by relying upon the facts of the case and precedents',[26] a process which seems entirely proper. He too described the difference between the offences as often 'negligible'.[27] The Attorney General also said –

> Members will be aware that at times there has been public disquiet about the perceived leniency of the small fine given to a driver of a vehicle involved in a crash that has resulted in a death. One of the reasons that this occurs is the court could not conclusively establish that the actions of the driver were dangerous rather than careless.[28]

In addition to bringing more drivers within the scope of culpable fault, the standard of proof for the new offence, driving 'without due care and attention', offers the possibility of doing away with the problems of conclusively proving difficult cases of dangerousness by substituting a lesser offence with a lower bar.

However, this ease may bring with it dangerous consequences. Public disquiet may, in fact, amplify.

The move to introduce a new offence had been building momentum for some time. Cathie Moloney's daughter, Courtney, died in a crash with her 17-year-old cousin, Scott, in 2006. The 16-year-old driver lost control of the vehicle and collided with a tree. He survived, as did one other passenger. At the time of the incident, he held only a learner's permit. Charged with contravening the conditions of his permit, he was not charged with Courtney or Scott's death, nor was he deprived of his permit.[29] Courtney's death set Cathie Moloney on a path of reform, lobbying that more charges should be introduced, such as 'contravening learner driver conditions causing death, injury or damage'.[30] While sympathetic to her grief, her proposal would have steered the focus away from the central issue; that is, the level of fault in the *manner* of the driving, not the tragic outcome. Moloney's proposal would have all but done away with a conduct element, bar contravening a permit. While there should be serious consequences for breaching a learner's permit, aligning the *contravention* of a permit with a homicide offence, where the causative nexus lies between the breach of conditions and the death seemed tenuous at best. The core of Cathie Moloney's understandable grievance is that her child was killed and the driver was not held to account, nor penalised in any way. The driver, who had completed only twenty-five hours of supervised driving, was driving the car along a gravel road when he lost traction and hit a tree.[31] Plainly, he lacked the experience to handle a vehicle under those circumstances, as many drivers would. The Coroner ruled the death an accident.

Moloney's campaign gained traction five years after her daughter died. In January 2011, former West Australian Coroner, Alastair Hope, released his findings in relation to the death of Jeremy Armstrong.[32] Armstrong was struck by a taxi driver, John Brennan, just after 5.00 am on Ocean Drive, Bunbury, on 14 December 2008. As the Coroner's report noted, 'visibility was particularly good and there were no nearby obstructions which could have impeded the ability of the driver of the motor vehicle from seeing the deceased'.[33] Armstrong was on the road when he was hit directly and head-on by Brennan.[34] The Coroner found that Armstrong 'must have been within Mr Brennan's line of vision for a significant period prior to the collision'.[35] There were no trees or vegetation obscuring his vision. For a driver keeping a proper lookout, at 185 centimetres tall Jeremy Armstrong was arguably there for all to see. A report provided by WA Police to the Coroner suggested that vegetation may have obstructed Brennan's vision. The Coroner described this suggestion as 'wholly without merit'. Inspection and photographs of the area plainly demonstrated that the site was clear of vegetation of any note.[36] Brennan actually stated in his police interview that the vegetation was so negligible that it 'wouldn't cover blind Freddy'.[37] There were no eyewitnesses.

Central to the inquest was the question of *how* Brennan ploughed directly into Armstrong, apparently without seeing him, as if he suddenly materialised from nowhere. The very limited evidence taken from the scene, and that which emerged at inquest, indicated that he made no attempt to avoid the collision, brake or, at minimum, slow down prior to impact.[38] While the paucity of evidence collected by police made the task of determining what occurred especially difficult, Coroner Hope suggested that Brennan might have fallen asleep, or was perhaps looking out of his rear view mirror and not paying attention. Brennan was driving the penultimate hour of a twelve-hour shift.[39]

The Coroner's findings were extensive, the bulk of his report concerning the failures of the officers involved. The police were heavily criticised for failing to adequately investigate the crash, document or capture evidence from the scene, in addition to blithely accepting Brennan's version of events. Coroner Hope noted that there was confusion and miscommunication between Major Crash Investigation and the South West Traffic Office regarding responsibility for, and potential follow-up of, the incident.⁴⁰ A series of systemic failures and delays made it impossible to contemplate charges against Brennan. The actions of the officers were contrary to routine procedures. Officer in Charge of South West Traffic Section, Sergeant Ashley Bean, was 'extremely critical' of the litany of failures and he accurately predicted adverse coverage from the Coroner and the public.⁴¹ While not in any way diminishing the magnitude of those failures, the history of West Australian prosecution outcomes demonstrates that a charge in such circumstances would have been extremely difficult, albeit not impossible, to mount. While Brennan hit a man who was apparently there for all to see, he was not, by any eyewitness account, driving dangerously, although that inference was open on the limited evidence.

In frustration, Coroner Hope emphasised that, far from being an isolated event, the failure to undertake the most 'basic investigative steps' following fatal collisions and treat crash sites as crime scenes had been a persistent problem in Western Australia, which he had repeatedly criticised over a decade.⁴² Amongst other things, he noted that police officers were ignoring the instructions of the Commissioner of Police.⁴³ As the police investigation failed to 'reach basic standards of competency', the officers involved failed to question Brennan's version of events and collect evidence from the scene, in addition to the lack of an eyewitness, the Coroner said that he was not able 'to determine whether the death arose by way of an unlawful homicide or as a result of an accident'.⁴⁴ On that basis, he delivered an open finding.⁴⁵

The Coroner recommended that consideration be given to amending WA's *Road Traffic Act* to introduce an offence in line with s 2B of the United Kingdom's *Road Traffic Act 1988*; that is, causing death by careless or inconsiderate driving.⁴⁶ It was this recommendation that Minister Harvey relied upon when recommending the offence to Parliament. The Coroner held it regrettable that no alternative offence was in place, of less gravitas than dangerous driving causing death, to charge those whose conduct fell below that of a reasonably prudent driver.⁴⁷

At the time Coroner Hope made his recommendation, he would not have had the opportunity to avail himself of the operation of UK's offence over an extended period, or the impact of like offences in other Australian jurisdictions. Had he, he may have expressed some reservations. In April 2015, almost four-and-a-half years later, the media announced Minister Harvey's intention to follow through on Hope's recommendation – 'WA drivers set to be hit with a new careless driving offence'.[48] The headline was emotively underscored by an image of Cathie Moloney holding a photograph of her dead daughter.

Perth barrister, Linda Black, of the WA Bar Association, was drawn into the fray. She told the press that the introduction of such an offence 'could see otherwise good drivers being severely punished'.[49] If seventy years of Western Australian sentences are any yardstick, Black's concerns regarding punitive sentencing are unlikely to come to fruition. Rarely have drivers been *severely* punished. Often they have barely been punished at all. The new offence does have the potential to bring the most trivial infractions within the scope of the law. While the benchmark of driving 'without due care and attention' could open the door to punitive action, there is no evidence to date of excessive, undue punishments.

Black's fundamental concern, similar to that of parliamentarians Johnson, Quigley and Goiran, is that a minor infraction could attract a significant penalty because of the fatal consequence, rather than the degree of *fault* demonstrated in the manner of the driving. As Black told the media – simply because a driver's actions may have precipitated an 'extraordinarily extreme outcome' does not necessitate that the law should deal with drivers in an 'extremely serious way'.[50] She noted that what the law *should* be addressing is the driving conduct – 'what is it that you have done and is your conduct worthy of that kind of punishment?'[51]

In the divergence between Harvey's concerns about 'insults' and Black's apprehensions of draconianism, there are other issues at stake. Hackneyed it may be, but if history has a habit of repeating itself, the government's best intentions may backfire. If past evidence offers any instruction, one of the greatest dangers of introducing yet another driving-occasioning-death offence is its inappropriate utilisation, in turn attenuating the nomenclature of *all* conduct, save for the most aberrant. This would be an outcome counterintuitive to the objective of elevating the seriousness and widening the scope of fault behind the wheel.

The introduction of dangerous driving causing death in 1974 saw a wide range of conduct, some which could *only* be described as criminally negligent, become *dangerous*. Thereafter, when a vehicle was involved, a charge of manslaughter became increasingly reserved for the homicidal driving Other, not prerequisite in the absence of a vehicle. The dilution of criminal negligence to dangerousness, in name and characterisation, was partially bolstered by inappropriately preferencing charges under the *Road Traffic Act* as opposed to the Code, and by shoring up the most aberrant conduct as *dangerous* by increasing the proscribed circumstances of aggravation. High-speed police chases and driving 45 km/h over the speed limit spring to mind.

Following the 2016 amendments, what was once appositely dangerous could potentially be diluted to careless, particularly if the poor investigative practices Coroner Hope complained of have continued, and if unambiguous guidelines and charging standards are not in place. In addition to these concerns, it is important to emphasise that momentary misjudgement and lapses in concentration can fall within the compass of dangerousness. The case law is resolutely clear that there is scope and precedent to elevate careless to dangerous, contingent on the context in which that driving occurs.[52] Yet, the danger is that a path-of-least-resistance approach to prosecutions, reluctance on behalf of jurors and inadequate training of officers, may in turn lead to only the most *aberrant* conduct being characterised as dangerous driving, in the same manner that vehicular manslaughter became a species apart. This would be a disastrous outcome. A great deal will rest on how the offence is utilised by police and prosecutors.

Since causing death by careless driving came into force in the UK in 2008, strong criticisms have emerged from a number of quarters. Some have argued that the sentencing regime is punitive and may lead to further tragedy in the shape of 'manifestly excessive custodial sentence[s]'.[53] Others have warned against retaliatory punishments for 'tragic driving errors'.[54] Perhaps such critics have little to fear. In 2015, the road safety charity, Brake, submitted that the availability of the lesser causing-death offence had led police and prosecutors to preference charges of causing death by careless driving over dangerous driving for ease of conviction, even in circumstances of significant aggravation.[55] Unfortunately, Brake cited few cases to support its contention. In an incident where a 14-year-old girl was killed by a speeding, drug-affected driver, the driver was charged with causing death by *careless* driving and received a four-month custodial term. He was released after eight weeks.[56] This example was not supported by further case studies in its submission, though Brake's website offered additional examples. On 3 October 2015, for instance, Bob Allaway was killed by a driver whose blood alcohol concentration was two-and-a-half times the legal limit. Andrew Crook was driving on the wrong side of the road when he collided with Allaway who was driving a motorbike. Crook pleaded guilty to causing death by *careless* driving while under the influence. Of his four-year-and-eight-month sentence, he was set to serve two-and-a-half years.[57] 'Careless' seems an erroneous characterisation of Crook's conduct.

Some legal scholarship presents a challenge to Brake's claims.[58] Using three police districts, Professor Sally Kyd examined case files and scrutinised decisions made by police and prosecutors in selecting appropriate charges over a two-year period following the introduction of the new offence, in conjunction with interviews.[59] Based on that evidence, Kyd found that the introduction of causing death by careless driving 'had little or no effect on the way in which prosecutors categorise bad driving resulting in a fatality'.[60] While she noted victim support groups' concerns that prosecutions for causing death by dangerous driving have 'fallen quite dramatically' since causing death by careless or inconsiderate driving was introduced, *her* findings suggested that charges were 'not generally being downgraded'.[61] On Kyd's early sample, it appeared that the availability of the new offence had reduced the overall rate of acquittals.[62]

Contrary to Kyd's early findings, more recent criticisms have emerged from less emotive quarters than victim support charities. In March 2016, the UK House of Commons Transport Committee on Road Traffic Law Enforcement released its findings.[63] Based on official statistics from England and Wales, the Committee's report demonstrated that there had been a *substantial* decline in the number of convictions for causing death by dangerous driving, from 241 in 2004, to 123 convictions in 2014.[64] The report further observed that, following the commencement of the new offence of causing death by careless driving in 2008, between 2009 and 2014, convictions for the new offence more than doubled, from eighty-one to 163.[65] Correspondingly, in the same period, convictions for causing death by dangerous driving fell. There were 225 convictions in 2009 and by 2014 that figure had dropped to 123.[66] The report held that, as the *aggregate* number of convictions had not appreciably declined, conduct which would have previously been brought before the courts as dangerous was now being downgraded to careless and inconsiderate. As such, the report recommended that the Justice Select Committee investigate the matter.[67] If such a trend were replicated in Western Australia, it would be a regressive step. In the brief time that has passed since the introduction of careless driving causing death in WA, such outcomes have not come to pass. However, only two years in and trouble was already afoot.

In August 2018, a Western Australian Police review revealed that the most severe penalty imposed to date for careless driving causing death was a suspended jail term.[68] At the end of August 2018, of the seven people charged where cases were finalised, not one driver had been sent to prison.[69] Penalties for causing death ranged from fines as low as $2,500 to $7,500, with two suspended terms of imprisonment and one intensive supervision order.⁷⁰ Equally, of the thirty-two offences of careless driving causing *grievous bodily harm*, no driver had been sent to jail, although the maximum fine imposed had been somewhat higher at $9,000.⁷¹ In fact, as of October 2018, only three offenders had been incarcerated, for terms of eight, nine and fourteen months.⁷² Surprisingly, all of those imprisoned were found guilty of careless driving causing *bodily harm*, not death or grievous bodily harm.⁷³ The Road Safety Minister, Michelle Roberts, advised that she was seeking advice from the Road Safety Commission on *strengthening* the legislation,⁷⁴ as though it were not robust enough. A keen supporter of the introduction of the new offence, Roberts seemed to apportion some blame for its apparent failure on the former government, as though the *government* were responsible for handing down, or failing to hand down, adequate penalties. According to Roberts, the government had 'promised' that the introduction of the new offence and its penalty regime 'would address concerns that those culpable for a road death or injury were not receiving adequate penalties'.⁷⁵ As she told the media, 'this didn't appear to be the case'.⁷⁶

The first charges brought under the new legislation were for the deaths of two passengers and the grievous bodily harm of another. On 9 December 2016, Zimo Li was driving near Wave Rock, 340 kilometres east of Perth, when he reportedly lost control of his car in the transition from a sealed to an unsealed section of road. The loss of control was *so* substantial that he rolled the vehicle and two passengers, not wearing seatbelts, were thrown from the car.⁷⁷ Li pleaded guilty. He received a suspended seven-month custodial term. He was disqualified from driving for three months.⁷⁸

The characterisation 'death driver' was employed to label Yanfang Yu, a 34-year-old woman who, on executing a right turn across a dual carriageway in September 2017, failed to see 90-year-old Wasyl Czwerenczuk's oncoming vehicle, crossing directly into his path.⁷⁹ Mr Czwerenczuk died twenty-five days later. He suffered 'horrific internal injuries', was reportedly in 'unbearable pain' and finally succumbed to death when his lungs collapsed.[80] Magistrate Benn characterised Yu's driving at the 'lower end of the range of culpability' and the fault as 'an instance in which Ms Yu, for whatever reason...*simply* did not see Mr Czwerenczuk's vehicle' [italics added].[81] While 'death driver' seemed an exaggerated portrayal, perhaps Ms Yu might have endeavoured to look harder. She was profoundly remorseful, cried throughout proceedings, offered profuse apologies and pleaded guilty. She was fined $5,000.[82]

Jan De Groote, a 79-year-old woman, was also fined. On 20 April 2018, executing a right-hand turn across a dual carriageway, De Groote failed to see a motorcyclist who tried to avoid her vehicle, but hit the passenger side.[83] Major Crash investigators appealed to the public for witnesses.[84] While the deceased, not named in the media, received emergency surgery for the traumatic head injury he sustained, he died seven days later. De Groote was fined $3,000.[85]

One of the most troubling cases to date was that of Che Curyer. On 23 December 2016, the 24-year-old L-plater was driving a utility vehicle with two passengers, about 1,000 kilometres east of Perth on Eyre Highway. It was 4.30 am, a rather unusual time to engage in supervised driving instruction. According to reports, the utility vehicle 'veered' off the highway and 'rolled several times', ceasing its trajectory in a ditch.[86] Curyer was reportedly tired, having slept only a few hours.[87] He apparently 'ran' from the crash scene and was located the following day, walking along the highway.[88] Back at the scene, 21-year-old Joanna Taylor was dead and her fiancé, Michael Nunez, was injured. Due to face court in November 2017, Curyer, a resident of South Australia, failed to appear. He was arrested and extradited.[89] On 18 July 2018, he pleaded guilty to careless driving causing death in the Perth Magistrate's Court. He was fined $2,500.

Notwithstanding the assertion that the new offence would rectify insults to bereaved loved ones, Joanna's parents seemed decidedly insulted. Channel Seven News headlined its interview with a description of the fine – 'inadequate and offensive'.[90] Joanna's mother, Jeanette Taylor, told the media that, 'everyone we've spoken to thinks the $2,500 fine is a joke'.[91] Joanna's father, Ken Taylor, indicated that the sentence fell well short of his expectations and the advice they had been given. 'We were expecting jail', he told the media. 'We had already been told (the maximum was) three years, now it is $2,500'.[92] His wife added that she believed the maximum three-year penalty was insufficient.[93] Just over one month later, Western Australian Police announced that they would appeal against the sentence.[94] On appeal in January 2019, Justice Curthoys described the fine as 'manifestly inadequate'.[95] He sentenced Curyer to nine months' imprisonment, but suspended the sentence.[96] In tears and disbelief, Jeanette Taylor told the media that Curyer had 'walked again for taking a life' and that she had 'no faith in the WA legal system'.[97] Indignant, Ken Taylor described it as 'a crock of shit'.[98]

While both the fine and suspended term of imprisonment imposed upon Curyer seem egregiously low, the Taylors' expectations seemed to have been falsely raised, not only on the basis of the maximum penalty and the possibility of that being imposed, but in the context of the scope of sentences handed down for dangerous driving and manslaughter to date. Despite the rhetoric, a $36,000 fine or up to three years in prison was *never* going to be imposed when regular cases of dangerous driving causing death would rarely receive such penalties, and some involving circumstances of aggravation might fall within that scope. As the author told the media, 'putting in place such sentencing provisions, without close regard to the history of sentences, raises unrealistic expectations in the community'.[99]

Plainly, if Melissa Waters could, with a blood alcohol concentration of 0.17%, kill an infant by ploughing across two lanes of traffic, up an embankment, through a fence and into a child's bedroom, thereby demolishing it, and receive three years and eight months in prison and be released after a year and ten months,[100] it is hard to imagine how Curyer could have received a comparable term. Or, more recently, consider the conduct and sentence in Aine Marie McGrath's case. McGrath veered across *four* lanes of traffic on the freeway, at speeds estimated at over 100 km/h and, following an exchange of text messages with her boyfriend, the last received twelve seconds before the first emergency call was made, killed her colleague. For dangerous driving causing death, she received three years and eight months' imprisonment, with parole eligibility set at twenty-two months.[101]

The Nepia-Keelan case bears some similarities to Curyer's. The defendant was, at twenty-three, of a similar age *and* a learner driver. The cases differ in that Nepia-Keelan had a blood alcohol concentration of 0.107% and was exceeding the speed limit between 30 and 50 km/h. He pleaded guilty to dangerous driving occasioning death, two counts of dangerous driving occasioning bodily harm, drink-driving and contravening his learner's permit. He was sentenced to four years' imprisonment, with a minimum non-parole period of two years.[102]

Save for another era of advocacy, as in the past when the judiciary and Crown argued it necessary to impose sentences commensurate with which the legislature and the community regarded deaths occasioned by the use of motor vehicles,[103] advocacy that brought about higher penalties for the most serious offenders, the status quo looks set to continue. Irrespective of the scope of penalties afforded by the legislature, sentences *cannot* and *will not* increase unless a comprehensive re-evaluation of sentencing occurs across the *entire* spectrum of fault, and particularly if sentences for 'ordinary' dangerous conduct continue to remain stubbornly static.

Sentences aside, and while purely speculative without crime scene evidence, of additional interest in the Li and Curyer cases are the charges laid. In traversing from a sealed to an unsealed section of road, Li lost control and rolled the vehicle. Experience would suggest that, in order to *roll* the vehicle, he had likely failed to modify his driving in accordance with the circumstances and was travelling at some speed – potentially meeting the benchmark of dangerousness. Again, in the absence of crime scene evidence and the testimony of surviving passengers, whether the driving constituted a *serious* breach of proper conduct is not possible to determine. However, despite the lack of evidence made public, the case does bring to mind the High Court's observations in *King v The Queen* in 2012 —

> it may be that in many if not most cases dangerous driving is a manifestation of negligence in the sense of carelessness. It may also be a manifestation of deliberate risk-taking behaviour. It may be in some circumstances where particular attention is required to the road and to other road users, momentary inattention will result in a manner of driving which is dangerous...'[104]

Again speculative, but notably Curyer veered off a highway, rolled the vehicle *several* times and ended up in a ditch. Evidence from the crash scene would be of particular interest, particularly tyre marks, evidence of braking (if any), distance travelled and the vehicle's trajectory. It is hard to conceive that the manner of Curyer's driving was but a simple omission of due care and attention. Notably, numerous cases of driving while tired have been successfully prosecuted as dangerous driving causing death and some have resulted in a custodial term.[105]

Tragic outcomes aside, driving without due care and attention would be unlikely to produce such an extraordinary trajectory. One fears that the Curyer and Li cases already point to the inappropriate employ of carelessness, where in fact dangerous driving could have been contemplated. Carelessness may be at risk of becoming the partial reserve of cases with particular investigative and evidential difficulties. Worse still, it may become the repository of lenient prosecutorial discretion. In light of the growing acceptance that the danger and devastation occasioned by the mismanagement of vehicles is unacceptable, West Australians might have been better served by continuing to widen the scope of what constitutes dangerous conduct and sentence within the *extensive* range afforded by the legislature. Without clear charging standards and guidelines, the inappropriate employ of careless driving causing death may inadvertently undermine the goal of underscoring the seriousness of the conduct, dilute charges, and fail to rectify, if not worsen, the 'insult' to the bereaved. The price of netting drivers who previously fell through the ostensible cracks in the law may prove very high.

A crash that occurred in late 2015 would see the Western Australian Parliament introduce a new offence in the name of yet another beloved daughter. In November that year, 19-year-old Charlotte Pemberton was violently killed.[106] Her grieving father, Wayne Pemberton, spoke to the media, initially insisting that any driver who was blatantly irresponsible and killed someone on the roads should be automatically subject to a minimum ten-year term.[107] The Pemberton family became vocal advocates for amending the law.[108] Premier McGowan and Police Minister Roberts were 'shocked' by the sentence, a sentence 'completely out of kilter' with community expectations.[109] While it was undoubtedly out of kilter with public sentiment, it was not out of kilter with trends in sentencing.

Motorcyclist, Dylan James Adams, ploughed into an intersection in Forrestfield at speed, colliding with Joshua Gallagher, Charlotte's boyfriend. Charlotte was in the front passenger seat of Joshua's car. She was but two minutes from home, but died two hours later in hospital. Adams was travelling at 94 km/h per hour in a 60 km/h zone.[110] Some estimates were 6 km/h higher.[111] It was not possible to establish with certainty that Adams was travelling at 45 km/h or more over the limit, thus his offence fell outside of the aggravating circumstance provisions and therefore the maximum twenty-year penalty.[112] Reports on Adams' behaviour at the crash scene underscored appraisals of his character. A member of the Rebels bikie gang, he seemed more concerned about his gang paraphernalia than the lives of his victims, insisting that paramedics should not cut his Rebels vest.[113] Adams was not licensed to drive a motorcycle.[114]

CARELESS DRIVING CAUSING DEATH AND CHARLOTTE'S LAW

Adams pleaded guilty to dangerous driving causing death. On 21 March 2017, he was sentenced to four years and three months' imprisonment, with eligibility for parole in just over two years. Judge McCann formed the opinion that a five-year penalty was in order, but gave Adams the benefit of a reduction in sentence in recognition of his plea.[115] Adams was also convicted of an additional count of no authority to drive. For the latter he was fined $200.[116] Judge McCann spoke of the 'wilfulness' of Adams' conduct and his apparent 'cold-blooded decision to endanger people'.[117] Speaking to the media, Charlotte's father described his family's 'heart-ripping, brain-torturing' grief.[118] Minister Roberts and Premier McGowan felt that the 'penalty did not come close enough' to the ten-year maximum and requested that the Director for Public Prosecutions review the sentence in light of other case outcomes,[119] initially urging an appeal.[120] Not surprisingly, the advice from Public Prosecutions was that the 'penalty was within the sentencing range' and that an appeal might in fact risk a *reduction* in penalty.[121] Wayne Pemberton could not conceive how the sentence reflected the magnitude of the conduct or the value of human life. Like so many loved ones before him, he asked of the sentence – 'How does that equate to my daughter's life?'[122]

In context, Adams' head sentence was reasonably significant. He was not intoxicated, or driving a stolen vehicle or under police pursuit, factors which would not have lent support to an appeal. Nonetheless, his status as an 'outlaw motorcycle gang member'[123] and his hostility at the scene, including yelling at paramedics and refusing a blood test, did much to engender the public to the grief of Charlotte's parents and their subsequent campaign, as did the fact that Adams had a history of traffic offending.

Nearly three years after Ms Pemberton was killed, the WA Parliament passed Charlotte's law, otherwise known as the *Road Traffic Amendment (Driving Offences) Act 2018* (WA). Charlotte's law amended West Australia's *Road Traffic Act* and *Road Traffic (Authorisation to Drive) Act 2008*. In essence, the amendments targeted two aspects of Adams' offending – his speed and that he was not licensed to drive a motorcycle – and made both circumstances of aggravation and thus liable to a maximum term of imprisonment of twenty years. In regard to speed, the amendments quite sensibly reduced the 45 km/h circumstance of aggravation to 30 km/h.[124] On authority to drive, the changes were comprehensive. Those who had never held any form of licence, or were not licensed to drive, or had applied for but been refused a licence, or were disqualified at the time of the incident, or were required to drive with an alcohol interlocking device and failed to do so, or were in breach of a prescribed authorisation (such an extraordinary licence holder driving outside of authorised hours) would now, were they found guilty of dangerous driving causing death, have committed the offence in a circumstance of aggravation, thus exposing them to the maximum penalty.[125]

The Bill's passage through Parliament was swift. It received unanimous support, with some small disclaimers. Members stood, one after the other, commending the Bill and offering sincere condolences and congratulations to the Pemberton family for their tenacity in the face of devastating grief. Those who rose to speak invariably stated that sentences were entirely out of touch with community expectations. With the circumstances of aggravation broadened, apparently drivers were now going to spend a long time in jail and feel the full force of the law.[126] The Pemberton family's loss was said not to be in vain.[127]

In the context of the merits of increasing terms of imprisonment by expanding the circumstances of aggravation, of particular interest was a case cited by Member Cassie Rowe. The apparent irony of the case's outcome seemed lost on Rowe, nor did it attract commentary from her colleagues. Citing Tony Kentwell who told the media, 'we are the ones who now have to serve the life sentence, but these drivers get almost nothing',[128] Ms Rowe noted the case of Amiel James Tittums, a 35-year-old father of two who, travelling at a speed of up to 165 km/h in a 90 km/h zone, killed 27-year-old Cowen Joseph Kentwell, 23-year-old Felicity Jane Pallett and 31-year-old Michael Hook.[129]

Tittums had a blood alcohol concentration of 0.130% and traces of valium, doxylamine and methylamphetamine in his blood.[130] He ploughed into the rear of Ms Pallett's Holden Commodore, forcing her car off the road into trees and rupturing its fuel tank. The car burst into flames.[131] From the point of impact, Amiel Tittums' vehicle continued to travel 82 metres.[132] He abandoned his vehicle and three victims at the scene and walked 1.5 kilometres home, where he showered and went to bed.[133] He did not notify anyone of the crash.

Tittums was charged with three counts of *aggravated* dangerous driving causing death, failure to report the incident and failure to render assistance.[134] He initially lied to police, claiming he had not driven the vehicle and, despite extensive bruising consistent with a seatbelt, was not injured.[135] Tittums pleaded guilty, notably not at the first available opportunity.[136] On appeal, his total sentence was increased, although the terms for the death were reduced and made wholly concurrent. He ultimately received three sentences of six years for each of the deceased, to be served concurrently, with two further sentences of four years and another two on the other remaining charges, the former to be served cumulatively on the six years and the latter concurrent. With a total sentence of ten years, he was made eligible for parole after eight.[137]

Importantly Tittums was convicted of three counts of *aggravated* dangerous driving causing death. Ms Rowe cited the case as an apparent failure of justice, yet simultaneously argued that the Charlotte's law provisions, which increased the circumstances of aggravation for speed and no authority to drive, would ensure that the 'full force of the law' would come down upon drivers and 'strong penalties' would now apply.[138] The circumstances of aggravation under Charlotte's law would apparently ensure that drivers received strong penalties. Given Tittums killed three people and was sentenced *under* the aggravating provisions, it is hard to see how. Notwithstanding, when questioned by Member Peter Katsambanis on what Adams' sentence *might* have been under the new laws and in light of community expectations, Minister

Roberts quite surprisingly stated that she expected a judge could potentially double the sentence to eight-and-a-half years. Such comments raise unrealistic expectations and show scant regard for sentencing precedents across the spectrum of fault.

On this anticipated sentence of eight-and-a-half years for speeding without a motorbike licence, one might consider the likelihood of the Minister's predictions against the outcome in the Antony Fogarty manslaughter case in 2014. Fogarty was engaged in a prolonged high-speed police chase. He ran several red lights at speeds of up to 170 km/h. He had never held a driver's licence. Driving a stolen vehicle, he was heavily under the influence of methamphetamine and cannabis. He told paramedics at the scene that he was not the driver – 'the bastard ran off'.[139] In monitored telephone calls whilst on remand, Fogarty disclosed that he was in fact the driver. Kulpdeep Singh, a taxi driver, had just collected Dr Sean Barrett from Perth airport. In the collision between Fogarty and Singh's vehicles, the taxi burst into flames. Fogarty pleaded guilty to two counts of manslaughter and a raft of other offences. He was sentenced to eleven years' imprisonment, with nine years non-parole.[140] Clearly, Dylan Adams' conduct in the spectrum of fault was nowhere approaching that of Antony Fogarty's. Despite parliamentarians' expectations, it is hard to imagine how, in the current environment, his sentence could either. Sentences *cannot* increase unless there is a wholesale shift in sentencing across the board.

In closing, on considering Charlotte's law, former Senior Crown Prosecutor turned parliamentarian, Shadow Attorney General Michael Mischin, made a number of significant observations. He did firmly state, however, that his observations were not a bar to supporting the amendments.[141] Mischin noted an ongoing piecemeal approach, whereby governments kept 'tweaking' circumstances of aggravation, returning to the legislation repeatedly.[142] While he noted this might be 'expeditious', he was ultimately concerned that it was 'counterproductive'.[143] He thought it would be preferable to take the approach that the maximum imposable term was set at twenty years and to 'let the courts impose penalties within that range'.[144] While he *hoped* that Charlotte's law would have an impact of modifying driver's behaviour, he doubted the likelihood of 'exercising people's minds in deterring them from poor driving'.[145] One equally doubts the likelihood of it delivering the penalties predicted.

Conclusion

A lesser species of homicide

Since 1925, when national fatality statistics were first compiled, until the time of writing, in the order of 225,000 people have died or been *killed* on Australian roads. On the matter of killed, in 2016 the Tasmanian Sentencing Advisory Council suggested that sentences for driving-causing-death offences and vehicular manslaughter should be 'appropriate',[1] a position that should equally apply to all State and Territory jurisdictions. The Council in turn observed that its statement raised the obvious question – 'appropriate to what?'[2] The short answer – sentences *should* be appropriate and proportionate to a driver's degree of fault or failure. Should that fault, failure, act or omission be so significant as to bring the driver within the scope of censure, sentences should also reflect the quantum of harm.

Historically, in the case of 'road deaths', a phrase that disguises human agency in addition to the often reckless and violent nature of offences, charges laid and sentences imposed fell manifestly short of *appropriate*. Where a vehicle was involved, notions of *appropriate* and *proportionate* were contentious. What constituted conduct worthy of censure was highly contested ground, muddied by our love affair with the vehicle, our *right* to drive, and tacit tolerance of risk-taking behaviours, including speeding and drink-driving. Of course, notions of 'accident' and crime are culturally contingent, and acutely so when so many people participate in the very transport system in which those deaths or killings occur, a fact that made the boundaries of blameworthiness difficult to shift. Displacing the residual category 'accident', and its understudy, misfortune, in favour of foreseeable risk and culpable fault was an extremely difficult battle, a battle fought hard by road safety campaigners, police, prosecutors, legislators, medicos and many members of the judiciary. Affecting change in normative driving culture has been a long journey. Over the last seven decades the scope of liability behind the wheel has widened considerably. In the twenty-first century, conduct that would rarely have seen the light of a twentieth-century courtroom, such as fatigue, momentary inattention and distraction, have become grounds for charges. Sentences, however, remain a more complex matter.

From the mid to late twentieth century, there were palpable tensions regarding vehicular homicide's criminal status. Indeed its status declined as the century wore on. That the fatal consequences were unintended presented a significant obstacle to perceptions of criminality, as did the age and antecedents of defendants brought before the courts. The fact that driving dangerously or negligently was not uncommon was at odds with the notion that *real* crime was the preserve of the socially deviant. Ubiquity undermined gravitas. Measures of *appropriate* and *proportionate* were also hampered by dominant constructions of masculinity and its insidious relationship with risk-taking. Speeding, drink-driving and commonplace recklessness proved difficult in the courts, where mercy prevailed and attitudes were slow to shift, but shift they have. Affecting change in cases involving fatigued driving, failure to modify driving in accordance with the changing road conditions, and keeping a proper lookout for non-motorised road users were comparatively herculean tasks.

CONCLUSION

The difficulties were not purely cultural. The legal test of what a 'reasonable' driver might do, or the objective, point-of-view-of-the-bystander yardstick for dangerous driving have been exacting standards. It is not simply the case that the law treated drivers with reckless leniency, although it has. The criterion 'reasonable' presented a significant obstacle when being *unreasonable* was all too common. Despite the valiant efforts of many prosecutors, the benchmark of culpable fault was a bar juries initially set detrimentally high. As the twentieth century wore on, efforts to ratchet that bar downwards were accompanied by other less desirable consequences. While the criminal justice system challenged society's most basic assumptions about 'accidents', it paradoxically contributed to and underscored a culture that positioned vehicular homicide as a much lesser species than any other, save for, in the twenty-first century, the most aberrant and utterly homicidal driver.

Between the mid-1940s and the mid-1970s, Australia's peak fatality decades, a driver's conduct typically had to be altogether exceptional in order to be charged. Anything less than the most grave conduct proved futile. Aggravating circumstances were generally mandatory and even the very worst of those was not sufficient to secure the condemnation of juries. The Crown did attempt to test a small number of failure-to-keep-a-proper-lookout cases, where those failures were particularly serious, but those charges were unsuccessful, even when the driver was three sheets to the wind. Men brought before the courts were given enormous latitude and a generous dose of reasonable doubt, particularly when they were young. Of 174 drivers convicted, 172 of them male, only thirty-eight were imprisoned for two or more years, with the highest *head* sentence of four years imposed only twice. A mere twenty were convicted of manslaughter. Following the High Court's judgment in 1952,[3] both negligent driving causing death and manslaughter required proof of *criminal* negligence, yet juries favoured the lesser offence. Nonetheless, the Crown was resolute in its determination; the State continued to charge drivers with manslaughter. As against the anxiety about the 'road toll', the rhetoric in the community and the courts, and penalties for other forms of involuntary manslaughter or worst still, vehicle theft, sentences were remarkably low. Alarmingly, they were set to further decline.

The introduction of dangerous driving causing death in 1974 was designed to free the courts from the 'bonds' of criminal negligence,[4] bonds acquired as a result of the High Court in *Callaghan v R*.[5] In some respects, the emancipation backfired. The purpose of the new offence, as was the case with s 291A in 1946, was to make it easier to secure convictions by widening the scope of liability and creating an alternative, lesser offence to manslaughter. Yet, the outcome was not so straightforward. With alarming frequency, very serious factual circumstances, circumstances previously characterised as criminal negligence, started to come before the courts under the banner of dangerous driving causing death. The new offence became the chief repository for high-end risk-taking. As the 1980s dawned, rarely were drivers *criminally negligent*. Rather, by legislative stroke and prosecutorial ease, the majority became *dangerous*, were they liable at all, and *dangerous* they stayed. Compared with the Crown's resolute approach over the previous thirty years, the late 1970s and 1980s seemed marked by defeat, underscored by the *Road Traffic Act's* emphasis on fines and summary judgment. From thereon, rarely was it that drivers had failed to use *reasonable care* and take *reasonable precautions*, despite that they might have been speeding, blind drunk and on the wrong side of the road with their headlights off. Now, they were driving in a manner *dangerous* to the public.

This watering down of the characterisation of *all* driving that resulted in death was not the legislature's objective. Dangerousness was not instituted as a substitute for manslaughter. The purpose of introducing another driving-causing-death offence was to widen the compass of culpability and bring more drivers within the ambit of the law, not to dilute the nomenclature of all driving conduct. There were, however, some positive developments. In the late 1970s, drivers who demonstrated lapses in judgment and *transitory* instances of bad driving were charged, although the anecdotal evidence suggests that this was infrequent. In 1974, West Australian barrister Leo Wood accurately observed that the law did 'not punish a person for a momentary lapse, for an error of judgment, for a miscalculation'.[6] The problem was that momentary lapses and errors in judgement were very generous categories. In order to be prosecuted, aggravating circumstances were typically mandatory, a requirement grossly disproportionate to the quantum of harm the mismanagement of vehicles posed and one *not* requisite for other forms of homicide.

Dangerous driving causing death would not have been so profoundly at odds with broadening the scope of criminal liability behind the wheel, were it not for the way the offence was utilised in practice. Had it been reserved for lesser degrees of fault than manslaughter, the offence might have properly served its intended purpose. Yet, from its introduction, dangerous driving causing death could be tried summarily, with statutory emphasis favouring expedited procedure as the primary course of action. The bulk of prosecutions quickly devolved to the lower courts where fines were customary. Prior to the introduction of the *Road Traffic Act*, 25 per cent of convicted drivers received a non-custodial term. After 1974 and until the end of the twentieth century, drivers were routinely fined for killing other road users in circumstances of aggravation. While it was entirely reasonable that cases at the very low end of the spectrum should be dealt with summarily, expedited procedures were not reserved for such circumstances. Summary judgment and its penalty regime were applied to the most serious of cases. Astonishingly, summary judgment remained in place for almost forty years. It was finally abolished in 2011. That aggravated dangerous driving came to dominate prosecutions under s 59(1) of the *Road Traffic Act*, and were subject to fines or short custodial sentences, in practical terms left little latitude to prosecute and sentence lesser degrees of dangerousness.

In the final decade of the twentieth century, road safety campaigns began to draw persistent attention to the fatal and tragic consequences of the mismanagement of vehicles, affecting change in driving culture. Campaign strategies flourished with even more funds and fervour in the 2000s. Yet, those efforts seemed somewhat undermined by trifling penalties, the practice of issuing extraordinary licences to recidivist 'traffic' offenders and the classification of the most serious cases as 'dangerous'.

While the penalty regime under the *Road Traffic Act* led to trivial fines for *dangerous* drivers, custodial terms for manslaughter remained erroneously constrained on the basis of the judgment in *Laporte v R* in 1970.[7] Thereafter, the judiciary held that *no* driver had ever received a sentence of more than four years and thus the courts were shackled by history. This fallacious claim was reiterated up until 1995. Despite this flawed curtailing of sentences, change was afoot. Progressively more and more prosecutors and members of the judiciary mounted persuasive arguments for increasing penalties. In 1990, the State appealed against what was already, by the day's standards, a significant custodial term in *R v Stebbings* and found a sympathetic appellant court.[8] Drawing support from judgments across Australia, judgments that forcefully argued that sentences were failing to match the criminality, ubiquity and 'social evil' posed by the mismanagement of vehicles, the appellant court increased Stebbings' sentence to three years' imprisonment on each count of manslaughter, and two years on one count of dangerous driving causing grievous bodily harm. All sentences were to be served concurrently. *Laporte's* value as a sentencing guideline was all but buried. While the term in *Stebbings* now seems remarkably low, it was nonetheless a decisive moment, a moment that drew a line under the notion that a young man with good antecedents should not be incarcerated. Sentences of the same length *had* been handed down between the 1940s and 1970s for killing one person in ten instances, although those cases required a mosaic of aggravating circumstances, poor antecedents and a history of offending. After *Stebbings*, otherwise respectable young men and women *could* be sent to jail. Custodial terms for manslaughter began to increase.

Following a wave of public protest in the early 1990s and a knee-jerk legislative response, drivers who came before the courts with extensive histories of criminal and 'traffic' offending, who were driving stolen vehicles and under police pursuit began to receive greater sentences than ever before. A peak in sentencing in manslaughter cases and those involving stolen vehicles in the 1990s paved the way for higher sentences in very serious circumstances thereafter. A concurrent shift in approaches to multiple fatalities, whereby drivers began to be charged with and sentenced for each decedent, even if only partially concurrently, was another factor in the upwards trend in custodial terms. Yet, these increased head sentences of between six to twelve years, later underscored by Jess' law, were reserved for offenders that readily fit the criminal archetype. Unfortunately, this focus on the exceptional did little to draw much needed attention to 'ordinary' dangerous drivers.

In drink-driving cases, the landscape changed dramatically with the introduction of Jess' law in 2004. Thereafter, drivers with a blood alcohol concentration of 0.15% or more were *deemed* dangerous and thereby responsible for the death. Guilty pleas followed. The deeming provision put an end to the difficulty of prosecuting drivers who *appeared* to be managing the vehicle right up until the crash instant, or where there was no witness to the manner of the driving. Drivers with a blood alcohol concentration of 0.15% or more, or those that had committed the offence in other circumstances of aggravation – driving a stolen vehicle, exceeding the speed limit by more than 45 km/h or engaging in a police pursuit – would also, in theory, be exposed to a twenty-year term. In many instances, arguably not enough, the aggravated sentencing provisions had an impact on increasing terms of imprisonment. Prior to 2004, it was inconceivable that one aggravating feature alone could result in a significant custodial term.

For all other dangerous drivers, Jess' law left the status quo intact – their cases could still be heard summarily. The maximum custodial penalty on indictment remained set at four years. The amendments underlined the most *exceptional* conduct and labelled it *dangerous*. That the penalty provisions suggested equivalence between manslaughter and aggravated dangerous driving causing death, helped seal vehicular homicide's status as a species apart. Cases with significant circumstances of aggravation were 'dangerous', not 'manslaughter'. Deaths occasioned by the use of motor vehicles seemed to be a species *sui generis*.

While in many respects constructive, the amendments were yet another inadvertent step in the history of attrition. Dangerous driving had to be utterly exceptional to be significantly blameworthy, not requisite for other forms of involuntary homicide. Thus, it was enacted that the worst offender, the *real* offender, was a speeding hoon or intoxicated thief who goaded police. By simultaneously failing to address 'ordinary' dangerous driving, the 2004 amendments underscored the fact that, in order to be considered significantly at fault and meaningfully penalised, one had to drive in an *extraordinary* manner. The increase in the maximum custodial penalty for non-aggravated dangerous driving, from four years to ten in 2008, went some way towards addressing this disjuncture, although it has affected little in the way of sentencing. The 2004 amendments also buttressed the existing provision that driving a stolen vehicle and causing a death was a much, much worse offence than killing someone in your own car, reflecting little about the *manner of the driving*, but, seemingly, the inherent value of property and the insolence of those inclined to steal it.

That Jess' law left summary judgment, fines and the maximum penalty for 'ordinary' dangerous driving on indictment intact, did little to draw attention to the duty of care required in the day-to-day management of vehicles. As sentences for more serious cases tended to fall within the statutory penalty for ordinary dangerousness, this meant that such terms could never be applied to a 'regular' dangerous driver, including those whose conduct fell short of the aggravating provisions by the slimmest of margins. It is here where distress and outrage about sentences seem the most

CONCLUSION

palpable in the community. In circumstances that fall just short of the aggravating provisions, such as in the case of Charlotte Pemberton in 2015, sentences have remained static.

Putting to one side some recent demands, such as a mandatory minimum term of ten years irrespective of the level of fault,[9] sentences do remain out of step with the scope and discretion afforded to the courts by the legislature and broader community sentiment. However, that terms in *aggravated* dangerous driving and manslaughter cases became fixed as low as the sentence imposed on Melissa Waters,[10] released on parole after a year and ten months, and, in others, between five to ten years for the most aberrant of conduct, has left very little scope for judges dealing with the average, yet *very* dangerous driver. The broadening of the circumstances of aggravation under Charlotte's law in 2018 is unlikely to affect much change unless there is a wholesale upwards shift in sentences across the board.

Despite best intentions, the operation of negligent and dangerous driving causing death over the last seven decades has been, in many instances, a startling chronicle of the attrition of the taxonomy of culpable fault behind the wheel. In light of this history, the introduction of careless driving causing death in 2016 is not without risks. Given what was once criminally negligent became, in most instances, dangerous, it is conceivable that dangerousness may be diluted to carelessness. While a conviction for careless driving occasioning death might ease the distress of a bereaved family where the driver would have previously been acquitted, it is likely to offer cold comfort in cases where charges are downgraded. Were that to occur in WA as it has in other jurisdictions it would damage efforts, underway for decades, to expand the scope of culpable fault behind the wheel. Still, it is too early to tell. Nevertheless, other outcomes are already clear. In the courts, careless driving causing death is delivering sentences that loved ones are deeming derisory and insulting. In the absence of a wholesale re-evaluation of sentencing, this will only continue.

The chorus of disapproval about sentences is not the preserve of the predictably outraged bereaved, a punitive public, or tough-on-crime governments looking to shore up election votes. Far from being a recent phenomenon, the question of appropriate penalties has attracted a tremendous amount of judicial consideration across the nation's courtrooms for decades. Judges and prosecutors have lamented the bloodshed, one of the 'most serious social problems causing loss of life',[11] the magnitude of the costs and drivers' reckless indifference, increasingly drawing attention to vehicular harm as a serious species of crime and, often, violence. In this overdue but mounting recognition, more and more observers have come to argue that the gravity of offences are not being reflected in penalties, particularly against that afforded by successive parliaments. In turn, many have called for more *appropriate* penalties, penalties in accordance with community values; not vigilante values, but values that reflect contemporaneous conceptions of the degree of the fault and its consequences. Sentences are, after all, in part a reflection of the community's view of the seriousness of the wrong and, over time, that view has shifted. Our weddedness to the machine and its ostensible freedoms, to tolerance of risk-taking and its relationship to dominant constructions of masculinity, and to *cause* rather than *accident*, have slowly shifted, as have verdicts. Penalties remain, however, another matter.

While many judges have persuasively argued that penalties have failed to reflect the gravity of the conduct and its consequences, the sentences imposed still remain low, often shamefully low, save for the most archetypal offender. However, judges are constrained by trends in sentencing. Not until a wholesale revision of penalties occurs across the entire spectrum of driving conduct can meaningful change occur. Unless 'ordinary' dangerous driving comes to be sentenced as a significant offence, so the status quo will remain. Consequential change will not be secured by instituting yet more and more alternative driving-occasioning-death offences, if they in turn water down the nomenclature of all conduct in order to catch those slipping through the net. Rather, the sense of what constitutes danger and criminal negligence should expand as it did over the late twentieth and early twenty-first centuries, when speed and heavy intoxication, once the subject of fines, came to be understood as more serious offences. Change *would* be achieved by cementing understandings that the mismanagement of a vehicle is as dangerous or negligent as discharging a firearm in a public precinct, rather than the idea that one must be drunk, excessively speeding, unlicensed, disqualified or driving a stolen car to be considered a truly serious offender. As the Shadow Attorney General Michael Mischin observed, 'tweaking' the circumstances of aggravation might be ultimately 'counterproductive'.[12]

Sadly, the weight of evidence explored throughout this book supports the claims made by surviving loved ones at the beginning. Contrary to the efforts of legislators, and often *because of*, deaths occasioned by the use of motor vehicles *have* been treated as a much lesser species of homicide. Overwhelmingly, charges laid and sentences imposed have not erred on the side of appropriate or proportionate. For a complex set of reasons, legal and social, drivers brought before the courts have been the beneficiaries of tremendous leniency. There is little reason to believe this to be some peculiar Western Australian phenomenon. Impressions from other jurisdictions, in Australia and overseas, suggest that the landscape appears remarkably similar.

Despite persistent judicial pleas and the carefully crafted reasoning evident in reported judgments, the preponderance of sentences across the seven decades examined in this book could only be described as inadequate. Decades on and *still* judges continue to lament that sentences are not reflecting community values, the intention of the legislature or the degree of culpable fault. It is time they did. Of course, loved ones customarily report that a penalty is never enough, but in the case of deaths on the roads, sentences and charges have *invariably* not been enough. Not only have charges, if laid, and sentences imposed been distressing to victims' families, they have been detrimental to efforts to elevate the seriousness of the wrong, the duty of care of *all* drivers, and the offence's criminal status. The anticipated positive impacts of recent amendments to the *Road Traffic Act* are yet to materialise and one suspects are unlikely to do so. Until they do, we are likely to remain caught where we began, in the accidental truth of Gary Numan's catchy assertion – 'nothing seems right in cars'.[13] Indeed, very little does.

APPENDICES

Table A1

Table A1 is compiled from the criminal indictment registers and record books of the Supreme Court of Western Australia. It lists all cases of interest that came before the Court from the introduction of negligent driving causing death in 1946, until the advent of the *Road Traffic Act* in 1974.

Cases were deemed to be of interest on the following grounds – defendants were charged with unlawful killing, manslaughter, or negligent driving causing death. Prosecutions initiated as wilful murder or murder which were downgraded to manslaughter were excluded. Dangerous driving causing death was not an offence during the period, nor was there an offence of reckless driving causing death, though court transcribers employed these phrases in the records. Whichever phrase is employed, it refers only to the s 291A offence, negligent driving causing death.

Remarks and notations often gave clues that a case involved a vehicle. When the Crown declined to proceed after the committal hearing but before the commencement of trial, cases were also

APPENDICES

omitted. Thus, the table reflects prosecutions in the period, rather than charges laid. Coronial inquests and indictments are identified underneath the date of committal. Case numbers are listed where available. The table employs the style, language and terminology used within the primary source materials.

Table A2

Table A2 lists all convictions and sentences for negligent driving causing death and vehicular manslaughter from 1946 until late 1974. It is compiled from the criminal indictment registers and record books of the Supreme Court of Western Australia. A total of 174 defendants were convicted across the period, only two of them female. Vehicular manslaughter cases could typically be determined by the notations regarding licence disqualification in the indictment registers and record books. Where there was doubt, case files were reviewed in order to provide clarification. If the uncertainty could not be resolved by recourse to the case file, convictions were omitted. The table employs the style, language and terminology used within the primary source materials. It facilitates an appreciation of the penalties imposed across the period.

Table A3

Table A3 is compiled from the criminal indictment registers and record books of the Supreme Court of Western Australia. It lists cases of interest that came before the Court from the introduction of dangerous driving causing death in late 1974, to mid-1981 when the State Records Office holdings of Supreme Court records cease.

Cases were recorded on the following bases – defendants were charged with unlawful killing, manslaughter or dangerous driving causing death pursuant to s 59(1) of the *Road Traffic Act*. By the 1970s, it was possible to determine with greater certainty when a manslaughter case was vehicular. As in Table A1, prosecutions that were initiated as wilful murder or murder which were downgraded to manslaughter were excluded. The table employs the style, language and terminology used within the primary source materials.

If a defendant was acquitted of manslaughter, it was not possible to determine from the record books whether the case involved a vehicle. Where reference to an indictment file established that a case was non-vehicular, those cases were excluded from the table. This exclusion involved nineteen non-vehicular cases. This is contrary to the approach adopted in Table A1, where non-vehicular cases are included to facilitate sentencing comparisons between vehicular and non-vehicular manslaughter. Again, when the Crown declined to proceed after the committal hearing and before the commencement of trial, cases were also excluded. For that reason, the table reflects prosecutions rather than charges laid. Case numbers are listed where available.

The Western Australian *Road Traffic Act* received assent in December 1974, though dangerous driving causing death did not become fully operational until mid-1975. The alternative offence of negligent driving causing death under s 291A of the Code remained intact due to a delay in the promulgation of the *Road Traffic Act's* penalties. Notwithstanding, after dangerous driving causing death became operational in mid-1975, record keepers and court participants frequently interchanged the phrase dangerous driving causing death with negligent or reckless driving causing death. That interchange was incorrect. Whichever phrase is employed, transcribers are referring to the offence under s 59(1) of the *Road Traffic Act*.

Key
* Indicates a sampled vehicular case file
^ Indicates a sampled non-vehicular case file
† Indicates a case file of significance that could not be located
+ Indicates offences likely brought under the former s 291A provisions, due to the delay in the promulgation of the *Road Traffic Act's* penalties

TABLE A1: SUPREME COURT INDICTMENTS, 1946–1974: CASES OF INTEREST WITH SAMPLED FILES MARKED

	Name and case no.	Offence	Committal and trial dates	Plea	Verdict, sentence and remarks
1.	A.J.C. 7,807*	Manslaughter	13 June 1946 (Coronial inquest) 8–9 July 1946	Not guilty	Not guilty Jury add rider – 'The jury add a rider that the street lighting at the scene is still quite inadequate and that the proper authority be notified accordingly'
2.	W.M. 7,812*	Manslaughter	24 June 1946 (Coronial inquest & indictment) 7 August 1946	Not guilty	Not guilty
3.	A.J.G. 7,814^	Manslaughter	8 July 1946 12 August 1946	Not guilty	Not guilty
4.	G.T.B. 7,853*	Manslaughter	6 November 1946 (Coronial inquest & indictment) 9–10 December 1946	Not guilty	Not guilty of manslaughter – Guilty of negligent driving causing death Bond – £100 & surety – £100 Disqualified from holding a driver's licence for the remainder of the current licence period and the following two periods
5.	A.K. 7,893^	Manslaughter	4 February 1947 6–7 March 1947	Not guilty	Not guilty
6.	R.F.A. 7,899*	Manslaughter	6 March 1947 (Coronial inquest) 3 April 1947	Not guilty	Not guilty
7.	L.W.S. 7,920*	Manslaughter	20 May 1947 (Coronial inquest & indictment) 5 & 16 June 1947	Not guilty	Not guilty of manslaughter – Guilty of reckless or dangerous driving causing death Jury recommend mercy 9 months' imprisonment with hard labour
8.	A.H.B. 7,921*	Manslaughter	21 May 1947 (Coronial inquest & indictment) 9–13 & 16 June 1947	Not guilty	Guilty 3 years' imprisonment with hard labour

TABLE A1: SUPREME COURT INDICTMENTS, 1946–1974

	Name and case no.	Offence	Committal and trial dates	Plea	Verdict, sentence and remarks
9.	D.I.H. 7,925^	Manslaughter	11 April 1947 3–4 July 1947	Not guilty	Not guilty
10.	A.H.P. 1	Manslaughter	14 August 1947 30 October 1947	Not guilty	Not guilty
11.	J.H.W. 8,012 8,022*	Manslaughter	23 February 1948 (Coronial inquest & indictment) 4–5 May 1948	Not guilty	Not guilty
12.	J.W.K. 8,044*	Manslaughter	17 June 1948 (Coronial inquest & indictment) 12–13 July 1948	Not guilty	Guilty Jury recommend mercy 12 months' imprisonment with hard labour Permanent licence disqualification
13.	M.J.N. 8,136*	Manslaughter	8 December 1948 (Coronial inquest) 2 March 1949	Not guilty	Not guilty of manslaughter – Guilty of negligent driving causing death Jury recommend mercy Bond – £50
14.	J.M.T. 6†	Manslaughter	4 January 1949 21 March 1949	Not guilty	Not guilty of manslaughter – Guilty of negligent driving causing death Jury recommend mercy Bond – £100 Bond breached 1953 – 1 year's imprisonment with hard labour
15.	A.C.E.D 8,146*	Manslaughter	3 February 1949 (Coronial inquest) 11–12 & 21 April 1949	Not guilty	Guilty Jury recommend mercy 3 years' imprisonment with hard labour
16.	J.C. 8,226*	Manslaughter	21 October 1949 (Coronial inquest & indictment) 10–11 November 1949	Not guilty	Not guilty of manslaughter – Guilty of negligent driving causing death Jury strongly recommend mercy 15 months' imprisonment with hard labour

TABLE A1: SUPREME COURT INDICTMENTS, 1946–1974

	Name and case no.	Offence	Committal and trial dates	Plea	Verdict, sentence and remarks
17.	J.W.T. 8,252 8,267*	Negligent driving causing death	2 November 1949 (Coronial inquest & indictment)	Not guilty	Jury disagreed Remanded for retrial
			8 December 1949		
			Retrial 7–8 February 1950		Not guilty
18.	W.A.B. 8,275*	Manslaughter	25 January 1950 (Coronial inquest & indictment)	Not guilty	Not guilty of manslaughter – Guilty of dangerous driving causing death Recognisance – £50 & surety – £50
			16–17, 20–21, 27 February & 1 March 1950		
19.	H.C.M. 8,298*	Negligent driving causing death	21 February 1950 (Coronial inquest & indictment)	Not guilty	Not guilty
			8–9 & 24 March 1950		
20.	D.V.J.^	Manslaughter	28 November 1949	Not guilty	Guilty Jury strongly recommend mercy Bond – £100
			27 July 1950		
21.	D.C. 8,347*	Negligent driving causing death	1 June 1950 (Coronial inquest)	Not guilty	Not guilty
			4 July 1950		
22.	E.J.H 8,349*	Negligent driving causing death	4 July 1950 (Coronial inquest & indictment)	Not guilty	Not guilty
			7 July 1950		
23.	H.A.H. 8,356*	Manslaughter	28 June 1950 2 August 1950	Not guilty to manslaughter Guilty to negligent driving causing death	Guilty of negligent driving causing death (as per plea) Bond – £50 & surety – £50 Bond conditions: a) cancellation of any current driver's licences b) declaration that unfit to hold any kind of driver's licence in the future c) prohibited from driving or attempting to drive any kind of vehicle in the future. Attempt or actual infringement of a condition may invoke detention

TABLE A1: SUPREME COURT INDICTMENTS, 1946–1974

	Name and case no.	Offence	Committal and trial dates	Plea	Verdict, sentence and remarks
24.	L.K.H. 8,357*	Negligent driving causing death	13 July 1950 (Coronial inquest & indictment)	Not guilty	Not guilty
			2 August 1950		
25.	N.T.J. 8,360 8,388*	Negligent driving causing death	18 July 1950 (Coronial inquest)	Not guilty	Not guilty
			10 August 1950 & 18 September 1950		
26.	S.M. 8,413*	Negligent driving causing death	17 October 1950 (Coronial inquest & indictment)	Not guilty	Not guilty
			16–17 & 20 November 1950		
27.	J.W.B.*	Negligent driving causing death	3 November 1950 (Coronial inquest & indictment)	Not guilty	Not guilty
		(Initially charged with manslaughter)	5–6 December 1950		
28.	B.B.M. 8,446*	Manslaughter	13 December 1950 (Coronial inquest)	Not guilty	Adjourned
			6 February 1951		
		Manslaughter	7–8 March 1951		Not guilty
29.	G.S.J. 8,436*	Manslaughter	6 November 1950 (Coronial inquest & indictment)	Not guilty	Not guilty
			6 February 1951		
30.	F.O.B. 8,445*	Manslaughter	31 January 1951 (Coronial inquest & indictment)	Not guilty	Not guilty of manslaughter – Guilty of negligent driving causing death 2 years' imprisonment with hard labour
			6 March 1951		
31.	O.S. 8,476*	Negligent driving causing death	17 April 1951 (Coronial inquest & indictment)	Not guilty	Guilty 2 years' imprisonment with hard labour
			2 May 1951		

TABLE A1: SUPREME COURT INDICTMENTS, 1946–1974

Name and case no.	Offence	Committal and trial dates	Plea	Verdict, sentence and remarks
32. B.D.S.M. 8,487*	Negligent driving causing death	20 April 1951 (Coronial inquest & indictment) 5 June 1951	Not guilty	Guilty 15 months' imprisonment with hard labour
33. E.B.H. 8,492^	Manslaughter	20 June 1951 6 July 1951	Not guilty	Not guilty
34. J.H. 8,494*	Manslaughter	18 June 1951 (Coronial inquest & indictment) 10 July 1951	Not guilty	Not guilty
35. J.W.G. 8,511*	Manslaughter	16 August 1951 (Coronial inquest & indictment) 13–14 September 1951	Not guilty	Not guilty
36. E.O. 8,539*	Manslaughter	14 November 1951 (Coronial inquest & indictment) 6–7 December 1951	Not guilty	Not guilty Jury add rider – measures should be taken to make the turn safer for oncoming traffic
37. L.S.D.G. 8,540*	Manslaughter	21 November 1951 (Coronial inquest & indictment) 10 December 1951	Not guilty	Not guilty
38. W.R.N. 8	Manslaughter	21 November 1951 4 February 1952	Not guilty	Not guilty of manslaughter – Guilty of negligent driving causing death 9 months' imprisonment with hard labour
39. W.H.T. 6	Manslaughter	19 December 1951 21 February 1952	Not guilty	Not guilty
40. E.V. 5	Manslaughter	27 March 1952 19 June 1952	Not guilty	Not guilty of manslaughter – Guilty of negligent driving causing death 10 months' imprisonment with hard labour Recommendation that licence not be renewed for 2 years

TABLE A1: SUPREME COURT INDICTMENTS, 1946–1974

	Name and case no.	Offence	Committal and trial dates	Plea	Verdict, sentence and remarks
41.	D.C.G. 8,647*	Manslaughter	6 June 1952 (Coronial inquest & indictment) 3 July 1952	Not guilty	Not guilty of manslaughter – Guilty of negligent driving causing death 18 months' imprisonment with hard labour
42.	J.W.C. 8,690 (Callaghan)*	Manslaughter	16 July 1952 (Coronial inquest & indictment) 13–14 August 1952	Not guilty	Not guilty of manslaughter – Guilty of negligent driving causing death 2 years' imprisonment with hard labour Released on bail pending appeal Sentence quashed by the High Court, 29 October 1952
43.	G.B.C. 8,739*	Manslaughter	16 September 1952 (Coronial inquest & indictment) 5 November 1952	Not guilty	Not guilty
44.	G.I.B. 8,742*	Manslaughter	15 August 1952 (Coronial inquest & indictment) 10 November 1952	Not guilty	Not guilty of manslaughter – Guilty of negligent driving causing death Jury recommend mercy 3 months' imprisonment with hard labour
45.	F.W.P. 8,745*	Manslaughter	2 October 1952 (Coronial inquest & indictment) 13 November 1952	Not guilty	Not guilty
46.	L.W.B. 8,747*	Manslaughter	7 October 1952 (Coronial inquest & indictment) 18 November 1952	Not guilty	Not guilty Jury add rider – 'The evidence established that the vehicle driven by the accused was not roadworthy both as regards brakes and visibility. The jury consider the company concerned have a responsibility to the public and its employees to maintain the safety factor of its transport'

TABLE A1: SUPREME COURT INDICTMENTS, 1946–1974

	Name and case no.	Offence	Committal and trial dates	Plea	Verdict, sentence and remarks
47.	J.H.P.P. 8,830	Manslaughter	11 December 1952	Not guilty	Adjourned
			11 February 1953		
		Manslaughter	4–5 March 1953		Jury disagreed
			Retrial 8–9 April 1953		Not guilty of manslaughter – Guilty of negligent driving causing death 4 months' imprisonment with hard labour
48.	R.E.S. 4	Manslaughter	26 March 1953	Not guilty	Not guilty of manslaughter – Guilty of reckless driving or negligence causing death 12 months' imprisonment with hard labour
			30 April 1953		
49.	R.M. 8,918	Manslaughter	16 April 1953	Not guilty	Not guilty
			7 May 1953		
50.	A.P.	Manslaughter	(Committal date unclear)	Not guilty	Not guilty
			1 September 1953		
51.	O.C. 8,991*	Manslaughter	24 July 1953 (Coronial inquest & indictment)	Not guilty	Not guilty
			3 September 1953		
52.	F.P.N. 9,029*	Negligent driving causing death	19 October 1953 (Coronial inquest & indictment)	Not guilty	Not guilty
			9–10 November 1953		
53.	W.R.P. 9,040	Manslaughter	29 October 1953	Not guilty	Not guilty of manslaughter – Guilty of dangerous driving causing death 6 months' imprisonment
			4 December 1953		
54.	P.D C. 9,094^	Manslaughter	27 January 1954	Not guilty	Guilty 15 months' imprisonment with hard labour
			18 March 1954		
55.	B.M. 9,155^	Manslaughter	1 May 1954	Not guilty	Guilty Jury recommend mercy 12 months' imprisonment
			16 June 1954		

TABLE A1: SUPREME COURT INDICTMENTS, 1946–1974

	Name and case no.	Offence	Committal and trial dates	Plea	Verdict, sentence and remarks
56.	G.N. 9,178	Manslaughter	26 May 1954 8 July 1954	Not guilty	Not guilty of manslaughter – Guilty of negligent driving causing death 9 months' imprisonment with hard labour Recommend that special consideration be given to prisoner by prison medical advisers to ensure, insofar as possible, prisoner may suffer no ill effects as result of imprisonment
57.	K.C.T. 9,183	Manslaughter	23 June 1954 22 July 1954	Not guilty	Not guilty
58.	W.F.C. 10	Manslaughter	1 July 1954 30 July 1954	Not guilty	Not guilty
59.	L.J.D. 11	Manslaughter	30 April 1954 3 August 1954	Not guilty	Not guilty
60.	R.H.L. 9,259*	Manslaughter	30 August 1954 (Coronial inquest & indictment) 7 October 1954	Not guilty	Not guilty of manslaughter – Guilty of dangerous driving causing death 12 months' imprisonment
61.	E.F.G. 9,331	Manslaughter	15 December 1954 12 February 1955 Retrial 3–4 March 1955	Not guilty	Jury disagreed Adjourned Not guilty
62.	G.W.B. 9,303*	Manslaughter	9 & 28 March 1955 (Coronial inquest) 4 May 1955	Not guilty	Guilty 3 years' imprisonment with hard labour
63.	B.R.H. 9,428*	Manslaughter	3 May 1955 (Coronial inquest) 10 June 1955	Not guilty	Not guilty
64.	D.J. 9,461	Manslaughter	6 July 1955 3 August 1955	Not guilty	Not guilty

TABLE A1: SUPREME COURT INDICTMENTS, 1946–1974

Name and case no.	Offence	Committal and trial dates	Plea	Verdict, sentence and remarks
65. R.F.M. 9,502	Manslaughter	14 September 1955 6 October 1955	Not guilty	Not guilty
66. R.L.D. (Name unclear) 9,503	Manslaughter	15 September 1955 7 & 10 October 1955	Not guilty	Not guilty of manslaughter – Guilty of dangerous driving causing death Jury strongly recommend mercy on account of youth 4 months' imprisonment with hard labour Driver's licence cancelled Banned from holding any driver's licence for 10 years
67. E.B.S. 9,545	Manslaughter	27 October 1955 14–15 December 1955	Not guilty	Not guilty of manslaughter – Guilty of dangerous driving causing death 9 months' imprisonment
68. J.W. 2	Unlawful killing	9 December 1955 22 March 1956	Not guilty	Not guilty
69. L.C.N. 9,604	Manslaughter	24 February 1956 6 April 1956	Not guilty	Not guilty
70. B.J.T. 9,606*	Manslaughter	31 January 1956 (Coronial inquest) 10–11 April 1956	Not guilty	Not guilty of manslaughter – Guilty of dangerous driving causing death Jury strongly recommend mercy on account of youth Recommendation that driver's licence be cancelled until he reaches more mature years Bond – £100 Disqualified from holding any driver's licence for life
71. L.G.F. 9,607	Manslaughter	16 March 1956 12–13 April 1956	Not guilty	Not guilty of manslaughter – Guilty of dangerous driving causing death 4 months' imprisonment with hard labour Disqualified from holding any driver's licence for 5 years
72. J.W.N.D. 9,622	Manslaughter	29 March 1956 3–4 May 1956	Not guilty	Not guilty

TABLE A1: SUPREME COURT INDICTMENTS, 1946–1974

	Name and case no.	Offence	Committal and trial dates	Plea	Verdict, sentence and remarks
73.	L.L.L. 9,623*	Manslaughter	26 March 1956 (Coronial inquest) 8–9 May 1956	Not guilty	Not guilty of manslaughter – Guilty of dangerous driving causing death 12 months' imprisonment with hard labour Motorcycle licence suspended for 5 years Disqualified from obtaining any licence for 5 years
74.	J.R.B. 9,636*	Manslaughter	2 May 1956 (Coronial inquest & indictment) 7–8 June 1956	Not guilty	Not guilty
75.	C.E.B. 9,637	Manslaughter	2 May 1956 11–13 June 1956	Not guilty	Not guilty
76.	K.G.T. 9,638	Manslaughter	20 April 1956 14–15 June 1956	Not guilty	Not guilty
77.	R.E.M. 9,640	Manslaughter	11 May 1956 19 June 1956	Not guilty	Not guilty
78.	D.C. 9,643	Manslaughter	8 June 1956 25–26 June 1956	Not guilty	Not guilty of manslaughter – Guilty of dangerous driving causing death 8 months' imprisonment
79.	K.C. 9,656	Manslaughter	24 May 1956 10 July 1956	Not guilty	Not guilty
80.	G.V.G. 9,681	Manslaughter	22 June 1956 9 August 1956	Not guilty	Not guilty of manslaughter – Guilty of dangerous driving causing death Jury strongly recommend mercy Bond – £50 Indefinite licence disqualification
81.	R.G.M. 9,682	Manslaughter	10 July 1956 13 August 1956	Not guilty	Not guilty
82.	W.W.D. 3	Manslaughter	8 October 1956 15 November 1956	Not guilty	Not guilty of manslaughter – Guilty of dangerous driving causing death 12 months' imprisonment with hard labour Recommendation sentence be served at Pardelup Prison Farm

TABLE A1: SUPREME COURT INDICTMENTS, 1946–1974

Name and case no.	Offence	Committal and trial dates	Plea	Verdict, sentence and remarks
83. D.J.O. 9,739*	Manslaughter	20 September 1956 (Coronial inquest & indictment)	Not guilty	Not guilty
		19 November 1956		
84. J.L.S. 9,753	Manslaughter	26 October 1956	Not guilty	Not guilty of manslaughter – Guilty of dangerous driving causing death
		13 December 1956		9 months' imprisonment
85. G.I. 9,756	Manslaughter	22 October 1956	Not guilty	Not guilty
		19 December 1956		
86. D.D.M. 9,789*	Manslaughter	21 December 1956 (Coronial inquest & indictment)	Not guilty	Not guilty
		8 February 1957		
87. A.C.S. 9,813	Manslaughter	1 February 1957	Not guilty	Not guilty
		7–8 March 1957		
88. N.W.G. 9,820	Manslaughter	25 February 1957	Not guilty	Not guilty
		3 April 1957		
89. J.E.C. 9,841*	Manslaughter	20 & 29 March 1957 (Coronial inquest & indictment)	Not guilty	Not guilty
		20 & 29 April 1957		
90. A.F.C. 9,842	Manslaughter	6 March 1957	Not guilty	Jury disagreed Remanded for retrial
		14–15 May 1957		
		4 June 1957		Nolle prosequi
91. F.R. 5	Manslaughter	1 October 1957	Not guilty	Not guilty
		1 November 1957		
92. B.W.W. 7	Manslaughter	30 September 1957	Not guilty	Not guilty
		5 November 1957		
93. A.S. 4	Manslaughter	28 October 1957	Not guilty	Not guilty
		14 November 1957		

TABLE A1: SUPREME COURT INDICTMENTS, 1946–1974

	Name and case no.	Offence	Committal and trial dates	Plea	Verdict, sentence and remarks
94.	D.I.M. 9,969	Manslaughter	12 December 1957 5 February 1958	Not guilty	Not guilty
95.	E.M. 10,008*	Manslaughter	14 March 1958 (Coronial inquest & indictment) 17 April 1958	Not guilty	Not guilty of manslaughter – Guilty of negligent driving causing death 3 months' imprisonment with hard labour
96.	M.R.S. 10,009	Manslaughter	6 March 1958 21 April 1958	Not guilty	Not guilty of manslaughter – Guilty of negligent driving causing death 6 months' imprisonment with hard labour
97.	T.S.C. 1	Manslaughter	26 February 1958 1 May 1958	Not guilty	Not guilty
98.	S.J.V.I. 10,032^	Manslaughter	18 April 1958 19 May 1958	Not guilty	Not guilty
99.	N.K. 10,054*	Manslaughter	6 May 1958 (Coronial inquest & indictment) 12 June 1958	Not guilty	Not guilty of manslaughter – Guilty of dangerous driving causing death 12 months' imprisonment
100.	D.A.J. 10,051	Manslaughter	5–6 April 1958 23 & 30 April 1958	Not guilty	Jury disagreed Adjourned
		Manslaughter	Retrial 2–3 July 1958	Not guilty	Not guilty of manslaughter – Guilty of dangerous driving causing death Jury recommend mercy 4 months' imprisonment with hard labour At expiration of sentence, disqualified from applying for a driver's licence for a further 5 years
101.	L.G.W. 10,088*	Manslaughter	15–16 July 1958 (Coronial inquest & indictment) 21 August 1958	Not guilty	Guilty Jury strongly recommend mercy owing to youth Bond – £50 All existing driver's licences cancelled Disqualified from holding any driving licence for life

TABLE A1: SUPREME COURT INDICTMENTS, 1946–1974

Name and case no.	Offence	Committal and trial dates	Plea	Verdict, sentence and remarks
102. R.E.O. 10,118	Manslaughter	18 September 1958 13 October 1958	Not guilty	Not guilty
103. E.D.D. 3	Manslaughter	11 November 1958 21 January 1959	Not guilty	Not guilty
104. F.G.D. 10,160*	Manslaughter	4 December 1958 (Coronial inquest & indictment) 10 February 1959	Guilty	Guilty 18 months' imprisonment with hard labour Driver's licence suspended Disqualified from holding a licence for 5 years
105. L.J.T. 10,162	Manslaughter	12 January 1959 16 February 1959	Not guilty	Not guilty of manslaughter – Guilty of negligent driving causing death Driver's licence suspended Disqualified from holding another licence for 5 years
106. G.H.M.	Manslaughter	5 November 1958 18 February 1959	Not guilty	Not guilty of manslaughter – Guilty of dangerous driving causing death Jury strongly recommend mercy Bond – £100 – for 2 years
107. R.E.P. 10,179*	Manslaughter	8 December 1958 (Coronial inquest & indictment) 9–10 March 1959	Not guilty	Not guilty
108. W.J.E. 10,193*	Manslaughter	26 February 1959 (Coronial inquest) 11–12 May 1959 2 June 1959	Not guilty	Jury disagreed Remanded for retrial Nolle prosequi
109. J.A.W. 10,223	Manslaughter	1 May 1959 9 June 1959	Not guilty	Not guilty
110. A.F. 10,226	Manslaughter	(Committal date unclear) 18–19 June 1959	Not guilty	Not guilty of manslaughter – Guilty of negligent driving causing death 6 months' imprisonment with hard labour Indefinite licence disqualification

TABLE A1: SUPREME COURT INDICTMENTS, 1946–1974

	Name and case no.	Offence	Committal and trial dates	Plea	Verdict, sentence and remarks
111.	J.P.S. 10,251	Manslaughter (2 counts)	3 June 1959 6 August 1959	Not guilty	Not guilty of manslaughter – Guilty of negligent driving causing death (1 count) Fined £180 Driver's licence cancelled Disqualified from holding a licence for further 3 years
112.	C.H.S. 5 & 7	Manslaughter	9 February 1959 19 August 1959	Not guilty	Not guilty
113.	J.M. (Name unclear) 8	Manslaughter	8 June 1959 19 August 1959	Not guilty	Not guilty
114.	F.G.P. 10,254	Manslaughter	13 July 1959 21 August 1959	Not guilty	Not guilty
115.	J.J.K. 10,267*	Manslaughter	11 August 1959 (Coronial inquest & indictment) 3 September 1959	Not guilty to manslaughter Guilty to negligent driving causing death	Guilty of negligent driving causing death (as per plea) 9 months' imprisonment with hard labour Driver's licence cancelled Licence not to be reissued for 5 years
116.	G.S. 2	Manslaughter	1 September 1959 22 October 1959	Not guilty	Not guilty
117.	R.J.S. 10,294	Manslaughter	30 September 1959 11 November 1959	Not guilty	Not guilty
118.	W.A.G.S.	Manslaughter	21 September 1959 18 November 1959	Not guilty	Not guilty
119.	H.C.C. 10,311*	Manslaughter	6 November 1959 (Coronial inquest & indictment) 2 December 1959	Not guilty	Not guilty
120.	C.A.L. 10,338	Manslaughter	1 December 1959 16 February 1960	Not guilty	Not guilty
121.	R.B. 13	Manslaughter	9 February 1960 17 February 1960	Not guilty	Not guilty

TABLE A1: SUPREME COURT INDICTMENTS, 1946–1974

Name and case no.	Offence	Committal and trial dates	Plea	Verdict, sentence and remarks
122. R.M.B. 10,371^	Manslaughter	1 March 1960 6 April 1960	Not guilty	Not guilty
123. B.J.M. 10,372*	Manslaughter	19 February 1960 (Coronial inquest & indictment) 11–12 April 1960	Not guilty	Guilty 6 months' imprisonment with hard labour
124. H.J.S. 5	Manslaughter	28 March 1960 28 April 1960	Not guilty	Not guilty
125. B.B. 10,385	Manslaughter	24 March 1960 3–4 May 1960	Not guilty	Not guilty
126. V.U. 10,373	Manslaughter	23 February 1960 16 May 1960	Not guilty	Not guilty
127. N.T.N. 10,391*	Manslaughter	23 March 1960 (Coronial inquest & indictment) 25 May 1960	Not guilty	Not guilty
128. S.F.M. 10,390	Manslaughter	17 March 1960 13 & 16 May 1960	Not guilty	Not guilty of manslaughter – Guilty of negligent driving causing death Fined £50 Driver's licence suspended for 2 years
129. A.K.A. 10,393*	Manslaughter	19 May 1960 (Coronial inquest & indictment) 7 June 1960	Not guilty to manslaughter Guilty to negligent driving causing death	Guilty of negligent driving causing death (as per plea) Bond – £100 & surety – £100 – for 3 years Driver's licence suspended for 2 years
130. R.M. 10,402	Manslaughter	28 April 1960 8–9 June 1960	Not guilty	Not guilty
131. G.E.D 10,416	Manslaughter	31 May 1960 5 July 1960	Not guilty	Not guilty

TABLE A1: SUPREME COURT INDICTMENTS, 1946–1974

	Name and case no.	Offence	Committal and trial dates	Plea	Verdict, sentence and remarks
132.	F.X.I. 10,417*	Manslaughter	15 & 20 June 1960 11–13 July 1960	Not guilty	Not guilty of manslaughter – Guilty of negligent driving causing death 15 months' imprisonment with hard labour Driver's licence cancelled for 3 years Leave to appeal - Denied
133.	A.F.H. 1	Unlawful killing	15 June 1960 28 July 1960	Not guilty to manslaughter Guilty to dangerous driving causing death	Guilty of dangerous driving causing death (as per plea) 6 months' imprisonment Driver's licence suspended for 12 months after expiration of sentence
134.	M.V.C. 10,432*	Manslaughter	21 June 1960 (Coronial inquest & indictment) 3 August 1960	Not guilty	Not guilty
135.	D.T.C.W 10,433	Manslaughter	20 May 1960 4 August 1960	Not guilty to manslaughter Guilty to dangerous driving causing death	Guilty of dangerous driving causing death (as per plea) 12 months' imprisonment with hard labour Disqualified from holding a driver's licence for 3 years
136.	C.C 3	Unlawful killing	29 July 1960 18 August 1960	Not guilty	Not guilty
137.	W.E.T. 3	Unlawful killing	2 August 1960 21 October 1960	Not guilty	Not guilty
138.	R.G.M. 5	Manslaughter	16 November 1960 24 November 1960	Not guilty	Not guilty
139.	A.J.C.	Unlawful killing	27 January 1961 15–17 March 1961	Not guilty	Not guilty of manslaughter – Guilty of negligent driving causing death 12 months' imprisonment with hard labour Disqualified from obtaining a driver's licence for 12 months from expiration of term of imprisonment

TABLE A1: SUPREME COURT INDICTMENTS, 1946–1974

Name and case no.	Offence	Committal and trial dates	Plea	Verdict, sentence and remarks
140. R.J.F. 10,556*	Manslaughter	21 March 1961 20 April 1961	Not guilty to manslaughter Guilty to negligent driving causing death	Guilty of negligent driving causing death (as per plea) Fined £350 Recognisance – £200 & surety – 5 years Driver's licence suspended for 3 years
141. P. (otherwise known as) N. (First name recorded only) 1	Manslaughter	8 February 1961 26 April 1961	Not guilty	Not guilty
142. A.V. 10,576	Manslaughter	14 & 29 March 1961 10 May 1961	Not guilty	Not guilty of manslaughter – Guilty of reckless driving causing death Fined £200 Disqualified from holding a driver's licence for 3 years
143. M.E.T. 1	Unlawful killing	20 March 1961 24 May 1961	Not guilty	Not guilty
144. E.H. 10,593^	Manslaughter	18 May 1961 8 June 1961	Not guilty	Not guilty
145. L.D. 2	Unlawful killing	24 April 1961 21 June 1961	Not guilty	Not guilty
146. G.J.B. 4*	Unlawful killing	21 April 1961 26–28 June 1961	Not guilty	Not guilty of manslaughter – Guilty of negligent driving causing death 12 months' imprisonment with hard labour Disqualified from holding or obtaining a driver's licence for 12 months from release
147. R.K.O. 10,617	Manslaughter	16 & 23 June 1961 2 August 1961	Not guilty	Not guilty of manslaughter – Guilty of negligent driving causing death 6 months' imprisonment with hard labour Indefinite disqualification
148. N.F.H. 10,619	Manslaughter	19–31 May & 4 July 1961 17 August 1961	Not guilty	Not guilty

TABLE A1: SUPREME COURT INDICTMENTS, 1946–1974

	Name and case no.	Offence	Committal and trial dates	Plea	Verdict, sentence and remarks
149.	A.P. 10,636 10,637	Manslaughter (2 counts)	27 July 1961 7 September 1961	Not guilty	Not guilty
150.	R.G.G. 10,638	Manslaughter	7 August 1961 11 September 1961	Not guilty	Not guilty
151.	W.G.C. 10,642	Manslaughter	29 June 1961 14 September 1961	Not guilty	Not guilty
152.	B.N.S. 10,677*	Manslaughter	4 October 1961 30 November & 1 December 1961	Not guilty	Not guilty
153.	N.J.W. 6	Manslaughter	16 October 1961 24 November 1961	Not guilty	Not guilty
154.	J.E.J. 10,690*	Manslaughter	20 September 1961 18 December 1961	Not guilty	Not guilty
155.	W.D. (Name unclear) 10,707	Manslaughter	29 December 1961 12–13 February 1962	Not guilty	Not guilty of manslaughter – Guilty of reckless driving causing death 6 months' imprisonment with hard labour Disqualified from holding a driver's licence for 3 years from release
156.	J.M.S. 10,710*	Manslaughter	18 January 1962 15–16 & 19 February 1962	Not guilty	Not guilty
157.	A.G. 1	Manslaughter	2 February 1962 20 March 1962	Not guilty	Not guilty of manslaughter – Guilty of negligent driving causing death Bond – £50 – for 2 years Breach of bond – sentenced 17 March 1964 18 months' imprisonment Disqualified from holding a driver's licence for 7 years Appealed term of licence disqualification – 15 November 1967 – disqualification revoked 20 November 1967

TABLE A1: SUPREME COURT INDICTMENTS, 1946–1974

Name and case no.	Offence	Committal and trial dates	Plea	Verdict, sentence and remarks
158. J.H. 10,760*	Manslaughter (2 counts)	28 May 1962 28 May 1962	Not guilty to manslaughter Guilty to negligent driving causing death	Guilty of negligent driving causing death (1 count) (as per plea) 2 years' imprisonment with hard labour Licence disqualified for 7 years 2nd count adjourned to next sittings with view to entering a nolle prosequi
159. R.J.T. 10,761	Manslaughter	14 May 1962 21–22 June 1962	Not guilty	Not guilty
160. H.J.H. 10,779	Manslaughter	15 May 1962 25 June 1962	Not guilty	Not guilty of manslaughter – Guilty of reckless driving causing death 9 months' imprisonment with hard labour Disqualified from holding a driver's licence for 5 years from date of release
161. A.R.N. 2	Manslaughter	10 April 1962 18 July 1962	Not guilty	Not guilty
162. B.B.T. 3	Manslaughter	16 June 1962 19 July 1962	Not guilty	Not guilty by a majority
163. W.R.F. 10,786	Manslaughter	23 May 1962 23–24 July 1962	Not guilty	Not guilty
164. G.J.F 10,789*	Manslaughter	2 May 1962 25 July 1962	Not guilty to manslaughter Guilty to negligent driving causing death	Guilty of negligent driving causing death (as per plea) Bond – £50 for 3 years Driver's licence disqualified for 5 years
165. J.L.T.	Manslaughter	30 July 1962 24 August 1962	Not guilty	Not guilty

TABLE A1: SUPREME COURT INDICTMENTS, 1946–1974

Name and case no.	Offence	Committal and trial dates	Plea	Verdict, sentence and remarks
166. C.W.N.	Manslaughter	10 July 1962 28 August 1962	Not guilty	Not guilty of manslaughter – Guilty of negligent driving causing death 2 years' imprisonment with hard labour Disqualified from holding any driver's licence for life Appealed against sentence – appeal dismissed
167. W.A.C.	Manslaughter	11 June 1962 18 September 1962	Not guilty	Not guilty
168. R.B.H. 10,846^	Manslaughter	3 September 1962 2 October 1962	Guilty	Guilty 4 years' imprisonment with hard labour
169. P.J.A. 4	Manslaughter	27 September 1962 18 October 1962	Not guilty	Not guilty
170. S.B. 10,873	Manslaughter	15 October 1962 8–9 November 1962	Not guilty	Not guilty
171. L.R.L. 5, 1	Manslaughter Manslaughter	24 August 1962 29 August 1962 12 November 1962	 Not guilty	Adjourned Not guilty of manslaughter – Guilty of dangerous driving causing death Fined £100 Driver's licence suspended Disqualified from holding any licence for 2 years
172. K.H. 10,875*	Manslaughter	16 October 1962 19 November 1962	Not guilty	Not guilty
173. R.C. 10,941^	Manslaughter	30 January 1963 12–15 March 1963	Not guilty	Guilty Jury recommend mercy Fined £200
174. G.H.C. 10,941^	Manslaughter	30 January 1963 12–15 March 1963	Not guilty	Guilty Jury recommend mercy Fined £100

TABLE A1: SUPREME COURT INDICTMENTS, 1946–1974

Name and case no.	Offence	Committal and trial dates	Plea	Verdict, sentence and remarks
175. F.F. 10,942*	Manslaughter	1 February 1963 18 March 1963	Not guilty	Not guilty
176. J.K.C. 10,959	Manslaughter	13 March 1963 April 1963 (Trial date unclear)	Not guilty	Not guilty of manslaughter – Guilty of negligent control of a vehicle causing death Jury strongly recommend mercy Fined £300 Driver's licence suspended Disqualified from holding a driver's licence for 2 years
177. F.R.O. 10,978	Manslaughter	1 April 1963 9 May 1963	Not guilty	Not guilty
178. J.M. (Middle name unclear) 28/63	Manslaughter	29 April 1963 22–25 May 1963	Not guilty	Not guilty of manslaughter – Guilty of negligent driving causing death Jury recommend mercy 12 months' imprisonment with hard labour, followed by indeterminate detention Driver's licence cancelled Disqualified from obtaining any type of licence for 10 years Leave to appeal denied 25 July 1963
179. J.H. 11,011*	Manslaughter	24 April 1963 26 June 1963	Not guilty	Not guilty of manslaughter – Guilty of negligent driving causing death Jury recommend mercy Bond – £100 & surety – £100 for 10 years Driver's licence suspended Disqualified from holding a licence for 10 years
180. G. (Surname unclear)	Manslaughter	26 June 1963 3–4 September 1963	Not guilty	Not guilty of manslaughter – Guilty of reckless driving causing death Fined £200 Disqualified from holding a driver's licence for 5 years
181. T.D. 11,083	Manslaughter	28 August 1963 9–10 October 1963	Not guilty	Not guilty of manslaughter – Guilty of reckless driving causing death 6 months' imprisonment with hard labour Driver's licence suspended Disqualified from holding a licence for 7 years after release

TABLE A1: SUPREME COURT INDICTMENTS, 1946–1974

	Name and case no.	Offence	Committal and trial dates	Plea	Verdict, sentence and remarks
182.	R.J.M. 11,104	Manslaughter	23 August 1963 6–7 November 1963	Not guilty	Not guilty
183.	L.J.S. 11,105	Manslaughter	22 October 1963 13 November 1963	Not guilty	Not guilty of manslaughter – Guilty of negligent driving causing death Jury strongly recommend mercy 4 months' imprisonment with hard labour Driver's licence cancelled Disqualified from holding a licence for 5 years
184.	R.F. 8	Manslaughter	(Dates unclear)	Not guilty	(Notations unclear)
185.	M.R. 11,130*	Manslaughter	7 November 1963 4–5 December 1963	Not guilty	Not guilty
186.	B.H.S. 11,131	Manslaughter	23 October 1963 11–12 December 1963	Not guilty	Not guilty
187.	A.H. 11,150	Manslaughter	13 January 1964 7 February 1964	Not guilty	Not guilty of manslaughter – Guilty of negligent driving causing death Fined £250 Driver's licence suspended Disqualified from holding a licence for life
188.	W.W.V. 11,151*	Manslaughter	7 December 1963 11–12 February 1964	Not guilty	Guilty 18 months' imprisonment with hard labour Driver's licence suspended Disqualified from holding a licence for 5 years
189.	M.J.C. 11,154*	Manslaughter	13 January 1964 19 February 1964	Not guilty	Not guilty
190.	J.F. 1	Unlawful killing	9 December 1963 25 February 1964	Not guilty	Not guilty

TABLE A1: SUPREME COURT INDICTMENTS, 1946–1974

Name and case no.	Offence	Committal and trial dates	Plea	Verdict, sentence and remarks
191. K.J.M. 3	Manslaughter	30 January 1964 3–4 March 1964	Not guilty	Not guilty of manslaughter – Guilty of negligent driving causing death Jury recommend mercy 9 months' imprisonment with hard labour Driver's licence suspended Disqualified from holding a licence for 10 years
192. O.L.W. 11,184	Manslaughter	16 December 1963 11–12 March 1964	Not guilty	Not guilty
193. E.L.B. 11,206	Manslaughter	28 February 1964 29–30 April 1964	Not guilty	Not guilty
194. C.W.H. 11,263*	Manslaughter	24 June 1964 23–24 July 1964	Not guilty	Possibility of trial being prejudiced Jury discharged – case adjourned
	Manslaughter	Retrial 11–12 August 1964	Not guilty	Not guilty
195. A.P. 11,264*	Manslaughter	17 June 1964 29 July 1964	Not guilty	Guilty 2 years' imprisonment with hard labour Disqualified from obtaining a driver's licence for 10 years
196. M.O.S.	Manslaughter	13 May 1964 4 August 1964	Not guilty to manslaughter Guilty to negligent driving causing death	Guilty of negligent driving causing death (as per plea) Fined £350 Driver's licence suspended until expiration Disqualified from obtaining a licence for 5 years
197. A.K. 40/04	Manslaughter	22 July 1964 25–26 August 1964	Not guilty	Not guilty
198. P.A.O. 11,292^	Manslaughter	27 July 1964 9–10 September 1964	Not guilty	Not guilty
199. K.J.D.	Manslaughter	12 August 1964 16 September 1964	Not guilty	Not guilty

TABLE A1: SUPREME COURT INDICTMENTS, 1946–1974

Name and case no.	Offence	Committal and trial dates	Plea	Verdict, sentence and remarks
200. A.G. 11,295	Manslaughter	10 August 1964 18 & 21 September 1964	Not guilty	Not guilty
201. J.W.S. 11,305	Manslaughter	2 September 1964 6 October 1964	Not guilty	Not guilty of manslaughter – Guilty of negligent driving causing death Bond – £50 for 5 years Driver's licence cancelled Disqualified from holding a licence for 10 years
202. C.T.A 11,320	Manslaughter	9 October 1964 10–11 October 1964	Not guilty	Not guilty of manslaughter – Guilty of reckless driving causing death Fined £100 Bond – £250 & surety – £250 for 5 years Driver's licence suspended for 10 years
203. J.B.J.R. 11,320	Manslaughter	20 October 1964 10 November 1964	Not guilty to manslaughter Guilty to reckless driving causing death	Guilty of reckless driving causing death (as per plea) 2 years' imprisonment, minimum term 9 months before eligible for parole Driver's licence suspended for 10 years
204. J.P.G. 11,322*	Manslaughter (2 counts)	12 October 1964 19–20 October 1964	Not guilty	Not guilty of manslaughter – Guilty of reckless driving causing death (1 count) 18 months' imprisonment, minimum term 6 months before eligible for parole Driver's licence suspended for 10 years 2nd count – nolle prosequi Application for review of licence suspension – 25 November 1964 – denied
205. E.A.N. 11,344	Manslaughter	7 January 1965 10 February 1965	Not guilty to manslaughter Guilty to reckless driving causing death	Guilty of reckless driving causing death (as per plea) 6 months' imprisonment with hard labour

TABLE A1: SUPREME COURT INDICTMENTS, 1946–1974

Name and case no.	Offence	Committal and trial dates	Plea	Verdict, sentence and remarks
206. L.G.H. 11,345*	Manslaughter	14 January 1965 11 February 1965	Not guilty to manslaughter Guilty to reckless driving causing death	Guilty of reckless driving causing death (as per plea) Fined £250 Driver's licence suspended Disqualified from holding a licence for 5 years
207. I.M.	Manslaughter	(Date unclear) 17 February 1965	Not guilty	Not guilty
208. R.G.	Manslaughter	(Date unclear) 11 March 1965	Not guilty	Not guilty of manslaughter – Guilty of dangerous driving causing death 2 years' imprisonment, minimum term 18 months before eligible for parole
209. A.W.†	Manslaughter	(Date unclear) 14 March 1965	Guilty	Guilty 12 months' imprisonment with hard labour
210. C.H.D. 11,421	Manslaughter	5 April 1965 27–28 May 1965	Not guilty	Not guilty of manslaughter – Guilty of reckless driving causing death 4 months' imprisonment
211. S.M.Q. 3	Manslaughter	14 April 1965 15 June 1965	Not guilty	Not guilty of manslaughter – Guilty of reckless driving causing death 10 months' imprisonment
212. N.M. 5	Manslaughter	18 May 1965 16–17 June 1965	Not guilty	Not guilty of manslaughter – Guilty of reckless driving causing death 2 years' imprisonment, minimum term 15 months before eligible for parole
213. P.M.L. 11,457*	Manslaughter	4 June 1965 8 July 1965	Not guilty to manslaughter Guilty to dangerous driving causing death	Guilty of dangerous driving causing death (as per plea) 12 months' imprisonment with hard labour, minimum term 6 months before eligible for parole Disqualified from holding a driver's licence for 10 years
214. F.P.F. 11,462	Manslaughter	17 June 1965 26 July 1965	Not guilty	Not guilty of manslaughter – Guilty of dangerous driving causing death 12 months' imprisonment with hard labour, minimum term 6 months before eligible for parole Disqualified from holding a driver's licence for 10 years

TABLE A1: SUPREME COURT INDICTMENTS, 1946–1974

Name and case no.	Offence	Committal and trial dates	Plea	Verdict, sentence and remarks
215. S.H. 11,491*	Unlawful killing	3 August 1965 13–15 August 1965	Not guilty	Not guilty of manslaughter – Guilty of negligent driving causing death 2 years' imprisonment with hard labour, minimum term 15 months before eligible for parole Driver's licence cancelled Disqualified from holding a licence for 8 years
216. R.D.S. 11,460 & 11,464*	Manslaughter Manslaughter Unlawful killing	11 June 1965 20 September 1965	Not guilty	Adjourned to August Adjourned to September Guilty of manslaughter 2 years' imprisonment with hard labour, minimum term 12 months before eligible for parole
217. D.A.W. 11,534*	Manslaughter	30 July 1965 7 October 1965	Not guilty	Not guilty of manslaughter – Guilty of negligent driving causing death 3 years' imprisonment with hard labour, minimum term 18 months before eligible for parole Driver's licence cancelled Ineligible to obtain a licence for 15 years
218. A.H.S. 11,514	Unlawful killing	23 July 1965 21–22 October 1965	Not guilty	Not guilty
219. R.H. 2	Manslaughter	7 October 1965 25–26 October 1965	Not guilty	Not guilty
220. P.R.V.S. 1	Unlawful killing	5 October 1965 2–3 November 1965	Not guilty	Guilty of manslaughter 2 years' imprisonment with hard labour, minimum term 18 months before eligible for parole Driver's licence cancelled Disqualified from holding a licence for 8 years
221. R.T.S. 2	Unlawful killing	4 August 1965 3 November 1965	Not guilty	Not guilty of manslaughter – Guilty of negligent driving causing death 18 months' imprisonment with hard labour, minimum term 9 months before eligible for parole Disqualified from holding a driver's licence for 5 years

TABLE A1: SUPREME COURT INDICTMENTS, 1946–1974

Name and case no.	Offence	Committal and trial dates	Plea	Verdict, sentence and remarks
222. H.G. 6	Manslaughter	23 August 1965 17 November 1965	Not guilty	Not guilty of manslaughter – Guilty of negligent driving causing death 9 months' imprisonment with hard labour
223. D.H.S. 11,564*	Manslaughter	23 November 1965 17 December 1965	Not guilty	Not guilty
224. A.J.P. 11,620	Unlawful killing	8 February 1966 14–15 March 1966	Not guilty	Not guilty of manslaughter – Guilty of negligent driving causing death 12 months' imprisonment with hard labour, minimum term 6 months before eligible for parole Existing driver's licence cancelled Declared ineligible to hold a licence for 5 years
225. J.W.R.	Manslaughter	15 March 1966 (Trial date unclear)	Not guilty	Not guilty
226. G.J.P. 11,621	Unlawful killing	11 November 1965 17–18 March 1966	Not guilty	Not guilty
227. J.R. 11,627^	Manslaughter	20 December 1965 5 April 1966	Guilty	Guilty 5 years' imprisonment with hard labour, minimum term 18 months before eligible for parole
228. L.M. 11,654*	Manslaughter	21 April 1966 19 May 1966	Not guilty	Not guilty
229. N.W.R. 3	Manslaughter	24 March 1966 4–5 May 1966	Not guilty	Not guilty of manslaughter – Guilty of reckless driving causing death 2 years' imprisonment, no minimum term Cumulative on present sentences Disqualified from holding a driver's licence for 12 years
230. F.K.G. 5	Manslaughter	21 January 1966 9–10 May 1966	Not guilty	Not guilty
231. G.K.	Manslaughter	9 March 1966 14 June 1966	Not guilty	Not guilty

TABLE A1: SUPREME COURT INDICTMENTS, 1946–1974

	Name and case no.	Offence	Committal and trial dates	Plea	Verdict, sentence and remarks
232.	R.L.M.S. 1	Manslaughter	17 January 1966 6 March 1966	Not guilty	Not guilty
233.	S.J. (Middle name unclear) 11,693	Manslaughter	16 May 1966 28–29 July 1966	Not guilty	Not guilty of manslaughter – Guilty of dangerous driving causing death 12 months' imprisonment with hard labour, minimum term 6 months before eligible for parole Driver's licence suspended Disqualified from obtaining a licence for a further period of 5 years Application for an extraordinary licence heard on 15 February 1971 – granted
234.	E.J.H. 11,695	Manslaughter	29 June 1966 19 & 22 August 1966	Not guilty	Not guilty of manslaughter – Guilty of negligent driving causing death 18 months' imprisonment with hard labour, minimum term 9 months before eligible for parole Driver's licence cancelled Disqualified from holding a licence for 5 years
235.	A.J.B. 11,696	Manslaughter	30 June 1966 24 August 1966	Not guilty	Not guilty of manslaughter – Guilty of negligent driving causing death 2 years' imprisonment with hard labour, minimum term 12 months before eligible for parole Driver's licence cancelled Disqualified from holding a licence for 5 years
236.	K.S.W. 11,697	Manslaughter	22 June 1966 25 August 1966	Not guilty	Not guilty of manslaughter – Guilty of negligent driving causing death 18 months' imprisonment with hard labour, minimum term 9 months before eligible for parole Driver's licence cancelled Disqualified from holding a licence for 5 years

TABLE A1: SUPREME COURT INDICTMENTS, 1946–1974

Name and case no.	Offence	Committal and trial dates	Plea	Verdict, sentence and remarks
237. D.J.B. 11,699*	Manslaughter	29 June 1966 1 July 1966 1–2 September 1966	Not guilty	Not guilty of manslaughter – Guilty of negligent driving causing death 3 years' probation on following conditions: 1) abstain from violation of the law 2) within 24 hours after this date report to the Chief Probation Officer personally 3) carry out the lawful instructions of the Probation Officer 4) report and receive visits as directed by the Probation Officer 5) notify the Probation Officer within 48 hours of any changes of your address or employment during the Probation period Driver's licence cancelled Disqualified from holding a licence for 5 years
238. I.G.C. 5	Manslaughter	7 October 1966 1–2 November 1966	Not guilty	Not guilty manslaughter – Guilty of negligent driving causing death Jury strongly recommend mercy 9 months' imprisonment with hard labour
239. J.U. 11,778^	Manslaughter	26 October 1966 6 December 1966	Guilty	Guilty 7 years' imprisonment, minimum term 4 years before eligible for parole
240. R.H.W. 11,782*	Manslaughter	8 November 1966 6 December 1966	Not guilty to manslaughter Guilty to reckless driving causing death	Not guilty of manslaughter – Guilty of reckless driving causing death (as per plea) 2 years' imprisonment Driver's licence suspended Disqualified from holding a licence for 12 years
241. M.Z. 11,785*	Manslaughter	22 November 1966 14 December 1966	Not guilty	Not guilty

TABLE A1: SUPREME COURT INDICTMENTS, 1946–1974

Name and case no.	Offence	Committal and trial dates	Plea	Verdict, sentence and remarks
242. A.S. 11,808	Manslaughter	28 November 1966 8–9 February 1967	Not guilty	Not guilty of manslaughter – Guilty of dangerous driving causing death 12 months' imprisonment with hard labour Disqualified from holding a driver's licence for 5 years Extraordinary licence application heard 20 March 1970 – granted
243. P.L.W. 11,814	Manslaughter	5 January 1967 2 March 1967	Not guilty to manslaughter Guilty to dangerous driving causing death	Guilty of dangerous driving causing death (as per plea) 12 months' imprisonment with hard labour Disqualified from holding a driver's licence for 5 years
244. R.N.S. 11,815*	Manslaughter	5 December 1966 2 March 1967	Not guilty to manslaughter Guilty to dangerous driving causing death	Guilty of dangerous driving causing death (as per plea) 12 months' imprisonment with hard labour Disqualified from holding a driver's licence for 5 years
245. A.J.W. 11,828	Manslaughter	21 January 1967 29–30 March 1967	Not guilty	Not guilty of manslaughter – Guilty of reckless driving causing death 18 months' imprisonment, minimum term 6 months before eligible for parole Driver's licence cancelled Disqualified from obtaining licence for 7 years
246. J.D.W. 11,849	Manslaughter	23 February 1967 17–18 April 1967	Not guilty	Not guilty of manslaughter – Guilty of reckless and dangerous driving causing death 15 months' imprisonment with hard labour, minimum term 6 months before eligible for parole
247. L.H. 11,851	Manslaughter	31 March 1967 3–4 May 1967	Not guilty	Not guilty
248. R.E. 1^	Unlawful killing	21 February 1967 24–25 July 1967	Not guilty	Guilty of manslaughter Jury recommend mercy 5 years' imprisonment with hard labour, minimum term 3 years to be served before eligible for parole

TABLE A1: SUPREME COURT INDICTMENTS, 1946–1974

Name and case no.	Offence	Committal and trial dates	Plea	Verdict, sentence and remarks
249. R.H. 11,914	Manslaughter	23 June 1967 8 August 1967	Not guilty to manslaughter Guilty to reckless driving causing death	Guilty of reckless driving causing death (as per plea) 18 months' imprisonment, minimum term 3 months before eligible for parole Driver's licence suspended Disqualified from obtaining a licence for 5 years
250. F.T.D. 11,904	Manslaughter	12 June 1967 15–16 August 1967	Not guilty	Not guilty manslaughter – Guilty of reckless driving causing death 18 months' imprisonment, minimum term 3 months before eligible for parole Driver's licence suspended Disqualified from obtaining a licence for 5 years
251. B. (First name unclear) 11,974^	Unlawful killing	20 September 1967 10 November 1967	Guilty	Guilty of manslaughter 5 years' probation on following conditions: 1) abstain from violation of law 2) within 24 hours after this date report to Chief Probation Officer personally 3) carry out lawful instructions of the Probation Officer 4) report and receive visits as directed by Probation Officer 5) notify Probation Officer within 48 hours of change of address or change of employment during the Probation period
252. C.J.F. 12,002*	Manslaughter	11 October 1967 13 November 1967	Not guilty to manslaughter Guilty to negligent driving causing death	Guilty of negligent driving causing death (as per plea) 18 months' imprisonment with hard labour, minimum term 6 months before eligible for parole Concurrent with sentences now serving Driver's licence cancelled Disqualified from holding a licence for 10 years
253. D.C.B.W. 82/67	Manslaughter	20 September 1967 28 November 1967	Not guilty	Not guilty

TABLE A1: SUPREME COURT INDICTMENTS, 1946–1974

Name and case no.	Offence	Committal and trial dates	Plea	Verdict, sentence and remarks
254. H.J.C.	Unlawful killing	12 October 1967 6–7 December 1967	Not guilty	Not guilty manslaughter – Guilty of negligent driving causing death 18 months' imprisonment with hard labour, minimum term 6 months before eligible for parole
255. P.G.N. 12,021*	Manslaughter	9 November 1967 13 December 1967	Not guilty	Not guilty
256. B.A.H. 12,064	Manslaughter	19 December 1967 18–19 March 1968	Not guilty	Not guilty manslaughter – Guilty of negligent driving causing death 18 months' imprisonment with hard labour, minimum term 6 months before eligible for parole Driver's licence cancelled Disqualified from driving for 3 years
257. J.C. 12,141	Manslaughter	8 March 1968 1 May 1968	Not guilty	Not guilty
258. W.D.W. 12,166	Manslaughter	27 March 1968 8 May 1968	Not guilty to manslaughter Guilty to dangerous driving causing death	Guilty of dangerous driving causing death (as per plea) 18 months' imprisonment with hard labour, minimum term 6 months before eligible for parole Disqualified from holding a driver's licence for 10 years
259. K.A.B. 12,171	Manslaughter	29 March 1968 9 May 1968	Not guilty	Not guilty
260. J.J. 12,175	Manslaughter	21 March 1968 23 May 1968	Not guilty	Not guilty
261. C.S.H. 8/68	Manslaughter	29 April 1968 4 June 1968	Not guilty to manslaughter Guilty to reckless driving causing death	Guilty of reckless driving causing death (as per plea) 3 years' imprisonment, minimum term 12 months before eligible for parole Driver's licence cancelled Disqualified from obtaining a licence for 10 years

TABLE A1: SUPREME COURT INDICTMENTS, 1946–1974

Name and case no.	Offence	Committal and trial dates	Plea	Verdict, sentence and remarks
262. M.M. 12,201	Unlawful killing	16 June 1968 6–7, 11 & 13 June 1968	Not guilty	Not guilty of manslaughter – Guilty of negligent driving causing death 18 months' imprisonment with hard labour, minimum term 8 months before eligible for parole Driver's licence cancelled Disqualified from obtaining a licence for 5 years
263. C.M.F. 4	Manslaughter	6 November 1967 12 June 1968	Not guilty	Not guilty
264. R.B.C.W. 12,321	Manslaughter	13 August 1968 17–18 September 1968	Not guilty	Not guilty of manslaughter – Guilty of reckless driving causing death Fined $500 Driver's licence cancelled Disqualified from obtaining a licence for 7 years
265. H.F. 12,315*	Manslaughter	31 July 1968 20 September 1968	Not guilty	Not guilty
266. C.J.R. 12,320*	Manslaughter	17 September 1968 8–9 October 1968	Not guilty	Not guilty
267. D.W.W. 12,321^	Manslaughter	23 August 1968 21 October 1968	Not guilty	Not guilty
268. E.W. 12,374*	Manslaughter	27 June 1968 25–26 November 1968	Not guilty	Not guilty
269. G.N.M. 12,410*	Manslaughter	6 December 1968 12–13 February 1969	Not guilty	Not guilty of manslaughter – Guilty of negligent driving causing death 18 months' imprisonment with hard labour, minimum term 8 months before eligible for parole Driver's licence cancelled Disqualified from holding a licence for 5 years
270. F.L.M. 12,414	Manslaughter	26 November 1968 26–27 February 1969	Not guilty	Not guilty

TABLE A1: SUPREME COURT INDICTMENTS, 1946–1974

Name and case no.	Offence	Committal and trial dates	Plea	Verdict, sentence and remarks
271. R.K.W.	Manslaughter	3 December 1968 4–5 March 1969	Not guilty	Not guilty
272. J.W.N. 12,486*	Manslaughter	14 February 1969 17 March 1969	Not guilty to manslaughter Guilty to dangerous driving causing death	Guilty of dangerous driving causing death (as per plea) 18 months' imprisonment with hard labour, minimum term 9 months before eligible for parole Disqualified from holding a driver's licence for 5 years
273. R.A.S. 12,516	Dangerous driving causing death and Breach of Probation	5 March 1969 17 April 1969	Guilty both counts	Guilty of dangerous driving causing death and breach of probation (as per plea) 1st charge – 2 years' imprisonment, minimum term 9 months before eligible for parole Driver's licence cancelled Disqualified from holding a licence for 5 years 2nd charge – 12 months' imprisonment, minimum term 3 months before eligible for parole Cumulative on previous sentence
12,517	Manslaughter (2nd deceased)			Nolle prosequi
274. E.J.V. 12,521*	Manslaughter	10 March 1969 30 April & 1 May 1969	Not guilty	Not guilty of manslaughter – Guilty of reckless driving causing death 3 years' imprisonment, minimum term 12 months before eligible for parole Driver's licence suspended for 7 years
275. W.L.	Negligent driving causing death & Unlawfully doing grievous bodily harm	(Committal date unclear) 6 May 1969	Not guilty	Not guilty both counts
276. B.F.L. 12,526	Manslaughter	26 March 1969 8 May 1969	Not guilty	Not guilty of manslaughter – Guilty of reckless driving causing death Indeterminate detention – reformatory prison Disqualified from obtaining a driver's licence for 10 years

TABLE A1: SUPREME COURT INDICTMENTS, 1946–1974

Name and case no.	Offence	Committal and trial dates	Plea	Verdict, sentence and remarks
277. A.N.	Manslaughter	31 March 1969 10 June 1969	Not guilty	Not guilty
278. G.P.S. 12,598	Manslaughter	28 April 1969 16 June 1969	Not guilty	Not guilty
279. A.J.M. 12, 633	Unlawful killing	22 May 1969 28–29 July 1969	Not guilty	Not guilty
280. G.P.C. 12,635*	Unlawful killing	13 June 1969 30–31 July 1969	Not guilty	Not guilty
281. W.J.M. 68/1969	Manslaughter	13 June 1969 5–6 August 1969	Not guilty	Not guilty
282. R.L.C. 12,637	Manslaughter	4 July 1969 7 August 1969	Not guilty	Not guilty
283. V.P.L. (Laporte)†	Unlawful killing	7 March 1969 13–14 May 1969	Not guilty	Jury disagreed Defendant remanded Bail allowed – bond – $2,000
	Manslaughter	Retrial 21–22 August 1969		Guilty 4 years' imprisonment with hard labour, minimum term 18 months before eligible for parole Current driver's licence suspended until expiry Disqualified from obtaining a licence for 7 years Leave to appeal granted Appeal allowed Sentence reduced – 2 years' imprisonment, minimum term 9 months before eligible for parole
284. B.O.S.Q. 12,685	Manslaughter	2 September 1969 22–23 September 1969	Not guilty	Not guilty
285. G.I. 12,778	Manslaughter	5 November 1969 8–9 December 1969	Not guilty	Not guilty

TABLE A1: SUPREME COURT INDICTMENTS, 1946–1974

Name and case no.	Offence	Committal and trial dates	Plea	Verdict, sentence and remarks
286. B.B. 1	Unlawful killing	17 November 1969 18–19 December 1969	Not guilty	Not guilty
287. N.M.C.†	Unlawful killing	4 November 1969 22 December 1969	Not guilty	Guilty of manslaughter 3 years' probation
288. W.W.W. 12,808*	Manslaughter	23 December 1969 4 February 1970	Not guilty to manslaughter Guilty to dangerous driving causing death	Guilty of dangerous driving causing death (as per plea) 5 years' probation Driver's licence cancelled Ineligible to hold a licence for 5 years
289. O.N.H. 12,858*	Manslaughter	3 February 1970 5–6 March 1970	Not guilty	Not guilty of manslaughter – Guilty of reckless driving causing death 3 years' imprisonment, minimum term 18 months before eligible for parole Disqualified from obtaining a licence for 5 years following release
290. K.W. 12,862	Manslaughter	28 January 1970 16–17 March 1970	Not guilty	Not guilty of manslaughter – Guilty of reckless driving causing death 9 months' imprisonment – minimum term Disqualified from obtaining a driver's licence for 2 years following release
291. M.W.B.E. 12,865*	Manslaughter	4 February 1970 25–26 March 1970	Not guilty	Not guilty
292. E.H.T. 12,834	Unlawful killing	30 January 1970 9–10 April 1970	Not guilty	Not guilty of manslaughter – Guilty of negligent driving causing death 18 months' imprisonment, minimum term 9 months before eligible for parole Driver's licence cancelled Disqualified from holding a licence for 5 years

TABLE A1: SUPREME COURT INDICTMENTS, 1946–1974

Name and case no.	Offence	Committal and trial dates	Plea	Verdict, sentence and remarks
293. S.R.B. 12,870	Unlawful killing (2 counts)	13 March 1970 14–15 April 1970	Not guilty	Guilty of manslaughter (1 count) 2 years' imprisonment, minimum term 9 months before eligible for parole Driver's licence cancelled Disqualified from holding a licence for 6 years Nolle prosequi – 2nd count
294. C.A.S.B. 12,864	Unlawful killing	19 February 1970 4 May 1970	Not guilty	Not guilty of manslaughter – Guilty of negligent driving causing death 15 months' imprisonment, minimum term 8 months before eligible for parole Driver's licence cancelled Disqualified from holding a licence for 5 years
295. F.J.H.	Unlawful killing	16 April 1970 12 May 1970	Not guilty to manslaughter Guilty to dangerous driving causing death	Guilty of dangerous driving causing death (as per plea) 2 years' imprisonment with hard labour, minimum term 9 months before eligible for parole Disqualified from holding a driver's licence for life
296. S.R.B. 2/1970	Unlawful killing	31 March 1970 8 June 1970	Not guilty	Not guilty of manslaughter – Guilty of reckless driving causing death Jury strongly recommend mercy 2 years' imprisonment, minimum term 12 months before eligible for parole Prohibited from holding a driver's licence for 3 years from the expiry of present suspended licence
297. C.F.C. 2/1970	Unlawful killing	31 March 1970 9 June 1970	Not guilty	Not guilty
298. K.W.F.	Manslaughter (2 counts)	6 May 1970 15–16 June 1970	Not guilty	Not guilty of manslaughter – Guilty of reckless driving causing death (1 count) 12 months' imprisonment, no minimum term Driver's licence suspended Disqualified from holding a licence for 5 years from release 2nd indictment adjourned sine die

TABLE A1: SUPREME COURT INDICTMENTS, 1946–1974

Name and case no.	Offence	Committal and trial dates	Plea	Verdict, sentence and remarks
299. A.R.B. 12,879*	Manslaughter	20 May 1970 16–17 June 1970	Not guilty	Not guilty
300. R.B.J.C.	Unlawful killing	8 July 1970 9 July 1970	Not guilty	Not guilty
301. A.P.C. 35/1970*	Manslaughter	13 July 1970 4–5 August 1970	Not guilty	Not guilty of manslaughter – Guilty of dangerous driving causing death Fined $1,000 Driver's licence suspended Disqualified from holding a licence for 10 years
302. T.B.N. 12,886^	Manslaughter	14 July 1970 11–12 August 1970	Not guilty	Guilty 5 years' imprisonment, minimum term 2 years before eligible for parole
303. S.G.H. 12,889	Manslaughter	13 August 1970 4 September 1970	Not guilty	Not guilty of manslaughter – Guilty of reckless driving causing death 18 months' imprisonment, minimum term 9 months before eligible for parole Driver's licence cancelled
304. J.R.J.	Unlawful killing	30 July 1970 7–8 September 1970	Not guilty	Not guilty
305. A.M.B.*	Unlawful killing	1 September 1970 8 September 1970	Not guilty	Not guilty of manslaughter – Guilty of negligent driving causing death Fined $1,000 Driver's licence cancelled Disqualified from holding a licence for 7 years Extraordinary licence application – 29 September 1972 – Disqualification order revoked
306. G.C.B. 12,893*	Manslaughter	23 July 1970 17–18 September 1970	Not guilty	Not guilty

TABLE A1: SUPREME COURT INDICTMENTS, 1946–1974

Name and case no.	Offence	Committal and trial dates	Plea	Verdict, sentence and remarks
307. R.E.M. 12,895	Unlawful killing	22 July 1970 24 September 1970	Not guilty to manslaughter Guilty to dangerous driving causing death	Guilty of dangerous driving causing death (as per plea) 18 months' imprisonment, minimum term 12 months before eligible for parole Driver's licence cancelled Disqualified from holding a licence for 7 years
308. B.J.D. 12,905	Manslaughter	7 October 1970 19–20 November 1970	Not guilty	Not guilty of manslaughter – Guilty of negligent driving causing death 12 months' imprisonment, minimum term 3 months before eligible for parole Driver's licence suspended Disqualified from holding a licence for 7 years
309. S.V.	Manslaughter	21 September 1970 1 December 1970	Not guilty	Not guilty
310. M.B.	Manslaughter	29 October 1970 2 December 1970	Not guilty	Not guilty of manslaughter – Guilty of negligent driving causing death 12 months' imprisonment, minimum term 8 months before eligible for parole Driver's licence suspended Disqualified from holding a licence for 7 years
311. T.B. 12,924*	Unlawful killing (2 counts)	21 January 1971	Not guilty	Not guilty 2nd count adjourned Nolle prosequi – 2nd count
312. A.E.B.	Manslaughter (2 counts)	27 August 1970 16 February 1971	Not guilty to manslaughter Guilty to dangerous driving causing death	Guilty of dangerous driving causing death (as per plea) (1 count) Bond – $500 – for 3 years
313. K.A.H. 12,919	Unlawful killing	11 January 1971 16–17 February 1971	Not guilty	Not guilty

TABLE A1: SUPREME COURT INDICTMENTS, 1946–1974

Name and case no.	Offence	Committal and trial dates	Plea	Verdict, sentence and remarks
314. G.N.C. 12,926	Unlawful killing (2 counts)	10 February 1971 18–19 March 1971	Not guilty	Not guilty of manslaughter – Guilty of negligent driving causing death (1 count) 9 months' imprisonment, minimum term 3 months before eligible for parole Disqualified from holding a driver's licence for 3 years
315. R.L.A. 12,929	Unlawful killing	10 February 1971 29 March 1971	Not guilty	Not guilty of manslaughter – Guilty of negligent driving causing death 9 months' imprisonment, minimum term 2 months before eligible for parole Driver's licence cancelled Disqualified from holding a licence for a period of 5 years
316. H.J.	Manslaughter	10 March 1971 27 April 1971	Not guilty	Not guilty
317. B.J.W.*	Unlawful killing	5 March 1971 3 May 1971	Not guilty to manslaughter Guilty to negligent driving causing death	Guilty of negligent driving causing death (as per plea) 17 months' imprisonment, minimum term 8 months before eligible for parole Driver's licence cancelled Disqualified from holding a licence for life
318. L.R.H. 12,940*	Manslaughter	23 March 1971 4–5 May 1971	Not guilty	Not guilty
319. V.J.K. 12,946	Manslaughter	27 April 1971 8–9 June 1971	Not guilty	Not guilty of manslaughter – Guilty of reckless driving causing death 2 years' imprisonment, minimum term 8 months before eligible for parole Disqualified from obtaining a driver's licence for 5 years from date of release
320. E.A.L.†	Manslaughter	5 April 1971 30 June 1971	None recorded	Adjourned to September 1971 (No further notations)

TABLE A1: SUPREME COURT INDICTMENTS, 1946–1974

Name and case no.	Offence	Committal and trial dates	Plea	Verdict, sentence and remarks
321. R.N.P. 12,959	Manslaughter	1 June 1971 26 July 1971	Not guilty to manslaughter Guilty to dangerous driving causing death	Guilty of dangerous driving causing death (as per plea) 6 months' imprisonment with hard labour Driver's licence suspended until expiry Disqualified from holding a licence for 5 years from date of release
322. M.E.T. 12,959	Manslaughter	18 June 1971 26–28 July 1971	Not guilty	Not guilty of manslaughter – Guilty of reckless driving causing death 6 months' imprisonment with hard labour Driver's licence suspended until expiry Disqualified from holding a licence for 5 years following release
323. J.M.V.D.B. 12,961	Manslaughter	8 June 1971 29–30 July 1971	Not guilty	Not guilty
324. G.I.N.	Manslaughter	28 June 1971 3–4 August 1971	Not guilty	Not guilty
325. J.R.R. 9/1971	Manslaughter	2 April 1971 11–12 August 1971	Not guilty	Not guilty
326. D.S.A.S. 12,967	Unlawful killing	13 July 1971 30–31 August 1971	Not guilty	Not guilty
327. A.V.P. 12,965^	Unlawful killing	13 July 1971 19 August 1971	Not guilty	Not guilty
328. A.S. 12,968^	Unlawful killing	22 June 1971 1–3 & 6 September 1971	Not guilty	Guilty of manslaughter 3 years' imprisonment with hard labour, minimum term 5 months before eligible for parole
329. V.I.P. 12,968	Unlawful killing	22 June 1971 1–3 & 6 September 1971	Not guilty	Not guilty
330. A.B.S. 12,973*	Manslaughter	2 September 1971 21–22 October 1971	Not guilty	Not guilty

TABLE A1: SUPREME COURT INDICTMENTS, 1946–1974

Name and case no.	Offence	Committal and trial dates	Plea	Verdict, sentence and remarks
331. J.T.E. 12,977	Manslaughter	4 October 1971 9 November 1971	Not guilty to manslaughter Guilty to reckless driving causing death	Guilty of reckless driving causing death (as per plea) 2 years' imprisonment, minimum term 6 months before eligible for parole Driver's licence suspended Disqualified from holding a licence for 5 years
332. R.S.M. 12,982*	Manslaughter	23 September 1971 18 November 1971	Not guilty	Guilty 3 years' imprisonment, minimum term 9 months before eligible for parole Disqualified from obtaining a driver's licence for 7 years
333. D.L.B.V. 2	Manslaughter	24 September 1971 30 November & 1 December 1971	Not guilty	Not guilty of manslaughter – Guilty of reckless driving causing death 3 years' imprisonment, minimum term 12 months before eligible for parole
334. G.J.M. 7*	Manslaughter	10 January 1972 15 February 1972	Not guilty	Not guilty of manslaughter – Guilty of reckless driving causing death Jury strongly recommend mercy Fined $300 Driver's licence cancelled Disqualified from holding a licence for 5 years
335. R.R.R. 12,996	Unlawful killing	11 January 1972 15–16 February 1972	Not guilty	Not guilty
336. A.W.B. 12,999	Unlawful killing	28 October 1971 16–17 March 1972	Not guilty	Not guilty
337. W.G.W. 13,005*	Manslaughter	9 March 1972 10–11 April 1972	Not guilty	Not guilty of manslaughter – Guilty of reckless driving causing death 3 years' imprisonment, minimum term 2 years before eligible for parole Concurrent with sentence now serving Driver's licence cancelled Not eligible to obtain a licence for 5 years following release

TABLE A1: SUPREME COURT INDICTMENTS, 1946–1974

Name and case no.	Offence	Committal and trial dates	Plea	Verdict, sentence and remarks
338. A.C.H. 13,008^	Manslaughter	10 January 1972 24 April 1972	Not guilty	Guilty 8 years' imprisonment, minimum term 5 years before eligible for parole
339. R.S. 2^	Manslaughter	14 April 1972 3 May 1972	Guilty	Guilty 6 months' imprisonment
340. W.G.G. 13,013	Unlawful killing	17 February 1972 3–4 May 1972	Not guilty	Not guilty
341. R.S.B. 13,019^	Manslaughter	8 May 1972 6 June 1972	Guilty	Guilty 5 years' imprisonment, minimum term 2½ years before eligible for parole
342. R.J.B. 13,021	Manslaughter	13 April 1972 7–9 June 1972	Not guilty	Not guilty of manslaughter – Guilty of dangerous driving causing death 12 months' imprisonment, minimum term 6 months before eligible for parole
343. R.G.C. 7/72	Unlawful killing	12 June 1972 25–27 June 1972	Not guilty	Not guilty
344. H.R.B. 25/1972	Manslaughter	16 June 1972 1–2 August 1972	Not guilty	Not guilty of manslaughter – Guilty of negligent driving causing death Jury strongly recommend mercy 6 months' imprisonment with hard labour Disqualified from holding a driver's licence for 5 years
345. T.D.K. 13,045	Unlawful killing	22 August 1972 3 October 1972	Not guilty to manslaughter Guilty to dangerous driving causing death	Guilty of dangerous driving causing death (as per plea) 2 years' imprisonment, minimum term 1 year before eligible for parole Driver's licence cancelled Disqualified from holding a licence for 7 years
346. P.R.C. 2	Manslaughter	8 August 1972 5–6 October 1972	Not guilty	Not guilty
347. B.W.P.*	Manslaughter (2 counts)	6 September 1972 12–13 October 1972	Not guilty	Not guilty (count 1) 2nd count – bond

TABLE A1: SUPREME COURT INDICTMENTS, 1946–1974

Name and case no.	Offence	Committal and trial dates	Plea	Verdict, sentence and remarks
348. S.S.^	Manslaughter	21 September 1972 16–17 October 1972	Not guilty	Not guilty
349. R.D.R. 13,048	Unlawful killing	1 September 1972 24–25 October 1972	Not guilty	Not guilty of manslaughter – Guilty of dangerous driving causing death 18 months' imprisonment, minimum term 6 months before eligible for parole Driver's licence cancelled for 5 years
350. G.D.D. 13,049	Unlawful killing	14 August 1972 26–27 October 1972	Not guilty	Not guilty
351. B.R.J. 13,054*	Manslaughter	15 September 1972 20–22 November 1972	Not guilty	Not guilty
352. A.I.F. 4/73	Manslaughter	4 January 1973 15 February 1973	Not guilty	Not guilty of manslaughter – Guilty of negligent driving causing death 18 months' imprisonment, minimum term 2 months before eligible for parole (having regard to 6 weeks already spent in custody) Present driver's licence (if any) cancelled Disqualified from holding a licence for 5 years
353. M.D.H 9/73	Manslaughter	6 February 1973 7 March 1973	Not guilty	Not guilty of manslaughter – Guilty of negligent driving causing death 12 months' imprisonment with hard labour, minimum term 3 months before eligible for parole Driver's licence disqualified for 5 years from date of expiry of present disqualification
354. D.G.C. A1/73^	Unlawful killing	11 October 1972 13–14 March 1973	Not guilty	Guilty of manslaughter 3 years' imprisonment, minimum term 12 months before eligible for parole

TABLE A1: SUPREME COURT INDICTMENTS, 1946–1974

Name and case no.	Offence	Committal and trial dates	Plea	Verdict, sentence and remarks
355. C.F.C. W2/73*	Manslaughter	15 March 1973 10–12 April 1973	Not guilty	Guilty 4 years' imprisonment, minimum term 18 months before eligible for parole Driver's licence suspended Disqualified from holding a licence for 4 years
356. K.H. 14/73	Unlawful killing	15 February 1973 26 April 1973	Not guilty	Not guilty
357. G.T.E. 3/73	Manslaughter	20 December 1972 12–13 February 1973	Not guilty	Not guilty 2nd count of manslaughter adjourned
8/73	Manslaughter			Nolle prosequi
358. L.D.S. 21/1973	Manslaughter	4 April 1973 17–18 May 1973	Not guilty	Not guilty of manslaughter – Guilty of reckless driving causing death 6 months' imprisonment Driver's licence cancelled Disqualified from holding a licence for 5 years
359. G.E.D. 27/1973	Manslaughter	18 April 1973 15 June 1973	Not guilty	Not guilty
360. K.G.M. 29/1973	Manslaughter	17 April 1973 20–21 June 1973	Not guilty	Not guilty
361. R.W.S. 23/1973	Manslaughter	10 April 1973 21 June 1973	Not guilty to manslaughter Guilty to reckless driving causing death	Guilty of reckless driving causing death (as per plea) 2 years' imprisonment, minimum term 6 months before eligible for parole Disqualified from obtaining a driver's licence for 5 years
362. G.A.H.	Manslaughter	18 April 1973 19 July 1973	Not guilty	Not guilty of manslaughter – Guilty of negligent driving causing death Fined $500 Disqualified from holding a driver's licence for 5 years
363. R.A.J. 46/73*	Unlawful killing	29 June 1973 31 July & 1 August 1973	Not guilty	Not guilty

TABLE A1: SUPREME COURT INDICTMENTS, 1946–1974

Name and case no.	Offence	Committal and trial dates	Plea	Verdict, sentence and remarks
364. G.J.T. 40/73	Manslaughter	27 June 1973 30 August 1973	Not guilty	Not guilty of manslaughter – Guilty of negligent driving causing death Fined $700 Disqualified from holding a driver's licence for 5 years
365. R.A.A.*	Manslaughter	24 August 1973 9–10 October 1973	Not guilty	Not guilty of manslaughter - Guilty of negligent driving causing death Jury strongly recommend mercy Fined $500 Driver's licence suspended Disqualified from holding or obtaining a licence for 3 years
366. A.C. 51/73*	Unlawful killing	(Committal date not recorded) 11 October 1973	Not guilty	Not guilty
367. R.M. 10/73*	Manslaughter	20 October 1973 1 November 1973	Not guilty	Guilty Bond – $500 & surety – $500 for 3 years Driver's licence cancelled Disqualified from holding a licence for 3 years
368. K.A.S. 26/1973	Manslaughter	18 April 1973 7–8 November 1973	Not guilty	Not guilty
369. R.L.F. 56/1973	Manslaughter	24 September 1973 12–13 November 1973	Not guilty	Not guilty of manslaughter – Guilty of reckless driving causing death 2 years' probation Driver's licence suspended Disqualified from obtaining a licence for 3 years
370. A.R.T. 57/1973	Manslaughter	12 October 1973 15–16 November 1973	Not guilty	Not guilty
371. B.L.W. 57/73	Manslaughter	12 November 1973 4–5 December 1973	Not guilty	Guilty 3 years' probation Driver's licence suspended Disqualified from holding licence for 3 years Conditional that he undertake a refresher course on responsible driving before reapplying for driver's licence in 3 years' time

TABLE A1: SUPREME COURT INDICTMENTS, 1946–1974

Name and case no.	Offence	Committal and trial dates	Plea	Verdict, sentence and remarks
372. L.M.K. 61/73†	Manslaughter	16 October 1973 13 December 1973	Not guilty	Not guilty
373. M.J.F. 63/73	Manslaughter	23 October 1973 19–20 December 1973	Not guilty	Not guilty of manslaughter – Guilty of reckless driving causing death 2 years' imprisonment, minimum term 6 months before eligible for parole Driver's licence cancelled Disqualified from holding a licence for 5 years
374. N.C. 3/74	Manslaughter	23 November 1973 5 February 1974	Not guilty	Not guilty of manslaughter – Guilty of negligent driving causing death 18 months' imprisonment, minimum term 5 months before eligible for parole Driver's licence cancelled Disqualified from holding a licence for 5 years
375. B.J.B. 11/74*	Manslaughter	24 January 1974 19–20 February 1974	Not guilty to manslaughter Guilty to negligent driving causing death	Guilty of negligent driving causing death (as per plea) 18 months' imprisonment, minimum term 5 months before eligible for parole Driver's licence (if any) cancelled Disqualified from holding a licence for 5 years
376. B.R.S. 18†	Unlawful killing	6 February 1974 6–7 March 1974	Not guilty	Not guilty
377. T.J.H. 19	Unlawful killing	4 February 1974 11–12 March 1974	Not guilty	Not guilty
378. C.P.M. 21/74*	Manslaughter	25 February 1974 12–13 March 1974	Not guilty	Not guilty
379. A.C.H. 20	Unlawful killing	29 January 1974 13 March 1974	Not guilty to manslaughter Guilty to negligent driving causing death	Guilty of negligent driving causing death (as per plea) 15 months' imprisonment, minimum term 4 months before eligible for parole Disqualified from holding a driver's licence for 5 years No action on breach of probation

TABLE A1: SUPREME COURT INDICTMENTS, 1946–1974

Name and case no.	Offence	Committal and trial dates	Plea	Verdict, sentence and remarks
380. J.M.P. 27/74†	Manslaughter	12 February 1974 2 April 1974	Guilty	Guilty 3½ years' imprisonment, minimum term 15 months before eligible for parole
381. M.L. 39/74	Manslaughter	12 December 1973 8–9 April 1974	Not guilty	Not guilty of manslaughter – Guilty of negligent driving causing death Recognisance – $50 – for 3 years
382. J.W. 32/74	Manslaughter	14 February 1974 8–9 April 1974	Not guilty	Not guilty
383. B.A., J.A., F.F., B.R. & J.W. (Joint prosecution) 49/74	Unlawful killing	22 February 1974 14–16 May 1974	Not guilty	Not guilty
384. J.F.H.W. 46/74	Manslaughter	5 April 1974 29–31 May 1974	Not guilty	Not guilty
385. M.A.J. 29/74*	Unlawful killing	11 February 1974 4 June 1974	Not guilty to manslaughter Guilty to negligent driving causing death	Guilty of negligent driving causing death (as per plea) 2 years' imprisonment, minimum term 9 months before eligible for parole Permanent licence disqualification
386. L.J.J. 57/74	Manslaughter	29 April 1974 10–11 June 1974	Not guilty	Not guilty
387. R.S.A. 59/74	Manslaughter	29 April 1974 20–21 June 1974	Not guilty	Not guilty of manslaughter – Guilty of negligent driving causing death Fined $500 Driver's licence suspended for 5 years Disqualified from obtaining a licence for 5 years
388. A.P.J. 60/74	Manslaughter	2 May 1974 24 June 1974	Not guilty	Not guilty
389. S.N. 56/74†	Manslaughter	22 April 1974 18–19 July 1974	Not guilty	Guilty 2 years' imprisonment, minimum terms 3 months before eligible for parole
390. M.T. 64/74	Manslaughter	6 May 1974 24–25 July 1974	Not guilty	Not guilty

TABLE A1: SUPREME COURT INDICTMENTS, 1946–1974

Name and case no.	Offence	Committal and trial dates	Plea	Verdict, sentence and remarks
391. I.G.R. 75/74	Manslaughter	7 June 1974 15–16 & 19 August 1974	Not guilty	Not guilty of manslaughter – Guilty of reckless driving causing death 6 months' imprisonment Driver's licence cancelled Disqualified from obtaining a licence for 5 years
392. D.R.P. 92/74^	Unlawful killing	12 June 1974 10–11 September 1974	Not guilty	Not guilty
393. M.J.S. 89/74†	Manslaughter	15 July 1974 16–17 September 1974	Not guilty	Guilty 2 years' imprisonment, minimum term 9 months before eligible for parole Driver's licence cancelled Disqualified from holding a licence for 5 years
394. H.D.M. 93/74*	Unlawful killing	9 August 1974 12–13 September 1974	Not guilty	Guilty of manslaughter 2 years' imprisonment, minimum term 12 months before eligible for parole Driver's licence cancelled Disqualified from holding a licence for 5 years
395. R.W.F. 90/74	Manslaughter	30 July 1974 26 September 1974	Guilty to dangerous and reckless driving causing death	Guilty of dangerous driving causing death (as per plea) 18 months' imprisonment, minimum term 6 months before eligible for parole Driver's licence cancelled Disqualified from holding a licence for 5 years
396. J.A.S.M. 79/74	Manslaughter	3 May 1974 4–5 November 1974	Not guilty	Not guilty
397. J.C.B. 100/74	Dangerous driving causing death	Unknown 5 November 1974	Guilty	Guilty 18 months' imprisonment, minimum term 3 months before eligible for parole Disqualified from holding or obtaining a licence for 5 years

TABLE A1: SUPREME COURT INDICTMENTS, 1946–1974

Name and case no.	Offence	Committal and trial dates	Plea	Verdict, sentence and remarks
398. B.K.W. 109/74†	Manslaughter	4 October 1974 5 November 1974	Guilty	Guilty 3 years' imprisonment, minimum term 6 months before eligible for parole
399. T.C.W. 109/74†	Manslaughter	4 October 1974 5 November 1974	Guilty	Guilty 3 years' imprisonment, minimum term 6 months before eligible for parole
400. K.R.B. 106/74^	Unlawful killing	9 October 1974 11–13 November 1974	Not guilty	Guilty of manslaughter 18 months' probation
401. S.H.B. 106/74†	Unlawful killing	9 October 1974 11–13 November 1974	Not guilty	Guilty of manslaughter 18 months' probation
402. C.D.A.	Unlawful killing	9 September 1974 14–15 November 1974	Not guilty	Not guilty
403. L.B. 11/74^	Manslaughter	20 November 1974 17 December 1974	Not guilty	Not guilty

TABLE A2: CONVICTIONS AND SENTENCES, 1946–1974: VEHICULAR MANSLAUGHTER AND NEGLIGENT DRIVING CAUSING DEATH

	Name	Offence	Year	Plea	Verdict, sentence and remarks
1.	G.T.B.	Manslaughter	1946	Not guilty	Not guilty of manslaughter – Guilty of negligent driving causing death Bond – £100 & surety – £100 Disqualified from holding a driver's licence for the remainder of the current licence period and the following two periods
2.	L.W.S.	Manslaughter	1947	Not guilty	Not guilty of manslaughter – Guilty of reckless or dangerous driving causing death Jury recommend mercy 9 months' imprisonment with hard labour
3.	A.H.B.	Manslaughter	1947	Not guilty	Guilty 3 years' imprisonment with hard labour
4.	J.W.K.	Manslaughter	1948	Not guilty	Guilty Jury recommend mercy 12 months' imprisonment with hard labour Permanent licence disqualification
5.	M.J.N.	Manslaughter	1949	Not guilty	Not guilty of manslaughter – Guilty of negligent driving causing death Jury recommend mercy Bond – £50
6.	J.M.T.	Manslaughter	1949	Not guilty	Not guilty of manslaughter – Guilty of negligent driving causing death Jury recommend mercy Bond – £100 Bond breached 1953 – 1 year's imprisonment with hard labour
7.	A.C.E.D	Manslaughter	1949	Not guilty	Guilty Jury recommend mercy 3 years' imprisonment with hard labour
8.	J.C.	Manslaughter	1949	Not guilty	Not guilty of manslaughter – Guilty of negligent driving causing death Jury strongly recommend mercy 15 months' imprisonment with hard labour
9.	W.A.B.	Manslaughter	1950	Not guilty	Not guilty of manslaughter – Guilty of dangerous driving causing death Recognisance – £50 & surety – £50

TABLE A2: CONVICTIONS AND SENTENCES, 1946–1974

	Name	Offence	Year	Plea	Verdict, sentence and remarks
10.	H.A.H.	Manslaughter	1950	Not guilty to manslaughter Guilty to negligent driving causing death	Guilty of negligent driving causing death Bond – £50 & surety – £50 Bond conditions: a) cancellation of any current driver's licences b) declaration that unfit to hold any kind of driver's licence in the future c) prohibited from driving or attempting to drive any kind of vehicle in the future. Attempt or actual infringement of a condition may invoke detention
11.	F.O.B.	Manslaughter	1951	Not guilty	Not guilty of manslaughter – Guilty of negligent driving causing death 2 years' imprisonment with hard labour
12.	O.S.	Negligent driving causing death	1951	Not guilty	Guilty 2 years' imprisonment with hard labour
13.	B.D.S.M.	Negligent driving causing death	1951	Not guilty	Guilty 15 months' imprisonment with hard labour
14.	W.R.N.	Manslaughter	1952	Not guilty	Not guilty of manslaughter – Guilty of negligent driving causing death 9 months' imprisonment with hard labour
15.	E.V.	Manslaughter	1952	Not guilty	Not guilty of manslaughter – Guilty of negligent driving causing death 10 months' imprisonment with hard labour Recommendation that licence not be renewed for 2 years
16.	D.C.G.	Manslaughter	1952	Not guilty	Not guilty of manslaughter – Guilty of negligent driving causing death 18 months' imprisonment with hard labour
17.	J.W.C. (Callaghan)	Manslaughter	1952	Not guilty	Not guilty of manslaughter – Guilty of negligent driving causing death 2 years' imprisonment with hard labour Released on bail pending appeal Appealed to WA Court of Criminal Appeal – dismissed Appealed to the High Court of Australia – sentence quashed
18.	G.I.B.	Manslaughter	1952	Not guilty	Not guilty of manslaughter – Guilty of negligent driving causing death Jury recommend mercy 3 months' imprisonment with hard labour

TABLE A2: CONVICTIONS AND SENTENCES, 1946–1974

	Name	Offence	Year	Plea	Verdict, sentence and remarks
19.	J.H.P.P.	Manslaughter	1953	Not guilty	Not guilty of manslaughter – Guilty of negligent driving causing death 4 months' imprisonment with hard labour
20.	R.E.S.	Manslaughter	1953	Not guilty	Not guilty of manslaughter – Guilty of reckless driving or negligence causing death 12 months' imprisonment with hard labour
21.	W.R.P.	Manslaughter	1953	Not guilty	Not guilty of manslaughter – Guilty of dangerous driving causing death 6 months' imprisonment
22.	G.N.	Manslaughter	1954	Not guilty	Not guilty of manslaughter – Guilty of negligent driving causing death 9 months' imprisonment with hard labour
23.	R.H.L.	Manslaughter	1954	Not guilty	Not guilty of manslaughter – Guilty of dangerous driving causing death 12 months' imprisonment
24.	G.W.B.	Manslaughter	1955	Not guilty	Guilty 3 years' imprisonment with hard labour
25.	R.L.D. (Name unclear)	Manslaughter	1955	Not guilty	Not guilty of manslaughter – Guilty of dangerous driving causing death Jury strongly recommend mercy on account of youth 4 months' imprisonment with hard labour Driver's licence cancelled Banned from holding any driver's licence for 10 years
26.	E.B.S.	Manslaughter	1955	Not guilty	Not guilty of manslaughter – Guilty of dangerous driving causing death 9 months' imprisonment
27.	B.J.T.	Manslaughter	1956	Not guilty	Not guilty of manslaughter – Guilty of dangerous driving causing death Jury strongly recommend mercy on account of youth Bond – £100 Disqualified from holding any driver's licence for life
28.	L.G.F.	Manslaughter	1956	Not guilty	Not guilty of manslaughter – Guilty of dangerous driving causing death 4 months' imprisonment with hard labour Disqualified from holding any driver's licence for 5 years

TABLE A2: CONVICTIONS AND SENTENCES, 1946–1974

	Name	Offence	Year	Plea	Verdict, sentence and remarks
29.	L.L.L.	Manslaughter	1956	Not guilty	Not guilty of manslaughter – Guilty of dangerous driving causing death 12 months' imprisonment with hard labour Motorcycle licence suspended for 5 years Disqualified from obtaining any licence for 5 years
30.	D.C.	Manslaughter	1956	Not guilty	Not guilty of manslaughter – Guilty of dangerous driving causing death 8 months' imprisonment
31.	G.V.G.	Manslaughter	1956	Not guilty	Not guilty of manslaughter – Guilty of dangerous driving causing death Jury strongly recommend mercy Bond – £50 Indefinite licence disqualification
32.	W.W.D.	Manslaughter	1956	Not guilty	Not guilty of manslaughter – Guilty of dangerous driving causing death 12 months' imprisonment with hard labour
33.	J.L.S.	Manslaughter	1956	Not guilty	Not guilty of manslaughter – Guilty of dangerous driving causing death 9 months' imprisonment
34.	E.M.	Manslaughter	1958	Not guilty	Not guilty of manslaughter – Guilty of negligent driving causing death 3 months' imprisonment with hard labour
35.	M.R.S.	Manslaughter	1958	Not guilty	Not guilty of manslaughter – Guilty of negligent driving causing death 6 months' imprisonment with hard labour
36.	N.K.	Manslaughter	1958	Not guilty	Not guilty of manslaughter – Guilty of dangerous driving causing death 12 months' imprisonment
37.	D.A.J.	Manslaughter	1958	Not guilty	Not guilty of manslaughter – Guilty of dangerous driving causing death Jury recommend mercy 4 months' imprisonment with hard labour At expiration of sentence, disqualified from applying for a driver's licence for a further 5 years
38.	L.G.W.	Manslaughter	1958	Not guilty	Guilty Jury strongly recommend mercy owing to youth Bond – £50 All existing driver's licences cancelled Disqualified from holding any driving licence for life

TABLE A2: CONVICTIONS AND SENTENCES, 1946–1974

	Name	Offence	Year	Plea	Verdict, sentence and remarks
39.	F.G.D.	Manslaughter	1959	Guilty	Guilty 18 months' imprisonment with hard labour Driver's licence suspended Disqualified from holding a licence for 5 years
40.	L.J.T	Manslaughter	1959	Not guilty	Not guilty of manslaughter – Guilty of negligent driving causing death Driver's licence suspended Disqualified from holding another licence for 5 years
41.	G.H.M.	Manslaughter	1959	Not guilty	Not guilty of manslaughter – Guilty of dangerous driving causing death Jury strongly recommend mercy Bond – £100 – for 2 years
42.	A.F.	Manslaughter	1959	Not guilty	Not guilty of manslaughter – Guilty of negligent driving causing death 6 months' imprisonment with hard labour Indefinite licence disqualification
43.	J.P.S.	Manslaughter (2 counts)	1959	Not guilty	Not guilty of manslaughter – Guilty of negligent driving causing death (1 count) Fined £180 Driver's licence cancelled Disqualified from holding a licence for further 3 years
44.	J.J.K.	Manslaughter	1959	Not guilty to manslaughter Guilty to negligent driving causing death	Guilty of negligent driving causing death 9 months' imprisonment with hard labour Driver's licence cancelled Licence not to be reissued for 5 years
45.	B.J.M.	Manslaughter	1960	Not guilty	Guilty 6 months' imprisonment with hard labour
46.	S.F.M.	Manslaughter	1960	Not guilty	Not guilty of manslaughter – Guilty of negligent driving causing death Fined £50 Driver's licence suspended for 2 years
47.	A.K.A.	Manslaughter	1960	Not guilty to manslaughter Guilty to negligent driving causing death	Guilty of negligent driving causing death Bond – £100 & surety – £100 – for 3 years Driver's licence suspended for 2 years

TABLE A2: CONVICTIONS AND SENTENCES, 1946–1974

	Name	Offence	Year	Plea	Verdict, sentence and remarks
48.	F.X.I.	Manslaughter	1960	Not guilty	Not guilty of manslaughter – Guilty of negligent driving causing death 15 months' imprisonment with hard labour Driver's licence cancelled for 3 years
49.	A.F.H.	Unlawful killing	1960	Not guilty to manslaughter Guilty to dangerous driving causing death	Guilty of dangerous driving causing death 6 months' imprisonment Driver's licence suspended for 12 months after expiration of sentence
50.	D.T.C.W.	Manslaughter	1960	Not guilty to manslaughter Guilty to dangerous driving causing death	Guilty of dangerous driving causing death 12 months' imprisonment with hard labour Disqualified from holding a driver's licence for 3 years
51.	A.J.C.	Unlawful killing	1961	Not guilty	Not guilty of manslaughter – Guilty of negligent driving causing death 12 months' imprisonment with hard labour Disqualified from obtaining a driver's licence for 12 months from expiration of term of imprisonment
52.	R.J.F.	Manslaughter	1961	Not guilty to manslaughter Guilty to negligent driving causing death	Guilty of negligent driving causing death Fined £350 Recognisance – £200 & surety – for 5 years Driver's licence suspended for 3 years
53.	A.V.	Manslaughter	1961	Not guilty	Not guilty of manslaughter – Guilty of reckless driving causing death Fined £200 Disqualified from holding a driver's licence for 3 years
54.	G.J.B.	Unlawful killing	1961	Not guilty	Not guilty of manslaughter – Guilty of negligent driving causing death 12 months' imprisonment with hard labour Disqualified from holding or obtaining a driver's licence for 12 months from release
55.	R.K.O.	Manslaughter	1961	Not guilty	Not guilty of manslaughter – Guilty of negligent driving causing death 6 months' imprisonment with hard labour Indefinite disqualification

TABLE A2: CONVICTIONS AND SENTENCES, 1946–1974

	Name	Offence	Year	Plea	Verdict, sentence and remarks
56.	W.D. (Name unclear)	Manslaughter	1962	Not guilty	Not guilty of manslaughter – Guilty of reckless driving causing death 6 months' imprisonment with hard labour Disqualified from holding a driver's licence for 3 years from release
57.	A.G.	Manslaughter	1962	Not guilty	Not guilty of manslaughter – Guilty of negligent driving causing death Bond – £50 – for 2 years Breach of bond – sentenced 17 March 1964 18 months' imprisonment Disqualified from holding a driver's licence for 7 years Appealed term of licence disqualification – 15 November 1967 – disqualification revoked 20 November 1967
58.	J.H.	Manslaughter (2 counts)	1962	Not guilty to manslaughter Guilty to negligent driving causing death	Guilty of negligent driving causing death (1 count) 2 years' imprisonment with hard labour Licence disqualified for 7 years
59.	H.J.H.	Manslaughter	1962	Not guilty	Not guilty of manslaughter – Guilty of reckless driving causing death 9 months' imprisonment with hard labour Disqualified from holding a driver's licence for 5 years from date of release
60.	G.J.F	Manslaughter	1962	Not guilty to manslaughter Guilty to negligent driving causing death	Guilty of negligent driving causing death Bond – £50 – for 3 years Driver's licence disqualified for 5 years
61.	C.W.N.	Manslaughter	1962	Not guilty	Not guilty of manslaughter – Guilty of negligent driving causing death 2 years' imprisonment with hard labour Disqualified from holding any driver's licence for life
62.	L.R.L.	Manslaughter	1962	Not guilty	Not guilty of manslaughter – Guilty of dangerous driving causing death Fined £100 Driver's licence suspended Disqualified from holding any licence for 2 years

TABLE A2: CONVICTIONS AND SENTENCES, 1946–1974

	Name	Offence	Year	Plea	Verdict, sentence and remarks
63.	J.K.C.	Manslaughter	1963	Not guilty	Not guilty of manslaughter – Guilty of negligent control of a vehicle causing death Jury strongly recommend mercy Fined £300 Driver's licence suspended Disqualified from holding a driver's licence for 2 years
64.	J.M. (Middle name unclear)	Manslaughter	1963	Not guilty	Not guilty of manslaughter – Guilty of negligent driving causing death Jury recommend mercy 12 months' imprisonment with hard labour, followed by indeterminate detention Driver's licence cancelled Disqualified from obtaining any type of licence for 10 years Leave to appeal denied 25 July 1963
65.	J.H.	Manslaughter	1963	Not guilty	Not guilty of manslaughter – Guilty of negligent driving causing death Jury recommend mercy Bond – £100 & surety – £100 for 10 years Driver's licence suspended Disqualified from holding a licence for 10 years
66.	G. (Surname unclear)	Manslaughter	1963	Not guilty	Not guilty of manslaughter – Guilty of reckless driving causing death Fined £200 Disqualified from holding a driver's licence for 5 years
67.	T.D.	Manslaughter	1963	Not guilty	Not guilty of manslaughter – Guilty of reckless driving causing death 6 months' imprisonment with hard labour Driver's licence suspended Disqualified from holding a licence for 7 years after release
68.	L.J.S.	Manslaughter	1963	Not guilty	Not guilty of manslaughter – Guilty of negligent driving causing death Jury strongly recommend mercy 4 months' imprisonment with hard labour Driver's licence cancelled Disqualified from holding a licence for 5 years
69.	A.H.	Manslaughter	1964	Not guilty	Not guilty of manslaughter – Guilty of negligent driving causing death Fined £250 Driver's licence suspended Disqualified from holding a licence for life

TABLE A2: CONVICTIONS AND SENTENCES, 1946–1974

	Name	Offence	Year	Plea	Verdict, sentence and remarks
70.	W.W.V.	Manslaughter	1964	Not guilty	Guilty 18 months' imprisonment with hard labour Driver's licence suspended Disqualified from holding a licence for 5 years
71.	K.J.M.	Manslaughter	1964	Not guilty	Not guilty of manslaughter – Guilty of negligent driving causing death Jury recommend mercy 9 months' imprisonment with hard labour Driver's licence suspended Disqualified from holding a licence for 10 years
72.	A.P.	Manslaughter	1964	Not guilty	Guilty 2 years' imprisonment with hard labour Disqualified from obtaining a driver's licence for 10 years
73.	M.O.S.	Manslaughter	1964	Not guilty to manslaughter Guilty to negligent driving causing death	Guilty of negligent driving causing death Fined £350 Driver's licence suspended until expiration Disqualified from obtaining a licence for 5 years
74.	J.W.S.	Manslaughter	1964	Not guilty	Not guilty of manslaughter – Guilty of negligent driving causing death Bond – £50 – for 5 years Driver's licence cancelled Disqualified from holding a licence for 10 years
75.	C.T.A	Manslaughter	1964	Not guilty	Not guilty of manslaughter – Guilty of reckless driving causing death Fined £100 Bond – £250 & surety – £250 for 5 years Driver's licence suspended for 10 years
76.	J.B.J.R.	Manslaughter	1964	Not guilty to manslaughter Guilty to reckless driving causing death	Guilty of reckless driving causing death 2 years' imprisonment, minimum term 9 months before eligible for parole Driver's licence suspended for 10 years
77.	J.P.G.	Manslaughter (2 counts)	1964	Not guilty	Not guilty of manslaughter – Guilty of reckless driving causing death (1 count) 18 months' imprisonment, minimum term 6 months before eligible for parole Driver's licence suspended for 10 years 2nd count – nolle prosequi Application for review of licence suspension – 25 November 1964 – denied

TABLE A2: CONVICTIONS AND SENTENCES, 1946–1974

	Name	Offence	Year	Plea	Verdict, sentence and remarks
78.	E.A.N.	Manslaughter	1965	Not guilty to manslaughter Guilty to reckless driving causing death	Guilty of reckless driving causing death 6 months' imprisonment with hard labour
79.	L.G.H.	Manslaughter	1965	Not guilty to manslaughter Guilty to reckless driving causing death	Guilty of reckless driving causing death Fined £250 Driver's licence suspended Disqualified from holding a licence for 5 years
80.	R.G.	Manslaughter	1965	Not guilty	Not guilty of manslaughter – Guilty of dangerous driving causing death 2 years' imprisonment, minimum term 18 months before eligible for parole
81.	C.H.D.	Manslaughter	1965	Not guilty	Not guilty of manslaughter – Guilty of reckless driving causing death 4 months' imprisonment
82.	S.M.Q.	Manslaughter	1965	Not guilty	Not guilty of manslaughter – Guilty of reckless driving causing death 10 months' imprisonment
83.	N.M.	Manslaughter	1965	Not guilty	Not guilty of manslaughter – Guilty of reckless driving causing death 2 years' imprisonment, minimum term 15 months before eligible for parole
84.	P.M.L.	Manslaughter	1965	Not guilty to manslaughter Guilty to dangerous driving causing death	Guilty of dangerous driving causing death 12 months' imprisonment with hard labour, minimum term 6 months before eligible for parole Disqualified from holding a driver's licence for 10 years
85.	F.P.F.	Manslaughter	1965	Not guilty	Not guilty of manslaughter – Guilty of dangerous driving causing death 12 months' imprisonment with hard labour, minimum term 6 months before eligible for parole Disqualified from holding a driver's licence for 10 years
86.	S.H.	Unlawful killing	1965	Not guilty	Not guilty of manslaughter – Guilty of negligent driving causing death 2 years' imprisonment with hard labour, minimum term 15 months before eligible for parole Driver's licence cancelled Disqualified from holding a licence for 8 years

TABLE A2: CONVICTIONS AND SENTENCES, 1946–1974

	Name	Offence	Year	Plea	Verdict, sentence and remarks
87.	R.D.S.	Manslaughter	1965	Not guilty	Guilty 2 years' imprisonment with hard labour Not eligible for parole for 12 months
88.	D.A.W.	Manslaughter	1965	Not guilty	Not guilty of manslaughter – Guilty of negligent driving causing death 3 years' imprisonment with hard labour, minimum term 18 months before eligible for parole Driver's licence cancelled Ineligible to obtain a licence for 15 years
89.	P.R.V.S.	Unlawful killing	1965	Not guilty	Guilty of manslaughter 2 years' imprisonment with hard labour, minimum term 18 months before eligible for parole Driver's licence cancelled Disqualified from holding a licence for 8 years
90.	R.T.S.	Unlawful killing	1965	Not guilty	Not guilty of manslaughter – Guilty of negligent driving causing death 18 months' imprisonment with hard labour, minimum term 9 months before eligible for parole Disqualified from holding a driver's licence for 5 years
91.	H.G.	Manslaughter	1965	Not guilty	Not guilty of manslaughter – Guilty of negligent driving causing death 9 months' imprisonment with hard labour
92.	A.J.P.	Unlawful killing	1966	Not guilty	Not guilty of manslaughter – Guilty of negligent driving causing death 12 months' imprisonment with hard labour, minimum term 6 months before eligible for parole Existing driver's licence cancelled Declared ineligible to hold a licence for 5 years
93.	N.W.R.	Manslaughter	1966	Not guilty	Not guilty of manslaughter – Guilty of reckless driving causing death 2 years' imprisonment, no minimum term Cumulative on present sentences Disqualified from holding a driver's licence for 12 years

TABLE A2: CONVICTIONS AND SENTENCES, 1946–1974

	Name	Offence	Year	Plea	Verdict, sentence and remarks
94.	S.J. (Middle name unclear)	Manslaughter	1966	Not guilty	Not guilty of manslaughter – Guilty of dangerous driving causing death 12 months' imprisonment with hard labour, minimum term 6 months before eligible for parole Driver's licence suspended Disqualified from obtaining a licence for a further period of 5 years Application for an extraordinary licence heard on 15 February 1971 – granted
95.	E.J.H.	Manslaughter	1966	Not guilty	Not guilty of manslaughter – Guilty of negligent driving causing death 18 months' imprisonment with hard labour, minimum term 9 months before eligible for parole Driver's licence cancelled Disqualified from holding a licence for 5 years
96.	A.J.B.	Manslaughter	1966	Not guilty	Not guilty of manslaughter – Guilty of negligent driving causing death 2 years' imprisonment with hard labour, minimum term 12 months before eligible for parole Driver's licence cancelled Disqualified from holding a licence for 5 years
97.	K.S.W.	Manslaughter	1966	Not guilty	Not guilty of manslaughter – Guilty of negligent driving causing death 18 months' imprisonment with hard labour, minimum term 9 months before eligible for parole Driver's licence cancelled Disqualified from holding a licence for 5 years
98.	D.J.B.	Manslaughter	1966	Not guilty	Not guilty of manslaughter – Guilty of negligent driving causing death 3 years' probation on following conditions: 1) abstain from violation of the law 2) within 24 hours after this date report to the Chief Probation Officer personally 3) carry out the lawful instructions of the Probation Officer 4) report and receive visits as directed by the Probation Officer 5) notify the Probation Officer within 48 hours of any changes of your address or employment during the Probation period Driver's licence cancelled Disqualified from holding a licence for 5 years

TABLE A2: CONVICTIONS AND SENTENCES, 1946–1974

	Name	Offence	Year	Plea	Verdict, sentence and remarks
99.	I.G.C.	Manslaughter	1966	Not guilty	Not guilty of manslaughter – Guilty of negligent driving causing death Jury strongly recommend mercy 9 months' imprisonment with hard labour
100.	R.H.W.	Manslaughter	1966	Not guilty to manslaughter Guilty to reckless driving causing death	Guilty of reckless driving causing death 2 years' imprisonment Driver's licence suspended Disqualified from holding a licence for 12 years
101.	A.S.	Manslaughter	1967	Not guilty	Not guilty of manslaughter – Guilty of dangerous driving causing death 12 months' imprisonment with hard labour Disqualified from holding a driver's licence for 5 years Extraordinary licence application heard 20 March 1970 – granted
102.	P.L.W.	Manslaughter	1967	Not guilty to manslaughter Guilty to dangerous driving causing death	Guilty of dangerous driving causing death 12 months' imprisonment with hard labour Disqualified from holding a driver's licence for 5 years
103.	R.N.S.	Manslaughter	1967	Not guilty to manslaughter Guilty to dangerous driving causing death	Guilty of dangerous driving causing death 12 months' imprisonment with hard labour Disqualified from holding a driver's licence for 5 years
104.	A.J.W.	Manslaughter	1967	Not guilty	Not guilty of manslaughter – Guilty of reckless driving causing death 18 months' imprisonment, minimum term 6 months before eligible for parole Driver's licence cancelled Disqualified from obtaining licence for 7 years
105.	J.D.W.	Manslaughter	1967	Not guilty	Not guilty of manslaughter – Guilty of reckless and dangerous driving causing death 15 months' imprisonment with hard labour, minimum term 6 months before eligible for parole

TABLE A2: CONVICTIONS AND SENTENCES, 1946–1974

	Name	Offence	Year	Plea	Verdict, sentence and remarks
106.	R.H.	Manslaughter	1967	Not guilty to manslaughter Guilty to reckless driving causing death	Guilty of reckless driving causing death 18 months' imprisonment, minimum term 3 months before eligible for parole Driver's licence suspended Disqualified from obtaining a licence for 5 years
107.	F.T.D.	Manslaughter	1967	Not guilty	Not guilty manslaughter – Guilty of reckless driving causing death 18 months' imprisonment, minimum term 3 months before eligible for parole Driver's licence suspended Disqualified from obtaining a licence for 5 years
108.	C.J.F.	Manslaughter	1967	Not guilty to manslaughter Guilty to negligent driving causing death	Guilty of negligent driving causing death 18 months' imprisonment with hard labour, minimum term 6 months before eligible for parole Concurrent with sentences now serving Driver's licence cancelled Disqualified from holding a licence for 10 years
109.	H.J.C.	Unlawful killing	1967	Not guilty	Not guilty manslaughter – Guilty of negligent driving causing death 18 months' imprisonment with hard labour, minimum term 6 months before eligible for parole
110.	B.A.H.	Manslaughter	1968	Not guilty	Not guilty manslaughter – Guilty of negligent driving causing death 18 months' imprisonment with hard labour, minimum term 6 months before eligible for parole Driver's licence cancelled Disqualified from driving for 3 years
111.	W.D.W.	Manslaughter	1968	Not guilty to manslaughter Guilty to dangerous driving causing death	Guilty of dangerous driving causing death 18 months' imprisonment with hard labour, minimum term 6 months before eligible for parole Disqualified from holding a driver's licence for 10 years
112.	C.S.H.	Manslaughter	1968	Not guilty to manslaughter Guilty to reckless driving causing death	Guilty of reckless driving causing death 3 years' imprisonment, minimum term 12 months before eligible for parole Driver's licence cancelled Disqualified from obtaining a licence for 10 years

TABLE A2: CONVICTIONS AND SENTENCES, 1946–1974

Name	Offence	Year	Plea	Verdict, sentence and remarks
113. M.M.	Unlawful killing	1968	Not guilty	Not guilty of manslaughter – Guilty of negligent driving causing death 18 months' imprisonment with hard labour, minimum term 8 months before eligible for parole Driver's licence cancelled Disqualified from obtaining a licence for 5 years
114. R.B.C.W.	Manslaughter	1968	Not guilty	Not guilty of manslaughter – Guilty of reckless driving causing death Fined $500 Driver's licence cancelled Disqualified from obtaining a licence for 7 years
115. G.N.M.	Manslaughter	1969	Not guilty	Not guilty of manslaughter – Guilty of negligent driving causing death 18 months' imprisonment with hard labour, minimum term 8 months before eligible for parole Driver's licence cancelled Disqualified from holding a licence for 5 years
116. J.W.N.	Manslaughter	1969	Not guilty to manslaughter Guilty to dangerous driving causing death	Guilty of dangerous driving causing death 18 months' imprisonment with hard labour, minimum term 9 months before eligible for parole Disqualified from holding a driver's licence for 5 years
117. R.A.S.	Dangerous driving causing death and Breach of Probation	1969	Guilty both counts	Guilty of dangerous driving causing death and breach of probation 1st charge – 2 years' imprisonment, minimum term 9 months before eligible for parole Driver's licence cancelled Disqualified from holding a licence for 5 years 2nd charge – 12 months' imprisonment, minimum term 3 months before eligible for parole Cumulative on previous sentence
	Manslaughter (2nd deceased)			Nolle prosequi
118. E.J.V.	Manslaughter	1969	Not guilty	Not guilty of manslaughter – Guilty of reckless driving causing death 3 years' imprisonment, minimum term 12 months before eligible for parole Driver's licence suspended for 7 years

TABLE A2: CONVICTIONS AND SENTENCES, 1946–1974

	Name	Offence	Year	Plea	Verdict, sentence and remarks
119.	B.F.L.	Manslaughter	1969	Not guilty	Not guilty of manslaughter – Guilty of reckless driving causing death Indeterminate detention – reformatory prison Disqualified from obtaining a driver's licence for 10 years
120.	V.P.L. (Laporte)	Unlawful killing	1969	Not guilty	Jury disagreed Defendant remanded
		Manslaughter		Retrial	Guilty 4 years' imprisonment with hard labour, minimum term 18 months before eligible for parole Current driver's licence suspended until expiry Disqualified from obtaining a licence for 7 years
					Leave to appeal granted Appeal allowed Sentence reduced – 2 years' imprisonment, minimum term 9 months before eligible for parole
121.	W.W.W.	Manslaughter	1970	Not guilty to manslaughter Guilty to dangerous driving causing death	Guilty of dangerous driving causing death 5 years' probation Driver's licence cancelled Ineligible to hold a licence for 5 years
122.	O.N.H.	Manslaughter	1970	Not guilty	Not guilty of manslaughter – Guilty of reckless driving causing death 3 years' imprisonment, minimum term 18 months before eligible for parole Disqualified from obtaining a licence for 5 years following release
123.	K.W.	Manslaughter	1970	Not guilty	Not guilty of manslaughter – Guilty of reckless driving causing death 9 months' imprisonment – minimum term Disqualified from obtaining a driver's licence for 2 years following release
124.	E.H.T.	Unlawful killing	1970	Not guilty	Not guilty of manslaughter – Guilty of negligent driving causing death 18 months' imprisonment, minimum term 9 months before eligible for parole Driver's licence cancelled Disqualified from holding a licence for 5 years

TABLE A2: CONVICTIONS AND SENTENCES, 1946–1974

Name	Offence	Year	Plea	Verdict, sentence and remarks
125. S.R.B.	Unlawful killing (2 counts)	1970	Not guilty	Guilty of manslaughter (1 count) 2 years' imprisonment, minimum term 9 months before eligible for parole Driver's licence cancelled Disqualified from holding a licence for 6 years
				Nolle prosequi – 2nd count
126. C.A.S.B.	Unlawful killing	1970	Not guilty	Guilty of negligent driving causing death 15 months' imprisonment Minimum term during which not eligible for parole fixed at 8 months Driver's licence cancelled Disqualified from holding a licence for 5 years
127. F.J.H.	Unlawful killing	1970	Not guilty to manslaughter Guilty to dangerous driving causing death	Guilty of dangerous driving causing death 2 years' imprisonment with hard labour Minimum term of 9 months to be served before eligible for release on parole Disqualified from holding a driver's licence for life
128. S.R.B.	Unlawful killing	1970	Not guilty	Not guilty of manslaughter – Guilty of reckless driving causing death Jury strongly recommend mercy 2 years' imprisonment, minimum term 12 months before eligible for parole Prohibited from holding a driver's licence for 3 years from the expiry of present suspended licence
129. K.W.F.	Manslaughter (2 counts)	1970	Not guilty	Not guilty of manslaughter – Guilty of reckless driving causing death (1 count) 12 months' imprisonment, no minimum term Driver's licence suspended Disqualified from holding a licence for 5 years from release
				2nd indictment adjourned sine die
130. A.P.C.	Manslaughter	1970	Not guilty	Not guilty of manslaughter – Guilty of dangerous driving causing death Fined $1,000 Driver's licence suspended Disqualified from holding a licence for 10 years
131. S.G.H.	Manslaughter	1970	Not guilty	Not guilty of manslaughter – Guilty of reckless driving causing death 18 months' imprisonment, minimum term 9 months before eligible for parole Driver's licence cancelled

TABLE A2: CONVICTIONS AND SENTENCES, 1946–1974

	Name	Offence	Year	Plea	Verdict, sentence and remarks
132.	A.M.B.	Unlawful killing	1970	Not guilty	Not guilty of manslaughter – Guilty of negligent driving causing death Fined $1,000 Driver's licence cancelled Disqualified from holding a licence for 7 years
					Extraordinary licence application – 29 September 1972 – Disqualification order revoked
133.	R.E.M.	Unlawful killing	1970	Not guilty to manslaughter Guilty to dangerous driving causing death	Guilty of dangerous driving causing death 18 months' imprisonment, minimum term 12 months before eligible for parole Driver's licence cancelled Disqualified from holding a licence for 7 years
134.	B.J.D.	Manslaughter	1970	Not guilty	Not guilty of manslaughter – Guilty of negligent driving causing death 12 months' imprisonment, minimum term 3 months before eligible for parole Driver's licence suspended Disqualified from holding a licence for 7 years
135.	M.B.	Manslaughter	1970	Not guilty	Not guilty of manslaughter – Guilty of negligent driving causing death 12 months' imprisonment, minimum term 8 months before eligible for parole Driver's licence suspended Disqualified from holding a licence for 7 years
136.	A.E.B.	Manslaughter (2 counts)	1971	Not guilty to manslaughter Guilty to dangerous driving causing death	Guilty of dangerous driving causing death (1 count) Bond – $500 – for 3 years
137.	G.N.C.	Unlawful killing (2 counts)	1971	Not guilty	Not guilty of manslaughter – Guilty of negligent driving causing death (1 count) 9 months' imprisonment, minimum term 3 months before eligible for parole Disqualified from holding a driver's licence for 3 years
138.	R.L.A.	Unlawful killing	1971	Not guilty	Not guilty of manslaughter – Guilty of negligent driving causing death 9 months' imprisonment, minimum term 2 months before eligible for parole Driver's licence cancelled Disqualified from holding a licence for a period of 5 years

TABLE A2: CONVICTIONS AND SENTENCES, 1946–1974

	Name	Offence	Year	Plea	Verdict, sentence and remarks
139.	B.J.W.	Unlawful killing	1971	Not guilty to manslaughter Guilty to negligent driving causing death	Guilty of negligent driving causing death 17 months' imprisonment, minimum term 8 months before eligible for parole Driver's licence cancelled Disqualified from holding a licence for life
140.	V.J.K.	Manslaughter	1971	Not guilty	Not guilty of manslaughter – Guilty of reckless driving causing death 2 years' imprisonment, minimum term 8 months before eligible for parole Disqualified from obtaining a driver's licence for 5 years from date of release
141.	R.N.P.	Manslaughter	1971	Not guilty to manslaughter Guilty to dangerous driving causing death	Guilty of dangerous driving causing death 6 months' imprisonment with hard labour Driver's licence suspended until expiry Disqualified from holding a licence for 5 years from date of release
142.	M.E.T.	Manslaughter	1971	Not guilty	Not guilty of manslaughter – Guilty of reckless driving causing death 6 months' imprisonment with hard labour Driver's licence suspended until expiry Disqualified from holding a licence for 5 years following release
143.	J.T.E.	Manslaughter	1971	Not guilty to manslaughter Guilty to reckless driving causing death	Guilty of reckless driving causing death 2 years' imprisonment, minimum term 6 months before eligible for parole Driver's licence suspended Disqualified from holding a licence for 5 years
144.	R.S.M.	Manslaughter	1971	Not guilty	Guilty 3 years' imprisonment, minimum term 9 months before eligible for parole Disqualified from obtaining a driver's licence for 7 years
145.	D.L.B.V.	Manslaughter	1971	Not guilty	Not guilty of manslaughter – Guilty of reckless driving causing death 3 years' imprisonment, minimum term 12 months before eligible for parole
146.	G.J.M.	Manslaughter	1972	Not guilty	Not guilty of manslaughter – Guilty of reckless driving causing death Jury strongly recommend mercy Fined $300 Driver's licence cancelled Disqualified from holding a licence for 5 years

TABLE A2: CONVICTIONS AND SENTENCES, 1946–1974

	Name	Offence	Year	Plea	Verdict, sentence and remarks
147.	W.G.W.	Manslaughter	1972	Not guilty	Not guilty of manslaughter – Guilty of reckless driving causing death 3 years' imprisonment, minimum term 2 years before eligible for parole Concurrent with sentence now serving Driver's licence cancelled Not eligible to obtain a licence for 5 years following release
148.	R.J.B.	Manslaughter	1972	Not guilty	Not guilty of manslaughter – Guilty of dangerous driving causing death 12 months' imprisonment, minimum term 6 months before eligible for parole
149.	H.R.B.	Manslaughter	1972	Not guilty	Not guilty of manslaughter – Guilty of negligent driving causing death Jury strongly recommend mercy 6 months' imprisonment with hard labour Disqualified from holding a driver's licence for 5 years
150.	T.D.K.	Unlawful killing	1972	Not guilty to manslaughter Guilty to dangerous driving causing death	Guilty of dangerous driving causing death 2 years' imprisonment, minimum term 1 year before eligible for parole Driver's licence cancelled Disqualified from holding a licence for 7 years
151.	R.D.R.	Unlawful killing	1972	Not guilty	Not guilty of manslaughter – Guilty of dangerous driving causing death 18 months' imprisonment, minimum term 6 months before eligible for parole Driver's licence cancelled for 5 years
152.	A.I.F.	Manslaughter	1973	Not guilty	Not guilty of manslaughter – Guilty of negligent driving causing death 18 months' imprisonment, minimum term 2 months before eligible for parole Driver's licence (if any) cancelled Disqualified from holding a licence for 5 years
153.	M.D.H.	Manslaughter	1973	Not guilty	Not guilty of manslaughter – Guilty of negligent driving causing death 12 months' imprisonment with hard labour, minimum term 3 months before eligible for parole Driver's licence disqualified for 5 years from date of expiry of present disqualification

TABLE A2: CONVICTIONS AND SENTENCES, 1946–1974

Name	Offence	Year	Plea	Verdict, sentence and remarks
154. C.F.C.	Manslaughter	1973	Not guilty	Guilty 4 years' imprisonment, minimum term 18 months before eligible for parole Driver's licence suspended Disqualified from holding a licence for 4 years
155. L.D.S.	Manslaughter	1973	Not guilty	Not guilty of manslaughter – Guilty of reckless driving causing death 6 months' imprisonment Driver's licence cancelled Disqualified from holding a licence for 5 years
156. R.W.S.	Manslaughter	1973	Not guilty to manslaughter Guilty to reckless driving causing death	Guilty of reckless driving causing death 2 years' imprisonment, minimum term 6 months before eligible for parole Disqualified from obtaining a driver's licence for 5 years
157. G.A.H.	Manslaughter	1973	Not guilty	Not guilty of manslaughter – Guilty of negligent driving causing death Fined $500 Disqualified from holding a driver's licence for 5 years
158. G.J.T.	Manslaughter	1973	Not guilty	Not guilty of manslaughter – Guilty of negligent driving causing death Fined $700 Disqualified from holding a driver's licence for 5 years
159. R.A.A.	Manslaughter	1973	Not guilty	Not guilty of manslaughter – Guilty of negligent driving causing death Jury strongly recommend mercy Fined $500 Driver's licence suspended Disqualified from holding or obtaining a licence for 3 years
160. R.M.	Manslaughter	1973	Not guilty	Guilty Bond – $500 & surety – $500 for 3 years Driver's licence cancelled Disqualified from holding a licence for 3 years
161. R.L.F.	Manslaughter	1973	Not guilty	Not guilty of manslaughter – Guilty of reckless driving causing death 2 years' probation Driver's licence suspended Disqualified from obtaining a licence for 3 years

TABLE A2: CONVICTIONS AND SENTENCES, 1946–1974

	Name	Offence	Year	Plea	Verdict, sentence and remarks
162.	B.L.W.	Manslaughter	1973	Not guilty	Guilty 3 years' probation Driver's licence suspended Disqualified from holding a licence for 3 years Conditional that he undertake a refresher course on responsible driving before reapplying for driver's licence in 3 years' time
163.	M.J.F.	Manslaughter	1973	Not guilty	Not guilty of manslaughter – Guilty of reckless driving causing death 2 years' imprisonment, minimum term 6 months before eligible for parole Driver's licence cancelled Disqualified from holding a licence for 5 years
164.	N.C.	Manslaughter	1974	Not guilty	Not guilty of manslaughter – Guilty of negligent driving causing death 18 months' imprisonment, minimum term 5 months before eligible for parole Driver's licence cancelled Disqualified from holding a licence for 5 years
165.	B.J.B.	Manslaughter	1974	Not guilty to manslaughter Guilty to negligent driving causing death	Guilty of negligent driving causing death 18 months' imprisonment, minimum term 5 months before eligible for parole Driver's licence (if any) cancelled Disqualified from holding a licence for 5 years
166.	A.C.H.	Unlawful killing	1974	Not guilty to manslaughter Guilty to negligent driving causing death	Guilty of negligent driving causing death 15 months' imprisonment, minimum term 4 months before eligible for parole Disqualified from holding a driver's licence for 5 years No action on breach of probation
167.	M.L.	Manslaughter	1974	Not guilty	Not guilty of manslaughter – Guilty of negligent driving causing death Recognisance – $50 – for 3 years
168.	M.A.J.	Unlawful killing	1974	Not guilty to manslaughter Guilty to negligent driving causing death	Guilty of negligent driving causing death 2 years' imprisonment, minimum term 9 months before eligible for parole Permanent licence disqualification
169.	R.S.A.	Manslaughter	1974	Not guilty	Not guilty of manslaughter – Guilty of negligent driving causing death Fined $500 Driver's licence suspended for 5 years Disqualified from obtaining a licence for 5 years

TABLE A2: CONVICTIONS AND SENTENCES, 1946–1974

	Name	Offence	Year	Plea	Verdict, sentence and remarks
170.	I.G.R.	Manslaughter	1974	Not guilty	Not guilty of manslaughter – Guilty of reckless driving causing death 6 months' imprisonment Driver's licence cancelled Disqualified from obtaining a licence for 5 years
171.	M.J.S.	Manslaughter	1974	Not guilty	Guilty 2 years' imprisonment, minimum term 9 months before eligible for parole Driver's licence cancelled Disqualified from holding a licence for 5 years
172.	H.D.M.	Unlawful killing	1974	Not guilty	Guilty of manslaughter 2 years' imprisonment, minimum term 12 months before eligible for parole Driver's licence cancelled Disqualified from holding a licence for 5 years
173.	R.W.F.	Manslaughter	1974	Not guilty to manslaughter Guilty to dangerous and reckless driving causing death	Guilty of dangerous driving causing death 18 months' imprisonment, minimum term 6 months before eligible for parole Driver's licence cancelled Disqualified from holding a licence for 5 years
174.	J.C.B.	Dangerous driving causing death	1974	Guilty	Guilty 18 months' imprisonment, minimum term 3 months before eligible for parole Disqualified from holding or obtaining a licence for 5 years

TABLE A3: SUPREME COURT INDICTMENTS, 1975–1981: CASES OF INTEREST WITH SAMPLED FILES MARKED

	Name and case no.	Offence	Committal and trial dates	Plea	Verdict, sentence and remarks
1.	B.J.P. 19/75+	Manslaughter	22 January 1975 5–6 March 1975	Not guilty	Not guilty of manslaughter – Guilty of negligent driving causing death 3 years' probation Driver's licence cancelled Disqualified from holding or obtaining a driver's licence for 5 years from date of conviction
2.	B.F.P. 1/75+*	Manslaughter	14 November 1974 4–5 February 1975	Not guilty	Not guilty
3.	M.J.F. 2/75+	Manslaughter	6 November 1975 25 February 1975	Not guilty to manslaughter Guilty to reckless driving causing death	Guilty of reckless driving causing death (as per plea) 12 months' imprisonment, minimum term 3 months before eligible for parole Driver's licence cancelled Disqualified from holding a licence for 3 years
4.	K.W.H. 6/1975+	Manslaughter	18 December 1974 17–18 February 1975	Not guilty	Not guilty of manslaughter – Guilty of reckless driving causing death 2 years' imprisonment, minimum term 6 months before eligible for parole Disqualified from holding a licence for 5 years Appeal Order of Court of Criminal Appeal 21 April 1975 Custodial term set aside Fined $500
5.	J.R. 8/75+	Manslaughter	15 January 1975 20–21 February 1975	Not guilty	Not guilty of manslaughter – Guilty of reckless driving causing death Fined $1,000 Driver's licence cancelled Disqualified from holding a licence for 5 years

TABLE A3: SUPREME COURT INDICTMENTS, 1975–1981

	Name and case no.	Offence	Committal and trial dates	Plea	Verdict, sentence and remarks
6.	M.S.P. 40/75+*	Manslaughter	10 April 1975 9–10 June 1975	Not guilty	Guilty Fined $750 Driver's licence suspended Disqualified from holding or obtaining a licence for 3 years
7.	B.J.P. 42/75+	Manslaughter	(Committal date unclear) April 1975 23–24 June 1975	Not guilty	Not guilty of manslaughter – Guilty of negligent driving causing death Fined $750 Driver's licence suspended Disqualified from holding or obtaining a licence for 3 years
8.	A.J.T. 18/75	Dangerous driving causing death (Initially charged with unlawful killing)	17 March 1975 28 July 1975	Guilty	Guilty Lesser plea accepted by Court Indeterminate detention – reformatory prison Driver's licence cancelled Disqualified from holding a licence for 5 years
9.	T.C.A. 48/75	Manslaughter	18 April 1975 17 July 1975	Not guilty to manslaughter Guilty to reckless driving causing death	Guilty of reckless driving causing death (as per plea) Fined $1,000 Driver's licence suspended Disqualified from obtaining a licence for 7 years
10.	B.D. 50/75	Manslaughter	28 February 1975 22–24 July 1975	Not guilty	Not guilty
11.	T.K.A. (Order of first and second names unclear) 52/75	Manslaughter	15 May 1975 28–29 July 1975	Not guilty	Not guilty
12.	M.T.F. 75/75	Manslaughter	11 July 1975 12 August 1975	Not guilty	Not guilty of manslaughter – Guilty of reckless driving causing death Bond – $500 & surety $500 – for 5 years Driver's licence cancelled Disqualified from obtaining a licence for 5 years

TABLE A3: SUPREME COURT INDICTMENTS, 1975–1981

	Name and case no.	Offence	Committal and trial dates	Plea	Verdict, sentence and remarks
13.	M.C.S. 84/75	Unlawful killing	3 August 1975 15 August 1975	Not guilty	Remanded
		Manslaughter	22–23 September 1975		Not guilty of manslaughter – Guilty of negligent driving causing death Recognisance – $500 – for 2 years
14.	A.M.K. 93/75	Unlawful killing	21 August 1975 8 October 1975	Not guilty	Not guilty
15.	W.K.B. 84/75	Manslaughter	15 July 1975 10 September 1975	Not guilty to manslaughter Guilty to reckless driving causing death	Guilty of reckless driving causing death (as per plea) 12 months' imprisonment followed by indeterminate detention Cumulative on sentences now serving Disqualified from obtaining a driver's licence for 7 years
16.	P.J.N. 88/75	Manslaughter	22 July 1975 29 September 1975	Not guilty	Not guilty of manslaughter – Guilty of reckless driving causing death Fined $500 Driver's licence suspended Disqualified from obtaining a licence for 3 years
17.	R.H. 1/76	Unlawful killing	27 November 1975 13 January 1976	Not guilty	Remanded
		Unlawful killing	23–24 February 1976	Not guilty	Not guilty
18.	R.J.M. 16/76	Unlawful killing	13 January 1976 16 February 1976	Not guilty	Not guilty
19.	B.D.S. & T.R.R. 41/76 (Joint prosecution)*	Manslaughter	17 February 1976 12–14 April 1976	Not guilty	Not guilty of manslaughter – Guilty of dangerous driving causing death Each 4 years' probation Driver's licences cancelled Disqualified from holding or obtaining driver's licences for 4 years

TABLE A3: SUPREME COURT INDICTMENTS, 1975–1981

Name and case no.	Offence	Committal and trial dates	Plea	Verdict, sentence and remarks
20. T.J.S. 46/76*	Manslaughter	23 February 1976 13 April 1976	Not guilty to manslaughter Guilty to dangerous driving causing death	Guilty of dangerous driving causing death (as per plea) 2 years' imprisonment with hard labour, minimum term 4 months before eligible for parole Disqualified from holding a driver's licence for 3 years
21. E.G. 17/76	Dangerous driving causing death	27 October 1975 7–9 April 1976	Not guilty	Guilty Fined $1,500 Disqualified from holding a driver's licence for 4 years Leave to appeal – denied
22. C.E.P. 78/76	Unlawful killing	25 May 1976 4–6 August 1976	Not guilty	Not guilty of manslaughter – Guilty of dangerous driving causing death 18 months' imprisonment, minimum term 6 months before eligible for parole Driver's licence cancelled Disqualified from holding or obtaining a licence for 3 years from date of release
23. D.A.H. 78/76	Unlawful killing	25 May 1976 4–6 August 1976	Not guilty	Not guilty of manslaughter – Guilty of dangerous driving causing death 18 months' imprisonment, minimum term 6 months before eligible for parole Driver's licence cancelled Disqualified from holding or obtaining a licence for 3 years from date of release
24. J.E.W.E. 81/76*	Unlawful killing	5 May 1976 26–29 July 1976	Not guilty	Guilty of manslaughter 5 years' imprisonment, minimum term 17 months before eligible for parole Driver's licence suspended Disqualified from holding or obtaining a licence for 7 years
25. C.R. 94/76	Manslaughter	5 July 1976 23–25 July 1976	Not guilty	Not guilty
26. G.R.F. 75/76	Manslaughter	27 May 1976 31 August & 1–2 September 1976	Not guilty	Not guilty

TABLE A3: SUPREME COURT INDICTMENTS, 1975–1981

	Name and case no.	Offence	Committal and trial dates	Plea	Verdict, sentence and remarks
27.	C.J.P.	Dangerous driving causing death	16 July 1976	Not guilty	Adjourned (No further notations)
28.	S.R.D. 95/76	Unlawful killing	30 June 1976 16 August 1976	Not guilty	Not guilty
29.	G.L.O. 112/76	Unlawful killing	6 August 1976 22–23 September 1976	Not guilty	Not guilty of manslaughter – Guilty of dangerous driving causing death Jury strongly recommend mercy 2 years' imprisonment, minimum term 1 year before eligible for parole Disqualified from holding a driver's licence for 5 years from date of release
30.	K.S. 3/1977	Manslaughter	2 December 1976 19–20 January 1977	Not guilty	Not guilty
31.	I.B.F. 94/77	Manslaughter	12 July 1977 22–23 September 1977	Not guilty	Not guilty of manslaughter – Guilty of dangerous driving causing death 3 years' probation Community service order – 200 hours to be completed within 12 months Driver's licence cancelled Disqualified from holding a licence for 5 years
32.	J.R.L. 135/1977	Manslaughter	17 November 1977 7–9 December 1977	Not guilty	Not guilty of manslaughter – Guilty of dangerous driving causing death Fined $1,000 Driver's licence cancelled Disqualified from holding a driver's licence for 2 years
33.	P.D. 135/1977	Manslaughter	18 October 1977 7–8 December 1977	Not guilty	Not guilty
34.	P.R. 24/78	Manslaughter	15 December 1977 13 February 1978	Not guilty	Not guilty
35.	S.R.A. 34/78	Unlawful killing	19 January 1978 13 March 1978	Not guilty to manslaughter Guilty to dangerous driving causing death	Guilty of dangerous driving causing death (as per plea) Fined $4,000 Disqualified from holding or obtaining a driver's licence for 5 years

TABLE A3: SUPREME COURT INDICTMENTS, 1975–1981

	Name and case no.	Offence	Committal and trial dates	Plea	Verdict, sentence and remarks
36.	D.W.M. 38/78	Unlawful killing	23 January 1978 22 March 1978	Not guilty to manslaughter Guilty to dangerous driving causing death	Guilty of dangerous driving causing death (as per plea) 18 months' imprisonment, minimum term 9 months before eligible for parole Disqualified from holding or obtaining a driver's licence for 5 years
37.	S.K., J.S. & A.L.S. 137/78 (Joint prosecution)*	Manslaughter	26 May 1978 11–15 & 18 September 1978	Not guilty (all defendants)	S.K. – Guilty J.S. and A.L.S. – Not guilty of manslaughter – Guilty of dangerous driving causing death S.K. – 2 years' imprisonment, minimum term 4½ months before eligible for parole J.S. – Fined $1,500 A.L.S. – 12 months' imprisonment, minimum term 2 months before eligible for parole All driving licences suspended All offenders disqualified from holding or obtaining a licence for 5 years
38.	G.E.F. 197/78	Manslaughter	26 September 1978 18–19 December 1978	Not guilty	Not guilty
39.	M.N.A. 6/79	Unlawful killing	9 November 1978 8 January 1979	Not guilty	Remanded
			5 February 1979	Not guilty	Not guilty
40.	A.M.C. 67/79*	Unlawful killing	23 November 1978 19–20 March 1979	Not guilty	Guilty of manslaughter 5 years' imprisonment, minimum term 3 years before eligible for parole Driver's licence cancelled Disqualified from holding or obtaining a licence for life
41.	S.J.M. 49/79	Manslaughter	15 February 1979 29–30 May 1979	Not guilty	Not guilty of manslaughter – Guilty of dangerous driving causing death Fined $2,500 Community service order – 100 hours Driver's licence cancelled Disqualified from holding a licence for 5 years

TABLE A3: SUPREME COURT INDICTMENTS, 1975–1981

	Name and case no.	Offence	Committal and trial dates	Plea	Verdict, sentence and remarks
42.	L.M.D. 193/79	Unlawful killing	22 August 1979	None taken	Remanded
			1 November 1979		
		Manslaughter	6 December 1979	Not guilty to manslaughter Guilty to dangerous driving causing death	Guilty of dangerous driving causing death (as per plea) 3 years' imprisonment, minimum term 1 year before eligible for parole Disqualified from obtaining a driver's licence for 5 years from date of release
43.	D.R.B. & I.P.S. 203/79 (Joint prosecution)	Manslaughter	18 September 1979 27–29 February 1980	Not guilty	Not guilty of manslaughter – Guilty of dangerous driving causing death Each 3 years' probation Community service order – 200 hours Disqualified from holding or obtaining a driver's licence for 5 years to commence at expiration of any present period of disqualification
					Defendant I.P.S. Appeal – allowed CCA 28/1980 Conviction quashed, orders set aside
44.	D.M. 3/80	Unlawful killing	7 November 1979 14 January 1980	Not guilty	Adjourned Bail (No further notations)
45.	G.K.S. 6/80	Manslaughter	14 November 1979	None taken	Not guilty
			14 January & 1 February 1980	Not guilty	
			25–26 February 1980		
46.	G.G 23/80	Manslaughter	13 December 1979	Not guilty	Not guilty
			4 February 1980		
			30 April & 1 May 1980		

TABLE A3: SUPREME COURT INDICTMENTS, 1975–1981

Name and case no.	Offence	Committal and trial dates	Plea	Verdict, sentence and remarks
47. W.D.T. 66/80	Unlawful killing	10 April 1980 12 May 1980	Not guilty	Jury disagreed Remanded
		11–12 August 1980	Not guilty	Not guilty
48. R.J.D. 45/80	Unlawful killing	22 February 1980 14 April 1980	Not guilty	Remanded
		12–13 June 1980		Not guilty
49. V.J.P. 51/80	Unlawful killing	30 January 1980 (Trial date not recorded)	Not guilty	Guilty of manslaughter 2½ years' imprisonment, minimum term 1 year before eligible for parole Disqualified from holding a driver's licence for 5 years from date of release
50. J.L.F. 67/80	Unlawful killing	9 December 1980 7 May 1980	No plea taken	Remanded
		5–6 June 1980	Not guilty	Not guilty
51. M.D.B. 75/80	Manslaughter	9 April 1980 9 June 1980	Guilty	Guilty Fined $1,000 Disqualified from driving for 5 years 200 hours of community service to be completed within 12 months
52. G.S.C. 85/80	Manslaughter	19 May 1980 30–31 July 1980	Not guilty	Guilty 4 years' imprisonment, minimum term 2 years before eligible for parole Driver's licence cancelled Disqualified from holding a driver's licence for life
53. G.A.T.C. 110/80*	Manslaughter	26 June 1980 29–30 September 1980	Not guilty	Guilty 12 months' imprisonment, no minimum term fixed Driver's licence cancelled Disqualified from holding a licence for 3 years Appeal – granted Court of Criminal Appeal 107/80 Conviction quashed, orders set aside Remanded on bail to appear before the District Court, 3 February, 1981 for retrial

TABLE A3: SUPREME COURT INDICTMENTS, 1975–1981

	Name and case no.	Offence	Committal and trial dates	Plea	Verdict, sentence and remarks
54.	I.T.A.M. 137/80	Dangerous driving causing death	5 September 1980 3 November 1980	Guilty	Guilty 8 months' imprisonment Disqualified from holding a driver's licence for five years to take effect from date of release from custody
55.	P.J.S. 136/80	Unlawful killing	1 September 1980 19 November 1980	Not guilty to manslaughter Guilty to dangerous driving causing death	Guilty of dangerous driving causing death (as per plea) 9 months' imprisonment Disqualified from holding a driver's licence for 5 years from date of release
56.	T.J.A. 140/80	Manslaughter	29 September 1980 19–21 November 1980	Not guilty	Not guilty of manslaughter – Guilty of dangerous driving causing death 8 months' imprisonment
57.	R.J.T. 140/80	Manslaughter	29 September 1980 19–21 November 1980	Not guilty	Not guilty
58.	M.E.H.W. 10/82 11/82	Manslaughter (2 counts)	30 October 1981 11 January 1982 10 March 1982	Not guilty	Not guilty 29 March 1982 – 2nd count - nolle prosequi
59.	J.D.F. 133/81	Manslaughter	16 June 1981 24–25 September 1981	Not guilty	Not guilty of manslaughter – Guilty of dangerous driving causing death Fined $1,250
60.	R.C.C. 131/81	Unlawful killing	18 June 1981 2–3 September 1981	Not guilty	Guilty of manslaughter 18 months' imprisonment, minimum term 5 months before eligible for parole Driving licence suspended Disqualified from driving for 3 years
61.	J.P.F.G. 148/81	Unlawful killing	10 July 1981 24 August 1981	Not guilty	Not guilty of manslaughter – Guilty of dangerous driving causing death 12 months' imprisonment, minimum term 3 months before eligible for parole

TABLE A3: SUPREME COURT INDICTMENTS, 1975–1981

Name and case no.	Offence	Committal and trial dates	Plea	Verdict, sentence and remarks
62. P.D.F. 94/81	Unlawful killing	22 April 1981	Guilty to manslaughter	Guilty of manslaughter (as per plea) 4 years' imprisonment, minimum term 2 years before eligible for parole Disqualified from holding a driver's licence for 5 years
				Appeal – granted Court of Criminal Appeal 89/81 Sentence varied to 3 years' imprisonment, minimum term 10 months before eligible for parole Time spent in custody to be taken into account
63. W.F.C.	Unlawful killing	26 March 1981 22–23 June 1981	Not guilty	Not guilty

NOTES

Introduction: Law, 'accidents' and the 'road toll'

1. Transport Accident Commission, 'Girlfriend', 1989, available online at <https://www.youtube.com/watch?v=TfhR5w5uYWs>, accessed: 4 January 2019.
2. The Triffids, 'Wide Open Road', *Born Sandy Devotional*, Mushroom Records, 1986.
3. Cold Chisel, 'Flame Trees', *Twentieth Century*, WEA, 1984.
4. AC/DC, 'Highway to Hell', *Highway to Hell*, Albert Productions, 1979.
5. AC/DC, 'Ride On', *Dirty Deeds Done Dirt Cheap*, Albert Productions, 1977.
6. Golden Earring, 'Radar Love', *Moontan*, Track Records Ltd., 1973.
7. The Cars, 'Drive', *Heartbeat City*, Elektra Records, 1984.
8. The Smiths, 'There is a Light That Never Goes Out', *The Queen is Dead*, Rough Trade Records, 1986.
9. Kiss, 'Detroit Rock City', *Destroyer*, Casablanca Records, 1976.
10. Steppenwolf, 'Born to be Wild', *Steppenwolf*, ABC Dunhill Records, 1968.
11. ZZ Top, 'Arrested for Driving While Blind', *Tejas*, London Records, 1976; Sammy Hagar, 'I Can't Drive 55', *VOA*, Geffen Records, 1984; Eagles, 'Take it Easy', *Eagles*, Asylum Records, 1972; Metallica, 'Fuel', *Reload*, Elektra Records, 1997; Jackson Browne, 'Running on Empty', *Running on Empty*, Asylum Records, 1977; The Doobie Brothers, 'Rockin' Down the Highway', *Toulouse Street*, Warner Bros. Records, 1972; Van Halen, 'Panama', *1984*, Warner Music Group, 1984; Meat Loaf, 'Bat Out of Hell', *Bat Out of Hell*, Cleveland International/Epic Records, 1977; Mötley Crüe, 'Kickstart My Heart', *Dr. Feelgood*, Elektra Records, 1989.
12. Deep Purple, 'Highway Star', *Machine Head*, EMI (UK), 1972; Led Zeppelin, 'Trampled Underfoot', *Physical Graffiti*, Swan Song Records, 1975; Prince, 'Little Red Corvette', *1999*, Warner Bros., 1983.
13. Queen, 'I'm in Love with My Car', *A Night at the Opera*, EMI Records (UK), 1975.
14. Bruce Springsteen, 'Born to Run', *Born to Run*, Columbia Records, 1975.

NOTES TO THE INTRODUCTION

15 Bruce Springsteen, 'Thunder Road', *Born to Run*, Columbia Records, 1975, and Bruce Springsteen, 'Racing in the Street', *Darkness on the Edge of Town*, Columbia Records, 1978.
16 Jimmy Barnes, 'Driving Wheels', *Freight Train Heart*, Mushroom Records, 1987.
17 ibid.
18 R. Browning, 'Where are the protests?', *British Medical Journal*, vol. 324, 11 May 2002, p. 1165.
19 Gary Numan, 'Cars', *The Pleasure Principle*, Beggars Banquet Records, 1979.
20 L. Breen, *Silenced Voices: Grief Following Road Traffic Crashes*, Saarbrucken, VDM Verlag, 2008; World Health Organization (WHO) & Association for Safe International Road Travel (ASIRT), *Faces behind the figures: voices of road traffic victims and their families*, WHO, Switzerland, 2007; Federation of European Road Traffic Victims (FEVR), *Impact of road death and injury: research into the principal causes of the decline in quality of life and living standard suffered by road crash victims and victim families: Proposal for improvements*, Geneva, FEVR, 1995; J. H. Lord, 'America's Number One Killer: Vehicular Crashes', in K. J. Doka (ed.), *Living With Grief After Sudden Loss: Suicide, Homicide, Accident, Heart Attack, Stroke*, Hospice Foundation of America, Washington, 1996, pp. 25–39; N. Tehrani, 'Road Victim Trauma: an investigation of the impact on the injured and bereaved', *Counselling Psychology Quarterly*, vol. 17, no. 4, 2004, pp. 361–73; M. Mitchell, 'Death and Injury on the Road', in M. Mitchell (ed.), *The Aftermath of Road Accidents: Psychological, social and legal consequences of an everyday trauma*, Routledge, London, 1997, pp. 3–14; C. Corbett, *Car Crime*, Willan Publishing, Devon, 2003, pp. 149–55.
21 WHO & ASIRT, *Faces behind the figures*.
22 L. Breen, 'Silenced Voices: Experiences of Grief Following Road Traffic Crashes in Western Australia', PhD thesis (Psychology), Faculty of Computing, Health and Sciences, Edith Cowan University, 2006, pp. 150–1.
23 FEVR, *Impact of road death and injury*, pp. 4–5.
24 G. Taylor & R. Walsh, 'Killer drivers must pay a higher price', *West Australian*, 25–26 March 2017, pp. 6–7.
25 ibid.
26 G. Knowles, 'Charlotte's Law: Wayne and Jackie Pemberton want other families to avoid their suffering', *West Australian*, 21 June 2018, <https://thewest.com.au/news/wa/charlottes-law-wayne-and-jackie-pemberton-want-other-families-to-avoid-their-suffering-ng-b88872523z,>, accessed: 23 June 2018.
27 Taylor & Walsh, 'Killer drivers must pay a higher price', p. 6.
28 Sentencing Advisory Council, *Sentencing of Driving Offences that Result in Death or Injury: Consultation Paper*, Sentencing Advisory Council Tasmania, Hobart, 2016, pp. 80–3.
29 E. Gramenz, 'Sarah Paino's death: Jail terms for dangerous driving offences appropriate, Government told', *ABC News*, 26 April 2017, <http://www.abc.net.au/news/2017-04-26/sarah-paino-jail-terms-for-dangerous-driving-appropriate-sac/8471768>, accessed: 25 May 2017.
30 K. King, 'A Lesser Species of Homicide – Manslaughter, Negligent and Dangerous Driving Causing Death: The Prosecution of Drivers in Western

Australia, 1946–2011', PhD thesis, University of Western Australia, 2014, pp. 25–7.

31   J. W. Knott, 'Speed, Modernity and the Motor Car: The Making of the 1909 Motor Traffic Act in New South Wales', *Australian Historical Studies*, vol. 26, no. 103, 1994, p. 241; J. S. Dean, *Murder Most Foul: A study of the road deaths problem*, George Allen & Unwin Ltd, Great Britain, 1947, pp. 7, 23, 79; K. Richardson, *The British Motor Industry, 1896–1939*, Macmillan, London, 1977, pp. 178–80; H. Perkin, *The Age of the Automobile*, Quartet Books, London, 1976, p. 138. For critical discussion, see B. H. Lerner, *One for the Road: Drunk Driving Since 1900*, The Johns Hopkins University Press, Baltimore, 2011, pp. 10–11, 44, 128–32, 136–45.

32   J. J. Leeming, *Road Accidents: Prevent or Punish?*, Cassell, London, 1969, pp. 35, 105, 206–7, 213; P. J. Fitzgerald, 'Road Traffic Law as the Lawyer Sees it', in Leeming, *Road Accidents*, p. 157–75; J. O'Connell & A. Myers, *Safety Last: An Indictment of the Auto Industry*, Random House, New York, 1966, p. 34; S. Birney, *Australia on Wheels: Early Beginnings to the Present Day*, Bullion Books, Silverwater, 1989, pp. 20, 42; Richardson, *The British Motor Industry*, p. 12; R. Flower & M. W. Jones, *100 Years of Motoring: An RAC Social History of the Car*, Royal Automobile Club in association with McGraw–Hill, Croydon, 1981, p. 154; J. Goode, *Smoke, Smell and Clatter: The Revolutionary Story of Motoring in Australia*, Lansdowne Press Pty Ltd, Melbourne, 1969, p. 29.

33   A. Aird, *The Automotive Nightmare*, Hutchinson & Co, London, 1972, p. 183.

34   D. Brown, *Traffic Offences: An examination of the principles of law governing offences committed by motorists on the road in Australia*, Sydney, Butterworths, 1983, p. 101.

35   D. Brown, *Traffic Offences and Accidents: An examination of the principles of law governing offences and negligence by motorists on the roads in Australia*, Butterworths, North Ryde, 1996, p. 74 and Law Reform Commission of Victoria, *Death Caused by Dangerous Driving*, Discussion Paper No. 21, Law Reform Commission of Victoria, Melbourne, 1991, p. 14.

36   P. Mugliston, S. Ainsworth & H. Colebatch, *Traffic law in Western Australia*, LexisNexis Butterworths, Chatswood, 2007; D. Brown, *Traffic Offences*; D. Brown, *Traffic Offences and Accidents*, LexisNexis, Chatswood, 2006; O. Mazengarb, *Mazengarb's Negligence on the highway: law and practice in Australia*, Butterworths, Sydney, 1957.

37   Law Reform Commission of Western Australia, *Report: Manslaughter or Dangerous Driving causing Death*, Project No. 17, Law Reform Commission of Western Australia, Perth, August 1970; Law Reform Commission of Victoria, *Death Caused by Dangerous Driving*; Law Reform Commission of Western Australia, *Review of the Law of Homicide: Final Report*, Law Reform Commission of Western Australia, Perth, 2007, pp. 118–32; Sentencing Advisory Council, *Sentencing of Driving Offences that Result in Death or Injury: Consultation Paper*; Sentencing Advisory Council, *Sentencing of Driving Offences that Result in Death or Injury: Final Report*, No. 8, Sentencing Advisory Council Tasmania, Hobart, 2017.

38   R. Cooter & B. Luckin, 'Accidents in History: An Introduction', in R. Cooter & B. Luckin (eds.), *Accidents in History: Injuries, fatalities and social relations*, Rodopi, Amsterdam, 1997, p. 4.

NOTES TO THE INTRODUCTION

39 Department of Infrastructure, Transport, Regional Development and Local Government, *Road deaths in Australia 1925–2008*, Information Sheet 38, Bureau of Infrastructure, Transport and Regional Economics, Canberra, 2010, p. 3.
40 See <https://en.wikipedia.org/wiki/List_of_motor_vehicle_deaths_in_Australia_by_year>, accessed: 1 December 2016; <https://bitre.gov.au/publications/ongoing/road_deaths_australia_monthly_bulletins.aspx>, accessed: 15 December 2016; <https://bitre.gov.au/publications/ongoing/rda/files/RDA_Dec_2018.pdf>, accessed: 18 January 2019.
41 J. Clark, 'Wild behaviour: Infernal Machines and Serious Accidents', *National Library of Australia News*, vol. 7, no. 5, 1997, p. 3.
42 Crash data was collected as early as 1911 in some Australian jurisdictions. The compilation of national statistics commenced in 1925.
43 Western Australian Police Department – 005 059 V1, 'Accidents: Police attendance at Traffic Accidents', State Records Office of Western Australia (SROWA), WAS 488, CONS 5931 and 1961/3992, 'Traffic Accidents: Police Attending', SROWA, WAS 76, CONS 1910.
44 Department of Infrastructure, Transport, Regional Development and Local Government, *Road deaths in Australia 1925–2008*. See Table, 'Road crash casualties and rates, Australia, 1925–2008', at p. 7. See also Table 2, 'Road fatalities by State and Territory 1950–97', in Federal Office of Road Safety, *The history of road fatalities in Australia*, Monograph 23, Federal Office of Road Safety, Canberra, 1998, p. 4.
45 Federal Office of Road Safety, *Road traffic accident data and rates: Australia, States and Territories 1925 to 1981*, Australian Government Publishing Service, Canberra, 1984, p. v.
46 N. Faith, *Crash: The limits of car safety*, Boxtree, London, 1997, p. 13.
47 WHO, *World report on road traffic injury prevention*, WHO, Geneva, 2004, p. 33.
48 ibid., p. 3.
49 WHO, *Global status report on road safety 2018*, WHO, Geneva, 2018, p. vii.
50 ibid. See also p. 5.
51 WHO, *Global status report on road safety 2013: supporting a decade of action*, WHO, Geneva, 2013, p. 7.
52 ibid., p. 6.
53 ibid., p. 7.
54 ibid., p. vii.
55 WHO & ASIRT, *Faces behind the figures*, p. 1.
56 J. C. Furnas, 'And Sudden Death', *Reader's Digest* (USA), vol. 27, August 1935, p. 21.
57 ibid., p. 24.
58 Australian Broadcasting Commission (ABC), *The Gruen Transfer*, ABC Television, Season 1, Episode 7, 'Road Safety', 9 July 2008.
59 R. Davis, *Death on the Streets: Cars and the Mythology of Road Safety*, Leading Edge Press and Publishing Ltd, North Yorkshire, 1992/93, p. 59.
60 Commonwealth Bureau of Census and Statistics, *Official Year Book of the Commonwealth of Australia, No. 37, 1946 and 1947*, Commonwealth Bureau of Census and Statistics, Canberra, 1949, p. 786.

NOTES TO THE INTRODUCTION

61 Transport Accident Commission, 'Pictures of You', 2008, available online at <https://www.youtube.com/watch?v=DOYEuEiNBKE>, accessed: 30 December 2016.

62 G. Fletcher, *Rethinking Criminal Law*, Oxford University Press, Oxford, 2000, p. 238 and S. Cunningham, 'Vehicular Homicide: Need for a Special Offence?', in C. M. V. Clarkson & S. Cunningham (eds.), *Criminal Liability for Non-Aggressive Death*, Ashgate, Aldershot, 2008, pp. 107–8.

63 D. Luria, 'Death on the Highway: Reckless Driving as Murder', *Oregon Law Review*, vol. 67, 1988, p. 812. See also Lerner, *One for the Road: Drunk Driving Since 1900*, pp. 16, 148.

64 Luria, 'Death on the Highway', pp. 804–5.

65 S. Yeo, *Fault in Homicide: towards a schematic approach to the fault elements for murder and involuntary manslaughter in England, Australia and India*, Federation Press in association with the Institute of Criminology, University of Sydney, Leichhardt, 1997, p. 11.

66 Law Reform Commission of Victoria, *Death Caused by Dangerous Driving*, Discussion Paper No. 21, p. 21.

67 'Berlin drag racers sentenced to life in prison for murder', *Deutsche Welle*, 26 March 2019, <https://p.dw.com/p/3Ff9E> accessed: 30 October 2019.

68 Royal Automobile Club of Western Australia (RAC), *The Road Patrol: The Official Journal of the Royal*, RAC, 10 September 1946, p. 4.

69 *West Australian*, 12 February 1960, p. 7.

70 J. Green, 'Accidents: the remnants of a modern classificatory system', in Cooter & Luckin (eds.), *Accidents in History*, p. 50.

71 Personal communication, email from Dr P. Conole, Historian, Western Australia Police, to K. King, 3 May 2011.

72 WHO, *World report on road traffic injury prevention*, p. 7.

73 Cooter & Luckin, 'Accidents in History: An Introduction', p. 12.

74 Breen, 'Silenced Voices: Experiences of Grief Following Road Traffic Crashes in Western Australia', p. 143 and WHO, *World report on road traffic injury prevention*, pp. 9–11.

75 Davis, *Death on the Streets*, p. 95.

76 S. J. Ball-Rokeach, M. Hale, A. Schaffer, L. Porras, P. Harris & M. Drayton, 'Changing the Media Production Process: From Aggressive to Injury-Sensitive Traffic Crash Stories', in D. P. Demers & K. Viswanath (eds.), *Mass media, social control, and social change: A Macrosocial perspective*, Iowa State University Press, Ames, 1999, p. 231.

77 WHO, *World report on road traffic injury prevention*, p. 10 and Corbett, *Car Crime*, p. 116.

78 Breen, 'Silenced Voices: Experiences of Grief Following Road Traffic Crashes in Western Australia', pp. 143–51.

79 Corbett, *Car Crime*, pp. 3, 34–5.

80 ibid., pp. 34–5.

81 ibid., p. 34.

82 S. Cunningham, *Driving Offences: Law, Policy and Practice*, Ashgate Publishing Limited, Hampshire, 2008, p. 1 and Corbett, *Car Crime*, pp. xiii, 3–4.

NOTES TO THE INTRODUCTION

83 For example, see Corbett, *Car Crime* and Cunningham, *Driving Offences*.
84 Davis, *Death on the Streets*, p. 119.
85 A sentiment borrowed from Professor of Law, A. J. McClurg, who spoke of 'valuing the dead to help the living', in A. J. McClurg, 'Dead sorrow: a story about loss and a new theory of wrongful death damages', *Boston University Law Review*, vol. 85, no. 1, 2005, p. 33.

Chapter One: Manslaughter and negligent driving causing death, 1946–1974

1 *Callaghan v R* (1952) 87 CLR 115.
2 Via s 2 of *Criminal Code Amendment Act, 1945* (WA).
3 Letter from Mr Dunphy, Crown Solicitor, to Minister for Justice, 28 July 1943, Crown Law Department – 1934/3780, 'Crown Prosecutors: Criminal Code re amendment of, to make it an offence when driving a vehicle to cause the death of, or bodily harm to another, by failing to use reasonable care', State Records Office of Western Australia (SROWA), WAS 2664, CONS 1042.
4 D. Brown, *Traffic Offences and Accidents*, Butterworths, Sydney, 1996, p. 74. New South Wales and Victoria introduced similar offences in 1951 and 1958 respectively.
5 'Road Accidents: A Bad Month', *West Australian*, 5 December 1945, p. 6.
6 Commonwealth Bureau of Census and Statistics, *Official Year Book of the Commonwealth of Australia, No. 37, 1946 and 1947*, Commonwealth Bureau of Census and Statistics, Canberra, 1949, pp. 782, 784.
7 *R v A.J.C.* (1946), *R v W.M.* (1946), *R v G.T.B* (1946).
8 Section 3 of the *Criminal Code Amendment Act, 1945* (WA) amended s 595 of the Code and provided that, on an indictment for manslaughter, the jury could alternatively convict the defendant of negligent driving causing death.
9 R. McDonald, *Parliamentary Debates (Hansard)*, Western Australia, Legislative Assembly, 17 November 1945, pp. 1707–8.
10 ibid., p. 1708.
11 ibid. H. S. W. Parker, Legislative Council, 28 November 1945, p. 2264.
12 ibid., G. Fraser, 29 November 1945, p. 2305.
13 S. Cunningham, *Driving Offences: Law, Policy and Practice*, Ashgate Publishing Limited, Hampshire, 2008, p. 97.
14 For example, see O. Mazengarb, *Mazengarb's Negligence on the highway: law and practice in Australia*, Butterworths, Sydney, 1957, p. 488; Cunningham, *Driving Offences*, p. 97; Law Reform Commission of Western Australia, *Review of the Law of Homicide: Final Report*, Law Reform Commission of Western Australia, Perth, 2007, p. 120; J. V. Barry, 'Foreword', in W. R. Warden, *Juggernaut: Slaughter on the Australian Roads*, A. H. & A. W. Reed, Sydney, 1968, p. xv; A. Ashworth, '"Manslaughter": Generic or Nominate Offences?', in C. M .V. Clarkson & S. Cunningham (Eds.), *Criminal Liability for Non-Aggressive Death*, Ashgate, Aldershot, 2008, p. 245; *R v Stebbings* (1990) 4 WAR 538 at 544; *R v Calder; ex parte Attorney General* [1987] 1 Qd R 348, (1986) 22 A Crim R 62 at 63–4, 68–9.

NOTES TO CHAPTER ONE

15 *R v R.D.S.* (1965), trial transcript, p. 70.
16 D. Brown, *Traffic Offences: An examination of the principles of law governing offences committed by motorists on the roads in Australia*, Butterworths, North Ryde, 1983, p. 101.
17 ibid. See also letter from the Crown Solicitor to the Minister for Justice, 12 July 1943, Crown Law Department – 'Crown Prosecutors: Criminal Code re amendment of, to make it an offence when driving a vehicle to cause the death of, or bodily harm to another, by failing to use reasonable care', SROWA.
18 A. Kaladelfos & M. Finnane, Prosecution Project data, Western Australian Supreme Court, 2016. Many thanks to Dr Kaladelfos and Professor Finnane for this invaluable information. For further information on The Prosecution Project, see <https://prosecutionproject.griffith.edu.au>.
19 'An open letter to a hit and run driver', in Royal Automobile Club of Western Australia (RAC), *The Road Patrol: The Official Journal of the Royal Automobile Club of Western Australia*, RAC, Perth, September 1946, p. 16.
20 Western Australian Police Department – 1967/0564 v6, 'Police Department (Traffic Office) – Traffic Act & Regulations – Inquiries and Suggestions', SROWA, WAS 76, CONS 251, folio 106, p. 2.
21 Letter from Mr T. G. Paterson, Chairman of the Australian Road Safety Council, to Mr T. Anderson, Western Australian Commissioner of Police, received 2 July 1954, with attached report – 'Straight talks to bad drivers: Outline of suggested advertising campaign for 1954–1955', prepared by the Commonwealth Advertising Division, October 1953 and Western Australian Police Department – 1954/1593 v2, 'Australian Road Safety Council – Proposed formation of Policy file', SROWA, WAS 76, CONS 430.
22 RAC, *The Road Patrol*, RAC, Perth, July 1950, p. 18.
23 Western Australian Police Department – vol 6, 'Police Department (Traffic Office) – Traffic Act & Regulations – Inquiries and Suggestions', SROWA and Western Australian Police Department – 68 0548 V2, 'Suggestions for the improvement of Road Safety and reduction of Road Toll', SROWA, WAS 77, CONS 3439.
24 National Safety Council of Western Australia, Collection of photographs, BA 840/83, vol. 357, J. S. Battye Library of West Australian History.
25 See 1964 brochure, 'The Beacon', p. 3, National Safety Council of Western Australia, Collection of material relating to various divisions of the National Safety Council of Western Australia, Printed ephemera, PR8972, J. S. Battye Library of West Australian History.
26 L. Wood, *R v G.C.B.* (1970), trial transcript, pp. 80–1.
27 Western Australian Police Department – v2, 'Australian Road Safety Council – Proposed formation of Policy file', SROWA.
28 Covering letter with draft confidential report from Commissioner of Police to Inspector Duggan, 30 May 1968, Western Australian Police Department – 1962/1377, 'Fatal Traffic Accidents: Investigation by members of CIB', SROWA, WAS 76, CONS 1910.

29 B. Elliot & D. South, *The development and assessment of a drink-driving campaign: a case study*, Department of Transport, Office of Road Safety, Australian Government Publishing Service, Canberra, 1985, p. 18.
30 A. Terry, *The Motor Vehicle, Society and the Law*, CCH Australia, North Ryde, New South Wales, 1983, p. 56.
31 R. Davis, *Death on the Streets: Cars and the Mythology of Road Safety*, Leading Edge Press & Publishing Ltd, North Yorkshire, 1992/93, p. 25.
32 C. Corbett, *Car Crime*, Willan Publishing, Devon, 2003, p. 191.
33 *R v J.E.W.E.* (1976), trial transcript, p. 275.
34 *R v F.F.* (1963), trial transcript, pp. 64–5.
35 Section 23 of the Code originally stated that the defence of accident was subject to the provisions relating to negligent acts and omissions, meaning that the defence of accident was precluded on a charge based in a breach of a duty.
36 R. McDonald, *Parliamentary Debates*, Western Australia, Legislative Assembly, 17 November 1945, p. 1708. Despite the fact that the new homicide offence, s 291A, was added to the Code in 1946, legislators did not *formally* amend the definition of unlawful killing to encompass the offence until 1972, via s 9 of the *Criminal Code Amendment Act, 1972*.
37 Law Reform Commission of Western Australia, *Review of the Law of Homicide: Final Report*, pp. 87–8.
38 S. Yeo, *Fault in Homicide: towards a schematic approach to the fault elements for murder and involuntary manslaughter in England, Australia and India*, Federation Press in association with the Institute of Criminology, University of Sydney, Leichhardt, 1997, pp. 3–4, 199, 204–7.
39 Brown, *Traffic Offences*, p. 95.
40 C. Cook, R. Creyke, R. Geddes & D. Hamer, *Laying Down the Law*, LexisNexis Butterworths, New South Wales, 2005, p. 240.
41 Pursuant to s 266 of the Code.
42 Law Reform Commission of Western Australia, *Review of the Law of Homicide: Final Report*, p. 91.
43 ibid., pp. 92, 97. See also Brown, *Traffic Offences*, pp. 95–6.
44 A. Webster, 'Recklessness: Awareness, indifference or belief?', *Criminal Law Journal*, vol. 31, no. 5, 2007, p. 273.
45 Law Reform Commission of Western Australia, *Review of the Law of Homicide: Final Report*, pp. 71, 92.
46 Cunningham, *Driving Offences*, p. 199. For further discussion see, for example, M. Moran, *Rethinking the Reasonable Person: An Egalitarian Reconstruction of the Objective Standard*, Oxford University Press, Oxford, 2003 and J. Horder, 'Can the Law Do Without the Reasonable Person?', *University of Toronto Law Journal*, vol. 55, no. 2, 2005, pp. 253–69.
47 *R v C.W.H.* (1964), trial transcript, pp. 192–3.
48 Brown, *Traffic Offences*, p. 95.
49 Lord Hewart, C. J., in *R v Bateman* (1925) 19 Cr App R 8 at 10–12.
50 C. Wells, 'Look Hard and See More', *The Modern Law Review*, vol. 47, no. 1, 1984, pp. 102–3.

NOTES TO CHAPTER ONE

51 Law Reform Commission of Western Australia, *Review of the Law of Homicide: Final Report*, p. 65 and Brown, *Traffic Offences*, p. 115. See also for discussion, *Nydam v The Queen* [1977] VR 430.
52 Yeo, *Fault in Homicide*, p. 200.
53 ibid., pp. 4, 198–201.
54 ibid., p. 199.
55 ibid., p. 205.
56 *R v B.W.P.* (1972), see submission of Mr Lane at p. 25 of 'Depositions of witnesses taken at Police Court, Narrogin on 6 September, 1972'; *R v H.F.* (1968), trial transcript, pp. 79–80; *R v R.A.J.* (1973), trial transcript, p. 4; *R v M.W.B.E* (1970), trial transcript, p. 137; *R v L.G.H.* (1965), trial transcript, p. 88; *R v D.H.S.* (1965), trial transcript pp. 90–1; *R v J.P.G.* (1964), trial transcript, p. 119; *R v A.P.* (1964), trial transcript, pp. 85, 87.
57 *Andrews v Director of Public Prosecutions* [1937] AC 576.
58 *R v Bateman* at 10–12.
59 *Andrews v Director of Public Prosecutions* at 583.
60 Brown, *Traffic Offences*, pp. 114–15.
61 Wells, 'Look Hard and See More', p. 101.
62 Yeo, *Fault in Homicide*, pp. 172, 200.
63 See correspondence in Crown Law Department – 'Crown Prosecutors: Criminal Code re amendment of, to make it an offence when driving a vehicle to cause the death of, or bodily harm to another, by failing to use reasonable care', SROWA and 'Criminal Code Amendment Act 1944: Private Members Bill introduced by Mr R McDonald to provide for lesser charge than manslaughter', SROWA.
64 Brown, *Traffic Offences*, p. 105 and Corbett, *Car Crime*, p. 17.
65 See s 11, *Road Traffic Act, 1930* (UK).
66 Crown Law Department – 'Crown Prosecutors: Criminal Code re amendment of, to make it an offence when driving a vehicle to cause the death of, or bodily harm to another, by failing to use reasonable care', SROWA and Crown Law Department – 1944/3007, 'Criminal Code Amendment Act 1944: Private Members Bill introduced by Mr R McDonald to provide for lesser charge than manslaughter', SROWA, WAS 2664, CONS 1042.
67 *R v Callaghan* (1952), deposition of H. S.
68 ibid. Deposition of Police Constable Fenton.
69 ibid. Deposition of Police Constable Hannaby.
70 ibid. Deposition of Police Constable Fenton.
71 ibid. Deposition of S. S.
72 ibid. For example, see deposition of D. F.
73 ibid. Report of Post-Mortem Examination.
74 ibid. Deposition of H. S.
75 ibid. Coroner's Statement of Findings.
76 ibid. Police Character Report with extract from Registers of Convictions attached, 22 July 1952.
77 ibid. Oath of C. Gibson filed on behalf of the appellant.
78 ibid. Orders of the Court of Criminal Appeal.

NOTES TO CHAPTER ONE

79 Callaghan v R at 117.
80 ibid. at 118.
81 ibid. at 119.
82 ibid. at 121.
83 ibid. at 124.
84 ibid. at 124–5.
85 Law Reform Commission of Western Australia, *Report: Manslaughter or Dangerous Driving causing Death*, Project No. 17, Law Reform Commission of Western Australia, Perth, August 1970, p. 4.
86 R v J.E.J. (1961), trial transcript, p. 100.
87 R v D.A.W. (1965), trial transcript, pp. 88–9.
88 R v W.G.W. (1972), trial transcript, p. 87.
89 R v F.F. (1963), trial transcript, pp. 79–80.
90 ibid., pp. 79–82.
91 R v F.F. (1963), trial transcript, pp. 79–80.
92 ibid., pp. 79–81.
93 ibid., p. 81.
94 ibid.
95 ibid.
96 ibid.
97 ibid., p. 82.
98 ibid.
99 R v J.M.T. (1949), R v J.W.T (1949), R v H.C.M (1950), R v D.C. (1950), R v N.T.J. (1950), R v E.J.H. (1950), R v S.M. (1950), R v L.K.H. (1950), R v J.W.B. (1950), R v B.D.S.M (1951), R v O.S. (1951), R v F.P.N. (1953), R v R.A.S. (1969), R v W.L. (1969), R v J.C.B. (1974).
100 R v F.P.N. (1953), R v R.A.S. (1969), R v W.L. (1969), R v J.C.B. (1974).
101 Law Reform Commission of Western Australia, *Working Paper: Manslaughter or Dangerous Driving causing Death*, Project No. 17, Law Reform Commission of Western Australia, Perth, June 1970, pp. 2–3.
102 R v C.J.R. (1968), trial transcript, p. 82.
103 Law Reform Commission of Western Australia, *Report: Manslaughter or Dangerous Driving causing Death*, p. 1.
104 Law Reform Commission of Western Australia, *Working Paper: Manslaughter or Dangerous Driving causing Death*, pp. 5–6.
105 Law Reform Commission of Western Australia, *Report: Manslaughter or Dangerous Driving causing Death*, p. 6.
106 Sentencing Advisory Council, *Maximum Penalty for Negligently Causing Serious Injury*, Sentencing Advisory Council Victoria, Melbourne, 2007, p. 20.
107 Law Reform Commission of Western Australia, *Report: Manslaughter or Dangerous Driving causing Death*, p. 6.
108 Law Reform Commission of Western Australia, *Working Paper: Manslaughter or Dangerous Driving causing Death*, pp. 5–6.
109 Law Reform Commission of Western Australia, *Report: Manslaughter or Dangerous Driving causing Death*, p. 7. There was one minor amendment. Section 11 of the *Criminal Code Amendment Act, 1972* (WA) modified s 291A so that the

offence became a failure to take reasonable care and use reasonable precautions in either 'the use or management' of a vehicle, as opposed to the previous 'use and management' of a vehicle.

110 Federal Office of Road Safety, *The history of road fatalities in Australia*, Monograph 23, Federal Office of Road Safety, Canberra, 1998, p. 4. The figure of 6,500 is an estimate based on Table 2 of the publication. State-by-State figures are not readily available before 1950. Between 1950 and 1974 there were 5,842 road fatalities in WA. On the basis that 142 people died in 1950 and, multiplying that by four to approximate the numbers between 1946 and 1950, equals a further 568 fatalities and thus a total 6,410 people killed.

111 Federal Office of Road Safety, *The History of Road Fatalities in Australia*, p. 4.

112 J. Clark, 'Wild behaviour: Infernal Machines and Serious Accidents', *National Library of Australia News*, vol. 7, no. 5, 1997, p. 4.

Chapter Two: An overview of Supreme Court trials, 1946–1974

1 See Albany Clerk of Courts – 1 & 2, 'Evidence Books – Children's Court', State Records Office of Western Australia (SROWA), WAS 1874, CONS 5393; Albany Clerk of Courts – 1, 2 & 3, 'Charge Sheets', SROWA, WAS 1875, CONS 5394; Perth Children's Court – 45–52, 'Charge Books', SROWA, WAS 343, CONS 2493; Yalgoo Clerk of Courts – 1, 'Magistrate's Evidence Book – Children's Court', SROWA, WAS 386, CONS 3811.

2 *R v R.S.M.* (1971).

3 See charges 698 to 706 in Perth Children's Court – 47, 'Charge Books', 1 January 1946 to 30 June 1946, SROWA. See also consecutive charges, commencing at charge number 345 on 2 March, Perth Children's Court – 45, 'Charge Books', 1 January 1945 to 30 June 1945, SROWA.

4 Report from Detective Sergeant Patterson to Inspector Hagan, 6 January 1966, Western Australian Police Department – 1962/1377, 'Fatal Traffic Accidents: Investigation by members of CIB', SROWA, WAS 76, CONS 1910.

5 Pursuant to s 42(2) of the *District Court of Western Australia Act, 1969* (WA).

6 Western Australian Police Department – 68 0548 V2, 'Suggestions for the improvement of Road Safety and reduction of Road Toll', SROWA, WAS 77, CONS 3439. See notation regarding the prosecution of James Lang in 1969 for the death of Alice Hallo under s 291A. The defendant's name was not discovered in the Supreme Court registers, suggesting that he was prosecuted in the District Court.

7 *Callaghan v R* (1952) 87 CLR 115.

8 Letter from Mr R. D. Wilson, Assistant Crown Prosecutor to Commissioner of Police, 13 October 1955, Western Australian Police Department – 'Fatal Traffic Accidents: Investigation by members of CIB', SROWA.

9 Examined case files which were the subject of a coronial inquest and/or coronial indictment are marked in Table A1 of the Appendices.

10 P. Conole, *Protect and Serve: A History of Policing in Western Australia*, Western Australia Police Service, Perth, 2002, p. 283 and <http://www.worldlibrary.org/articles/pat_rodriguez>, accessed: 5 January 2017.

NOTES TO CHAPTER TWO

11 Covering letter with report, 20 January 1966, Western Australian Police Department – 'Fatal Traffic Accidents: Investigation by members of CIB', SROWA.
12 ibid. Letter from Western Australian Police to Crown Prosecution Service, 5 January 1956.
13 On occasion, a charge was listed in the indictment books and registers as an 'unlawful killing'. This was somewhat ambiguous in that, pursuant to s 268 of the Code, all killings, be they wilful murder, murder or manslaughter, are unlawful unless authorised or excused by law. As the twentieth century wore on, indictments recorded as 'unlawful killings' were usually manslaughter charges.
14 *R v M.J.N.* (1949), *R v B.B.M* (1951), *R v B.D.S.M* (1951), *R v E.O.* (1951), *R v G.I.B.* (1952), *R v F.P.N.* (1953), *R v G.W.B.* (1955), *R v J.H.* (1962), *R v A.P.* (1964), *R v J.P.G.* (1964), *R v R.N.S.* (1966), *R v P.G.N.* (1967), *R v T.B.* (1971), *R v R.S.M.* (1971), *R v B.W.P.* (1972), *R v B.J.B.* (1974).
15 *R v M.V.C.* (1960).
16 Section 16 of the Western Australian Code originally stated that, 'A person cannot be twice punished, either under the provisions of this Code or under the provisions of any other law, for the same act or omission, except in the case where the act or omission is such that by means thereof he causes the death of another person, in which case he may be convicted of the offence of which he is guilty by reason of causing such death, notwithstanding that he has already been convicted of some other offence constituted by the act or omission'. The section was amended in 1977, via the *Criminal Code Amendment Act (No. 3) 1977* (WA), so that where 'an act or omission constitutes more than one offence a person may be convicted of each such offence but shall not be twice punished for the same act or omission'. The section was later repealed in favour of s 11 of Western Australia's *Sentencing Act 1995* (WA). For discussion, see V. Campbell & I. G. Campbell, 'Punishing Multiple Harms', *University of Queensland Law Journal*, vol. 17, no. 1, 1992, p. 20.
17 D. Brown, *Traffic Offences and Accidents: An examination of the principles of law governing offences and negligence by motorists on the roads in Australia*, Butterworths, North Ryde, 1996, p. 93.
18 Via the *Sentencing (Consequential Provisions Act) 1995* (WA) and the *Sentencing Act 1995* (WA). For discussion regarding multiple harms and appropriate punishment for consequences arising out of the same act or omission, see *Drage v The Queen* (1989) 44 A Crim R 352; *Phillips v Carbone (No 2)* (1992) 10 WAR 169; *Moore v The Queen* (1995) 15 WAR 87; *Eves v Western Australia* (2008) 49 MVR 259.
19 *R v J.M.T.* (1949), *R v J.W.T* (1949), *R v H.C.M* (1950), *R v D.C.* (1950), *R v N.T.J.* (1950), *R v E.J.H.* (1950), *R v S.M.* (1950), *R v L.K.H.* (1950), *R v J.W.B.* (1950), *R v B.D.S.M* (1951), *R v O.S.* (1951), *R v F.P.N.* (1953), *R v R.A.S.* (1969), *R v W.L.* (1969), *R v J.C.B.* (1974).
20 *R v S.R.B.* (1970), *R v R.S.M.* (1971), *R v C.F.C.* (1973), *R v R.S.M.* (1973), *R v B.L.W.* (1973), *R v M.J.S.* (1973), *R v H.D.M.* (1974).
21 Brief from the Solicitor General to the Minister for Justice, 14 August 1935 and Letter to Minister for Justice from Mr Dunphy, Crown Solicitor, 13 October 1939, Crown Law Department – 1934/3780, 'Crown Prosecutors: Criminal Code re amendment of, to make it an offence when driving a vehicle to cause

the death of, or bodily harm to another, by failing to use reasonable care',
SROWA, WAS 2664, CONS 1042.
22 There were seven cases in which defendants were found guilty of manslaughter where the case files could not be located. These matters were assumed to be non-vehicular, given the absence of notations regarding licence disqualification and, as such, have been included in the total twenty-two non-vehicular cases: *R v A.W.* (1965), *R v N.M.C.* (1969), *R v J.M.P* (1974), *R v S.N.* (1974), *R v B.K.W.* (1974), *R v T.C.W.* (1974), *R v S.H.B.* (1974). All other non-vehicular manslaughter convictions are as follows: *R v P.D.C.* (1954), *R v M* (1954), *R v R.B.H.* (1962), *R v G.C.* (1963), *R v J.R.* (1966), *R v J.U.* (1966), *R v R.E.* (1967), *R v S.B.* (1967), *R v T.B.N.* (1970), *R v A.S.* (1971), *R v A.C.H.* (1972), *R v R.S.* (1972), *R v R.S.B.* (1972), *R v D.G.C.* (1973), *R v K.R.B.* (1974).
23 *R v D.V.J.* (1950), *R v L.G.W.* (1958), *R v R.S.M.* (1973), *R v B.L.W.* (1973).
24 *R v Laporte* (1969) and *R v C.F.C.* (1973).
25 *Laporte v R* [1970] WAR 87 at 90.
26 *R v C.F.C.* (1973).
27 Western Australia, Committee of Inquiry into the Rate of Imprisonment, *Report of the Committee of Inquiry into the Rate of Imprisonment*, Committee of Inquiry into the Rate of Imprisonment, Perth, 1981, pp. 205–7.
28 *Offenders Probation and Parole Act, 1963* (WA).
29 Western Australia, Review of Remission and Parole, *Report of the Review of Remission and Parole*, Ministry of Justice, Government of Western Australia, Perth, March 1998, p. 3.
30 Pursuant to s 29 of the *Prisons Act 1981* (WA).
31 L. M. Friedman, *Crime and Punishment in American History*, Basic Books, New York, 1993, p. 4.
32 *R v A.H.B.* (1947), *R v A.C.E.D.* (1949), *R v G.W.B.* (1955), *R v D.A.W.* (1965), *R v C.S.H.* (1968), *R v E.J.V.* (1969), *R v O.N.H.* (1970), *R v D.L.B.V.* (1971), *R v R.S.M.* (1971), *R v W.G.W.* (1972).
33 *R v A.H.B.* (1947), *R v A.C.E.D.* (1949), *R v R.S.M.* (1971).
34 *R v F.O.B.* (1951), *R v J.W.C.* (1952), *R v J.H.* (1962), *R v C.W.N.* (1962), *R v A.P.* (1964), *R v J.B.R.* (1964), *R v R.D.S.* (1965), *R v R.G.* (1965), *R v M.M.* (1965), *R v S.H.* (1965), *R v P.R.V.S* (1965), *R v N.W.R.* (1966), *R v A.J.B.* (1966), *R v R.H.W.* (1966), *R v R.A.S* (1969), *R v K.W.* (1970), *R v S.R.B.* (1970), *R v F.J.H.* (1970), *R v S.B.* (1970), *R v V.K.* (1971), *R v J.T.E.* (1971), *R v R.W.S.* (1973), *R v M.F.* (1973), *R v M.A.J.* (1974), *R v H.D.M.* (1974), *R v M.J.S.* (1974).
35 For example, see *R v K.W.* (1949), *R v J.E.B.* (1950), *R v E.S.* (1951), *R v R.B.T.* (1952), *R v K.E.S.* (1952), *R v S.L.B.* (1952), *R v J.A.A.* (1954), *R v E.M.R.* (1955), *R v P.F.G.P.* (1956), *R v J.B.P.P.* (1958), *R v R.P.R.* (1967).
36 Newspaper clipping, 1 January 1969, Western Australian Police Department – 68 0548 V2, 'Suggestions for the improvement of Road Safety and reduction of Road Toll', SROWA, WAS 77, CONS 3439.
37 ibid. Western Australian Police Department, Media release, 14 July 1969 and various correspondence on file.
38 ibid. Letter from John Tunsey. While undated, the letter is clearly a response to the Government's 1969 public appeal.

39 ibid. See extensive correspondence on file. See also correspondence in Western Australian Police Department – 1964/1551 VI, 'Police Department (Traffic Office) Suggestions for the improvement of Road Safety and Reduction of Road Toll', SROWA, WAS 76, CONS 1911.
40 A non-custodial penalty was imposed in forty-three cases.
41 *R v B.L.W.* (1973).

Chapter Three: Supreme Court trials, 1946–1974

1   *R v E.J.H.* (1950), *R v H.C.C.* (1959), *R v F.F.* (1963).
2   For example, *R v K.H.* (1962), *R v G.P.C.* (1969), *R v G.C.B.* (1970).
3   For example, *R v J.W.G.* (1951), *R v B.R.H.* (1955), *R v F.G.D.* (1959), *R v J.E.J.* (1961), *R v F.F.* (1963).
4   *R v F.F.* (1963), trial transcript, p. 62.
5   For example, *R v L.G.W.* (1958), *R v H.D.M.* (1974), *R v L.R.H.* (1971), *R v A.H.B.* (1947), *R v R.A.J.* (1973), *R v L.R.H.* (1971), *R v R.D.S.* (1965).
6   For example, see *R v D.A.W.* (1965).
7   For example, *R v W.M.* (1946), *R v F.X.I.* (1960), *R v K.H.* (1962), *R v M.J.C.* (1964), *R v A.P.* (1964), *R v J.P.G.* (1964), *R v R.D.S.* (1965), *R v D.A.W.* (1965), *R v G.N.M.* (1969), *R v G.P.C.* (1969), *R v A.M.B.* (1970), *R v G.C.B.* (1970), *R v A.B.S.* (1971), *R v R.A.* (1973).
8   For example, *R v W.M.* (1946), *R v A.K.A.* (1960), *R v F.X.I.* (1960), *R v A.P.* (1964).
9   For example, *R v A.J.C.* (1946).
10 For example, *R v G.P.C.* (1969) and *R v A.B.S.* (1971).
11 For example, *R v J.W.T.* (1950), *R v K.H.* (1962), *R v J.P.G.* (1964), *R v W.W.V.* (1964), *R v M.J.C.* (1964), *R v A.P.* (1964), *R v R.D.S.* (1965), *R v P.G.N.* (1967), *R v C.J.R.* (1968), *R v G.P.C.* (1969), *R v G.N.M.* (1969), *R v M.W.B.E.* (1970), *R v G.C.B.* (1970), *R v G.J.M.* (1972), *R v M.A.J.* (1974).
12 *R v F.F.* (1963), trial transcript, pp. 62–3.
13 *R v D.J.B.* (1966), trial transcript, pp. 119–20.
14 *R v R.H.L.* (1954), extract from sentencing remarks.
15 *R v R.D.S.* (1965), trial transcript, p. 65.
16 *R v L.L.L.* (1956), deposition of A. S.
17 ibid. Deposition of Police Constable M. Screaigh.
18 ibid. Deposition of A. S. and Exhibit H, 'Statement of defendant'.
19 ibid. Deposition of A. S.
20 ibid. Report of Post-Mortem Examination and deposition of T. S.
21 ibid. Extract from sentencing remarks.
22 *R v F.G.D.* (1959).
23 ibid. Depositions of H. B., F. L., N. N., B. B., A. P., Police Constable H. Browner.
24 ibid. Depositions of A. P., N. N., F. L.
25 ibid. Depositions of Police Constables A. Prior and H. Browner.
26 ibid. Letter from Dr R. Bissett, Surgical Registrar, Fremantle Hospital, 21 November 1958.

NOTES TO CHAPTER THREE

27 *R v D.A.W.* (1965), trial transcript, p. 100.
28 ibid.
29 *R v G.J.F.* (1962) and *R v A.P.C.* (1970).
30 *R v B.J.M.* (1960), letter from C. G. D., 24 March 1960.
31 *R v R.H.W.* (1966), trial transcript, p. 5.
32 *R v A.P.* (1964), trial transcript, p. 86.
33 *R v G.S.J.* (1951), deposition of Police Constable W. Allen and *R v N.T.J.* (1950), deposition of Police Constable R. G. Vinicombe respectively.
34 *R v J.P.G.* (1964), trial transcript, p. 145.
35 *R v D.J.B.* (1966), trial transcript, p. 117.
36 *R v G.N.M.* (1969), extract from sentencing remarks.
37 *R v R.H.W.* (1966), extract from sentencing remarks.
38 *R v J.W.K.* (1948), extract from sentencing remarks.
39 *R v H.A.H.* (1950), extract from sentencing remarks.
40 *R v L.G.W.* (1958), extract from sentencing remarks.
41 *R v R.L.D.* (1955), *R v J.P.H.* (1963), *R v J.B.M.* (1963), *R v K.J.M.* (1964), *R v A.P.* (1964), *R v J.W.S.* (1964), *R v J.B.J.R.* (1964), *R v C.T.A.* (1964), *R v J.P.G.* (1964), *R v F.P.F.* (1965), *R v C.J.F.* (1967), *R v D.W.W.* (1968), *R v C.S.H.* (1968), *R v B.F.L.* (1969), *R v A.P.C.* (1970), *R v G.V.G.* (1956), *R v A.F.* (1959), *R v R.K.O.* (1961).
42 *R v N.W.R.* (1966), *R v R.H.W.* (1966), *R v D.A.W.* (1965) respectively.
43 Pursuant to s 668A of the Code inserted by the *Criminal Code Amendment Act (No. 2), 1956*.
44 For example, see *R v S.F.M.* (1960), *R v R.J.F.* (1961), *R v R.L.L.* (1962), *R v K.J.C.* (1963), *R v H.A.* (1964), *R v M.O.S.* (1964), *R v A.P.C.* (1970), *R v G.J.M.* (1972), *R v G.J.T.* (1973), *R v R.A.A.* (1973), *R v R.S.A.* (1974).
45 *R v M.A.J.* (1974), sentencing transcript, p. 2.
46 Pursuant to the *Criminal Code Amendment Act (No. 2), 1956*.
47 *R v J.W.K.* (1948), *R v H.A.H.* (1950), *R v B.J.T.* (1956), *R v L.G.W.* (1958), *R V C.W.N.* (1962), *R v A.H.* (1964), *R v F.J.H.* (1970), *R v B.J.W.* (1971), *R v M.A.J.* (1974).
48 D. Brown, *Traffic Offences: An examination of the principles of law governing offences committed by motorists on the road in Australia*, Sydney, Butterworths, 1983, p. 86.
49 *R v W.G.W.* (1972), trial transcript, p. 25 and notations in the indictment register.
50 ibid. See depositions of W. K. and G. H. and trial transcript, pp. 8–9.
51 ibid. See deposition of C. G. and W. K.
52 ibid. Report of Post-Mortem Examination.
53 ibid. Trial transcript, p. 99.
54 *R v M.A.J.* (1974). Justice Burt stated that the defendant had been convicted for driving without a licence on twelve occasions, which contradicted the Record of Traffic Convictions submitted to the Court for sentencing.
55 ibid. See Record of Traffic Convictions, 22 February 1974 and Record of Criminal Convictions of same.
56 ibid. See testimony of P. R.
57 ibid., see also deposition of J. H.

NOTES TO CHAPTER THREE

58 *R v J.P.G.* (1964), *R v S.H.* (1965), *R v A.S.* (1967), *R v M.M.* (1968), *R v W.W.W.* (1970), *R v A.M.B.* (1970), *R v G.J.T.* (1973).
59 *R v J.P.G.* (1964).
60 ibid. Deposition of U. V. and trial transcript, pp. 23–35.
61 ibid. Extract from sentencing remarks.
62 ibid. Deposition of Police Constable K. Wagstaff.
63 ibid. Reports of Post-Mortem Examination dated 17 and 18 August 1964.
64 ibid. Trial transcript, p. 146.
65 ibid. Extract from sentencing remarks.
66 ibid. Notice of Motion and Minute of Order.
67 The details concerning *R v A.M.B.* (1970) and the application for, and conditions of, his extraordinary licence were documented in the criminal record book. See Supreme Court of Western Australia – 4, 'Criminal Record Book 11', State Records Office of Western Australia (SROWA), WAS 49, CONS 4332, p. 256.
68 *R v E.J.V.* (1969), trial transcript, p. 124.
69 *R v S.H.* (1965), see judgment transcript on file.
70 ibid., pp. 9–10.
71 *R v A.C.* (1973) and *R v B.W.P.* (1972).
72 *R v J.H.W.* (1948), *R v W.W.V.* (1964), *R v C.F.C.* (1973).
73 *R v V.P.L.* (1969) and *R v C.F.C.* (1973).
74 *R v C.F.C.* (1973).
75 *R v W.W.V.* (1964), extract from sentencing remarks.
76 ibid. See deposition of K. W. and S. J. and opening remarks of Crown Prosecutor, Mr Parker, trial transcript, pp. 4–5.
77 Crown Prosecution Service, *Policy for Prosecuting cases of bad driving*, Crown Prosecution Service, London, 2007.
78 *R v W.W.V.* (1964), trial transcript, p. 121.
79 *R v W.M.* (1946), *R v J.W.T.* (1950), *R v O.C.* (1953), *R v B.R.H.* (1955), *R v B.J.T.* (1956), *R v D.J.O.* (1956), *R v E.M.* (1958), *R v L.G.W.* (1958), *R v J.J.K.* (1959), *R v A.K.A.* (1960), *R v F.X.I.* (1960), *R v K.H.* (1962), *R v J.H.* (1963), *R v M.J.C.* (1964), *R v J.P.G.* (1964), *R v P.G.N.* (1967), *R v J.W.N.* (1969), *R v G.P.C.* (1969), *R v W.W.W.* (1970), *R v G.C.B.* (1970), *R v B.J.W.* (1971), *R v A.B.S.* (1971), *R v G.J.M.* (1972), *R v B.W.P.* (1972), *R v R.A.J.* (1973), *R v R.A.A.* (1973), *R v R.S.M.* (1973), *R v C.P.M.* (1974), *R v M.A.J.* (1974).
80 For example, see *R v G.J.F* (1962), trial transcript, pp. 3–5; *R v K.H.* (1962), trial transcript, pp. 57, 61; *R v P.G.N.* (1967), trial transcript, p. 40; *R v J.W.N.* (1969), trial transcript, p. 5; *R v G.J.M.* (1972), extract from sentencing remarks.
81 *R v B.J.T.* (1956), *R v E.M.* (1958), *R v J.J.K.* (1959), *R v A.K.A.* (1960), *R v F.X.I.* (1960), *R v J.H.* (1963), *R v J.P.G.* (1964), *R v J.W.N.* (1969), *R v W.W.W.* (1970), *R v B.J.W.* (1971), *R v G.J.M.* (1972), *R v R.A.A.* (1973), *R v M.A.J.* (1974).
82 *R v L.G.W.* (1958) and *R v R.S.M.* (1973).
83 *R v B.J.T.* (1956), *R v J.H.* (1963), *R v G.J.M.* (1972), *R v R.A.A.* (1973).
84 With the exception of *R v C.F.C.* (1973).
85 *R v E.M.* (1958), Exhibit G, 'Statement of defendant'.
86 ibid. Deposition of M. A. S.
87 ibid. Report of Post-Mortem Examination.

NOTES TO CHAPTER THREE

88   ibid. Deposition of Police Constable V. T. Westwood.
89   ibid. Exhibit G, Coronial Inquest.
90   ibid. Extract from sentencing remarks.
91   ibid.
92   *R v B.J.T.* (1956), deposition of Police Constable R. Scott. At the time of the offence, the legal drinking age was 21.
93   ibid. Memo from Associate to Justice Wolff, 21 March 1956.
94   ibid. Depositions of Police Constables A. Frame and F. Scantlebury.
95   For example, see *R v P.G.N.* (1967), *R v G.C.B.* (1970), *R v F.X.I.* (1960).
96   *R v F.X.I.* (1960), trial transcript, pp. 22, 79.
97   *R v A.P.C.* (1970).
98   For example, see *R v M.R.* (1963), trial transcript, pp. 118, 128, 133–4.
99   *R v G.C.B.* (1970), trial transcript, p. 4.
100 ibid. Deposition of P. C. and trial transcript, pp. 12–14.
101 ibid. Trial transcript, p. 67.
102 ibid., p. 19.
103 ibid. Report of Post-Mortem Examination.
104 N. Faith, *Crash: The limits of car safety*, Boxtree, London, 1997, p. 5.
105 A. J. McClurg, 'Dead sorrow: a story about loss and a new theory of wrongful death damages', *Boston University Law Review*, vol. 85, no. 1, 2005, pp. 2–5.
106 *R v W.M.* (1946), Report of Post-Mortem Examination.
107 *R v D.C.* (1950), Report of Post-Mortem Examination.
108 ibid. See deposition of Dr P. Triplett.
109 *R v R.H.W.* (1966), Report of Post-Mortem Examination.
110 *R v D.C.G.* (1952), Report of Post-Mortem Examination and deposition of Police Constable K. Parnell.
111 *R v B.W.P.* (1972), Report of Post-Mortem Examination and deposition of G. D.
112 *R v E.W.* (1968), Report of Post-Mortem Examination and deposition of S. B.
113 *R v G.W.B.* (1955), deposition of F. L.
114 ibid. Deposition of Police Constable J. Rule.
115 ibid. Deposition of Paramedic T. Bellas.
116 ibid. Report of Post-Mortem Examination of pillion passenger, T. K.
117 ibid. Report of Post-Mortem Examination of deceased driver, M. J.
118 *R v O.N.H.* (1970), depositions of S. D. and R. L. G.
119 ibid. Deposition of S. D.
120 ibid. Report of Post-Mortem Examination.
121 L. Breen, *Silenced Voices: Grief Following Road Traffic Crashes*, Saarbrucken, VDM Verlag, 2008.
122 *R v A.J.C.* (1946), deposition of S. H. H.
123 ibid.
124 *R v D.C.* (1950) and *R v S.M.* (1950).
125 *R v L.G.H.* (1965), trial transcript, pp. 3–7, 84–5.
126 ibid. Report of Post-Mortem Examination.
127 ibid. Trial transcript, p. 99.
128 For example, see *R v B.J.T.* (1956), reference from President of the Hills Football Association, 27 March 1956.

129 ibid. Reference from Member for Guildford–Midland, 29 March 1956.
130 *R v J.W.N.* (1969), reference from R. S. B., Clancy Motors, 13 March 1969.
131 For example, see *R v R.J.F.* (1961), testimony of F. J. S. W., trial transcript, p. 5. See also *R v B.J.M.* (1960), reference from C. G. D., 24 March 1960.
132 *R v J.W.N.* (1969), letter from R. D. M., 14 March 1969.
133 ibid.
134 *R v B.J.M.* (1960), reference of Parish Priest E. L., Nedlands, 24 March 1960.
135 *R v F.X.I.* (1960), letter from defendant's wife, 19 September 1960.
136 *R v J.W.K.* (1948), letter from defendant's wife, 17 July 1948.
137 ibid.
138 *R v F.X.I.* (1960), letter from defendant's father, 13 September 1960.
139 *R v L.L.L.* (1956), letter from N. E. to Justice Jackson, 10 May 1956.

Chapter Four: One for the road, 1946–1974

1 *R v D.A.W.* (1965), Mr Walsh, trial transcript, p. 72.
2 ibid.
3 *R v J.C.* (1949), deposition of Sergeant A. Duperouzel.
4 ibid. Deposition of G. L. M.
5 ibid. Statement of defendant.
6 ibid. Deposition of Police Constable J. MacKenzie.
7 ibid. Deposition of Sergeant A. Duperouzel.
8 A. T. Pearson, 'Alcohol and fatal traffic accidents', *Medical Journal of Australia*, vol. 2, no. 5, 1957, pp. 166–7. Pearson's research was cited in numerous sources, including National Safety Council of Western Australia, *A case for the introduction of blood-alcohol tests in Western Australia*, National Safety Council of Western Australia, Perth, 1957, J. S. Battye Library of West Australian History and Road Traffic Authority of Western Australia & D. I. Smith, *An investigation to determine whether blood alcohol tests should be compulsory for all traffic accident casualties over the age of 15 years admitted to hospital in Western Australia*, Research and Statistics Division, Road Traffic Authority, Perth, 1975.
9 For instance see, B. H. Lerner, *One for the Road: Drunk Driving Since 1900*, The Johns Hopkins University Press, Baltimore, 2011, pp. 24–8; H. A. Heise, 'Alcohol and Automobile Accidents', *Journal of the American Medical Association*, vol. 103, no. 10, 1934, pp. 739–41; J. W. Cavett, 'The determination of alcohol in blood and other bodily fluids', *The Journal of Laboratory and Clinical Medicine*, vol. 23, no. 5, 1938, pp. 543–6; R. Andréasson & A. Wayne Jones, 'The life and work of Erik M.P. Widmark', *The American Journal of Forensic Medicine and Pathology*, vol. 17, no. 3, 1996, pp. 177–90; S. Selesnick, 'Alcoholic intoxication: Its diagnosis and medicolegal implications', *The Journal of the American Medical Association*, vol. 110, no. 11, 1938, pp. 775–8; R. L. Holcomb, 'Alcohol in relation to traffic accidents', *Journal of the American Medical Association*, vol. 110, no. 12, 1938, pp. 1076–85.
10 R. Wagnsson, K. Bjerver, G. Nelker, S. Rosell & J. Akerbladh-Rosell (eds.), *Alcohol and Road Traffic. Proceedings of the First international Conference*, Kugelbergs, Boktryckeri, 1951.

NOTES TO CHAPTER FOUR

11 G. Davison, *Car Wars: How the car won our hearts and conquered our cities*, Allen & Unwin, Crows Nest, 2004, p. 153.
12 For some examples, see K. Laybourn with D. Taylor, *The Battle for the Roads of Britain, Police, Motorists and the Law, c. 1890s to 1970s*, Palgrave Macmillan, Hampshire, 2015, pp. 82–3, 87–8, 114–16, 119–22; Lerner, *One for the Road: Drunk Driving Since 1900*, pp. 38–64; Davison, *Car Wars*, pp. 155–62; J. Clark, 'Road safety and the historical perspective: the Example of Women', *Roadwise*, vol. 13, no. 4, 2002, p. 20.
13 Letter from Mr T. G. Paterson, Chairman of the Australian Road Safety Council, to Mr T. Anderson, Western Australian Commissioner of Police, received 2 July 1954, with attached report – 'Straight talks to bad drivers: Outline of suggested advertising campaign for 1954–1955', prepared by the Commonwealth Advertising Division, October 1953, Western Australian Police Department – 1954/1593 v2, 'Australian Road Safety Council – Proposed formation of Policy file', State Records Office of Western Australia (SROWA), WAS 76, CONS 430.
14 Royal Automobile Club of Western Australia (RAC), *The Road Patrol*, RAC, Perth, 10 July 1946, p. 19 and 10 May 1946, pp. 3, 7. See also November 1946 edition, featuring an interview with the Western Australian Commissioner of Police.
15 *Western Mail*, 15 April 1954, p. 4.
16 *West Australian*, 21 May 1971, p. 17.
17 Western Australian Police Department files – VI, 'Police Department (Traffic Office) Suggestions for the improvement of Road Safety and Reduction of Road Toll', SROWA; 68 0548 V2, 'Suggestions for the improvement of Road Safety and reduction of Road Toll, SROWA, WAS 77, CONS 3439; 1967/0564 v6, 'Traffic Act & Regulations – Inquiries and Suggestions', SROWA, WAS 76, CONS 251; 1960/0907 V4, 'Traffic Branch – Drunken drivers: Policy', SROWA, WAS 77, CONS 3998.
18 RAC, *The Road Patrol*, vol. 13, no. 95, April 1969, p. 22.
19 ibid., January 1950, pp. 20–1.
20 ibid., 10 May 1946, p. 3.
21 RAC, Collection of material relating to the Royal Automobile Club, 'Driving is an art!', PR9402/1-18, Item, PR9402/20, J. S. Battye Library of West Australian History.
22 RAC, *The Road Patrol*, 10 April 1945, p. 5; 10 June 1945, p. 5; 10 August 1945, p. 15; February 1951, p. 48.
23 RAC, Collection of material relating to the Royal Automobile Club, Membership folder, PR9402/36-61, Item PR9402/58, J. S. Battye Library of West Australian History.
24 Davison made similar observations of Victorian parliamentarians in the 1950s in *Car Wars*, p. 157.
25 Channel Nine News, R. O'Connor, 27 March 1975, J. S. Battye Library of West Australian History, Video recording, State Film Archives Collection, E0383.
26 ibid.

NOTES TO CHAPTER FOUR

27 House of Representatives Standing Committee on Road Safety, *Alcohol, drugs and road safety: Report of the House of Representatives Standing Committee on Road Safety, May 1980,* Australian Government Publishing Service, Canberra, 1980, p. 18.
28 *R v R.S.M.* (1973), extract from trial transcript, p. 2.
29 Dr G. Brown, Henry Windsor Lecture 1972, 'Road Trauma – A Community Crisis', published in *The Medical Journal of Australia,* vol. 1, no. 14, 1972, p. 669.
30 Western Australian Police Department, 'Traffic Branch – Drunken drivers: Policy', folio 76, SROWA.
31 Letter from the Commissioner of Police to the Minister for Police, including test results from 1969, 27 February 1969, Western Australian Police Department – 1969/0346 V2, 'Traffic Office – Breathalyser Policy Volume 2', SROWA, WAS 77, CONS 3998.
32 Letter from Sergeant Bracken, Officer in Charge, Breathalyser Squad, Western Australian Police, to Justice M. D. Kirby, Chairman, Australian Law Reform Commission, 9 February 1976, Western Australian Police Department – 040 126 V1, 'Equipment – General – Breathalyser equipment-use-of-policy', SROWA, WAS 488, CONS 5907.
33 *R v K.H.* (1962), trial transcript, pp. 75–6.
34 *R v M.A.J.* (1974), extract from sentencing remarks, p. 2.
35 *R v C.P.M.* (1974), Exhibit D, 'Identification of Dead Body'.
36 ibid. See also Report of Post-Mortem Examination.
37 ibid. Deposition of B. L. B. and Statement of defendant.
38 ibid. Deposition of B. J. F.
39 ibid. Letter from Crown Law Department with attached affidavit of Dr Pocock to Messrs. Hudson, Henning and Goodman.
40 ibid. Statement of defendant.
41 For example, see *R v E.M.* (1958) and *R v W.W.W.* (1970).
42 For example, see *R v J.W.T.* (1950), *R v O.C.* (1953), *R v K.H.* (1962), *R v P.G.N.* (1967), *R v M.W.B.E.* (1970), *R v J.C.B.* (1970), *R v A.B.S.* (1971), *R v B.W.P.* (1972), *R v R.A.J.* (1973), *R v R.A.A.* (1973).
43 For example, see *R v J.W.T.* (1950), *R v O.C.* (1953), *R v B.J.T.* (1956), *R v E.M.* (1958), *R v W.W.W.* (1970), *R v G.J.M.* (1972).
44 *R v W.W.W.* (1970), Statement of defendant.
45 ibid. Deposition of Detective Sergeant B. Godfrey.
46 ibid. Report of Post-Mortem Examination.
47 ibid. Trial transcript, pp. 13–14.
48 For discussion, see *Koltasz v The Queen* [2003] WASCA 38, judgment text, para 40.
49 Pursuant to s 21 of *Traffic Act Amendment Act (No. 4), 1957* (WA) which introduced s 32A into the *Traffic Act, 1919* (WA).
50 See s 27(1) of the Western Australian *Traffic Act, 1919* as repealed and substituted by s 11 of *Traffic Act Amendment Act,* 1930 (WA), the substance of which later became s 32A.

NOTES TO CHAPTER FOUR

51 British Medical Association, *The Drinking Driver: The medico-legal investigation of the drinking driver: Report of a Special Committee of the British Medical Association*, British Medical Association, London, 1965, p. 7.
52 Western Australian Police Department – 040 126 VI, 'Equipment – General – Breathalyser equipment-use-of-policy', folios 175–6, August 1974, SROWA.
53 *R v B.N.S.* (1961), trial transcript, p. 45.
54 Instructions on conducting and recording a sobriety test including form P69B, folios 175–6, Western Australian Police Department – 040 126 VI, 'Equipment – General – Breathalyser equipment-use-of-policy', SROWA and Davison, *Car Wars*, pp. 154–5.
55 *R v G.T.B.* (1946), deposition of Dr B. Bladen.
56 ibid. Deposition of Police Constable G. I. Petterson.
57 ibid. Deposition of Paramedic J. Cameron.
58 ibid. Deposition of Police Constable G. I. Petterson.
59 ibid. Deposition of Police Constable C. Lawson.
60 ibid.
61 ibid.
62 ibid.
63 ibid. Deposition of R. C. A.
64 ibid. Coroner's Statement of Findings, 6 November 1946.
65 National Safety Council of Western Australia, *A case for the introduction of blood-alcohol tests in Western Australia*, pp. 4, 10, 14.
66 *R v L.S.D.G.* (1951).
67 ibid. See depositions of Dr A. T. Pearson and Dr B. Southern.
68 J. Lewis & B. Hirsh, 'Doctor, Driver and The Courts', *The British Medical Journal*, vol. 2, no. 5402, 1964, p. 189.
69 *R v J.R.B.* (1956), deposition of Dr N. Colyner, including cross-examination at inquest.
70 *R v W.W.V.* (1964), deposition of K. W.
71 ibid. See also trial transcript, pp. 20–3.
72 ibid. See testimony of S. J., trial transcript, p. 64.
73 ibid. Trial transcript, pp. 90–1.
74 ibid., pp. 4–5.
75 ibid. See Report of Post-Mortem Examination and testimony of Dr S. E. Benjamin, trial transcript, p. 61.
76 ibid. See testimonies of Drs S. E. Benjamin, B. Bolton and J. Marum, trial transcript, pp. 61–3, 65–6, 69–71 respectively.
77 ibid. See also depositions of Dr J. Marum and Dr B. Bolton.
78 ibid. Testimony of A. M., trial transcript, pp. 52–4.
79 ibid. Trial transcript, pp. 6–7.
80 ibid. Dr Benjamin's deposition and trial transcript, pp. 63–4.
81 ibid. Trial transcript, pp. 67–71.
82 ibid., pp. 69–71.
83 ibid., pp. 63–4.
84 ibid. Letter from Dr E. F. Fletcher to Justice Negus, 24 February 1964.
85 ibid. Extract from sentencing remarks.

86 This observation has also been made by others. For instance, see B. J. Elliot & D. R. South, *The development and assessment of a drink-driving campaign: a case study*, Department of Transport, Office of Road Safety, Australian Government Publishing Service, Canberra, 1985, p. 18; House of Representatives Standing Committee on Road Safety, *Alcohol, drugs and road safety: Report of the House of Representatives Standing Committee on Road Safety, May 1980*, Australian Government Publishing Service, Canberra, 1980, pp. 35–8; C. Corbett, *Car Crime*, Willan Publishing, Devon, 2003, p. 85.
87 *R v D.A.W.* (1965), trial transcript, pp. 62–5.
88 *R v A.B.S.* (1971), trial transcript, p. 71.
89 *R v R.J.F.* (1961), Exhibit G, Statement of defendant.
90 ibid. Report of Post-Mortem Examination.
91 ibid. Deposition of Police Constable G. MacGregor.
92 ibid. Deposition of Police Constable D. Anderson.
93 ibid. Sentencing transcript, pp. 2–3, 6.
94 ibid. Trial transcript, testimony of F. J. S. W., p. 5.
95 ibid. Testimony of R. J. H., pp. 5–6.
96 ibid. Sentencing transcript, pp. 3–4.
97 ibid. Extract from sentencing remarks.
98 *R v R.S.M.* (1971), Exhibit E, 'Statement of defendant'.
99 ibid. Reports of Post-Mortem Examination.
100 ibid. Deposition of B. B.
101 ibid. Deposition of A. F. and trial transcript, pp. 19–20.
102 ibid. Statement of defendant and trial transcript, pp. 37–8.
103 ibid. Deposition of W. J.
104 ibid. Trial transcript, p. 75.
105 ibid., p. 106.
106 ibid. Record of Criminal Convictions.
107 ibid. Record of Traffic Convictions.
108 ibid. Trial transcript, p. 96.
109 *R v C.J.F.* (1967), Exhibit J, 'Statement of defendant'.
110 ibid. See deposition of Police Constable K. Matthews.
111 ibid. See deposition of Sergeant W. Connolly.
112 ibid. See deposition of Police Constable K. Matthews.
113 ibid.
114 ibid.
115 ibid. See deposition of Sergeant W. Connolly.
116 ibid.
117 *R v B.J.W.* (1971), deposition of Traffic Inspector, Kalgoorlie Regional District Traffic Office.
118 *R v B.B.M.* (1951), deposition of O. R.
119 ibid. Deposition of C. J.
120 ibid. Deposition of Police Constable F. Wass.
121 ibid. Report of Post-Mortem Examination.
122 ibid. Deposition of T. T.
123 For example, see *R v B.D.S.M.* (1951) and *R v J.E.J.* (1961).

NOTES TO CHAPTER FOUR

124 For example, see *R v J.E.J.* (1961) where the deceased driver's blood alcohol concentration was 0.28%.
125 Via s 21 of *Traffic Act Amendment Act (No. 4), 1957* (WA) and *Blood Alcohol Test Regulations, 1958* (WA).
126 National Safety Council of Western Australia, *A case for the introduction of blood alcohol tests in Western Australia*, p. 5.
127 Anon., 'Drinking Drivers Dangerous as Well as Drunken Ones', *The Science News-Letter*, vol. 33, no. 13, 26 March 1938, p. 205.
128 British Medical Association, *Relation of alcohol to road accidents: Report of a Special Committee of the British Medical Association*, British Medical Association, London, 1960, p. 8; Anon., 'Under the Influence', *The British Medical Journal*, vol. 1, no. 5168, 1960, p. 256; British Medical Association, *The Drinking Driver: The medico-legal investigation of the drinking driver*; R. A. McFarland & R. C. Moore, 'Accidents and Accident Prevention', *Annual Review of Medicine*, vol. 13, no. 1, 1962, p. 380.
129 British Medical Association, *The Drinking Driver: The medico-legal investigation of the drinking driver*, p. 10.
130 Davison, *Car Wars*, p. 160.
131 R. F. Borkenstein, R. F. Crowther, R. P. Shumate, W. B. Ziel & R. Zylman, *The role of the drinking driver in traffic accidents*, Indiana University, Bloomington, 1964.
132 R. F. Borkenstein, R. F. Crowther, R. P. Shumate, W. B. Ziel & R. Zylman, *The role of the drinking driver in traffic accidents: the Grand Rapids Study*, Steintor-Verlag, Hamburg, 1974, pp. 70, 99, 100–2.
133 ibid., pp. 101–2. See also, Figure 6, 'Comparison of two estimates the relative risk of crash involvement as a function of BAC', adapted from Blomberg et al. (2005) and Borkenstein (1974)' in R. B. Voas & J. C. Lacey, *Alcohol and Highway Safety 2006: A Review of the State of Knowledge*, National Highway Traffic Safety Administration, Washington DC, 2011–2013, p. xxiv.
134 Borkenstein *et al*, *The role of the drinking driver in traffic accidents: the Grand Rapids Study*, p. 99.
135 For example, see Western Australian Police Department – V4, 'Traffic Branch – Drunken drivers: Policy', SROWA. See letters from Churches of Christ: Federal Conference Executive to Premier Brand, 14 November 1960 and Country Women's Association to Minister for Police, 8 June 1960.
136 ibid. Brief from the Commissioner of Police to Minister for Police – briefing response to correspondence from Churches of Christ to Premier Brand, folio 85.
137 See s 4 *Traffic Act Amendment Act (No. 3), 1965* (WA) and Report from Inspector Duggan, 21 February 1969, p. 2, Western Australian Police Department – V2, 'Traffic Office – Breathalyser Policy', SROWA.
138 *Blood Sampling and Analysis Regulations, 1966* (WA) and *Breath Analysis Regulations, 1966* (WA).
139 Report to Inspector Duggan, 21 February 1969, p. 2, Western Australian Police Department – V2, 'Traffic Office – Breathalyser Policy', SROWA.
140 See s 4 *Traffic Act Amendment Act (No. 3), 1965* (WA).

NOTES TO CHAPTER FOUR

141 Letter from Royal Perth Hospital's Deputy Administrator to the Crown Solicitor, 31 August 1967; letter from Fremantle Hospital Administration to Assistant Crown Solicitor, 7 September 1967; Royal Perth Hospital, Circular to staff – 'Police Requests for Blood Alcohol and breathalyser investigations', folio 82; letter from D. J. R. Snow, Acting Commissioner of Public Health, to G. MacKinnon MLC, 1 September 1967 – Public Health Department of Western Australia – 1958/1102, 'Regulations re blood sampling of persons under the influence of liquor', SROWA, WAS 268, CONS 2489.
142 ibid. Letter dated 2 October 1968.
143 Via s 5 of the *Traffic Act Amendment Act (No. 2), 1968* (WA).
144 Via s 9 of the *Road Traffic Amendment Act 1992* (WA).
145 Lerner, *One for the Road: Drunk Driving Since 1900*, p. xii.
146 British Medical Association, *The Drinking Driver: The medico-legal investigation of the drinking driver*, p. 11.
147 National Safety Council of Western Australia, *A case for the introduction of blood-alcohol tests in Western Australia*, p. 39; Western Australian Hotels Association, *Assessment on "the effectiveness" of blood alcohol limits in reducing traffic accidents*, Western Australian Hotels Association Incorporated, Leederville, 1983, at 4.2; Lerner, *One for the Road: Drunk Driving Since 1900*, p. 27.
148 Via s 2 of the *Motor Car (Driving Offence) Act* 1965 (VIC).
149 Pursuant to s 7 *Traffic Act Amendment Act (No. 2), 1968* (WA) which repealed ss 1 of s 32B. See also Report to Inspector Duggan, 21 February 1969, p. 2 and Report from Sergeant Woodley to Superintendent Monck, 25 June 1971, p. 3, Western Australian Police Department – V2, 'Traffic Office – Breathalyser Policy', SROWA.
150 *Road Traffic Amendment (Random Breath Tests) Act 1988* (WA). See also E. Cameron, 'The Development of Drink Driving Policy in Western Australia, 1990–1996', Honours dissertation (Politics), Faculty of Arts, Edith Cowan University, 1996, p. 4.
151 Pursuant to s 7 *Traffic Act Amendment Act (No. 2), 1968* (WA).
152 Report from Sergeant Woodley to Superintendent Monck, 25 June 1971; letter from Acting Commissioner of Police to Under Secretary for Law, 17 September 1971; letter from First Assistant Parliamentary Counsel to Acting Commissioner of Policy, 8 October 1971 – Western Australian Police Department – V2, 'Traffic Office – Breathalyser Policy', SROWA.
153 *Blood Alcohol Test Regulations, 1958* (WA). The usual means of analysis employed by the Government Chemical Laboratories was the widely accepted Kozelka and Hine method. Other methods that conformed to the regulations were also employed but Kozelka and Hine's was preferred. See also W. M. Laurie, Director of the Public Health Laboratory to UK Commissioner of Public Health, 26 August 1959, Public Health Department of Western Australia, 'Regulations re blood sampling of persons under the influence of liquor', SROWA.
154 Report to Inspector Duggan from Sergeant Woodley, 21 February 1969, p. 2, Western Australian Police Department – V2, 'Traffic Office – Breathalyser Policy', SROWA.
155 *R v G.C.B.* (1970), trial transcript, pp. 50–4.

NOTES TO CHAPTER FOUR

156 ibid. Deposition of Police Constable J. Gibson.
157 ibid. Trial transcript, pp. 68–70.
158 ibid., p. 67.
159 ibid., p. 64.
160 ibid. Deposition of Police Constable J. Gibson and trial transcript, p. 60.
161 ibid. Trial transcript, pp. 59–60.
162 ibid., p. 92.
163 ibid., p. 67.
164 ibid., p. 78.
165 ibid., pp. 78–9.
166 ibid., p. 86.
167 ibid., p. 87.
168 ibid., pp. 4, 92.
169 'Loophole in .08 Law, says Lawyer', *West Australian*, 3 April 1969.
170 Report to Inspector Duggan from Sergeant Woodley, 21 February 1969, p. 2, Western Australian Police Department – V2, 'Traffic Office – Breathalyser Policy', SROWA.
171 Pursuant to s 21 of *Traffic Act Amendment Act (No. 4), 1957* (WA).
172 *R v A.R.B.* (1970), trial transcript, p. 8.
173 ibid. Deposition of Police Constable D. Johnson.
174 ibid. Trial transcript, pp. 16–17.
175 ibid., pp. 18–19.
176 *R v G.N.M.* (1969), trial transcript, pp. 2–4.
177 ibid. Deposition of Police Constable K. Bracken.
178 ibid. Trial transcript, p. 4.
179 ibid., p. 6.
180 *R v E.J.V.* (1969).
181 ibid. Trial transcript, pp. 11–14, 20.
182 ibid., p. 12.
183 ibid., pp. 40–1.
184 ibid. Record of Criminal Convictions and Record of Traffic Convictions.
185 ibid. Trial transcript, pp. 31–4.
186 ibid., p. 10.
187 ibid., pp. 72–7.
188 ibid., pp. 33–5.
189 ibid., pp. 96–9.
190 ibid., p. 9.
191 ibid., pp. 2–4.
192 ibid., p. 93.
193 *R v B.W.P.* (1972), deposition of Senior Police Constable L. Thickbroom.
194 ibid. 'Reasons for ruling evidence inadmissible', 7 November 1972.
195 ibid., p. 2.
196 ibid., pp. 2–4.

NOTES TO CHAPTER FIVE

Chapter Five: Killing them softly, 1946–1974
1   For example, see K. Richardson, *The British Motor Industry, 1896–1939*, Macmillan, London, 1977, pp. 178–80; H. Perkin, *The Age of the Automobile*, Quartet Books, London, 1976, p. 138; J. S. Dean, *Murder Most Foul: A study of the road deaths problem*, George Allen & Unwin Ltd, Great Britain, 1947, pp. 23, 79; K. Laybourn with D. Taylor, *The Battle for the Roads of Britain, Police, Motorists and the Law, c. 1890s to 1970s*, Palgrave Macmillan, Hampshire, 2015, p. 73.
2   *R v A.J.C.* (1946), *R v G.T.B.* (1946), *R v R.F.A.* (1947), *R v A.H.B.* (1947), *R v J.W.K.* (1948), *R v J.C.* (1949), *R v W.A.B.* (1950), *R v E.J.H.* (1950), *R v N.T.J.* (1950), *R v S.M.* (1950), *R v J.W.B.* (1950), *R v G.S.J.* (1951), *R v O.S.* (1951), *R v D.C.G.* (1952), *R v J.W.C.* (1952), *R v L.L.L.* (1956), *R v J.R.B.* (1956), *R v D.D.M.* (1957), *R v J.E.C.* (1957), *R v N.K.* (1958), *R v F.G.D.* (1959), *R v R.E.P.* (1959), *R v J.W.E.* (1959), *R v B.J.M.* (1960), *R v N.T.N.* (1960), *R v R.J.F.* (1961), *R v B.N.S.* (1961), *R v C.W.H.* (1964), *R v P.M.L.* (1965), *R v D.H.S.* (1965), *R v L.M.* (1966), *R v D.J.B.* (1966), *R v M.Z.* (1966), *R v C.J.F.* (1967), *R v H.F.* (1968), *R v A.R.B.* (1970), *R v B.J.B.* (1974).
3   *R v A.H.B.* (1947), *R v W.A.B.* (1950), *R v D.D.M.* (1957), *R v N.K.* (1958), *R v R.E.P.* (1959), *R v B.J.M.* (1960), *R v C.W.H.* (1964), *R v B.J.B.* (1974).
4   *R v A.J.C.* (1946), *R v R.F.A.* (1947), *R v E.J.H.* (1950), *R v L.K.H.* (1950), *R v N.T.J.* (1950), *R v S.M.* (1950), *R v J.W.B.* (1950), *R v G.S.J.* (1951), *R v J.R.B.* (1956), *R v D.D.M.* (1957), *R v J.E.C.* (1957), *R v R.E.P.* (1959), *R v J.W.E.* (1959), *R v N.T.N.* (1960), *R v B.N.S.* (1961), *R v C.W.H.* (1964), *R v D.H.S.* (1965), *R v M.Z.* (1966), *R v L.M.* (1966), *R v H.F.* (1968), *R v A.R.B.* (1970).
5   'Hit-Run Search Drama', *Daily News*, 9 April 1947, p. 1.
6   *R v A.H.B.* (1947).
7   *R v A.H.B.* (1947), *R v W.A.B.* (1950), *R v N.K.* (1958), *R v B.J.M.* (1960), *R v B.J.B.* (1974).
8   For example, see *R v R.E.P.* (1959).
9   *R v N.K.* (1958), extract from Chief Justice Dwyer's sentencing remarks.
10 *R v A.J.C.* (1946), *R v G.T.B.* (1946), *R v R.F.A.* (1947), *R v A.H.B.* (1947), *R v J.W.B.* (1950), *R v G.S.J.* (1951), *R v O.S.* (1951), *R v J.W.C.* (1952), *R v L.L.L.* (1956), *R v J.R.B* (1956), *R v D.D.M.* (1957), *R v J.E.C.* (1957), *R v N.K.* (1958), *R v F.G.D.* (1959), *R v W.J.E.* (1959), *R v N.T.N.* (1960), *R v R.J.F.* (1961), *R v C.W.H.* (1964), *R v P.M.L.* (1965), *R v M.Z.* (1966), *R v L.M.* (1966), *R v H.F.* (1968), *R v A.R.B.* (1970), *R v B.J.B.* (1974).
11 *R v A.H.B.* (1947), *R v O.S.* (1951), *R v J.W.C.* (1952), *R v L.L.L.* (1956), *R v N.K.* (1958), *R v F.G.D.* (1959), *R v R.J.F.* (1961), *R v P.M.L.* (1965), *R v B.J.B.* (1974).
12 *R v W.A.B.* (1950), deposition of F. H. P.
13 ibid. Depositions of A. J. G., M. B. G., I. F. P., R. G.
14 ibid. Deposition of Police Constable I. L. Dunn.
15 ibid. Deposition of Sergeant A. W. White.
16 ibid. Justice Walker's notes for sentencing.
17 *R v B.J.M.* (1960), depositions of A. M., R. C., R. H.
18 ibid. Deposition of D. M.
19 ibid. Depositions of Police Constable S. Jackson and Detective J. Dalton.
20 ibid. Extract from sentencing remarks.

21 *R v N.K.* (1958), extract from sentencing remarks.
22 ibid.
23 ibid. Exhibit D, 'Statement of defendant'.
24 ibid.
25 ibid. Letter from G. C. Curlewis to C. B. Gibson with handwritten response and notations from Chief Justice Dwyer, 14 June 1958.
26 For example, see *R v M.Z.* (1966).
27 *R v C.W.H.* (1964).
28 ibid. Trial transcript, pp. 107–8.
29 ibid. Deposition of R. W.
30 ibid. Report of Post-Mortem Examination and depositions of R. W. and R. G.
31 ibid. Trial transcript, pp. 45–59.
32 ibid. Deposition of R. W.
33 ibid.
34 ibid. Deposition of Police Constable F. Spears.
35 ibid. Trial transcript, pp. 128–9. See also deposition of Sergeant R. Harris.
36 ibid. Deposition of Sergeant R. Harris.
37 ibid.
38 ibid. Deposition of Police Constable F. Spears.
39 ibid. Trial transcript, pp. 129–30.
40 ibid., p. 197.
41 ibid., p. 125.
42 ibid., pp. 80–1.
43 ibid., pp. 116–17.
44 ibid., pp. 67–9.
45 ibid., pp. 125–6.
46 ibid., p. 125.
47 ibid., p. 140.
48 ibid., p. 126.
49 ibid., p. 140.
50 ibid., p. 36.
51 ibid., pp. 36–44.
52 ibid. Deposition of R. W.
53 ibid. Trial transcript, p. 161.
54 ibid. See also pp. 113–15, 153–4.
55 ibid., p. 161.
56 ibid., pp. 161–2.
57 ibid., pp. 179–80, 185.
58 ibid., pp. 189–90.
59 ibid., p. 185.
60 ibid., p. 9.
61 ibid., p. 187.
62 ibid., pp. 149–51.
63 ibid., p. 149.
64 ibid., pp. 67–9, 149–51.
65 ibid., p. 5.

NOTES TO CHAPTER FIVE

66 ibid., pp. 67–9.
67 Letter from Sergeant Goodman to Inspector Daniels, 13 June 1967, Western Australian Police Department – 1962/1377, 'Fatal Traffic Accidents: Investigation by members of CIB', State Records Office of Western Australia (SROWA), WAS 76, CONS 1910.
68 *R v R.J.F.* (1961), depositions of G. W. and W. B.
69 *R v P.M.L.* (1965), depositions of R. J. W. and C. I. L.
70 ibid. Exhibit B, 'Statement of defendant'.
71 ibid. Trial transcript, pp. 3–5 and depositions of J. L. P. and G. M.
72 ibid. Trial transcript, p. 5.
73 *R v A.R.B.* (1970), Statement of defendant and trial transcript, p. 90.
74 ibid. Trial transcript, pp. 4, 53. See also deposition of M. R. H.
75 ibid. Trial transcript, pp. 4, 21, 35–6, 49–53.
76 ibid. Deposition of C. J.
77 ibid. Trial transcript, pp. 4, 21, 35–6, 49–53, 100–1, 126 and Statement of defendant.
78 ibid. Trial transcript, pp. 92–105.
79 ibid.
80 ibid., p. 128.
81 ibid. Affidavit of Dr D. Hainsworth and trial transcript, pp. 8–20.
82 ibid. Trial transcript, pp. 18–19.
83 *R v H.B.F.* (1968), trial transcript, p. 4.
84 ibid., p. 5.
85 ibid. See also p. 26.
86 ibid., p. 16.
87 ibid., p. 38.
88 ibid., pp. 53–9.
89 *R v H.B.F.* (1968), trial transcript, p. 63.
90 ibid., p. 29.
91 ibid., p. 66.
92 ibid., pp. 73–4.
93 ibid., p. 68.
94 ibid., pp. 73–4.
95 ibid., p. 69.
96 *R v M.Z.* (1966).
97 ibid. Trial transcript, pp. 50–2.
98 ibid., pp. 47–9.
99 ibid. Deposition of B. S.
100 ibid. Report of Post-Mortem Examination.
101 ibid. Statement of defendant from Inquest, 14 September 1966 and deposition of B. S.
102 ibid. Trial transcript, p. 19.
103 ibid., p. 3.
104 ibid., pp. 3–6, 73–80.
105 ibid., p. 78.
106 ibid., p. 79.

107 ibid., p. 73.
108 ibid.
109 ibid., p. 75.
110 ibid., p. 63.
111 ibid., p. 74.
112 ibid., p. 55.
113 ibid., pp. 59, 61.
114 ibid., p. 57.
115 ibid., p. 68.
116 ibid., p. 66.
117 ibid.
118 ibid., p. 86.
119 ibid. Extract from sentencing remarks.
120 *R v J.W.K.* (1948), *R v J.C.* (1949), *R v W.A.B.* (1950), *R v E.J.H.* (1950), *R v N.T.J.* (1950), *R v S.W.* (1950), *R v D.C.G.* (1952), *R v R.E.P.* (1959), *R v B.J.M.* (1960), *R v B.N.S.* (1961), *R v D.H.S.* (1965), *R v D.J.B.* (1966), *R v C.J.F.* (1967).
121 *R v J.W.K.* (1948), *R v J.C.* (1949), *R v W.A.B.* (1950), *R v D.C.G.* (1952), *R v B.J.M.* (1960), *R v D.J.B.* (1966), *R v C.J.F.* (1967).
122 *R v W.A.B.* (1950) and *R v D.J.B.* (1966).
123 For example, see *R v S.M.* (1950) and *R v D.H.S.* (1965).
124 *R v B.N.S.* (1961).
125 ibid. See depositions of R. D. and G. P.
126 ibid. Trial transcript, p. 110.
127 ibid. Deposition of G. P.
128 ibid. Trial transcript, p. 5.
129 ibid., p. 95.
130 ibid.
131 ibid. See deposition of G. P.
132 ibid.
133 ibid. Trial transcript, pp. 96, 110–12.
134 ibid., pp. 71, 103.
135 ibid., pp. 4, 126.
136 ibid., pp. 23–4.
137 ibid., pp. 109–10, 120.
138 ibid., pp. 56–7.
139 ibid., p. 58.
140 ibid., p. 4.
141 ibid., p. 118.
142 *R v D.H.S.* (1965), trial transcript, p. 88.
143 ibid. Depositions of I. M., N. H., B. W., F. C.
144 ibid. Trial transcript, p. 31.
145 ibid., pp. 3–4 and deposition of H. M.
146 ibid. Trial transcript, p. 89.
147 ibid., pp. 6–7.
148 ibid., p. 89.
149 ibid., p. 6.

150 ibid. Deposition of Police Constable P. Archibald.
151 ibid. Trial transcript, p. 57.
152 ibid. See also Exhibit N.
153 ibid. Trial transcript, pp. 73, 278.
154 ibid., p. 59.
155 ibid., p. 60.
156 ibid., pp. 60–7.
157 ibid., p. 60.
158 ibid., pp. 41, 50 and deposition of Police Constable P. Archibald.
159 ibid. Trial transcript, p. 50.
160 ibid., p. 68.
161 ibid., pp. 74–8.
162 *R v N.T.J.* (1950), Statement of defendant.
163 ibid. Depositions of P. R. M. and Police Constable R. G. Vinicombe.
164 ibid. Deposition of H. F. D. W.
165 ibid. Deposition of W. G. K.
166 ibid. Deposition of Police Constable R. G. Vinicombe.
167 ibid. Deposition of H. H. H.
168 ibid. Statement of defendant.
169 ibid. Exhibit B.
170 ibid. Deposition of Police Constable R. G. Vinicombe.
171 'Police Say Man Was Drinking Before Fatality', *Daily News*, 18 September 1950, p. 3.
172 Personal communication, email from K. King to L. Larment, Webmaster, OzBurials, 17 March 2016 and reply from L. Larment to K. King, 17 March 2016. His grave was later identified with a generic marker.
173 *R v M.Z.* (1966), trial transcript, p. 61.

Chapter Six: Dangerous driving causing death and the *Road Traffic Act 1974*

1   See s 5 of *Acts Amendment (Road Traffic) Act 1974* (WA).
2   Law Reform Commission of Western Australia, *Report: Manslaughter or Dangerous Driving causing Death*, Project No. 17, Law Reform Commission of Western Australia, Perth, August 1970, p. 6.
3   The *Road Traffic Act 1974* (WA) received assent on 3 December 1974, although s 59(1) did not become fully operational until mid-1975. The s 291A offence remained temporarily intact due to a delay in the promulgation of the Act's penalties. For discussion, see Justice Jones, *R v M.S.P.* (1975), trial transcript, p. 103.
4   *Callaghan v R* (1952) 87 CLR 115.
5   Pursuant to s 595A of the Code.
6   Via the *Road Traffic Amendment Act (No. 4) 1981* (WA). See also correspondence in Western Australian Police Department – 1981/0728, 'Road Traffic Authority/Police Amalgamation of', State Records Office of Western Australia (SROWA), WAS 76, CONS 4000; and Public Sector Management Office – 943528, 'Police

NOTES TO CHAPTER SIX

Department Road Traffic Authority Merger Steering Committee', SROWA, WAS 36, CONS 5864.
7   Royal Commission on the Police, Great Britain, *Final report: Royal Commission on the Police, 1962*, H. M. Stationery Office, London, 1962.
8   *Parliamentary Debates (Hansard)*, Western Australia, Legislative Assembly, 30 October 1974, pp. 2827–30, 2837; Legislative Assembly, 12 November 1974, pp. 2989–99; Legislative Council, 21 November 1974, pp. 3421–8.
9   ibid. T. H. Jones, Legislative Assembly, 24 October 1974, p. 2642, 12 November 1974, p. 2989; T. D. Evans, Legislative Assembly, 30 October 1974, p. 2808; D. K. Dans, Legislative Council, 21 November 1974, p. 3421.
10 ibid. T. H. Jones, Legislative Assembly, 12 November 1974, p. 2989.
11 ibid. D. K. Dans, Legislative Council, 21 November 1974, p. 3421.
12 ibid., G. E. Masters, p. 3427.
13 ibid. B. T. Burke, Legislative Assembly, 12 November 1974, p. 3001.
14 ibid., R. J. O'Connor, 30 and 31 October 1974, pp. 2837, 2887 respectively.
15 Letter from Superintendent Lee, Supervisor Accident Section, to Superintendent Cole, 10 August 1976, Western Australian Police Department – 76/7154, 'Nash Amanda May – Death of on July 24, 1976 – rider of pushbike that was struck from behind by vehicle driven by Michael John Roche in Bay View Terrace, Mosman Park', SROWA, WAS 76, CONS 3454.
16 ibid.
17 Law Reform Commission of Victoria, *Death Caused by Dangerous Driving*, Discussion Paper No. 21, Law Reform Commission of Victoria, Melbourne, 1991, p. 15.
18 T. A. Hartrey, *Parliamentary Debates*, Western Australia, Legislative Assembly, 30 October 1974, pp. 2825–8.
19 ibid., 12 November 1974, p. 2987.
20 ibid., 30 October 1974, p. 2825.
21 ibid., 15 October 1974, p. 2281.
22 ibid., 30 October 1974, pp. 2825–8.
23 ibid., p. 2825.
24 ibid., 12 November 1974, p. 2985.
25 ibid., 30 October 1974, pp. 2825–6.
26 ibid., 12 November 1974, p. 2985.
27 ibid., pp. 2985–6.
28 ibid., 30 October 1974, p. 2826 and 12 November 1974, p. 2986.
29 ibid., 12 November 1974, pp. 2987–8.
30 D. Brown, *Traffic Offences: An examination of the principles of law governing offences committed by motorists on the road in Australia*, Sydney, Butterworths, 1983, p. 112.
31 R. J. O'Connor, *Parliamentary Debates*, Western Australia, Legislative Assembly, 12 November 1974, p. 2988.
32 ibid.
33 *Smith v The Queen* [1976] WAR 97 at 103.
34 ibid.
35 Sometimes referred to as the 'year and a day rule', a common law rule abolished by statute in WA in 1991. See Law Reform Commission of Western Australia,

Review of the Law of Homicide: Final Report, Law Reform Commission of Western Australia, Perth, 2007, pp. 23, 27.
36 Pursuant to s 59(2)(b) of the *Road Traffic Act 1974* (WA).
37 ibid. Pursuant to s 59(2)(c).
38 Drawing on the judgment in *R v Spurge* [1961] 2 QB 205, where it was held that a mechanical defect of a vehicle could be relied upon as a defence to a charge of dangerous driving if the defect was in *no way* due to any fault on behalf of the driver. See also Western Australian Police Department – 078 7261 VI, 'Henson Yvonne Anne (passenger) Carey Pamela Betty (driver) Dths of on 22.10.78 respectively when veh. coll. with veh. driven by Robert Edwin Malcolm COOPER at intersect. Walter road & Iolanthe St', SROWA, WAS 488, CONS 5882.
39 Pursuant to s 25 of the Code. See also D. Brown, *Traffic Offences and Accidents*, Butterworths, Sydney, 1996, p. 81.
40 For example, see *Hill v Baxter* (1958) 1 QB 277 at 282–3.
41 Brown, *Traffic Offences and Accidents*, p. 81.
42 For example, see *Kitson v R* (1987) 5 MVR 228.
43 As per the facts in *R v Warner* [1980] Qd R 207.
44 Brown, *Traffic Offences and Accidents*, p. 79 and *Traffic Offences*, pp. 118–19.
45 *Kroon v The Queen* (1990) 55 SASR 476, (1990) 52 A Crim R 15. See A Crim R at 18, 30. See also *Jiminez v R* (1992) 173 CLR 572, Chief Justice Mason at 578–9.
46 Brown, *Traffic Offences*, p. 118.
47 Justice Jones, *R v J.E.W.E.* (1976), trial transcript, p. 246.
48 Pursuant to s 59(3) of the *Road Traffic Act 1974* (WA).
49 T. A. Hartrey, *Parliamentary Debates*, Western Australia, Legislative Assembly, 12 November 1974, p. 2985.
50 Summary judgment was abolished in 2011 via the *Manslaughter Legislation Amendment Act 2011* (WA).
51 Justice Wallace, *R v S.K., J.S. & A.L.S.* (1978), transcript of sentencing, 20 October 1978, p. 47.
52 Pursuant to s 59(3)(b) of the *Road Traffic Act 1974* (WA).
53 ibid. See s 59(3)(a).
54 Letter from Assistant Commissioner (Traffic) to Commissioner of Police, 11 August 1976, Western Australian Police Department – 'Nash Amanda May – Death of on July 24, 1976 – rider of pushbike that was struck from behind by vehicle driven by Michael John Roche in Bay View Terrace, Mosman Park', SROWA.
55 Via s 6 of the *Criminal Law Amendment Act 1992* (WA).
56 Pursuant to s 59(3)(b) of the *Road Traffic Act 1974* (WA) as at reprint, 4 April 1991. Available online at <https://www.legislation.wa.gov.au/legislation/prod/filestore.nsf/FileURL/mrdoc_17406.pdf/$FILE/Road%20Traffic%20Act%201974%20-%20%5B03-00-00%5D.pdf?OpenElement>, accessed: 15 January 2019.
57 ibid., s 59(3)(aa).
58 ibid. See s 59(1) and s 59(1)(3)(b).
59 Pursuant to s 297 of the Criminal Code as at reprint, 9 July 1974. Available online at <https://www.legislation.wa.gov.au/legislation/prod/filestore.nsf/FileURL/

mrdoc_17668.pdf/$FILE/Criminal%20Code%20Act%20Compilation%20 Act%201913%20-%20%5B02-01-00%5D.pdf?OpenElement>, accessed: 15 January 2019.

60 *Mitchell v The Queen* (1986) 4 MVR 347 at 347–8.
61 Law Reform Commission of Western Australia, *Summary Trial of Indictable Offences*, Law Reform Commission of Western Australia, Perth, 1970, pp. 5, 8–10.
62 Via s 12(b) of the *Road Traffic Act Amendment Act, 1978* (WA).
63 This provision was tested in *R v Krakouer* (2003) 30 SR (WA) 186.
64 See s 59(3), s 59(4), s 61(3)(a) and s 62 of the *Road Traffic Act 1974* (WA).
65 For instance, see *Criminal Code 1899* (Qld), *Crimes Act 1900* (ACT), *Crimes Act 1900* (NSW), *Criminal Code Act 1924* (Tas), *Criminal Law Consolidation Act 1935* (SA), *Crimes Act 1958* (Vic), *Criminal Code 1983* (NT). The NSW *Crimes Act* initially defined dangerous driving causing death as a misdemeanour.
66 Law Reform Commission of Western Australia, *Review of the Law of Homicide: An Issues Paper*, Law Reform Commission of Western Australia, Perth, 2006, p. 5.
67 Law Reform Commission of Western Australia, *Review of the Law of Homicide: Final Report*, p. 120.
68 J. J. Leeming, *Road Accidents: Prevent or Punish?*, Cassell, London, 1969, pp. 105, 213, 206–7 and P. J. Fitzgerald, 'Road Traffic Law as the Lawyer Sees it', in Leeming, *Road Accidents*, pp. 157–75.
69 Law Reform Commission of Western Australia, *Review of the Law of Homicide: Final Report*, p. 120.
70 *Smith v The Queen* [1976] WAR 97.
71 *Kaighin v The Queen* (1990) 1 WAR 390.
72 *Smith v The Queen* at 97, 99–101.
73 ibid. at 99.
74 ibid. at 101.
75 ibid. at 97, 99.
76 ibid. at 97–8.
77 ibid. at 99–102.
78 ibid. at 98. For further discussion, see *Nickisson v The Queen* [1963] WAR 114, *R v McBride* [1962] 2 QB 167, *R v Thorpe* [1972] 1 WLR 342. *Thorpe* gave some clarity to the issue in finding that it would be within the scope of *R v McBride* to admit evidence of blood alcohol concentration were it at, or in excess of, the limit prescribed by the legislation.
79 *Smith v The Queen* at 97, 102–5.
80 Principally, *R v Evans* [1963] 1 QB 412, *R v McBride* [1962] 2 QB 167, *McBride v R* (1966) 115 CLR 44, *R v Coventry* (1938) 59 CLR 633.
81 *McBride v R* at 50.
82 *Smith v The Queen* at 104–5.
83 ibid. at 97, 103–4.
84 ibid. at 104.
85 ibid.
86 ibid. at 105.

87 See *R v Coventry* at 637.
88 *McBride v R* at 50.
89 ibid.
90 N. Morgan & S. Yeo, 'Defining the fault elements of driving offences', *Singapore Academy of Law Journal*, vol. 19, 2007, p. 224.
91 *Smith v The Queen* at 105.
92 T. A. Hartrey, *Parliamentary Debates*, Western Australia, Legislative Assembly, 12 November 1974, p. 2985.
93 *Smith v The Queen* at 104 and *McBride v R* at 50–1.
94 *McBride v R* at 50.
95 ibid. at 47.
96 ibid. at 47, 51–2.
97 ibid. See also *R v Evans* at 418 and J. E. Hall Williams, 'Causing Death by Dangerous Driving: The Objective Test', *The Modern Law Review*, vol. 26, no. 4, 1963, p. 430.
98 See CIB report and various correspondence, Western Australian Police Department – 76/7065, 'Gojak, Josa; Gojak, Patricia Ann – Deaths of on March 27, 1976, driver and passenger respectivley [sic] whose vehicle was struck head on by vehicle driven by David Alan Humble when he was racing vehicle driven by Colin Edmond Parker on Marmion Avenue', SROWA, WAS 76, CONS 3454.
99 Pursuant to s 8 of the Code. Where two or more persons form a common intention to carry out an unlawful purpose (in this instance racing and driving dangerously in conjunction with one another) and an offence is committed in the *course* of that common purpose which was a *probable* consequence of that purpose, all parties are deemed to have committed the offence.
100 See CIB report, Western Australian Police Department – 'Gojak, Josa; Gojak, Patricia Ann – Deaths of on March 27, 1976, driver and passenger respectivley [sic] whose vehicle was struck head on by vehicle driven by David Alan Humble when he was racing vehicle driven by Colin Edmond Parker on Marmion Avenue', SROWA.
101 *R v Campbell* [No. 2] (1981) 6 A Crim R 208 at 208, 213.
102 ibid. at 213.
103 ibid.
104 ibid.
105 *Campbell v The Queen* (1980) 2 A Crim R 157 at 159–61.
106 *R v Campbell* [No. 2] at 208–9.
107 Law Reform Commission of Western Australia, *Working Paper: Manslaughter or Dangerous Driving causing Death*, Project No. 17, Law Reform Commission of Western Australia, Perth, June 1970, p. 6.
108 *McBride v R* at 50.
109 *R v J.E.W.E.* (1976), trial transcript, pp. 73–5 and deposition of S. J. O.
110 ibid. Trial transcript, pp. 38–40, 49.
111 ibid., pp. 38–40, 49, 58–9, 64–7, 86–8, 110–12.
112 ibid., pp. 38–40, 58–9.
113 ibid. See analysis reports and test results conducted by Government Chemical Laboratories.

NOTES TO CHAPTER SIX

114 ibid. Letter from Dr K. Grainger, Associate in Neurology, Royal Perth Hospital – 'To whom it may concern', 25 February 1976 and D. R. Daley 'Confidential: Probation Service Pre-sentence Report', 16 August 1976, p. 1.
115 ibid. Letter from Dr K. Grainger, Associate in Neurology, Royal Perth Hospital – 'To whom it may concern'.
116 ibid.
117 ibid. Trial transcript, pp. 3–20.
118 ibid., pp. 6, 10.
119 ibid., pp. 154–8.
120 ibid., p. 269.
121 ibid., pp. 269–70.
122 ibid.
123 ibid.
124 ibid.
125 ibid.
126 ibid., p. 246.
127 File note from Police Constable B. F. Hodgson, 28 December 1977, Western Australian Police Department – 76/7063, 'Edwards, Jean Margaret – Death of on March 28, 1976, passenger in vehicle driven by Colin George Pyer when vehicle turned in front of vehicle driven by Helen Margaret Shine at South West Highway & Picton Road, Picton', SROWA, WAS 76, CONS 3454.
128 ibid. Brief to Sergeant Greenaway from Sergeant Kimber, 11 May 1976 and Statement of Sergeant Kimber, 30 November 1976.
129 ibid. See also statement of Police Constable R. L. Pengilly, 12 May 1976.
130 ibid. For example, see statement of J. Bird, 28 March 1976.
131 ibid. Analysis reports and test results conducted by Government Chemical Laboratories.
132 ibid. Letter from Sergeant M. B. Warner to Senior Inspector Liddelow, 4 May 1977; letter from Senior Inspector Liddelow to Assistant Commissioner for Traffic, 10 May 1977; letter from Sergeant M. B. Warner to Sergeant Wilkinson, 15 November 1977.
133 ibid. Form 16, Coroner's Statement of Findings from inquest at Bunbury, 3 December 1976.
134 ibid. Letter from Crown Prosecutor M. J. Murray, Crown Law Department to Assistant Commissioner for Police, 31 May 1977 and letter from Sergeant Whitbread to Senior Inspector Dobie, 8 December 1976.
135 ibid. Letter from Superintendent L. Pages-Oliver to Assistant Commissioner of Traffic, 17 May 1977. Pyers was later charged with dangerous driving causing death. Following an adjournment of the proceedings, he entered a guilty plea and was placed on two years' probation and was disqualified from driving for one year.
136 CIB report and analysis reports and test results conducted by Government Chemical Laboratories, Western Australian Police Department – 76/7020, 'Craggs, Kathleen Francis – Death of on February 1, 1976, as pedestrian was struck by vehicle driven by Gary George White in Atkinson Street, Collie', SROWA, WAS 76, CONS 3454.

NOTES TO CHAPTER SIX

137 ibid. Statement of A. Rosewarne, 1 February 1976 and telex from Bunbury Police Station to Commissioner of Police, Superintendent in Charge, Road Traffic Authority, Perth, 1 February 1976, 21:00.
138 ibid. See also Statement of A. Thorne, 7 February 1976.
139 ibid. Statement of P. Ugle, 2 February 1976.
140 ibid. Letter from Police Constable W. J. Elkes to Sergeant M. B. Warner, 24 August 1976, and wireless message, Western Australia Police to Commissioner of Police, South Australia, 1 February 1976, requesting that Mrs E. Kent be notified that the Coroner declined to hold an inquest into the death of her daughter.
141 ibid. See letter from District Coroner J. M. Forrest to Superintendent Forkin, 8 September 1976.
142 CIB report, Western Australian Police Department – 76/7056, 'Wilson, Robert – Death of on March 10, 1976 passenger in vehicle driven by George Bernard Walker that collided with vehicle driven by Carmela Flemming at Renou and Station Streets, East Cannington', SROWA, WAS 76, CONS 3454.
143 ibid. Letter from Sergeant B. R. Illingworth, Prosecuting Branch to Senior Inspector L. Pages-Oliver, 1 July 1976.
144 ibid. Letter from Senior Inspector L. Pages-Oliver to Assistant Commissioner (Traffic), 1 July 1976.
145 ibid. Letter from Premier Court to Attorney General and Commissioner of Police, 1 July 1976, newspaper clipping of 30 June 1976 attached.
146 CIB report, Western Australian Police Department – 77/7251, 'Hewison, Malcolm Robert William – Death of on 1/12/1977, passenger in vehicle driven by Brett Clinton Bond who collided with SEC pole in Brockway Avenue, Graylands', SROWA, WAS 76, CONS 3454.
147 ibid. 'Reasons for decision, Special Magistrate – J.R. Standing (Police) – v – B.C. Bond'.
148 ibid.
149 CIB report and other correspondence on file, Western Australian Police Department – 75/7164, 'Smith, Kevin Michael – death of on August 6, 1975, passenger in vehicle driven by Jeremy Peter Finch, When vehicle collided with vehicle driven by Alan John Lewington. Finch then collided with stationary vehicle driven by Eric Victor Welsh in Belgravia Street and Alexander Road, Belmont', SROWA, WAS 76, CONS 3454.
150 CIB report and other correspondence, Western Australian Police Department – 77/7194, 'York Andrew Lawrence – Death of on September 17, 1977 passenger in vehicle driven by Bernice Evelyn York when vehicle collided with vehicle driven by John Frederick Lowndes at Holmes Place & Collick St', SROWA, WAS 76, CONS 3454. See also statement of decedent's father, F. York, 17 September 1977.
151 ibid. CIB report and other correspondence on file.
152 Western Australian Police Department – 'Craggs, Kathleen Francis – Death of on February 1, 1976, as pedestrian was struck by vehicle driven by Gary George White in Atkinson Street, Collie', SROWA.
153 CIB report, Western Australian Police Department – 'Nash Amanda May – Death of on July 24, 1976 – rider of pushbike that was struck from behind by

NOTES TO CHAPTER SIX

vehicle driven by Michael John Roche in Bay View Terrace, Mosman Park', SROWA. 'May' was not Ms Nash's actual middle name. She adopted 'May' in honour of her grandmother and told fellow students and teachers that it *was* her name. Personal communication, phone call, S. Nash (deceased's mother) and K. King, 24 February 2017.

154 Personal communication, phone call, S. Nash and K. King, 24 February 2017.
155 Deposition of T. Kailis, Western Australian Police Department – 'Nash Amanda May – Death of on July 24, 1976 – rider of pushbike that was struck from behind by vehicle driven by Michael John Roche in Bay View Terrace, Mosman Park', SROWA.
156 Personal communication, phone call, S. Nash and K. King, 24 February 2017.
157 ibid.
158 Deposition of G. Tilley, Western Australian Police Department – 'Nash Amanda May – Death of on July 24, 1976 – rider of pushbike that was struck from behind by vehicle driven by Michael John Roche in Bay View Terrace, Mosman Park', SROWA.
159 ibid. CIB file note.
160 ibid. Record of Interview, 8.50 am, Fremantle Police Station, 26 July 1976, pp. 2–4.
161 ibid.
162 ibid. CIB file note.
163 ibid. Record of Interview, 26 July 1976, pp. 8–9.
164 ibid., p. 6.
165 ibid., p. 14.
166 ibid., p. 9.
167 ibid. Letter from Assistant Commissioner of Traffic to Commissioner of Police, 11 August 1976 and letter from Superintendent Lee, Supervisor Accident Section to Superintendent Cole, 10 August 1976.
168 ibid. Letter from Assistant Commissioner of Traffic to Commissioner of Police, 11 August 1976.
169 ibid. Deposition of T. Kailis.
170 Report of Sergeant Peters, Accident Inquiry Section, 11 May 1978, Western Australian Police Department – 77/7213, 'Holland Luke Christopher Michael – Death of on October 22, 1977 when driver of a car collided with car driven by Michael Solonel [sic] at Railway Parade, Shenton Park', SROWA, WAS 76, CONS 3454.
171 ibid. Letter from Police Constable J. Crawford to Sergeant M. B. Warner, 17 April 1978.
172 CIB report and file notes, Western Australian Police Department – 76/7242, 'Afflick Christopher Rodney – Death of on November 21, 1976 passenger in vehicle driven by Christopher Anthony Corrigin that left Oceanic Drive, City Beach and collided with SEC pole', SROWA, WAS 76, CONS 3454.
173 Western Australian Police Department – 'Henson Yvonne Anne (passenger) Carey Pamela Betty (driver) Dths of on 22.10.78 respectively when veh. coll. with veh. driven by Robert Edwin Malcolm COOPER at intersect. Walter road & Iolanthe st', SROWA.

NOTES TO CHAPTER SIX

174 Letter from Assistant Commissioner (Traffic) to Commissioner of Police, 11 August 1976, Western Australian Police Department – 'Nash Amanda May – Death of on July 24, 1976 – rider of pushbike that was struck from behind by vehicle driven by Michael John Roche in Bay View Terrace, Mosman Park', SROWA.
175 *R v B.D.S. & T.R.R. (1976); R v S.K., J.S. & A.L.S.* (1978); *R v D.R.B. & I.P.S.* (1979).
176 See Table A3, Appendices.
177 *R v M.S.P.* (1974), *R v J.E.W.E.* (1976), *R v S.K.* (1978) [of *R v S.K., J.S. & A.L.S* – joint prosecution], *R v A.M.C.* (1978), *R v V.J.P.* (1980), *R v M.D.B.* (1980), *R v G.S.C.* (1980), *R v G.A.T.C.* (1980), *R v R.C.C.* (1981), *R v P.D.F.* (1981).
178 *R v K.W.H.* (1974), *R v M.J.F.* (1975), *R v A.J.T.* (1975), *R v W.K.B.* (1975), *R v T.J.S.* (1976), *R v C.E.P.* (1976), *R v D.A.H.* (1976), *R v G.L.O.* (1976), *R v D.W.M.* (1978), *R v S.K.* (1978), *R v A.L.S.* (1978), *R v L.M.D.* (1979), *R v I.T.A.M.* (1980), *R v T.J.A.* (1980), *R v P.J.S.* (1980), *R v J.P.F.G.* (1981).
179 See Table A3, Appendices.
180 *R v L.M.D.* (1979) in which the offender was sentenced to a custodial term of three years' imprisonment.
181 *R v M.S.P.* (1975) and *R v I.B.F.* (1977) respectively.
182 See Table A3, Appendices.
183 *R v S.R.A.* (1978).
184 *R v M.S.P.* (1975), trial transcript, pp. 59, 72.
185 ibid., p. 5.
186 ibid., pp. 88–9.
187 ibid., p. 81.
188 ibid., p. 5.
189 ibid., pp. 7–8.
190 ibid., p. 18.
191 ibid., pp. 73–3a.
192 ibid., p. 73.
193 Supreme Court of Western Australia: 4, 'Criminal Record Book 11', SROWA, WAS 49, CONS 4332; 5, 'Criminal Record Book 12', SROWA, WAS 49, CONS 4332; 6, 'Criminal Record Book 13', SROWA, WAS 49, CONS 4332.

Chapter Seven: Reconsidering *Laporte v R* and the maximum imposable penalty, 1970–2004

1 *Laporte v R* [1970] WAR 87.
2 *Veen v The Queen (No 1)* (1979) 143 CLR 458, *Veen v The Queen (No 2)* (1988) 164 CLR 465, *Hoare v The Queen* (1989) 167 CLR 348.
3 *Laporte v R* at 87, 89.
4 ibid. at 89 and *R v Watson* [1960] Qd R 332. The Western Australian appellant court failed to observe that the sentence in *Watson* was reduced on appeal to nine months.
5 *Laporte v R* at 89.

NOTES TO CHAPTER SEVEN

6 ibid. at 90.
7 ibid. at 89.
8 *Smith v The Queen* [1976] WAR 97.
9 *R v Guilfoyle* [1973] 2 All ER 844 and *Smith v The Queen* at 107.
10 *R v Guilfoyle* at 845.
11 *Smith v The Queen* at 107–8.
12 *R v A.H.B.* (1947), *R v A.C.E.D.* (1949), *R v G.W.B.* (1955), *R v D.A.W.* (1965), *R v E.J.V.* (1969), *R v R.S.M.* (1971), *R v W.G.W.* (1972).
13 For example, see Justice McLure in *Eves v Western Australia* (2008) 49 MVR 259. See judgment text, para 22.
14 *Ainsworth v D (A Child)* (1992) 7 WAR 102 at 115.
15 *The Queen v S (No 2) (A CHILD)* (1992) 7 WAR 434 at 445–6, *McKenna v The Queen* (1992) 7 WAR 455 at 460–1, *English v The Queen* (1995) 82 A Crim R 586 at 588. Note, counsel for the appellant in *McKenna* submitted that sentences imposed in motor vehicle manslaughter cases had spanned a range, with a maximum penalty of five years. Justice Rowland overlooked this assertion, stating that penalties have 'ranged through terms of imprisonment of up to four years' and that 'Counsel for the applicant relies on this assertion'. It seems unlikely that McKenna's representative had unearthed two unreported cases of the 1970s, examined in this book. In appealing against the sentence, it would not have been in his client's interest to draw attention to previous matters which had attracted higher penalties.
16 *R v A.M.C.* (1979), extract from sentencing remarks.
17 ibid. See Record of Criminal Convictions and Record of Traffic Convictions.
18 ibid. Deposition of E. T.
19 ibid.
20 ibid. Statement of defendant, 26 September 1978.
21 ibid. Deposition of G. F.
22 ibid. Deposition of Sergeant V. Smith.
23 Signed property list, 27 September 1978, Receipt of items recovered from crash scene, Western Australian Police Department – 078 7237 VI, 'Deaths of NOYCE, Dennis Wayne; NOYCE Albert George; NOYCE Mary Elva Maria – Fatal Traffic Accident', State Records Office of Western Australia (SROWA), WAS 488, CONS 5882.
24 *R v A.M.C.* (1979), extract from sentencing remarks and character reference on file.
25 *Hodgson v Thomson* (1985) 2 MVR 272.
26 *R v Browne* (1985) 2 MVR 135 at 135, 137–9.
27 *R v Street* (1986) 4 MVR 156 at 156.
28 *R v S.K., J.S. & A.L.S.* (1978), sentencing transcript, pp. 45, 12–18A.
29 ibid. Pre-sentence reports for A. L. S. and S. K. and sentencing transcript, p. 47.
30 ibid. S. K. admitted to driving at speeds of up to 80 mph (128.74 km/h) in his pre-sentencing report interview. See also deposition of H. M. H.
31 ibid. Deposition of L. M. J. M.
32 ibid. Pre-sentence report for S. K.
33 ibid. Pre-sentence report for A. L. S.

34 ibid. See also sentencing transcript, pp. 36–8.
35 ibid., p. 44.
36 ibid., pp. 44–5.
37 ibid. Pre-sentence reports for A. L. S. and S. K. and sentencing transcript, pp. 30–45.
38 ibid. Sentencing transcript, p. 47.
39 ibid. Pre-sentence report for J. S.
40 ibid. Sentencing transcript, pp. 44–5.
41 For example, see *R v L.L.L.* (1956), *R v E.M.* (1958), *R v F.G.D.* (1959), *R v B.J.B.* (1974).
42 Via s 7 of the *Criminal Law Amendment Act 1988* (WA). See Australian Law Reform Commission, *Sentencing*, ALRC Report Number 44, Australian Government Publishing Service, Canberra, 1988, p. 28.
43 *R v Stebbings* (1990) 4 WAR 538.
44 *Crawley v The Queen* (1981) 55 FLR 463, (1981) 36 ALR 241. See ALR at 242–3.
45 ibid. at 243–4.
46 ibid. at 244.
47 ibid. at 248.
48 ibid. at 246.
49 ibid. at 246.
50 ibid. at 247.
51 ibid. at 252.
52 ibid. at 255.
53 ibid. at 253.
54 ibid., Justice Sheppard citing his remarks in *Evans v Sharman* [1973] NSWSC, 135 NSW 39, 10 December 1973.
55 Australian Transport Safety Bureau, *Road crash casualties and rates, Australia, 1925 to 2005*, Australian Transport Safety Bureau, Canberra, 2006.
56 S. O'Connell, 'From Toad of Toad Hall to the "Death Drivers" of Belfast: An Exploratory History of "Joyriding"', *British Journal of Criminology*, vol. 46, no. 3, 2006, p. 456.
57 *Blair v Semple* (1989) 10 MVR 75.
58 M. Lang, 'Death-drive fines apt, court rules', *West Australian*, 8 November 1989, p. 14 and *Blair v Semple* at 75.
59 *Blair v Semple* at 75–7.
60 Lang, 'Death–drive fines apt, court rules'.
61 ibid. See also *Blair v Semple* at 77–9.
62 *Blair v Semple* at 81.
63 ibid. at 80, 82.
64 R. Bindon, 'Literate lesson in death case', *West Australian*, 17 November 1989, p. 10.
65 ibid. Three convictions for refusing a breathalyser were likely in error. According to the judgment on appeal, there were only two prior convictions. See *Blair v Semple* at 75.
66 *R v Stebbings* at 538–9.
67 ibid. at 539, 543.

68 ibid. at 540.
69 ibid. at 543–4.
70 ibid. at 544.
71 ibid. at 538–41.
72 ibid. at 541–2.
73 ibid. at 540.
74 ibid.
75 ibid. at 545.
76 ibid. at 540–1.
77 ibid. See also Justice Kennedy at 546–7.
78 *The Queen v S (No 2) (A CHILD)* at 446.
79 R v Stebbings at 538, 541.
80 R v A.H.B. (1947), R v A.C.E.D. (1949), R v G.W.B. (1955), R v D.A.W. (1965), R v C.S.H. (1968), R v E.J.V. (1969), R v O.N.H. (1970), R v D.L.B.V. (1971), R v R.S.M. (1971), R v W.G.W. (1972).
81 R v Stebbings at 546.
82 MADD was founded in the USA in 1980 and CADD in the UK in 1985. RID was established in the USA in 1978. RoadPeace and Brake were established in the UK in 1992 and 1995 respectively. For a detailed discussion of the history of MADD and RID, see B. H. Lerner, *One for the Road: Drunk Driving Since 1900*, The Johns Hopkins University Press, Baltimore, 2011, pp. 64–92.
83 C. Sidoti, 'The Commonwealth's responsibility for Aboriginal young offenders', in L. Atkinson & S. A. Gerull (eds.), *National Conference on Juvenile Justice: Proceedings of a conference held 22–24 September 1992*, Australian Institute of Criminology, Canberra, 1993, pp. 83–4.
84 L. Colyer, 'Get tough on young offenders', *West Australian*, 7 August 1991, p. 3.
85 'Thief should have watched my mother die', *Sunday Times*, 18 August 1991, p. 2.
86 J. Duffy, 'Family backs fatal chase', *West Australian*, 17 August 1991, p. 15 and H. Winterton, 'Murder charge in car crash death', *West Australian*, 19 August 1991, p. 3.
87 'Rally for Justice', *Sunday Times*, 18 August 1991, p. 31.
88 K. Brewster in association with SBS Independent, *Demons at Drivetime*, 1995. Available online at <http://aso.gov.au/titles/documentaries/demons–drivetime/credits/>, accessed: 1 August 2016. Reports on the number of people that attended the rally are conflicting. The media estimated that 15,000 to 20,000 attended, which others have suggested was inflated to 30,000 by rally organisers and supporters. See H. Jackson, 'Juvenile justice – the Western Australian experience', in Atkinson & Gerull (eds.), *National Conference on Juvenile Justice*, p. 88.
89 C. Stockwell, 'The role of the media in the juvenile justice debate in Western Australia', in Atkinson & Gerull (eds.), *National Conference on Juvenile Justice*, p. 279 and Brewster in association with SBS Independent, *Demons at Drivetime*, Clip 2, 'Rally for Justice', S. Mickler, interview.
90 Stockwell, 'The role of the media in the juvenile justice debate in Western Australia', p. 280.

NOTES TO CHAPTER SEVEN

91 Federal Office of Road Safety, *The history of road fatalities in Australia*, Monograph 23, Federal Office of Road Safety, Canberra, 1998, p. 4.
92 L. Jackson, 'Western Australia: tough and controversial laws for juvenile offenders', *Background Briefing* (transcript), Radio National, Australian Broadcasting Commission (ABC) Radio, 15 March 1992, p. 2.
93 Brewster in association with SBS Independent, *Demons at Drivetime*, Clip 2, 'Rally for Justice' and Jackson, 'Western Australia: tough and controversial laws for juvenile offenders', pp. 2–3.
94 Brewster in association with SBS Independent, *Demons at Drivetime*, Clip 2, 'Rally for Justice', S. Mickler, interview.
95 'MPs swamped by reform demands', *West Australian*, 21 August 1991, p. 2.
96 For example, see M. Wilkie, 'Crime (Serious and Repeat Offenders) Sentencing Act 1992: A Human Rights Perspective', *Western Australian Law Review*, vol. 22, 1992, pp. 187–96; R. White, 'Tough laws for hard-core politicians', *Alternative Law Journal*, vol. 17, 1992, pp. 58–60; A. Ashworth, 'Ways out of the Abyss? Reflections on punishment in Western Australia', *University of Western Australia Law Review*, vol. 22, 1992, pp. 257–71.
97 Brewster in association with SBS Independent, *Demons at Drivetime*, Clip 1, 'Howard Loves Controversy'.
98 ibid.
99 Brewster in association with SBS Independent, *Demons at Drivetime*, Clip 2, 'Rally for Justice'.
100 S. Mickler, 'Visions of disorder: media, police, Aboriginal youth and the politics of youth crime reporting', *Cultural Studies*, vol. 6, no. 3, 1992, p. 14.
101 Brewster in association with SBS Independent, *Demons at Drivetime*, Clip 2, 'Rally for Justice' and Jackson, 'Western Australia: tough and controversial laws for juvenile offenders'.
102 Stockwell, 'The role of the media in the juvenile justice debate in Western Australia', p. 281.
103 'Death crash sentence pathetic: Minister', *West Australian*, 20 August 1991, p. 11.
104 Stockwell, 'The role of the media in the juvenile justice debate in Western Australia', p. 283.
105 ibid. See also 'Death driver pleads guilty', *West Australian*, 15 February 1992, p. 9.
106 Jackson, 'Juvenile justice – the Western Australian experience', p. 88 and Jackson, 'Western Australia: tough and controversial laws for juvenile offenders', p. 2.
107 ibid. See Jackson, p. 2 of transcript.
108 A. Hurley & D. Pedley, 'Hardline on young criminals', *West Australian*, 6 January 1992, p. 5.
109 Stockwell, 'The role of the media in the juvenile justice debate in Western Australia', p. 283.
110 Hurley & Pedley, 'Hardline on young criminals'.
111 Stockwell, 'The role of the media in the juvenile justice debate in Western Australia', p. 283.
112 'Death crash sentence pathetic: Minister' and D. Chandler, 'Treat chase deaths as murder: MP', *West Australian*, 4 January 1992, p. 13.

NOTES TO CHAPTER SEVEN

113 Wilkie, 'Crime (Serious and Repeat Offenders) Sentencing Act 1992: A Human Rights Perspective' and Western Australian Parliament, Standing Committee on Legislation, *First report on the Crime (Serious and Repeat Offenders) Sentencing Act 1992 and the Criminal Law Amendment Act 1992*, Legislative Council, Perth, 1992.
114 Jackson, 'Western Australia: tough and controversial laws for juvenile offenders', pp. 1, 7.
115 'Memories of fatal Sunday never fade', *West Australian*, 7 October 1995, p. 4.
116 S. Yeap, 'Drink-driving takes its horrendous price', *West Australian*, 8 December 1989, p. 9 and 'Death driver's inner torment', *West Australian*, 7 October 1995, p. 4.
117 K. King, 'A Lesser Species of Homicide – Manslaughter, Negligent and Dangerous Driving Causing Death: The Prosecution of Drivers in Western Australia, 1946–2011', PhD thesis, University of Western Australia, 2014, p. 23.
118 Jackson, 'Western Australia: tough and controversial laws for juvenile offenders', p. 2.
119 *Ainsworth v D (A Child)* at 116.
120 *Punch v The Queen* (1993) 9 WAR 486 at 497.
121 *McKenna v The Queen* at 460.
122 *R v Calder; ex parte Attorney General* [1987] 1 Qd R 348, (1986) 22 A Crim R 62. See A Crim R at 71.
123 For example, see Justice Seaman in *The Queen v S (No 2) (A CHILD)* at 450.
124 Justice Wallwork citing Professor Harding, UWA Crime Research Centre, *Wood v The Queen* (2002) 130 A Crim R 518 at 521.
125 *The Queen v S (No 2) (A CHILD)* at 436.
126 ibid. at 434.
127 ibid. at 437–9.
128 ibid. at 436, 442, 450.
129 ibid. at 439–40.
130 ibid. at 447–9.
131 ibid. at 446.
132 ibid. at 447.
133 ibid. at 449.
134 ibid. at 450.
135 ibid. at 449–50.
136 ibid.
137 ibid. at 450, citing *R v Cascoe* [1970] 2 All ER 833.
138 ibid. at 451.
139 ibid. at 451–2.
140 ibid. at 452.
141 Pursuant to s 279(2) of the Code.
142 Law Reform Commission of Western Australia, *Review of the Law of Homicide: Final Report*, Law Reform Commission of Western Australia, Perth, 2007, p. 51.
143 ibid., p. 54.
144 *McKenna v The Queen* at 461 and *The Queen v S (No 2) (A CHILD)* at 442, 450.
145 *McKenna v The Queen* at 461, 467.

146 ibid. at 455.
147 ibid. at 464.
148 ibid.
149 ibid. at 456, 462.
150 ibid. at 457–8, 463.
151 ibid. at 463.
152 ibid. at 458, 463.
153 ibid. at 463–4, 474.
154 ibid. at 474.
155 ibid. at 455.
156 ibid. at 466.
157 ibid. at 456, 468.
158 *Punch v The Queen* at 490.
159 ibid. at 486.
160 ibid. at 488.
161 D. Kennedy, 'Death driver gets 10 years', *West Australian*, 18 February 1993, p. 9 and *Punch v The Queen* at 488–9.
162 *Punch v The Queen* at 490.
163 ibid. at 489.
164 ibid. at 491.
165 ibid. at 491–2.
166 ibid. at 499.
167 ibid. at 496–7.
168 ibid. at 500.
169 ibid. at 501.
170 *Clinch v The Queen* [1999] WASCA 57.
171 ibid., judgment text, para 5.
172 ibid., para 7.
173 ibid., paras 7–8.
174 ibid., para 8.
175 ibid., para 4.
176 ibid., paras 2, 4.
177 *White v The Queen* (2003) 39 MVR 157. See judgment text, para 38.
178 ibid., para 41.
179 ibid., para 15.
180 ibid., para 16.
181 ibid., para 14.
182 ibid., paras 2–3 and C. Manton, 'Man charged over couple's death in crash', *West Australian*, 7 October 2002, p. 5.
183 *White v The Queen*, paras 3, 12.
184 ibid., para 2.
185 ibid., para 4.
186 S. Cowan, 'Crash orphans sue death driver', *West Australian*, 26 September 2003, p. 5.
187 Manton, 'Man charged over couple's death in crash' and *White v The Queen*, para 4.

NOTES TO CHAPTER SEVEN

188 *White v The Queen*, para 6.
189 ibid., para 7.
190 ibid., para 13.
191 ibid., para 19.
192 ibid., para 26.
193 ibid., paras 42–4.
194 A. March, 'Detention term for young death driver', *West Australian*, 14 April 1992.
195 'Death driver jailed', *West Australian*, 15 August 1992, p. 5.
196 M. Barton, 'Death driver "on cannabis"' and B. Peace, 'Death driver gets 8 years', *West Australian*, 11 and 13 November 1999, p. 34 and p. 36 respectively.
197 Peace, 'Death driver gets 8 years'.
198 T. Hunter, 'Youth's driving killed his friends', *West Australian*, 14 April 1992, p. 31.
199 March, 'Detention term for young death driver'.
200 *Koltasz v The Queen* [2003] WASCA 38. See judgment text, para 41.
201 ibid., paras 7, 9.
202 ibid., para 45.
203 Justice Wallwork citing Professor Harding, UWA Crime Research Centre, *Wood v The Queen* at 521.
204 S. Cowan, 'Death driver walks free', *West Australian*, 25 April 2002, p. 5.
205 A. March, 'Death driver given probation', *West Australian*, 29 July 1992, p. 28.
206 L. Gosden, 'Fines for death drivers anger granddaughter', *West Australian*, 7 March 1996, p. 3.
207 'Death driver fined', *West Australian*, 7 September 1996, p. 5.
208 R. Gibson, 'Death driver gets special licence', *West Australian*, 30 January 1997, p. 3.
209 R. Gibson, 'Blind driver's risk kills two', *West Australian*, 29 July 1998, p. 13.
210 ibid.
211 *R v Jurisic* (1998) 45 NSWLR 209, (1998) 101 A Crim R 259.
212 ibid. See A Crim R at 259, 277–8.
213 For example, see *Koltasz v The Queen*, para 49 and *Wood v The Queen*, at 530, 543.
214 *Wood v The Queen* at 534.
215 ibid. at 523, 531.
216 ibid. at 532.
217 ibid. at 524.
218 ibid. at 523–4, 531–2, 537.
219 ibid. at 524.
220 ibid. at 538.
221 ibid. at 526.
222 ibid. at 531–2.
223 S. Cowan, 'Death driver "no criminal"', *West Australian*, 23 March 2002, p. 3.
224 'Death driver fined'.
225 *D'Amico v The Queen* (2000) 33 MVR 148. See judgment text, para 6.
226 ibid. See also paras 10–13.

227 ibid., paras 15–20.
228 G. Fang, 'Death driver calls police', *West Australian*, 25 November 1997, p. 11.
229 *D'Amico v The Queen*, paras 13, 22–3.
230 ibid., para 16.
231 ibid., para 44.
232 ibid., para 29.
233 ibid., paras 35–8.
234 For example, see Justice Murray in *Kay v The Queen* (2004) 147 A Crim R 401, (2004) 42 MVR 130. See A Crim R at 404–5 and Justice Miller at 412–13. See also Justice Wheeler in *Parsons v The Queen* (2000) 32 MVR 319, judgment text, paras 21–2.
235 Pursuant to s 5 of the *Criminal Law Amendment Act 1992* (WA) which amended s 378 of the Criminal Code.
236 *D'Amico v The Queen*, para 33.
237 *Parsons v The Queen*, para 19.
238 ibid., para 20.
239 ibid.
240 ibid., para 21.
241 ibid., para 22.
242 *Kay v The Queen* and D. Reed, '12 years for killer drunk driver', *West Australian*, 30 June 1999, p. 3.
243 Reed, '12 years for killer drunk driver'.
244 D. Reed, 'The Road to tragedy', *West Australian*, 30 June 1999, p. 3.
245 ibid. See also B. Pearce, 'I tried to stop drunk driver: wife', *West Australian*, 21 June 1999, p. 3.
246 Reed, '12 years for killer drunk driver'.
247 ibid.
248 Reed, 'The Road to tragedy'.
249 Pearce, 'I tried to stop drunk driver: wife'.
250 Reed, '12 years for killer drunk driver'.
251 *Kay v The Queen* at 401 and A. Calverley, 'Road train death driver jailed', *West Australian*, 1 October 2003, p. 40.
252 *Kay v The Queen* at 411.
253 ibid.
254 ibid. at 405.
255 ibid. at 406.
256 ibid. at 410.
257 ibid. at 401.
258 ibid. at 416.
259 ibid. at 412.
260 *Phillips v Carbone (No 2)* (1992) 10 WAR 169 at 175–7, 187.
261 ibid. at 169.
262 ibid. at 190.
263 *Kay v The Queen* at 416 and *R v Wilkins* (1988) 38 A Crim R 445 at 449–50.
264 ibid.
265 ibid.

NOTES TO CHAPTER EIGHT

266 *Kay v The Queen* at 417–18.
267 *R v Wilkins* at 450.
268 *Kay v The Queen* at 416–17.
269 *White v The Queen*, para 19 and *Kay v The Queen* at 417.
270 *Kay v The Queen* at 417 and *R v Snewin* (1997) 190 LSJS 487, (1997) 25 MVR 553.
271 *Kay v The Queen* at 417–18.
272 ibid. at 419.
273 ibid. at 401.
274 ibid. at 404.
275 ibid. at 405.
276 ibid.
277 ibid. at 412. See also A. Calverley, 'Death drivers may get more jail', *West Australian*, 5 October 2004, p. 15.
278 *Kay v The Queen* at 412–13.
279 ibid. at 413.
280 Calverley, 'Death drivers may get more jail'.
281 ibid.

Chapter Eight: Jess' law, 2004

1   N. Miraudo, 'Jess in our hearts forever', *West Australian*, 13 June 2009, p. 7.
2   A. Pownall & P. Perry, 'Serial drink driver to face court on four new charges', *West Australian*, 17 March 2010, p. 11.
3   J. A. McGinty, Attorney General, *Parliamentary Debates (Hansard)*, Western Australia, Legislative Assembly, 23 June 2004, pp. 4184–5 and G. Knowles, 'Call to jail banned serial drink-driver who killed', *West Australian*, 28 April 2009, p. 3.
4   R. Gibson, 'Drunk driver not guilty of killing girl', *West Australian*, 23 March 2006, p. 5.
5   J. A. McGinty, *Parliamentary Debates*, Western Australia, Legislative Assembly, 23 June 2004, p. 4184 and K. Hodson-Thomas, 17 August 2004, pp. 5005–6.
6   J. A. McGinty, Ministerial Media Statement, 'Deadly drunk drivers to be jailed under new laws', 13 June 2004, <https://www.mediastatements.wa.gov.au/Pages/Gallop/2004/06/Deadly-drunk-drivers-to-be-jailed-under-new-laws.aspx>, accessed: 27 April 2016 and J. A. McGinty, *Parliamentary Debates*, Western Australia, Legislative Assembly, 23 June 2004, pp. 4184–5.
7   'Death driver charged', *West Australian*, 8 October 2004, p. 4.
8   D. Le Grand, 'Bill to reverse onus of proof stalls', *West Australian*, 23 September 2004, p. 45.
9   K. Hodson-Thomas, *Parliamentary Debates*, Western Australia, Legislative Assembly, 17 August 2004, p. 5005.
10 ibid., J. A. McGinty, 23 June 2004, pp. 4184–5.
11 ibid. See also McGinty, Ministerial Media Statement, 'Deadly drunk drivers to be jailed under new laws'.
12 J. A. McGinty, Ministerial Media Statement, 'Jess' Law – deadly drunk drivers face 20 years' jail from January 1', 2 January 2005, <https://www.

NOTES TO CHAPTER EIGHT

mediastatements.wa.gov.au/Pages/Gallop/2005/01/Jess'-Law-deadly-drunk-drivers-face-20-years'-jail-from-January-1.aspx>, accessed: 27 April 2016.
13 'Death driver charged' and 'Charge to be contested', *West Australian*, 14 October 2004, p. 39.
14 'Drink-driver acquitted in landmark case', *ABC News*, 22 March 2006, <http://www.abc.net.au/news/2006-03-22/drink-driver-acquitted-in-landmark-case/825464>, accessed: 27 April 2016 and 'Not guilty plea in Jess case', *West Australian*, 4 March 2005, p. 4.
15 Gibson, 'Drunk driver not guilty of killing girl'.
16 'Drink-driver acquitted in landmark case'.
17 Knowles, 'Call to jail banned serial drink-driver who killed'.
18 N. Miraudo, 'Mum's mercy for fatal driver', *West Australian*, 2 May 2009, p. 15.
19 'Driver fined over 10-year-old girl's death', *ABC News*, 12 June 2009, <http://www.abc.net.au/news/2009-06-12/driver-fined-over-10-year-old-girls-death/1712398>, accessed: 27 April 2016.
20 ibid. See also N. Cox, 'Jess Meehan death-driver Miitchell [sic] Walsh-McDonald back in court', *Perth Now*, 16 March 2010, <http://www.perthnow.com.au/news/western-australia/jess-meehan-death-driver-miitchell-walsh-mcdonald-back-in-court/story-e6frg143-1225841388028>, accessed: 9 June 2012.
21 Miraudo, 'Jess is in our hearts forever'.
22 Pursuant to s 63(2)(b) & (c) of the *Road Traffic Act 1974* (WA).
23 Cox, 'Jess Meehan death-driver Miitchell [sic] Walsh-McDonald back in court'. See also Pownall & Perry, 'Serial drink driver to face court on four new charges'.
24 G. Stolley, 'Repeat driving offender walks free', *West Australian*, 13 May 2010, p. 4.
25 G. Wynne, 'Call to review extraordinary licences after serial drink driver caught again', *ABC News*, 30 July 2013, <https://www.abc.net.au/news/2013-07-30/call-to-review-extraordinary-licences-after-serial-drink-driver/4854484>, accessed: 25 April 2016.
26 P. Hickey, 'Serial drink driver gets extraordinary licence despite Government opposing decision', *Perth Now*, 3 August 2013, <http://www.perthnow.com.au/news/western-australia/serial-drink-driver-gets-extraordinary-licence-despite-government-opposing-decision/story-fnhocx03-1226690717624>, accessed: 13 September 2013.
27 P. Hickey, 'Serial drink-driver Mitchell Walsh McDonald admits 7th charge, fined $2800', *Perth Now*, 8 August 2013, <http://www.perthnow.com.au/news/western-australia/serial-drink-driver-mitchell-walsh-mcdonald-admits-7th-charge/story-fnhocx03-1226693607430>, accessed: 25 September 2013. The headline of the article contradicts the information contained therein. The total fines imposed were $2,850.
28 N. Cox, 'Perth traffic pest faces jail', *WA Today*, 16 April 2014, <http://www.watoday.com.au/wa-news/perth-traffic-pest-faces-jail-20140416-36rd3.html>, accessed: 23 April 2014.
29 N. Cox, 'Serial traffic pest Mitchell Walsh jailed for driving unlicensed', *WA Today*, 28 May 2014, <http://www.watoday.com.au/wa-news/serial-traffic-pest-mitchell-walsh-jailed-for-driving-unlicensed-20140528-zrr78.html>, accessed: 23 April 2016.

NOTES TO CHAPTER EIGHT

30 D. Emerson & G. Knowles, 'Killer driver Mitchell Walsh finally banned from WA roads', *West Australian*, 25 January 2018, <https://thewest.com.au/news/wa/killer-driver-mitchell-walsh-finally-banned-from-wa-roads-ng-b887240172>, accessed: 29 January 2018 and P. Hickey, 'Notorious WA drink-driver faces yet more charges', *WA Today*, 11 January 2018, <http://www.watoday.com.au/wa-news/notorious-wa-drinkdriver-faces-yet-more-charges-20180110-h0g7y6.html>, accessed: 20 January 2018.

31 S. Hampton, 'Mitchell Walsh jailed for 12 months for dishonesty offences', *West Australian*, 3 March 2018, <https://thewest.com.au/news/crime/mitchell-walsh-jailed-for-12-months-for-dishonesty-offences-ng-b887604382>, accessed: 3 July 2018.

32 T. Clarke, 'Killer driver Mitchell Walsh back in court', *West Australian*, 3 May 2019, <https://thewest.com.au/news/court-justice/killer-driver-mitchell-walsh-back-in-court-ng-b881187096z>, accessed: 31 July 2019.

33 K. Hodson-Thomas, *Parliamentary Debates*, Western Australia, Legislative Assembly, 17 August 2004, p. 5006.

34 ibid. M. J. Criddle, Legislative Council, 28 October 2004, citing the Western Australian Police Service submission, pp. 7463–4.

35 Appendix 2, 'Public Statement from the Western Australian Police Service', in Western Australian Parliament, Standing Committee on Legislation, *Report of the Standing Committee on Legislation in Relation to the Road Traffic Amendment (Dangerous Driving) Bill 2004*, Report no. 23, Standing Committee on Legislation, Perth, 2004, pp. 57–8.

36 Le Grand, 'Bill to reverse onus of proof stalls'. See also G. Watson, G. Cash and P. Foss, *Parliamentary Debates*, Western Australia, Legislative Council, 28 October 2004, pp. 7469–70, 7479–80.

37 D. J. Guise, *Parliamentary Debates*, Western Australia, Legislative Assembly, 17 August 2004, pp. 5008–9.

38 Road Safety Council, *2004 Annual Review of Arriving Safely – Road Safety Strategy for Western Australia, 2003–2007*, Government of Western Australia, December 2005.

39 D. J. Guise, *Parliamentary Debates*, Western Australia, Legislative Assembly, 17 August 2004, pp. 5008–9.

40 ibid., p. 5009.

41 ibid. P. Foss, Legislative Council, 28 October 2004, p. 7477.

42 D. Le Grand & R. Williams, 'Drink laws pass amid rowdy scenes', *West Australian*, 29 October 2004, p. 5.

43 McGinty, Ministerial Media Statement, 'Jess' Law – deadly drunk drivers face 20 years' jail from January 1'.

44 P. Foss and K. D. E. Travers, *Parliamentary Debates*, Western Australia, Legislative Council, 28 October 2004, pp. 7479, 7484 respectively.

45 P. Dowding, 'Draconian measures flawed and disordered', *West Australian*, 1 November 2004, p. 16.

46 L. Eliot, 'Lawyers hit out at "populist" laws', *West Australian*, 23 September 2004, p. 13.

47 ibid.

NOTES TO CHAPTER EIGHT

48 K. Hodson-Thomas, *Parliamentary Debates*, Western Australia, Legislative Assembly, 17 August 2004, p. 5006.
49 ibid. G. Cash, Legislative Council, 24 September 2004, pp. 6554–6.
50 Eliot, 'Lawyers hit out at "populist" laws'. See also Western Australian Parliament, Subcommittee of the Standing Committee on Legislation, 'Road Traffic Amendment (Dangerous Driving) Bill 2004: Transcript of evidence taken at Perth on Monday, 11 October 2004, Session One', G. Tannin SC, p. 3.
51 ibid. Western Australian Parliament, 'Road Traffic Amendment (Dangerous Driving) Bill 2004: Transcript of evidence taken at Perth on Monday, 11 October 2004, Session One', G. Tannin SC, p. 7.
52 *Parliamentary Debates*, Western Australia, Legislative Council, 21 September 2004, p. 6053.
53 Le Grand, 'Bill to reverse onus of proof stalls'; 'Drink-driving Bill's referral angers McGinty', *ABC News*, 22 September 2004, <http://www.abc.net.au/news/2004-09-22/drink-driving-bills-referral-angers-mcginty/556146>, accessed: 27 April 2016 and D. Le Grand, '"Shameful" McGinty wins quick review', *West Australian*, 25 September 2004, p. 49.
54 Le Grand, 'Bill to reverse onus of proof stalls'.
55 N. F. Moore, *Parliamentary Debates*, Western Australia, Legislative Council, 22 September 2004, p. 6268 and 24 September 2004, p. 6553.
56 ibid., J. A. Scott, 24 September 2004, pp. 6552, 6556.
57 ibid., G. Watson, 28 October 2004, pp. 7466–70 and D. Le Grand, 'Greens doubt puts cloud over drink-drive law', *West Australian*, 28 October 2004, p. 43.
58 P. Foss, *Parliamentary Debates*, Western Australia, Legislative Council, 24 September 2004, p. 6553.
59 ibid., G. Cash, pp. 6554–6.
60 ibid. K. Hodson-Thomas, Legislative Assembly, 17 August 2004, p. 5007; R. A. Ainsworth, Legislative Assembly, 17 August 2004, pp. 5009, 5011; T. K. Waldron, Legislative Assembly, 17 August 2004, p. 5013; S. E. Walker, Legislative Assembly, 17 August 2004, p. 5014; M. F. Board, Legislative Assembly, 17 August 2004, pp. 5015, 5019; M. J. Criddle, Legislative Council, 28 October 2004, pp. 7464, 7466.
61 ibid. T. H. Jones, Legislative Assembly, 12 November 1974, p. 2989.
62 ibid., T. K. Waldron, 17 August 2004, p. 5013.
63 Western Australian Parliament, Standing Committee on Legislation, *Report of the Standing Committee on Legislation in Relation to the Road Traffic Amendment (Dangerous Driving) Bill 2004*, p. iii.
64 Western Australian Parliament, Standing Committee on Legislation, *Sessional Report: An Overview of the Committee's Operations: Second Session of the Thirty-Sixth Parliament*, Report no. 26, Standing Committee on Legislation, Perth, 2004, p. 9.
65 *Smith v The Queen* [1976] WAR 97.
66 Law Reform Commission of Victoria, *Death Caused by Dangerous Driving*, Discussion Paper No. 21, pp. 8–9.
67 See s 52A(1) the *Crimes Act 1900* (NSW).

NOTES TO CHAPTER EIGHT

68 Western Australian Parliament, 'Road Traffic Amendment (Dangerous Driving) Bill 2004: Transcript of evidence taken at Perth on Monday, 11 October 2004, Session One', G. Tannin SC, p. 7.
69 M. M. Quirk, *Parliamentary Debates*, Western Australia, Legislative Assembly, 17 August 2004, p. 5013.
70 *Western Australia v Gibbs* (2009) 192 A Crim R 399 at 405–7.
71 Western Australian Parliament, Standing Committee on Legislation, *Report of the Standing Committee on Legislation in Relation to the Road Traffic Amendment (Dangerous Driving) Bill 2004*, p. 15.
72 *McBride v R* (1966) 115 CLR 44 at 50–1 and Western Australian Parliament, 'Road Traffic Amendment (Dangerous Driving) Bill 2004: Transcript of evidence taken at Perth on Monday, 11 October 2004, Session One', G. Tannin SC, p. 7.
73 Western Australian Parliament, Standing Committee on Legislation, *Report of the Standing Committee on Legislation in Relation to the Road Traffic Amendment (Dangerous Driving) Bill 2004*, p. 38.
74 J. A. McGinty, *Parliamentary Debates*, Western Australia, Legislative Assembly, 23 June, p. 4185. See also s 59B(1) and (2) of the *Road Traffic Act 1974* (WA).
75 *Western Australia v Gibbs* at 407.
76 G. Cash, *Parliamentary Debates*, Western Australia, Legislative Council, 28 October 2004, pp. 7473–4.
77 ibid., K. D. E. Travers, 28 October 2004, p. 7483.
78 Western Australian Parliament, Standing Committee on Legislation, *Report of the Standing Committee on Legislation in Relation to the Road Traffic Amendment (Dangerous Driving) Bill 2004*, p. 121.
79 S. E. Walker, *Parliamentary Debates*, Western Australia, Legislative Assembly, 17 August 2004, p. 5016.
80 Western Australian Parliament, 'Road Traffic Amendment (Dangerous Driving) Bill 2004: Transcript of evidence taken at Perth on Monday, 11 October 2004, Session One', G. Tannin SC, p. 9.
81 S. E. Walker, *Parliamentary Debates*, Western Australia, Legislative Assembly, 17 August 2004, p. 5014–15.
82 ibid., J. A. McGinty, 17 August 2004, p. 5016.
83 Via s 6(b) *Criminal Law Amendment Act 1992* (WA).
84 Via the *Criminal Law Amendment Act (No 2) 1982* (Qld) which amended s 328A and increased the penalty from five years to seven if the driver had a blood alcohol concentration of 0.15% or more.
85 Via s 3, Schedule 1 of the *Crimes (Dangerous Driving Offences) Amendment Act 1994*, which amended s 52A and s 52AA of the *Crimes Act 1900* (NSW).
86 Pursuant to s 19A(2)(a) and s 19A(2)(b) of the *Criminal Law Consolidation Act 1935* (SA).
87 Pursuant to s 59(3)(a)(i) of the *Road Traffic Act 1974* (WA).
88 ibid. See also s 59B(3).
89 M. H. Roberts, *Parliamentary Debates*, Western Australia, Legislative Assembly, 21 June 2018, pp. 3668–70.

NOTES TO CHAPTER EIGHT

90   See amendments to s 67 under s 10 of the *Road Traffic Amendment (Dangerous Driving) Act 2004* (WA).
91   Western Australian Parliament, Subcommittee of the Standing Committee on Legislation, 'Road Traffic Amendment (Dangerous Driving) Bill 2004: Transcript of evidence taken at Perth on Thursday, 14 October 2004', J. Prior, p. 2.
92   ibid., pp. 2–3.
93   Western Australian Parliament, Standing Committee on Legislation, *Report of the Standing Committee on Legislation in Relation to the Road Traffic Amendment (Dangerous Driving) Bill 2004*, p. 37.
94   Pursuant to s 59(B)(6) of the *Road Traffic Act 1974* (WA).
95   Western Australian Parliament, 'Road Traffic Amendment (Dangerous Driving) Bill 2004: Transcript of evidence taken at Perth on Monday, 11 October 2004, Session One', G. Tannin SC, p. 4.
96   Law Reform Commission of Western Australia, *Review of the Law of Homicide: Final Report*, Law Reform Commission of Western Australia, Perth, 2007, p. 122.
97   K. M. Chance, *Parliamentary Debates*, Western Australia, Legislative Council, 28 October 2004, p. 7501 and D. J. Guise, Legislative Assembly, 17 August 2004, pp. 5008–9.
98   ibid. K. M. Chance, Legislative Council, 28 October 2004, p. 7501.
99   Western Australian Parliament, 'Road Traffic Amendment (Dangerous Driving) Bill 2004: Transcript of evidence taken at Perth on Thursday, 14 October 2004', John Prior, pp. 2, 6.
100 ibid.
101 ibid. Transcript of evidence taken at Perth on Monday, 11 October 2004, Session One', G. Tannin SC, p. 10.
102 P. Embry, *Parliamentary Debates*, Western Australia, Legislative Council, 28 October 2004, p. 7507.
103 ibid. For example, see P. Foss, 28 October 2004, pp. 7480–1.
104 Western Australian Parliament, 'Road Traffic Amendment (Dangerous Driving) Bill 2004: Transcript of evidence taken at Perth on Thursday, 14 October 2004', J. Prior, p. 3.
105 ibid.
106 ibid.
107 ibid., p. 4.
108 ibid., pp. 4–5.
109 ibid., p. 5.
110 ibid., p. 9.
111 Western Australian Parliament, Standing Committee on Legislation, *Report of the Standing Committee on Legislation in Relation to the Road Traffic Amendment (Dangerous Driving) Bill 2004*. See Appendix 5, Memo dated 1 October 2004, pp. 89–95.
112 Western Australian Parliament, 'Road Traffic Amendment (Dangerous Driving) Bill 2004: Transcript of evidence taken at Perth on Thursday, 14 October 2004', J. Prior, pp. 9–10.

NOTES TO CHAPTER EIGHT

113 ibid., p. 4.
114 *Blair v Semple* (1989) 10 MVR 75.
115 ibid. at 77–9.
116 M. McGowan, *Parliamentary Debates*, Western Australia, Legislative Assembly, 17 August 2004, pp. 5011–12 and K. D. E. Travers, Legislative Council, 28 October 2004, pp. 7483–4. See also discussion between K. D. E. Travers and J. Prior in Western Australian Parliament, 'Road Traffic Amendment (Dangerous Driving) Bill 2004: Transcript of evidence taken at Perth on Thursday, 14 October 2004', J. Prior, p. 8. The evidence given by Prior to the Standing Committee indicated that the driver had a blood alcohol concentration of 0.171%, whereas McGowan stated in Parliament that the concentration was 0.161%.
117 M. McGowan, *Parliamentary Debates*, Western Australia, Legislative Assembly, 5 June 2003, p. 8282.
118 ibid., 17 August 2004, pp. 5011–12.
119 Western Australian Parliament, 'Road Traffic Amendment (Dangerous Driving) Bill 2004: Transcript of evidence taken at Perth on Monday, 11 October 2004, Session One', G. Tannin SC, p. 7.
120 ibid., p. 3.
121 G. Tannin cited by K. D. E. Travers, *Parliamentary Debates*, Western Australia, Legislative Council, 28 October 2004, p. 7483.
122 Western Australian Parliament, 'Road Traffic Amendment (Dangerous Driving) Bill 2004: Transcript of evidence taken at Perth on Monday, 11 October 2004, Session One', G. Tannin SC, p. 3.
123 ibid., p. 10.
124 ibid., p. 4.
125 K. D. E. Travers, *Parliamentary Debates*, Western Australia, Legislative Council, 28 October 2004, p. 7484.
126 ibid. T. K. Waldron, Legislative Assembly, 17 August 2004, p. 5014.
127 Western Australian Parliament, 'Road Traffic Amendment (Dangerous Driving) Bill 2004: Transcript of evidence taken at Perth on Monday, 11 October 2004, Session One', G. Tannin SC, p. 3; 'Transcript of evidence taken at Perth on Thursday, 14 October 2004', J. Prior. See also M. J. Criddle, *Parliamentary Debates*, Western Australia, Legislative Council, 28 October 2004, p. 7465.
128 Western Australian Parliament, 'Road Traffic Amendment (Dangerous Driving) Bill 2004: Transcript of evidence taken at Perth on Thursday, 14 October 2004', J. Prior, pp. 5–6 and Law Reform Commission of Western Australia, *Review of the Law of Homicide*, p. 124.
129 ibid.
130 Pursuant to s 12 of the *Road Traffic Amendment (Dangerous Driving) Act 2004* (WA).
131 Le Grand & Williams, 'Drink laws pass amid rowdy scenes'.
132 Personal communication – voicemail from Minister R. F. Johnson's office, received 9 February 2012, 4.24 pm following initial phone call from K. King, 8 February 2012; email from K. King to Minister for Transport, Housing and Emergency Services T. R. Buswell and Attorney General C. C. Porter, 7 June 2012; letter from Minister for Transport, Housing and Emergency Services

NOTES TO CHAPTER EIGHT

T. R. Buswell to K. King, received 14 June 2012 (no date, department reference 30–29270); letter from N. Lyhne, Managing Director, Department of Transport, to K. King, 23 July 2012.
133 Personal communication, letter from N. Lyhne, Department of Transport, 23 July 2012.

Chapter Nine: After Jess: Reflecting the value of human life?
1 Via s 38(3) of the *Criminal Law Amendment (Homicide) Act 2008* (WA) and A. Calverley, 'Death drivers may get more jail', *West Australian*, 5 October 2004, p. 15.
2 Via the *Manslaughter Legislation Amendment Act 2011* (WA). See also Attorney General C. C. Porter, Ministerial Media Statement, 'Crimes causing death given stronger penalties', 20 October 2011, <https://www.mediastatements.wa.gov.au/Pages/Barnett/2011/10/Crimes-causing-death-given-stronger-penalties.aspx>, accessed: 5 April 2017 and Royal Automobile Club of Western Australia (RAC), Media release, 'RAC welcomes new dangerous driving penalties', 20 October 2011.
3 M. Bennett, 'Death driver gets 3 years jail', 6 November 2009, *West Australian*, <https://au.news.yahoo.com/thewest/wa/a/6438888/death-driver-gets-3-years-jail/>, accessed: 8 June 2016.
4 ibid.
5 C. C. Porter, *Parliamentary Debates (Hansard)*, Western Australia, Legislative Assembly, 20 October 2011, p. 8497.
6 Porter, Ministerial Media Statement, 'Crimes causing death given stronger penalties'.
7 ibid.
8 ibid.
9 RAC, Media release, 'RAC welcomes new dangerous driving penalties'.
10 *Western Australia v Gibbs* (2009) 192 A Crim R 399 at 414.
11 ibid. at 420.
12 A. Hayward, 'Man pleads guilty to causing death', *Sydney Morning Herald*, 30 November 2007, <http://www.smh.com.au/national/man-pleads-guilty-to-causing-death-20071130-1e05.html>, accessed: 7 June 2016.
13 *Western Australia v Gibbs* at 420.
14 ibid. at 402.
15 Hayward, 'Man pleads guilty to causing death'.
16 *Western Australia v Gibbs* at 399.
17 ibid. at 400.
18 ibid. at 419–23.
19 ibid. at 419.
20 *Western Australia v Butler* [2009] WASCA 110.
21 *Western Australia v Mitchell* [2008] WASC 114.
22 *Western Australia v Butler*. See judgment text paras 2, 6, 48.
23 ibid., paras 2, 20.

NOTES TO CHAPTER NINE

24 T. Clarke, 'Grace's killer gets 44 months jail', *WA Today*, 13 November 2008, <http://www.watoday.com.au/wa-news/graces-killer-gets-44-months-jail-20081113-65yc.html> and T. Cardy, 'Baby Grace Moorby death driver jailed', *Perth Now*, 12 November 2008, <http://www.perthnow.com.au/news/baby-grace-death-driver-jailed/story-e6frg12c-1111118026864>, accessed: 20 June 2016.
25 *Western Australia v Butler*, paras 42, 48.
26 ibid., paras 6, 56.
27 T. Cardy, 'Baby Grace Moorby death driver jailed'.
28 *Penny v Western Australia* (2006) 33 WAR 48; *Farmer v Western Australia* [2007] WASCA 219; *Taylor v Western Australia* (2007) 177 A Crim R 81, (2007) 48 MVR 562; *Western Australia v Mitchell* [2008].
29 *Penny v Western Australia* at 55.
30 *Devine v Western Australia* (2010) 202 A Crim R 1, (2010) 55 MVR 486. See A Crim R at 6.
31 D. Reed, '12 years for killer drunk driver', *West Australian*, 30 June 1999, p. 3.
32 *McKenna v The Queen* (1992) 7 WAR 455; *Punch v The Queen* (1993) 9 WAR 486; *Clinch v The Queen* [1999] WASCA 57; Fox in D. Reed, '12 years for killer drunk driver'; *White v The Queen* (2003) 39 MVR 157.
33 *Brown v Western Australia* (2011) 207 A Crim R 533 and J. Menagh, 'Drugged driver sentenced to 11 years in jail for killing taxi driver and tourist', *ABC News*, 14 February 2014, <http://www.abc.net.au/news/2014-02-14/drugged-driver-jailed-for-killing-taxi-driver-and-tourist/5260682>, accessed: 12 May 2016.
34 E. Farcic, 'Nine years for intoxicated driver', *Kalgoorlie Miner*, 20 September 2018, <https://thewest.com.au/news/kalgoorlie-miner/nine-years-for-intoxicated-driver-ng-b889668887z>, accessed: 24 September 2018.
35 *Western Australia v Butler*, para 14.
36 J. Sapienza, 'Baby Grace's killer "genuinely remorseful"', *WA Today*, 25 June 2009, <http://www.watoday.com.au/wa-news/baby-graces-killer-genuinely-remorseful-20090625-cxnj.html>, accessed: 7 June 2016.
37 *Western Australia v Butler*, para 15.
38 ibid., paras 15–16.
39 ibid., paras 19–20.
40 ibid., para 27.
41 ibid., para 72.
42 ibid.
43 ibid., para 70.
44 ibid., para 59.
45 ibid., para 78.
46 ibid., para 79.
47 ibid., para 80.
48 Supreme Court of Western Australia, Media Statement, 'Supreme Court judge retires', 28 October 2009, <http://www.wabar.asn.au/images/Miller%20JA%20retirement%2028%20Oct%2009%20_4_.pdf>, accessed: 17 October 2016.
49 *Devine v Western Australia* at 3–4.
50 ibid. at 19–20.

51 ibid. at 7–8.
52 ibid. at 9.
53 ibid. at 3, 8–9.
54 T. Cardy, 'Judge blasts 200 km/h death driver Luke Devine', *Perth Now*, 18 August 2009, <http://www.perthnow.com.au/news/judge-blasts-200kmh-death-driver-luke-devine/story-e6frg12c-1225763267643>, accessed: 1 May 2016.
55 ibid.
56 ibid.
57 ibid.
58 *Devine v Western Australia* at 26.
59 ibid. at 1–2, 25.
60 *Barron v Western Australia* (2010) 55 MVR 123. See judgment text, paras 3–5.
61 ibid., para 6.
62 ibid., para 17.
63 ibid., para 16.
64 ibid., para 49.
65 A-J. Sanderson, *Parliamentary Debates*, Western Australia, Legislative Council, 3 December 2013, pp. 6978–9 and <http://pledgefornate.thewest.com.au/>, accessed: 4 July 2016.
66 B. Martin, 'Nate Dunbar died because of one decision', *West Australian, West Weekend Magazine*, <http://pledgefornate.thewest.com.au/decision.html>, accessed: 4 July 2016.
67 ibid.
68 'Melissa Waters jailed after crash which killed baby Nate Dunbar at Merriwa', *ABC News*, 24 September 2013, <http://www.abc.net.au/news/2013-09-24/drink-driver-jailed-after-crash-kills-baby/4978000>, accessed: 4 July 2016.
69 K. Campbell, 'Family's anger at Nate Dunbar drunk-drive killer's release on parole', 2 July 2015, *Perth Now*, <http://www.perthnow.com.au/news/western-australia/familys-anger-at-nate-dunbar-drunkdrive-killers-release-on-parole/news-story/b3098a5c44d0316148303bcc03d733a9>, accessed: 4 July 2016.
70 K. Emery, 'Parole for killer driver lashed', *West Australian*, 3 July 2015, <https://au.news.yahoo.com/thewest/wa/a/28651117/parole-for-nate-dunbar-driver-lashed/>, accessed: 4 July 2016.
71 K. Emery, 'Anger over parole for Nate Dunbar's killer', *West Australian*, 2 July 2015, <https://au.news.yahoo.com/thewest/wa/a/28641619/anger-over-early-release-for-driver-who-killed-nate-dunbar/>, accessed: 4 July 2016.
72 J. Menagh, 'Angry scenes as repeat drink-driver sentenced over Perth double fatal crash', *ABC News*, 31 October 2014, <http://www.abc.net.au/news/2014-10-31/repeat-drink-driver-sentenced-over-perth-double-fatal/5858638>, accessed: 4 July 2016 and A. Massey & G. Millmaci, 'Kill accused "drove drunk"', *West Australian*, 16 May 2014, <https://au.news.yahoo.com/thewest/wa/a/23552603/kill-accused-drove-drunk/>, accessed: 4 July 2016.
73 Massey & Millmaci, 'Kill accused "drove drunk"'.
74 Menagh, 'Angry scenes as repeat drink-driver sentenced over Perth double fatal crash'.

NOTES TO CHAPTER NINE

75 'Drink-driver Andrew Richmond reveals shame of causing deaths of two young men', *Perth Now*, 31 October 2014, <http://www.perthnow.com.au/news/western-australia/drinkdriver-andrew-richmond-reveals-shame-of-causing-deaths-of-two-young-men/news-story/ff60b641a729ce11f01e14eb3f108011>, accessed: 4 July 2016.
76 Menagh, 'Angry scenes as repeat drink-driver sentenced over Perth double fatal crash'.
77 'Drink-driver Andrew Richmond reveals shame of causing deaths of two young men'.
78 ibid.
79 Menagh, 'Angry scenes as repeat drink-driver sentenced over Perth double fatal crash'.
80 *Eves v Western Australia* (2008) 49 MVR 259. See judgment text, paras 18, 20, 45, 70–7.
81 ibid., paras 18, 54, 60, 83–4, 96.
82 ibid., para 54.
83 'Fatigued driver faces jail over triple fatality', *ABC News*, 3 May 2007, <http://www.abc.net.au/news/2007-05-03/fatigued-driver-faces-jail-over-triple-fatality/2538664>, accessed: 4 July 2016.
84 *Eves v Western Australia*, para 46.
85 ibid., para 48.
86 ibid., para 49.
87 ibid., para 50.
88 ibid., paras 97–8.
89 ibid., paras 48–9.
90 ibid., paras 32, 84, 123.
91 G. Stolley, 'Jail for fatal crash driver', *West Australian*, 5 March 2010, <https://au.news.yahoo.com/thewest/wa/a/6893583/jail-for-fatal-crash-driver/>, accessed: 19 October 2016.
92 ibid.
93 ibid.
94 A. Saunders, 'Three years jail 'inadequate' for death driver', *West Australian*, 4 December 2009, <https://au.news.yahoo.com/thewest/wa/a/6549973/three-years-jail-inadequate-for-death-driver/> and 'Victim's family furious at drag-race death driver penalty', *Perth Now*, 5 March 2010, <http://www.perthnow.com.au/news/victims-family-furious-at-drag-race-death-driver-penalty/story-e6frg12c-1225837509918>, accessed: 20 October 2016.
95 Stolley, 'Jail for fatal crash driver'.
96 'Victim's family furious at drag-race death driver penalty'.
97 K. Robertson, 'L-plater Cory Nepia-Keelan faces jail over Luke Beyer death', *Perth Now*, 17 February 2012, <http://www.dailytelegraph.com.au/learner-driver-admits-luke-beyer-deadly-driving-charge/story-fn6b3v4f-1226273983245> and K. Robertson, 'L-plater Cory Nepia-Keelan jailed for four years over Luke Beyer death', *Perth Now*, 17 February 2012, <http://www.perthnow.com.au/news/western-australia/learner-driver-admits-luke-beyer-deadly-driving-charge/story-e6frg13u-1226273699007>, accessed: 5 July 2016.

98   K. Campbell, 'Anger over death crash sentence', *West Australian*, 17 February 2012, <https://au.news.yahoo.com/thewest/wa/a/12939438/anger-over-death-crash-sentence/>, accessed: 5 July 2016.
99   'Drink-driver given four year sentence for teen's death', *WA Today*, 17 February 2012, <http://www.watoday.com.au/wa-news/drinkdriver-given-four-year-sentence-for-teens-death-20120217-1tdo1.html>, accessed: 5 July 2016.
100 Robertson, 'L-plater Cory Nepia-Keelan jailed for four years over Luke Beyer death' and 'Drink-driver given four year sentence for teen's death'.
101 Robertson, 'L-plater Cory Nepia-Keelan jailed for four years over Luke Beyer death'.
102 A. Banks & T. Clarke, 'Bid to get killer driver off the road', *West Australian*, 20 June 2015, <https://au.news.yahoo.com/thewest/wa/a/28504352/bid-to-get-killer-driver-off-road/> and T. Clarke, 'Drink-driver in fatal back on road', *West Australian*, 25 May 2015, <https://au.news.yahoo.com/thewest/wa/a/28212757/drink-driver-in-fatal-back-on-road/>, accessed: 5 July 2016.
103 Clarke, 'Drink-driver in fatal back on road'.
104 ibid.
105 ibid.
106 ibid.

Chapter Ten: A new offence – careless driving causing death – and another law for another girl – Charlotte's law

1   Road Traffic Legislation Amendment Bill (No. 2) 2015.
2   J. Butler, 'QLD Doubles Penalties For Driving Death Offences', *Ten Daily*, 14 June 2018, <https://tendaily.com.au/news/crime/a180614utf/qld-doubles-penalties-for-driving-death-offences-20180614>, accessed: 10 September 2018.
3   L. Martin, 'Distracted drivers who cause a fatal accident could go to jail under proposed new WA law', *ABC News*, 20 April 2015, <http://www.abc.net.au/news/2015-04-20/concerns-raised-over-tough-new-driving-laws/6407262>, accessed: 5 July 2015.
4   ibid.
5   L. M. Harvey, Ministerial Media Statement, 'Major traffic law changes to make roads safer', 11 November 2015, <https://www.mediastatements.wa.gov.au/Pages/Barnett/2015/11/Major-traffic-law-changes-to-make-roads-safer.aspx>, accessed: 21 November 2015.
6   R. J. Johnson, *Parliamentary Debates (Hansard)*, Western Australia, Legislative Assembly, 23 August 2016, p. 5066.
7   ibid.
8   ibid.
9   ibid., J. R. Quigley, pp. 5066–7.
10 ibid., p. 5067.
11 ibid., W. J. Johnston, p. 5069.
12 ibid., L. M. Harvey.
13 ibid.

NOTES TO CHAPTER TEN

14 ibid., p. 5070.
15 N. P. Goiran, *Parliamentary Debates*, Western Australia, Legislative Council, 13 September 2016, p. 5796.
16 ibid., p. 5797.
17 ibid. See also Sentencing Advisory Council, *Sentencing of Driving Offences that Result in Death or Injury: Consultation Paper*, Sentencing Advisory Council Tasmania, Hobart, 2016, p. 52.
18 N. P. Goiran, *Parliamentary Debates*, Western Australia, Legislative Council, 13 September 2016, p. 5797.
19 ibid.
20 For instance, see C. Bembridge, 'Proposed careless driving laws for WA motorists could water down penalties, academic warns', *ABC News*, 13 September 2016, <http://www.abc.net.au/news/2016-09-13/proposed-wa-careless-driving-laws-could-backfire-academic-says/7837412>, accessed: 6 October 2016 and radio interview, K. King, *ABC Drive with Barry Nicholls, ABC News*, 13 September 2016, 3.06 pm.
21 Bembridge, 'Proposed careless driving laws for WA motorists could water down penalties, academic warns'.
22 CIB report, Western Australian Police Department – 77/7251, 'Hewison, Malcolm Robert William – Death of on 1/12/1977, passenger in vehicle driven by Brett Clinton Bond who collided with SEC pole in Brockway Avenue, Graylands', State Records Office of Western Australia (SROWA), WAS 76, CONS 3454. See 'Reasons for decision, Special Magistrate – J.R. Standing (Police) – v – B.C. Bond'.
23 L. M. Harvey, *Parliamentary Debates*, Western Australia, Legislative Assembly, 11 November 2015, p. 8047.
24 ibid., 23 August 2016, p. 5065.
25 M. M. Mischin, *Parliamentary Debates*, Western Australia, Legislative Council, 6 September 2016, p. 5370.
26 ibid.
27 ibid.
28 ibid.
29 G. Loney, 'Car deaths inquest raise hope', *West Australian*, 26 January 2011, <https://au.news.yahoo.com/thewest/wa/a/8713743/car-deaths-inquest-raises-hope/>, accessed: 5 July 2015.
30 ibid.
31 ibid.
32 Western Australian State Coroner, A. N. Hope, *Record of Investigation into Death: Inquest into the death of Jeremy Graham Armstrong*, Ref. no. 29/10, 13 January 2011, Coroner's Court of Western Australia, Perth, 2011.
33 ibid., p. 2.
34 ibid., p. 5.
35 ibid., p. 23.
36 ibid., pp. 12–13.
37 ibid., p. 14.

38 ibid., p. 6.
39 ibid., pp. 23–4.
40 ibid., pp. 24–8.
41 ibid., p. 18–19.
42 ibid., p. 20–1.
43 ibid., p. 22.
44 ibid., pp. 24, 27.
45 ibid., p. 24.
46 ibid., pp. 25–6.
47 ibid., pp. 24–5.
48 P. Hickey, 'WA drivers set to be hit with a new careless driving offence', *Perth Now*, 19 April 2015, <http://www.perthnow.com.au/news/western-australia/wa-drivers-set-to-be-hit-with-a-new-careless-driving-offence/news-story/9688d402c373662d5714f5bb7942fe8c>, accessed: 5 July 2015.
49 Martin, 'Distracted drivers who cause a fatal accident could go to jail under proposed new WA law'.
50 ibid.
51 ibid.
52 *Wood v The Queen* (2002) 130 A Crim R 518 at 529; *Kay v The Queen* (2004) 147 A Crim R 401, (2004) 42 MVR 130, see A Crim R at 403; *McBride v R* (1966) 115 CLR 44; *Smith v The Queen* [1976] WAR 97; *King v The Queen* (2012) 245 CLR 588.
53 C. Newman, 'Death by Careless Driving; Sentencing Guidelines and the Custody Threshold', *Journal of Criminal Law*, vol. 74, no. 2, 2010, pp. 100–3.
54 ibid. See also M. Hirst, 'Causing death by driving and other offences: a question of balance', *Criminal Law Review*, no. 5, 2008, p. 343.
55 Brake, 'Ministry of Justice consultation on driving charges and penalties: Response from Brake, the road safety charity', 13 January 2015, p. 3, <http://www.brake.org.uk/assets/docs/pdf/MoJ-drivingchargespenalties-jan15.pdf>, accessed: 7 July 2016.
56 ibid., p. 2.
57 Brake, 'Roads to justice: real-life cases', <http://www.brake.org.uk/top-level/18-campaigns/1594-roads-to-justice-real-life-cases>, accessed: 7 October 2016; 'Drunk driver jailed for killing Long Preston motorcyclist', *BBC News*, 13 May 2016, <http://www.bbc.com/news/uk-england-36287701>; L. Allaway, 'Tougher sentences for drivers who kill other road users whilst drunk/drugged', Change.org online petition, <https://www.change.org/p/tougher-sentences-for-drivers-who-kill-other-road-users-whilst-driving-drunk>, accessed: 21 October 2016.
58 S. Kyd Cunningham, 'Has law reform policy been driven in the right direction? How the new causing death by driving offences are operating in practice', *Criminal Law Review*, no. 9, 2013, pp. 711–28.
59 ibid., pp. 712–14.
60 ibid., p. 714.
61 ibid.

62 ibid., pp. 715, 717.
63 House of Commons Transport Committee (UK), *Road Traffic Law Enforcement: Second Report of Session 2015–2016*, The Stationary Office Limited, London, 2016.
64 ibid., pp. 7–8.
65 ibid., p. 8.
66 ibid.
67 ibid.
68 G. Knowles, 'Careless driver law not tough enough: Police and Road Safety Minister Michelle Roberts', *West Australian*, 21 August 2018, <https://thewest.com.au/news/crime/careless-driver-law-not-tough-enough-police-and-road-safety-minister-michelle-roberts-ng-b88930029z/>, accessed: 22 August 2018.
69 I sincerely thank G. Knowles, former Chief Crime Reporter at the *West Australian*, for supplying me with details of recent sentences. Personal communication, email from G. Knowles to K. King, 17 August 2018, 2.58 pm; email from K. King to G. Knowles, 17 August 2018, 3.59 pm; email from G. Knowles to K. King, 18 August 2018, 4.11 pm; email from K. King to G. Knowles, 29 August 2018, 3.57 pm; email from G. Knowles to K. King, 31 August 2018, 4.37 pm; email from G. Knowles to K. King, 16 October 2018, 4.33 pm.
70 Personal communication, email from G. Knowles to K. King, 16 October 2018, 4.33 pm.
71 ibid.
72 ibid.
73 ibid.
74 Knowles, 'Careless driver law not tough enough: Police and Road Safety Minister Michelle Roberts'.
75 ibid.
76 ibid.
77 R. Walsh, 'Fatal crash charge under stiffer laws', *West Australian*, 16 December 2016, p. 29.
78 Personal communication, email from G. Knowles to K. King, 17 August 2018, 2.58 pm; email from K. King to G. Knowles, 17 August 2018, 3.59 pm; email from G. Knowles to K. King, 18 August 2018, 4.11 pm; email from K. King to G. Knowles, 29 August 2018, 3.57 pm; email from G. Knowles to K. King, 31 August 2018, 4.37 pm; email from G. Knowles to K. King, 16 October 2018, 4.33 pm.
79 S. Hampton, 'Death driver didn't see victim's car', *Perth Now*, 13 March 2018, <https://www.perthnow.com.au/news/wa/death-driver-didnt-see-victims-car-ng-b88773465z>, accessed: 14 March 2018.
80 ibid.
81 ibid.
82 ibid.
83 L. Roberts, 'Woman (79) fined after killing motorcyclist in Hamilton Hill Crash', *Fremantle Gazette*, 26 June 2018, <https://www.communitynews.com.au/fremantle-gazette/news/woman-79-fined-after-killing-motorcyclist-in-hamilton-hill-crash/>, accessed: 27 September 2018.

84 'Motorcyclist seriously injured in Hamilton Hill Crash', *Fremantle Gazette*, 23 April 2018, <https://www.communitynews.com.au/fremantle-gazette/news/motorcyclist-seriously-injured-hamilton-hill-crash/>, accessed: 27 September 2018.
85 ibid.
86 R. Walsh & J. Cutts, 'I'm sorry, as death driver is free to go', *West Australian*, 19 July 2018, <https://www.pressreader.com/australia/the-west-australian/20180719/281621011116047/>, accessed: 9 October 2018 and G. Knowles, 'Appeal over $2500 fine for driver in death case', *West Australian*, 15 August 2018, <https://thewest.com.au/news/crime/appeal-over-2500-fine-for-driver-in-death-case-ng-b889276552z>, accessed: 17 August 2018.
87 R. Walsh, 'Parents demand justice for daughter killed in crash', *West Australian*, 20 July 2018, <https://thewest.com.au/news/crime/parents-demand-justice-for-daughter-killed-in-crash-ng-b88901227z>, accessed: 9 October 2018 and E. Farcic, 'Family of Joanna Taylor devastated by killer crash driver Che Curyer's sentence', *West Australian*, 25 January 2019, <https://thewest.com.au/news/wa/family-of-joanna-taylor-devastated-by-killer-crash-driver-che-curyers-sentence-ng-b881084758z>, accessed: 29 January 2019.
88 Knowles, 'Appeal over $2500 fine for driver in death case'.
89 ibid. See also B. Lackey, '"You killed my daughter": Mother of woman, 21, killed by an L-plater screams in court as he is spared jail and handed just a $2500 fine – and the driver says HE deserves sympathy', *Daily Mail Australia*, 19 July 2018, <https://www.dailymail.co.uk/news/article-5967167/Outrage-L-plater-escapes-just-FINE-despite-killing-girl-crash.html>, accessed: 8 November 2018.
90 '"Inadequate and offensive": Family outraged by crash killer's punishment', *Seven News*, 19 July 2018, <https://au.news.yahoo.com/inadequate-offensive-family-outraged-crash-102855612.html>, accessed: 6 November 2018.
91 Knowles, 'Appeal over $2500 fine for driver in death case'.
92 R. Walsh & J. Cutts, 'Family outrage as killer driver escapes with fine', *Perth Now*, 18 July 2018, <https://www.perthnow.com.au/news/crime/family-outrage-as-killer-driver-escapes-with-fine-ng-b88900732z>, accessed: 9 October 2018.
93 Knowles, 'Appeal over $2500 fine for driver in death case'.
94 ibid.
95 Farcic, 'Family of Joanna Taylor devastated by killer crash driver Che Curyer's sentence'.
96 ibid.
97 ibid.
98 ibid.
99 Knowles, 'Careless driver law not tough enough: Police and Road Safety Minister Michelle Roberts'.
100 B. Martin, 'Nate Dunbar died because of one decision', *West Australian, West Weekend Magazine*, <http://pledgefornate.thewest.com.au/decision.html>, accessed: 4 July 2016 and K. Campbell, 'Family's anger at Nate Dunbar drunk-drive killer's release on parole', 2 July 2015, *Perth Now*, <http://www.perthnow.

NOTES TO CHAPTER TEN

com.au/news/western-australia/familys-anger-at-nate-dunbar-drunkdrive-killers-release-on-parole/news-story/b3098a5c44d0316148303bcc03d733a9>, accessed: 4 July 2016.

101 S. Hampton, 'Texting driver jailed for at least 22 months over Mitchell Freeway Crash that killed workmate', 18 October 2018, *West Australian*, <https://thewest.com.au/news/crime/texting-driver-jailed-for-at-least-22-months-over-mitchell-freeway-crash-that-killed-workmate-ng-b88995082z>, accessed: 23 October 2018.

102 K. Robertson, 'L-plater Cory Nepia-Keelan faces jail over Luke Beyer death', *Perth Now*, 17 February 2012, <http://www.dailytelegraph.com.au/learner-driver-admits-luke-beyer-deadly-driving-charge/story-fn6b3v4f-1226273983245>, accessed: 5 July 2016; K. Robertson, 'L-plater Cory Nepia-Keelan jailed for four years over Luke Beyer death', *Perth Now*, 17 February 2012, <http://www.perthnow.com.au/news/western-australia/learner-driver-admits-luke-beyer-deadly-driving-charge/story-e6frg13u-1226273699007>, accessed: 5 July 2016; K. Campbell, 'Anger over death crash sentence', *West Australian*, 17 February 2012, <https://au.news.yahoo.com/thewest/wa/a/12939438/anger-over-death-crash-sentence/>, accessed: 5 July 2016.

103 For example, see Crown Prosecutor Davies in *R v S.K., J.S. & A.L.S.* (1978), sentencing transcript, p. 40; Justice Sheppard in *Crawley v The Queen* (1981) 55 FLR 463, (1981) 36 ALR 241, see ALR at 253; Justice Derrington in *R v Calder; ex parte Attorney General* [1987] 1 Qd R 348, (1986) 22 A Crim R 62, see A Crim R at 71; Chief Justice Malcolm in *R v Stebbings* (1990) 4 WAR 538 at 540; Chief Justice Malcolm in *Ainsworth v D (A Child)* (1992) 7 WAR 102 at 116; Chief Justice Malcolm and Justice Seaman in *The Queen v S (No 2) (A CHILD)* (1992) 7 WAR 434 at 446–7, 449–50; Justice Seaman in *McKenna v The Queen* (1992) 7 WAR 455 at 466; Justices Murray and Anderson in *Punch v The Queen* (1993) 9 WAR 486 at 497, 501; Justice Miller in *Western Australia v Gibbs* (2009) 192 A Crim R 399 at 419; Justice Miller in *Western Australia v Butler* [2009] WASCA 110, paras 78–80.

104 *King v The Queen* (2012) 245 CLR 588 at 609.

105 *Wood v The Queen* (2002) 130 A Crim R 518.

106 S. Hampton, 'Rebel bikie jailed for crash that killed Charlotte Pemberton', *Perth Now*, 22 March 2017, <https://www.perthnow.com.au/news/wa/rebel-bikie-jailed-for-crash-that-killed-charlotte-pemberton-ng-59752a4e7529774bfa0813a1986fe0ac/>, accessed: 24 October 2018.

107 G. Taylor & R. Walsh, 'Killer drivers must pay a higher price', *West Australian*, 25–26 March 2017, pp. 6–7.

108 J. M. C. Stojkovski, *Parliamentary Debates*, Western Australia, Legislative Assembly, 21 August 2018, p. 4930.

109 ibid.

110 Hampton, 'Rebel bikie jailed for crash that killed Charlotte Pemberton' and S. Hampton, 'Bikie cared for Rebels' vest, not crash victims', *West Australian*, 22 March 2017, <https://thewest.com.au/news/perth/bikie-cared-for-rebels-vest-not-crash-victims-ng-b88421682z>, accessed: 24 October 2018.

NOTES TO CHAPTER TEN

111 S. Dawson, *Parliamentary Debates*, Western Australia, Legislative Council, 21 August 2018, p. 4860.
112 ibid.
113 Hampton, 'Rebel bikie jailed for crash that killed Charlotte Pemberton' and Hampton, 'Bikie cared for Rebels' vest, not crash victims'.
114 S. Dawson, *Parliamentary Debates*, Western Australia, Legislative Council, 21 August 2018, p. 4860 and 'Charlotte's Law needed to help protect drivers on WA roads', *West Australian*, 27 March 2017, <https://www.pressreader.com/australia/the-west-australian/20170327/281758449119875>, accessed: 26 October 2018.
115 M. H. Roberts, *Parliamentary Debates*, Western Australia, Legislative Assembly, 21 August 2018, p. 4933.
116 ibid. S. Dawson, Legislative Council, 21 August 2018, p. 4860.
117 ibid. M. H. Roberts citing Judge P. McCann, Legislative Assembly, 21 August 2018, p. 4933.
118 Hampton, 'Rebel bikie jailed for crash that killed Charlotte Pemberton'.
119 M. H. Roberts, *Parliamentary Debates*, Western Australia, Legislative Assembly, 21 August 2018, p. 4933.
120 Hampton, 'Rebel bikie jailed for crash that killed Charlotte Pemberton'.
121 M. H. Roberts, *Parliamentary Debates*, Western Australia, Legislative Assembly, 21 August 2018, p. 4933.
122 Hampton, 'Rebel bikie jailed for crash that killed Charlotte Pemberton'.
123 S. Dawson, *Parliamentary Debates*, Western Australia, Legislative Council, 21 August 2018, p. 4860.
124 Via s 4(3) of the *Road Traffic Amendment (Driving Offences) Act 2018* (WA).
125 M. H. Roberts, *Parliamentary Debates*, Western Australia, Legislative Assembly, 21 June 2018, p. 3669 and 21 August 2018, pp. 4934–5.
126 ibid. For example, see M. H. Roberts, 21 June 2018, p. 3670; C. M. Rowe, 21 August 2018, pp. 4928; J. M. C. Stojkovski, 21 August 2018, p. 4929; T. J. Healy, 21 August 2018, p. 4932; M. H. Roberts, 21 August 2018, pp. 4933–5, 4939; P. A. Katsambanis, pp. 4937, 4939.
127 ibid., J. M. C. Stojkovski, 21 August 2018, p. 4930.
128 ibid., C. M. Rowe, p. 4928.
129 G. Taylor, 'Grieving dad backs tougher car crash sentences', *West Australian*, 28 March 2017, <https://thewest.com.au/news/wa/grieving-dad-backs-tougher-sentences-ng-b88427314z>, accessed: 9 November 2018.
130 *Western Australia v Tittums* [2018] WASCA 23. See judgment text, para 11(j).
131 ibid., para 11(c).
132 ibid., para 11(d).
133 ibid., paras 11(e–f).
134 ibid., paras 3(a–e).
135 ibid., para 82.
136 ibid., para 15(a).
137 ibid., paras 110–16.
138 C. M. Rowe, *Parliamentary Debates*, Western Australia, Legislative Assembly, 21 August 2018, p. 4929.

NOTES TO THE CONCLUSION

139 N. Boddy, 'Fatal crash driver "high on drugs"', *West Australian*, 21 January 2014, <https://au.news.yahoo.com/thewest/wa/a/20914625/fatal-crash-driver-high-on-drugs-unlicensed/>, accessed: 19 October 2016.
140 ibid. See also J. Menagh, 'Drugged driver sentenced to 11 years in jail for killing taxi driver and tourist', *ABC News*, 14 February 2014, <http://www.abc.net.au/news/2014-02-14/drugged-driver-jailed-for-killing-taxi-driver-and-tourist/5260682>, accessed: 19 October 2016.
141 M. Mischin, *Parliamentary Debates*, Western Australia, Legislative Council, 30 August 2018, p. 5435.
142 ibid.
143 ibid.
144 ibid.
145 ibid.

Conclusion: A lesser species of homicide

1 Sentencing Advisory Council, *Sentencing of Driving Offences that Result in Death or Injury: Consultation Paper*, Sentencing Advisory Council Tasmania, Hobart, 2016, p. 7.
2 ibid.
3 *Callaghan v R* (1952) 87 CLR 115.
4 Letter from Superintendent Lee, Supervisor Accident Section, to Superintendent Cole, 10 August 1976, Western Australian Police Department – 76/7154, 'Nash Amanda May – Death of on July 24, 1976 – rider of pushbike that was struck from behind by vehicle driven by Michael John Roche in Bay View Terrace, Mosman Park', State Records Office of Western Australia (SROWA), WAS 76, CONS 3454.
5 *Callaghan v R* (1952).
6 *R v M.Z.* (1966), trial transcript, p. 61.
7 *Laporte v R* [1970] WAR 87.
8 *R v Stebbings* (1990) 4 WAR 538.
9 G. Taylor & R. Walsh, 'Killer drivers must pay a higher price', *West Australian*, 25–26 March 2017, pp. 6–7.
10 B. Martin, 'Nate Dunbar died because of one decision', *West Australian, West Weekend Magazine*, <http://pledgefornate.thewest.com.au/decision.html>, accessed: 4 July 2016.
11 Judge Stavrianou cited in K. Robertson, 'L-plater Cory Nepia-Keelan jailed for four years over Luke Beyer death', *Perth Now*, 17 February 2012, <http://www.perthnow.com.au/news/western-australia/learner-driver-admits-luke-beyer-deadly-driving-charge/story-e6frg13u-1226273699007>, accessed: 5 July 2016.
12 M. Mischin, *Parliamentary Debates (Hansard)*, Western Australia, Legislative Council, 30 August 2018, p. 5435.
13 Gary Numan, 'Cars', *The Pleasure Principle*, Beggars Banquet Records, 1979.

SELECT BIBLIOGRAPHY

ARCHIVAL

J. S. Battye Library of West Australian History

Channel Nine News, O'Connor, R., MLA, 27 March 1975, Video recording, State Film Archives Collection, E0383.

National Safety Council of Western Australia, *A case for the introduction of blood-alcohol tests in Western Australia*, National Safety Council of Western Australia, Perth, 1957.

National Safety Council of Western Australia, Collection of material relating to various divisions of the National Safety Council of Western Australia, Printed ephemera, PR8972.

National Safety Council of Western Australia, Collection of photographs, BA 840/83, vol. 357.

Royal Automobile Club of Western Australia (RAC), Collection of material relating to the Royal Automobile Club, PR9402.

State Records Office of Western Australia

Albany Clerk of Courts

1, 'Charge Sheets', SROWA, WAS 1875, CONS 5394.
2, 'Charge Sheets', SROWA, WAS 1875, CONS 5394.
3, 'Charge Sheets', SROWA, WAS 1875, CONS 5394.
1, 'Evidence Books – Children's Court', SROWA, WAS 1874, CONS 5393.
2, 'Evidence Books – Children's Court', SROWA, WAS 1874, CONS 5393.

SELECT BIBLIOGRAPHY

Crown Law Department
1944/3007, 'Criminal Code Amendment Act 1944: Private Members Bill introduced by Mr R McDonald to provide for lesser charge than manslaughter', SROWA, WAS 2664, CONS 1042.
1934/3780, 'Crown Prosecutors: Criminal Code re amendment of, to make it an offence when driving a vehicle to cause the death of, or bodily harm to another, by failing to use reasonable care', SROWA, WAS 2664, CONS 1042.
1957/06806, 'Traffic Act Amendment Act (No. 4) 1957: Preparation of Bill', SROWA, WAS 2664, CONS 6815.
1944/3353, 'Traffic Act Amendment Act of 1945 – Preparation of Bill', SROWA, WAS 2664, CONS 1042.
1937/00957, 'WA National Council of Women (Inc), Criminal Code: Suggesting an amendment of to give power to Judge to cancel or suspend drivers licenses of persons convicted of manslaughter', SROWA, WAS 2664, CONS 6815.

Perth Children's Court
45, 'Charge Books', SROWA, WAS 343, CONS 2493.
46, 'Charge Books', SROWA, WAS 343, CONS 2493.
47, 'Charge Books', SROWA, WAS 343, CONS 2493.
48, 'Charge Books', SROWA, WAS 343, CONS 2493.
49, 'Charge Books', SROWA, WAS 343, CONS 2493.
50, 'Charge Books', SROWA, WAS 343, CONS 2493.
51, 'Charge Books', SROWA, WAS 343, CONS 2493.
52, 'Charge Books', SROWA, WAS 343, CONS 2493.

Public Health Department of Western Australia
1958/1102, 'Regulations re blood sampling of persons under the influence of liquor', SROWA, WAS 268, CONS 2489.

Public Sector Management Office
943528, 'Committees: Police Department Road Traffic Authority Merger Steering Committee', SROWA, WAS 36, CONS 5864.

Supreme Court of Western Australia
05, 'Criminal Indictment Register 5', SROWA, WAS 49, CONS 3422.
1, 'Criminal Record Book 6', SROWA, WAS 49, CONS 4332.
2, 'Criminal Record Book 9', SROWA, WAS 49, CONS 4332.
3, 'Criminal Record Book 10', SROWA, WAS 49, CONS 4332.
4, 'Criminal Record Book 11', SROWA, WAS 49, CONS 4332.
5, 'Criminal Record Book 12', SROWA, WAS 49, CONS 4332.
6, 'Criminal Record Book 13', SROWA, WAS 49, CONS 4332.

SELECT BIBLIOGRAPHY

Files – Criminal indictment, 1946–1980, SROWA, WAS 122, CONS – 4216, 6141, 6143, 6146, 6147, 6148 and 6149. [Restricted access files.] In accordance with the access restrictions imposed by the Supreme Court of Western Australia, individual item numbers and full prosecution details cannot be listed. Sampled case files are listed using the initials of each defendant and year of prosecution.

R v A.J.C. (1946)
R v A.J.G. (1946)
R v A.K. (1947)
R v L.W.S. (1947)
R v D.I.H. (1947)
R v J.W.K. (1948)
R v A.C.E.D (1949)
R v J.W.T. (1950)
R v H.C.M. (1950)
R v D.C. (1950)
R v H.A.H. (1950)
R v N.T.J. (1950)
R v J.W.B. (1950)
R v G.S.J. (1951)
R v O.S. (1951)
R v E.B.H. (1951)
R v J.W.G. (1951)
R v L.S.D.G. (1951)
R v J.W.C. (1952)
R v G.I.B. (1952)
R v L.W.B. (1952)
R v O.C. (1953)
R v P.D C. (1954)
R v R.H.L. (1954)
R v G.W.B. (1955)
R v B.J.T. (1956)
R v J.R.B. (1956)
R v D.D.M. (1957)
R v J.B.P.P. (1958)
R v S.J.V.I. (1958)
R v L.G.W. (1958)
R v R.E.P. (1959)
R v J.J.K. (1959)
R v R.M.B. (1960)
R v N.T.N. (1960)
R v F.X.I. (1960)
R v R.J.F. (1961)
R v G.J.B. (1961)

R v W.M. (1946)
R v G.T.B. (1946)
R v R.F.A. (1947)
R v A.H.B. (1947)
R v J.H.W. (1948)
R v M.J.N. (1949)
R v J.C. (1949)
R v W.A.B. (1950)
R v D.V.J. (1950)
R v E.J.H. (1950)
R v L.K.H. (1950)
R v S.M. (1950)
R v B.B.M. (1951)
R v F.O.B. (1951)
R v B.D.S.M. (1951)
R v J.H. (1951)
R v E.O. (1951)
R v D.C.G. (1952)
R v G.B.C. (1952)
R v F.W.P. (1952)
R v R.B.T. (1952)
R v F.P.N. (1953)
R v M. (1954)*
R v E.M.R. (1955)
R v B.R.H. (1955)
R v L.L.L. (1956)
R v D.J.O. (1956)
R v J.E.C. (1957)
R v E.M. (1958)
R v N.K. (1958)
R v F.G.D. (1958)
R v W.J.E. (1959)
R v H.C.C. (1959)
R v B.J.M. (1960)
R v A.K.A. (1960)
R v M.V.C. (1960)
R v E.H. (1961)
R v B.N.S. (1961)

* First name not recorded in indictment register.

SELECT BIBLIOGRAPHY

R v J.E.J. (1961)
R v J.H. (1962)
R v R.B.H. (1962)
R v R.C. (1963)
R v F.F. (1963)
R v M.R. (1963)
R v M.J.C. (1964)
R v A.P. (1964)
R v J.P.G. (1964)
R v P.M.L. (1965)
R v D.A.W. (1965)
R v S.H. (1965)
R v J.R. (1966)
R v D.J.B. (1966)
R v R.H.W. (1966)
R v R.N.S. (1967)
R v B. (1967)*
R v R.P.R. (1967)
R v D.W.W. (1968)
R v G.N.M. (1969)
R v E.J.V. (1969)
R v G.P.C. (1969)
R v M.W.B.E. (1970)
R v A.P.C. (1970)
R v A.M.B. (1970)
R v G.C.B. (1970)
R v L.R.H. (1971)
R v A.S. (1971)
R v R.S.M. (1971)
R v W.G.W. (1972)
R v R.S. (1972)
R v B.W.P. (1972)
R v B.R.J. (1972)
R v C.F.C. (1973)
R v R.A.A. (1973)
R v R.M. (1973)
R v C.P.M. (1974)
R v D.R.P. (1974)
R v K.R.B. (1974)
R v L.B. (1974)
R v M.S.P. (1975)
R v T.J.S. (1976)
R v S.K., J.S. & A.L.S. (1978)
R v A.M.C. (1979)

R v J.M.S. (1962)
R v G.J.F. (1962)
R v K.H. (1962)
R v G.H.C. (1963)
R v J.H. (1963)
R v W.W.V. (1963)
R v C.W.H. (1964)
R v P.A.O. (1964)
R v L.G.H. (1965)
R v R.D.S. (1965)
R v D.H.S. (1965)
R v L.M. (1966)
R v J.U. (1966)
R v M.Z. (1966)
R v R.E. (1967)
R v C.J.F. (1967)
R v P.G.N. (1967)
R v H.F. (1968)
R v C.J.R. (1968)
R v E.W. (1968)
R v J.W.N. (1969)
R v W.W.W. (1970)
R v O.N.H. (1970)
R v A.R.B. (1970)
R v T.B.N. (1970)
R v T.B. (1971)
R v B.J.W. (1971)
R v A.V.P. (1971)
R v A.B.S. (1971)
R v G.J.M. (1972)
R v A.C.H. (1972)
R v R.S.B. (1972)
R v S.S. (1972)
R v D.G.C. (1973)
R v R.A.J. (1973)
R v A.C. (1973)
R v B.J.B. (1974)
R v M.A.J. (1974)
R v H.D.M. (1974)
R v B.F.P (1975)
R v B.D.S. & T.R.R. (1976)
R v J.E.W.E. (1976)
R v R.W.S. (1978)
R v G.A.T.C. (1980)

* First name not recorded in indictment register.

SELECT BIBLIOGRAPHY

Western Australian Police Department

005 059 V1, 'Accidents: Police attendance at Traffic Accidents', SROWA, WAS 488, CONS 5931.

76/7242, 'Afflick Christopher Rodney – Death of on November 21, 1976 passenger in vehicle driven by Christopher Anthony Corrigin that left Oceanic Drive, City Beach and collided with SEC pole', SROWA, WAS 76, CONS 3454.

1954/1593 v2, 'Australian Road Safety Council – Proposed formation of Policy file', SROWA, WAS 76, CONS 430.

76/7020, 'Craggs, Kathleen Francis – Death of on February 1, 1976, as pedestrian was struck by vehicle driven by Gary George White in Atkinson Street, Collie', SROWA, WAS 76, CONS 3454.

078 7237 vi, 'Deaths of NOYCE, Dennis Wayne; NOYCE Albert George; NOYCE Mary Elva Maria – Fatal Traffic Accident', SROWA, WAS 488, CONS 5882.

76/7063, 'Edwards, Jean Margaret – Death of on March 28, 1976, passenger in vehicle driven by Colin George Pyer when vehicle turned in front of vehicle driven by Helen Margaret Shine at South West Highway & Picton Road, Picton', SROWA, WAS 76, CONS 3454.

040 126 V2, 'Equipment: General – Breathalyser equipment – use-of-policy', SROWA, WAS 488, CONS 5907.

1962/1377, 'Fatal Traffic Accidents: Investigation by members of CIB', SROWA, WAS 76, CONS 1910.

76/7065, 'Gojak, Josa; Gojak, Patricia Ann – Deaths of on March 27, 1976, driver and passenger respectivley [sic] whose vehicle was struck head on by vehicle driven by David Alan Humble when he was racing vehicle driven by Colin Edmond Parker on Marmion Avenue', SROWA, WAS 76, CONS 3454.

078 7261 vi, 'Henson Yvonne Anne (passenger) Carey Pamela Betty (driver) Dths of on 22.10.78 respectively when veh. coll. with veh. driven by Robert Edwin Malcolm COOPER at intersect. Walter road & Iolanthe st', SROWA, WAS 488, CONS 5882.

77/7251, 'Hewison, Malcolm Robert William – Death of on 1/12/1977, passenger in vehicle driven by Brett Clinton Bond who collided with SEC pole in Brockway Avenue, Graylands', SROWA, WAS 76, CONS 3454.

77/7213, 'Holland Luke Christopher Michael – Death of on October 22, 1977 when driver of a car collided with car driven by Michael Solonel [sic] at Railway Parade, Shenton Park', SROWA, WAS 76, CONS 3454.

76/7154, 'Nash Amanda May – Death of on July 24, 1976 – rider of pushbike that was struck from behind by vehicle driven by Michael John Roche in Bay View Terrace, Mosman Park', SROWA, WAS 76, CONS 3454.

1967/0564 v6, 'Police Department (Traffic Office) – Traffic Act & Regulations – Inquiries and Suggestions', SROWA, WAS 76, CONS 251.

1981/0728, 'Road Traffic Authority/Police Amalgamation of', SROWA, WAS 76, CONS 4000.

SELECT BIBLIOGRAPHY

75/7164, 'Smith, Kevin Michael – death of on August 6, 1975, passenger in vehicle driven by Jeremy Peter Finch, When vehicle collided with vehicle driven by Alan John Lewington. Finch then collided with stationary vehicle driven by Eric Victor Welsh in Belgravia Street and Alexander Road, Belmont', SROWA, WAS 76, CONS 3454.

1964/1551 v1, 'Suggestions for the improvement of Road Safety and Reduction of Road Toll', SROWA, WAS 76, CONS 1911.

68 0548 V2, 'Suggestions for the improvement of Road Safety and Reduction of Road Toll', SROWA, WAS 77, CONS 3439.

1961/3992, 'Traffic Accidents: Police Attending', SROWA, WAS 76, CONS 1910.

1958/0483, 'Traffic Act and Regulations: Amendments and additions to', SROWA, WAS 76, CONS 1911.

1960/0907 V4, 'Traffic Branch – Drunken drivers: Policy', SROWA, WAS 77, CONS 3998.

1969/0346 V2, 'Traffic Office – Breathalyser Policy Volume 2', SROWA, WAS 77, CONS 3998.

76/7056, 'Wilson, Robert – Death of on March 10, 1976 passenger in vehicle driven by George Bernard Walker that collided with vehicle driven by Carmela Flemming at Renou and Station Streets, East Cannington', SROWA, WAS 76, CONS 3454.

77/7194, York Andrew Lawrence – Death of on September 17, 1977 passenger in vehicle driven by Bernice Evelyn York when vehicle collided with vehicle driven by John Frederick Lowndes at Holmes Place & Collick St', SROWA, WAS 76, CONS 3454.

Yalgoo Clerk of Courts
1, 'Magistrate's Evidence Book – Children's Court', SROWA, WAS 386, CONS 3811.

PUBLISHED SOURCES

Parliamentary and government

Attorney General McGinty, J., MLA, Ministerial Media Statement, 'Deadly drunk drivers to be jailed under new laws', 13 June 2004.

Attorney General McGinty, J., MLA, Ministerial Media Statement, 'Jess' Law – deadly drunk drivers face 20 years' jail from January 1', 2 January 2005.

Attorney General Porter, C. C., MLA, Ministerial Media Statement, 'Crimes causing death given stronger penalties', 20 October 2011.

Australian Law Reform Commission, *Sentencing*, Report Number 44, Australian Government Publishing Service, Canberra, 1988.

Australian Transport Safety Bureau, *Road crash casualties and rates, Australia, 1925 to 2005*, Australian Transport Safety Bureau, Canberra, 2006.

SELECT BIBLIOGRAPHY

Commonwealth Bureau of Census and Statistics, *Official Year Book of the Commonwealth of Australia, No. 37, 1946 and 1947*, Commonwealth Bureau of Census and Statistics, Canberra, 1949.

Crown Prosecution Service, *Policy for Prosecuting cases of bad driving*, Crown Prosecution Service, London, 2007.

Department of Infrastructure, Transport, Regional Development and Local Government, *Road deaths in Australia 1925–2008*, Information Sheet 38, Bureau of Infrastructure, Transport and Regional Economics, Canberra, 2010.

Elliot, B. J. & South, D. R., *The development and assessment of a drink-driving campaign: a case study*, Department of Transport, Office of Road Safety, Australian Government Publishing Service, Canberra, 1985.

Federal Office of Road Safety, *Road traffic accident data and rates: Australia, States and Territories 1925 to 1981*, Australian Government Publishing Service, Canberra, 1984.

Federal Office of Road Safety, *The history of road fatalities in Australia*, Monograph 23, Federal Office of Road Safety, Canberra, 1998.

House of Commons Transport Committee (UK), *Road Traffic Law Enforcement: Second Report of Session 2015–2016*, The Stationary Office Limited, London, 2016.

House of Representatives Standing Committee on Road Safety, *Alcohol, drugs and road safety: Report of the House of Representatives Standing Committee on Road Safety, May 1980*, Australian Government Publishing Service, Canberra, 1980.

Law Reform Commission of Victoria, *Death Caused by Dangerous Driving*, Discussion Paper No. 21, Law Reform Commission of Victoria, Melbourne, 1991.

Law Reform Commission of Victoria, *Death Caused by Dangerous Driving*, Report No. 45, Law Reform Commission of Victoria, Melbourne, 1992.

Law Reform Commission of Western Australia, *Report: Manslaughter or Dangerous Driving causing Death*, Project No. 17, Law Reform Commission of Western Australia, Perth, 1970.

Law Reform Commission of Western Australia, *Summary Trial of Indictable Offences*, Law Reform Commission of Western Australia, Perth, 1970.

Law Reform Commission of Western Australia, *Working Paper: Manslaughter or Dangerous Driving causing Death*, Project No. 17, Law Reform Commission of Western Australia, Perth, 1970.

Law Reform Commission of Western Australia, *Review of the Law of Homicide: An Issues Paper*, Law Reform Commission of Western Australia, Perth, 2006.

Law Reform Commission of Western Australia, *Review of the Law of Homicide: Final Report*, Law Reform Commission of Western Australia, Perth, 2007.

Parliament of the Commonwealth of Australia, Standing Committee on Road Safety, *Report on Road Safety generally: including drink driving, driver attitudes*

SELECT BIBLIOGRAPHY

and behaviour, speed, disregard of road law as a factor in crashes, Report of the House of Representatives, Australian Government Publishing Service, Canberra, 1984.

Parliamentary Commissioner for Administrative Investigations, *The Falsification of Random Breath Testing Statistics in the Western Australian Police Service*, Ombudsman Western Australia, Perth, WA, 2001.

Road Safety Council, *2004 Annual Review of Arriving Safely – Road Safety Strategy for Western Australia, 2003–2007*, Government of Western Australia, December 2005.

Road Traffic Authority of Western Australia & Smith, D. I., *An investigation to determine whether blood alcohol tests should be compulsory for all traffic accident casualties over the age of 15 years admitted to hospital in Western Australia*, Road Traffic Authority of Western Australia, Perth, 1975.

Royal Commission on the Police, Great Britain, *Final report: Royal Commission on the Police, 1962*, H. M. Stationery Office, London, 1962.

Sentencing Advisory Council, *Maximum Penalty for Negligently Causing Serious Injury*, Sentencing Advisory Council Victoria, Melbourne, 2007.

Sentencing Advisory Council, *Sentencing of Driving Offences that Result in Death or Injury: Consultation Paper*, Sentencing Advisory Council Tasmania, Hobart, 2016.

Sentencing Advisory Council, *Sentencing of Driving Offences that Result in Death or Injury: Final Report, No. 8*, Sentencing Advisory Council Tasmania, Hobart, 2017.

Voas, R. B. & Lacey, J. C., *Alcohol and Highway Safety 2006: A Review of the State of Knowledge*, National Highway Traffic Safety Administration, Washington DC, 2011–2013.

Western Australia, Committee of Inquiry into the Rate of Imprisonment, *Report of the Committee of Inquiry into the Rate of Imprisonment*, Committee of Inquiry into the Rate of Imprisonment, Perth, 1981.

Western Australia, Review of Remission and Parole, *Report of the Review of Remission and Parole*, Ministry of Justice, Government of Western Australia, Perth, March 1998.

Western Australian Parliament, *Parliamentary Debates (Hansard)*.

Western Australian Parliament, Standing Committee on Legislation, *First report on the Crime (Serious and Repeat Offenders) Sentencing Act 1992 and the Criminal Law Amendment Act 1992*, Legislative Council, Perth, 1992.

Western Australian Parliament, Standing Committee on Legislation, *Report of the Standing Committee on Legislation in Relation to the Road Traffic Amendment (Dangerous Driving) Bill 2004*, Report no. 23, Standing Committee on Legislation, Perth, 2004.

Western Australian Parliament, Standing Committee on Legislation, *Sessional Report: An Overview of the Committee's Operations: Second Session of the*

SELECT BIBLIOGRAPHY

Thirty-Sixth Parliament, Report no. 26, Standing Committee on Legislation, Perth, 2004.

Western Australian Parliament, Subcommittee of the Standing Committee on Legislation, 'Road Traffic Amendment (Dangerous Driving) Bill 2004: Transcript of evidence taken at Perth on Monday, 11 October 2004, Session One' and 'Road Traffic Amendment (Dangerous Driving) Bill 2004: Transcript of evidence taken at Perth on Thursday, 14 October 2004', Standing Committee on Legislation, Perth, 2004.

Western Australian State Coroner, Alastair N. Hope, *Record of Investigation into Death: Inquest into the death of Jeremy Graham Armstrong*, Ref. no. 29/10, 13 January 2011, Coroner's Court of Western Australia, Perth, 2011.

Books, chapters, articles and other reports

Aird, A., *The Automotive Nightmare*, Hutchinson & Co, London, 1972.

Andréasson, R. & Jones, A. W., 'The life and work of Erik M. P. Widmark', *The American Journal of Forensic Medicine and Pathology*, vol. 17, no. 3, 1996, pp. 177–90.

Anon., 'Drinking Drivers Dangerous as Well as Drunken Ones', *The Science News-Letter*, vol. 33, no. 13, 26 March 1938, p. 205.

Anon., 'Under the Influence', *The British Medical Journal*, vol. 1, no. 5168, 1960, pp. 256–7.

Ashworth, A., 'Ways out of the Abyss? Reflections on punishment in Western Australia', *University of Western Australia Law Review*, vol. 22, 1992, pp. 257–71.

Ashworth, A., 'Taking the Consequences', in Shute, S., Gardner, J. & Horder, J. (eds.), *Action and Value in Criminal Law*, Clarendon Press, Oxford, 1993, pp. 107–24.

Ashworth, A., '"Manslaughter": Generic or Nominate Offences?', in Clarkson, C. M. V. & Cunningham, S. (eds.), *Criminal Liability for Non-Aggressive Death*, Ashgate, Hampshire, 2008, pp. 235–48.

Ball-Rokeach, S. J., Hale, M., Schaffer, A., Porras, L., Harris, P. & Drayton, M., 'Changing the Media Production Process: From Aggressive to Injury-Sensitive Traffic Crash Stories', in Demers, D. & Viswanath, K. (eds.), *Mass media, social control, and social change: A Macrosocial perspective*, Iowa State University Press, Ames, 1999, pp. 229–62.

Barker, T. (ed.), *The Economic and Social Effects of the Spread of Motor Vehicles: An International Centenary Tribute*, Macmillan, Basingstoke, 1987.

Birney, S., *Australia on Wheels: Early Beginnings to the Present Day*, Bullion Books, Silverwater, 1989.

Birrell, J. H. W., 'Alcohol as a factor in Victorian road collisions', *Medical Journal of Australia*, vol. 1, no. 19, 1960, pp. 713–22.

Birrell, J. H. W., 'Alcohol and Road Accidents: Some Recent Developments', *Medical Journal of Australia*, vol. 1, 1964, pp. 265–70.

SELECT BIBLIOGRAPHY

Birrell, J. H. W., 'A preliminary note on the drinking driver in Victoria, Australia, since 1966', *Medicine, Science and the Law*, vol. 10, no. 1, 1970, pp. 38–41.

Borkenstein, R. F., Crowther, R. F., Shumate, R. P., Ziel, W. B. & Zylman, R., *The role of the drinking driver in traffic accidents*, Indiana University, Bloomington, 1964.

Borkenstein, R. F., Crowther, R. F., Shumate, R. P., Ziel, W. B. & Zylman, R., *The role of the drinking driver in traffic accidents: the Grand Rapids Study*, Steintor-Verlag, Hamburg, 1974.

Breen, L., *Silenced Voices: Grief Following Road Traffic Crashes*, Saarbrucken, VDM Verlag, 2008.

British Medical Association, *Relation of alcohol to road accidents: Report of a Special Committee of the British Medical Association*, British Medical Association, London, 1960.

British Medical Association, *Alcohol and Road Traffic: Proceedings of the Third International Conference on Alcohol and Road Traffic*, September 3–7, 1962, British Medical Association, London, 1963.

British Medical Association, *The Drinking Driver: The medico-legal investigation of the drinking driver: Report of a Special Committee of the British Medical Association*, British Medical Association, London, 1965.

Brown, D., *Traffic Offences: An examination of the principles of law governing offences committed by motorists on the roads in Australia*, Butterworths, North Ryde, 1983.

Brown, D., *Traffic Offences and Accidents: An examination of the principles of law governing offences and negligence by motorists on the roads in Australia*, Butterworths, North Ryde, 1996.

Brown, G., Henry Windsor Lecture 1972, 'Road Trauma – A Community Crisis', *The Medical Journal of Australia*, vol. 1, no. 14, 1972, p. 669.

Browning, R., 'Where are the protests?', *British Medical Journal*, vol. 324, 11 May 2002, p. 1165.

Campbell, V. & Campbell, I. G., 'Punishing Multiple Harms', *University of Queensland Law Journal*, vol. 17, no. 1, 1992, pp. 20–34.

Cavett, J. W., 'The determination of alcohol in blood and other bodily fluids', *The Journal of Laboratory and Clinical Medicine*, vol. 23, no. 5, 1938, pp. 543–6.

Clark, J., 'Wild behaviour: Infernal Machines and Serious Accidents', *National Library of Australia News*, vol. 7, no. 5, 1997, pp. 3–5.

Clark, J., 'Road safety and the historical perspective: the example of women', *Roadwise*, vol. 13, no. 4, 2002, pp. 19–22.

Clarkson, C. M. V. & Cunningham, S. (eds.), *Criminal Liability for Non-Aggressive Death*, Ashgate, Hampshire, 2008.

Conole, P., *Protect and Serve: A History of Policing in Western Australia*, Success Print, Bayswater, 2002.

Cook, C., Creyke, R., Geddes, R. & Hamer, D., *Laying Down the Law*, LexisNexis Butterworths, New South Wales, 2005.

SELECT BIBLIOGRAPHY

Cooter, R. & Luckin, B. (eds.), *Accidents in History: Injuries, fatalities and social relations*, Rodopi, Amsterdam, 1997.

Corbett, C., *Car Crime*, Willan Publishing, Devon, 2003.

Cunningham, S., 'Punishing drivers who kill: putting road safety first?', *Legal Studies*, vol. 27, no. 2, 2007, pp. 288–311.

Cunningham, S., *Driving Offences: Law, Policy and Practice*, Ashgate, Hampshire, 2008.

Cunningham, S. 'Vehicular Homicide: Need for a Special Offence?', in Clarkson, C. M. V. & Cunningham, S. (eds.), *Criminal Liability for Non-Aggressive Death*, Ashgate, Hampshire, 2008, pp. 96–123.

Davis, R., *Death on the Streets: Cars and the mythology of road safety*, Leading Edge Press & Publishing Ltd, North Yorkshire, 1992/1993.

Davison, G., *Car Wars: How the car won our hearts and conquered our cities*, Allen & Unwin, Crows Nest, 2004.

Dean, J. S., *Murder Most Foul: A study of the road deaths problem*, George Allen & Unwin Ltd, Great Britain, 1947.

Duff, R. A., 'Whose Luck Is It Anyway?', in Clarkson, C. M. & Cunningham, S. (eds.), *Criminal Liability for Non-Aggressive Death*, Ashgate, Hampshire, 2008, pp. 61–77.

Faith, N., *Crash: The limits of car safety*, Boxtree, London, 1997.

Federation of European Road Traffic Victims (FEVR), *Impact of road death and injury: research into the principal causes of the decline in quality of life and living standard suffered by road crash victims and victim families: Proposal for improvements*, Geneva, Federation of European Road Traffic Victims, 1995.

Fitzgerald, P. J., 'Road Traffic Law as the Lawyer Sees it', in Leeming, J. J. (ed.), *Road Accidents: Prevent or Punish?*, Cassell, London, 1969, pp. 157–75.

Fletcher, G., *Rethinking Criminal Law*, Oxford University Press, Oxford, 2000.

Friedman, L. M., *Crime and Punishment in American History*, Basic Books, New York, 1993.

Furnas, J. C., 'And Sudden Death', *Reader's Digest* (USA), vol. 27, August 1935, pp. 21–6.

Goode, J., *Smoke, Smell and Clatter: The Revolutionary Story of Motoring in Australia*, Lansdowne Press Pty Ltd, Melbourne, 1969.

Green, J., 'The medico-legal production of fatal accidents', *Sociology of Health & Illness*, vol. 14, no. 3, 1992, pp. 373–89.

Green, J., 'Accidents: the remnants of a modern classificatory system', in Cooter, R. & Luckin, B. (eds.), *Accidents in History: Injuries, fatalities and social relations*, Rodopi, Amsterdam, 1997, pp. 35–58.

Green, J., *Risk and Misfortune: A Social Construction of Accidents*, UCL Press, London, 1997.

Hall Williams, J. E., 'Causing Death by Dangerous Driving: The Objective Test', *The Modern Law Review*, vol. 26, no. 4, 1963, pp. 430–3.

SELECT BIBLIOGRAPHY

Heise, H. A., 'Alcohol and Automobile Accidents', *Journal of the American Medical Association*, vol. 103, no. 10, 1934, pp. 739–41.
Hirst, M., 'Causing death by driving and other offences: a question of balance', *Criminal Law Review*, no. 5, 2008, pp. 339–52.
Hodge, P. R., 'Fatal traffic accidents in Adelaide', *Medical Journal of Australia*, vol. 1, no. 9, 1962, pp. 309–14.
Holcomb, R. L., 'Alcohol in relation to traffic accidents', *Journal of the American Medical Association*, vol. 110, no. 12, 1938, pp. 1076–85.
Hood, R., *Sentencing the motoring offender: a study of magistrates' views and practices*, Heinemann, London, 1972.
Horder, J., 'Can the Law Do Without the Reasonable Person?', *University of Toronto Law Journal*, vol. 55, no. 2, 2005, pp. 253–69.
Jackson, H., 'Juvenile justice – the Western Australian experience', in Atkinson, L. & Gerull, S-A. (eds.), *National Conference on Juvenile Justice: Proceedings of a conference held 22–24 September 1992*, Australian Institute of Criminology, Canberra, 1993, pp. 85–95.
Knott, J. W., 'Speed, Modernity and the Motor Car: The Making of the 1909 Motor Traffic Act in New South Wales', *Australian Historical Studies*, vol. 26, no. 103, 1994, pp. 221–41.
Kyd Cunningham, S., 'Has law reform policy been driven in the right direction? How the new causing death by driving offences are operating in practice', *Criminal Law Review*, no. 9, 2013, pp. 711–28.
Laybourn, K. with Taylor, D., *The Battle for the Roads of Britain, Police, Motorists and the Law, c. 1890s to 1970s*, Palgrave Macmillan, Hampshire, 2015.
Leeming, J. J., *Road Accidents: Prevent or Punish?*, Cassell, London, 1969.
Lerner, B. H., *One for the Road: Drunk Driving Since 1900*, The Johns Hopkins University Press, Baltimore, 2011.
Levin, M. S., 'People v Watson: Drunk Driving Homicide: Murder or Enhanced Manslaughter?', *California Law Review*, vol. 71, no. 4, 1983, pp. 1298–323.
Lewis, J. & Hirsh, B., 'Doctor, Driver and the Courts', *The British Medical Journal*, vol. 2, no. 5402, 1964, pp. 189–90.
Lord, J. H., 'America's number one killer: Vehicular crashes', in Doka, K. J. (ed.), *Living with grief after sudden loss: Suicide, homicide, accident, heart attack, stroke*, Hospice Foundation of America, Washington, 1996, pp. 25–39.
Luckin, B., 'A Never–Ending Passing of the Buck? The Failure of Drink-driving Reform in Interwar Britain', *Contemporary British History*, vol. 24, no. 3, 2010, pp. 363–84.
Luria, D., 'Death on the Highway: Reckless Driving as Murder', *Oregon Law Review*, vol. 67, 1988, pp. 799–836.
Marshall, H., 'Alcohol: A Critical Review of the Literature, 1929–1940', *Psychological Bulletin*, vol. 38, no. 4, 1941, pp. 193–217.
Mazengarb, O. C., *Mazengarb's Negligence on the highway: law and practice in Australia*, Butterworths, Sydney, 1957.

SELECT BIBLIOGRAPHY

Mazengarb, O. C., *Mazengarb's law and practice relating to actions for negligence on the highway*, Butterworths, Sydney, 1962.

McClurg, A. J., 'Dead Sorrow: A Story about Loss and a New Theory of Wrongful Death Damages', *Boston University Law Review*, vol. 85, no. 1, 2005, pp. 1–51.

McFarland, R. A. & Moore, R. C., 'Accidents and Accident Prevention', *Annual Review of Medicine*, vol. 13, no. 1, 1962, pp. 371–88.

Mickler, S., 'Visions of disorder: media, police, Aboriginal youth and the politics of youth crime reporting', *Cultural Studies*, vol. 6, no. 3, 1992, pp. 322–36.

Mitchell, M. (ed.), *The Aftermath of Road Accidents: Psychological, social and legal consequences of an everyday trauma*, Routledge, London, 1997.

Moran, M., *Rethinking the Reasonable Person: An Egalitarian Reconstruction of the Objective Standard*, Oxford University Press, Oxford, 2003.

Morgan, N. & Yeo, S., 'Defining the fault elements of driving offences', *Singapore Academy of Law Journal*, vol. 19, 2007, pp. 205–30.

Mugliston, P., Ainsworth, S. & Colebatch, H., *Traffic law in Western Australia*, LexisNexis Butterworths, Chatswood, 2007.

Nader, R., *Unsafe at any speed: The designed-in dangers of the American automobile*, Grossman, New York, 1965.

Newman, C., 'Death by Careless Driving; Sentencing Guidelines and the Custody Threshold', *Journal of Criminal Law*, vol. 74, no. 2, 2010, pp. 100–3.

O'Connell, J. & Myers, A., *Safety Last: An Indictment of the Auto Industry*, Random House, New York, 1966.

O'Connell, S., *The car in British Society: Class, gender and motoring, 1896–1939*, Manchester University Press, Manchester, 1998.

O'Connell, S., 'From Toad of Toad Hall to the "Death Drivers" of Belfast: An exploratory history of "joyriding"', *British Journal of Criminology*, vol. 46, no. 3, 2006, pp. 455–69.

Pearson, A. T., 'Alcohol and fatal traffic accidents', *Medical Journal of Australia*, vol. 2, no. 5, 1957, pp. 166–7.

Perkin, H., *The Age of the Automobile*, Quartet Books, London, 1976.

Rae, J. B., *The American Automobile: A Brief History*, University of Chicago Press, Chicago, 1965.

Rechnitzer, G., 'Road crashes', in Selby, H. (ed.), *The Inquest Handbook*, The Federation Press, Sydney, 1998, pp. 80–106.

Richardson, K., *The British Motor Industry, 1896–1939*, Macmillan, London, 1977.

Selesnick, S., 'Alcoholic intoxication: Its diagnosis and medicolegal implications', *The Journal of the American Medical Association*, vol. 110, no. 11, 1938, pp. 775–8.

Shute, S., Gardner, J. & Horder, J. (eds.), *Action and Value in the Criminal Law*, Clarendon Press, Oxford, 1993.

Sidoti, C., 'The Commonwealth's responsibility for Aboriginal young offenders', in Atkinson, L. & Gerull, S-A. (eds.), *National Conference on Juvenile Justice:*

SELECT BIBLIOGRAPHY

Proceedings of a conference held 22–24 September 1992, Australian Institute of Criminology, Canberra, 1993, pp. 80–93.

Stockwell, C., 'The role of the media in the juvenile justice debate in Western Australia', in Atkinson, L. & Gerull, S-A. (eds.), *National Conference on Juvenile Justice: Proceedings of a conference held 22–24 September 1992*, Australian Institute of Criminology, Canberra, 1993, pp. 279–90.

Tehrani, N., 'Road Victim Trauma: an investigation of the impact on the injured and bereaved', *Counselling Psychology Quarterly*, vol. 17, no. 4, 2004, pp. 361–73.

Terry, A., *The Motor Vehicle, Society and the Law*, CCH Australia, North Ryde, New South Wales, 1983.

Wagnsson, R., Bjerver, K., Nelker, G., Rosell, S. & Akerbladh-Rosell, J. (eds.), *Alcohol and Road Traffic. Proceedings of the First international Conference*, Kugelbergs, Boktryckeri, 1951.

Warden, W. R., *Juggernaut: Slaughter on the Australian Roads*, A. H. & A. W. Reed, Sydney, 1968.

Webster, A., 'Recklessness: Awareness, indifference or belief?', *Criminal Law Journal*, vol. 31, no. 5, 2007, pp. 272–86.

Wells, C., 'Look Hard and See More', *The Modern Law Review*, vol. 47, no. 1, 1984, pp. 98–103.

Western Australian Hotels Association, *Assessment on "the effectiveness" of blood alcohol limits in reducing traffic accidents*, Western Australian Hotels Association Incorporated, Leederville, 1983.

White, A. R., 'Carelessness, Indifference and Recklessness', *The Modern Law Review*, vol. 24, no. 5, 1961, pp. 592–5.

White, R., 'Tough laws for hard-core politicians', *Alternative Law Journal*, vol. 17, 1992, pp. 58–60.

Wilkie, M., 'Crime (Serious and Repeat Offenders) Sentencing Act 1992: A Human Rights Perspective', *Western Australian Law Review*, vol. 22, 1992, pp. 187–96.

World Health Organization, *World report on road traffic injury prevention*, World Health Organization, Geneva, 2004.

World Health Organization, *Global status report on road safety 2013: supporting a decade of action*, World Health Organization, Geneva, 2013.

World Health Organization, *Global status report on road safety 2018*, World Health Organization, Geneva, 2018.

World Health Organization & Association for Safe International Road Travel, *Faces behind the figures: voices of road traffic victims and their families*, World Health Organization, Switzerland, 2007.

Yeo, S., *Fault in homicide: towards a schematic approach to the fault elements for murder and involuntary manslaughter in England, Australia and India*, Federation Press in association with the Institute of Criminology, University of Sydney, Leichhardt, 1997.

SELECT BIBLIOGRAPHY

Newspapers, media and periodicals

7 News
ABC News https://www.abc.net.au/news/
BBC News https://www.bbc.com/news
Community News https://www.communitynews.com.au
Daily Mail https://www.dailymail.co.uk/home.index.html
Daily News
Daily Telegraph https://www.dailytelegraph.com.au
Perth Now https://www.perthnow.com.au/
Sunday Times
Sydney Morning Herald https://www.smh.com.au/
The Road Patrol: the official magazine of the Royal Automobile Club of Western Australia
WA Today https://www.watoday.com.au/
West Australian https://thewest.com.au/
Western Mail

Other websites

Australasian Legal Information Institute http://www.austlii.edu.au/
Australian Screen https://aso.gov.au/
Brake: The road safety charity http://www.brake.org.uk/
FEVR: European Federation of Road Traffic Victims https://fevr.org/
MADD: Mothers Against Drunk Driving https://www.madd.org/
Parliament of Australia https://www.aph.gov.au/
Parliament of Western Australia http://www.parliament.wa.gov.au/WebCMS/WebCMS.nsf/index
RoadPeace http://www.roadpeace.org/
Royal Automobile Club of Western Australia (RAC) https://rac.com.au/about-rac/media
State Law Publisher https://www.slp.wa.gov.au/Index.html
Western Australian Government media statements https://www.mediastatements.wa.gov.au/Pages/Default.aspx
Western Australian Legislation https://www.legislation.wa.gov.au/
World Health Organization https://www.who.int/
YouTube https://www.youtube.com

SELECT BIBLIOGRAPHY

UNPUBLISHED MANUSCRIPTS

Theses and dissertations

Axup, I., 'The impact of motor car "accidents" on society in the State of Victoria, 1900–1950', Honours dissertation (History), Department of History, Monash University, 1988.

Breen, L., 'Silenced Voices: Experiences of Grief following Road Traffic Crashes in Western Australia', PhD thesis (Psychology), Faculty of Computing, Health and Sciences, Edith Cowan University, 2006.

Cameron, E., 'The Development of Drink Driving Policy in Western Australia, 1990–1996', Honours dissertation (Politics), Faculty of Arts, Edith Cowan University, 1996.

King, K., 'A Lesser Species of Homicide – Manslaughter, Negligent and Dangerous Driving Causing Death: The Prosecution of Drivers in Western Australia, 1946–2011', PhD thesis, University of Western Australia, 2014.

Voelcker, J., 'A Critical Review of the Legal Penalties for Drivers Who Kill Cyclists or Pedestrians', Honours dissertation, School for Policy Studies, University of Bristol, 2007.

INDEX

absence of eyewitness 65–6, 79, 80, 100, 102, 106–7, 109, 125–8, 211, 218–19, 232, 242–3, 244–6, 269
'accidents', *see* terminology
advocacy
   by coroners 43–4
   by Crown and judiciary 51–3, 55–7, 64–5, 160, 163, 165–73, 174–7, 182–9, 191, 197–8, 200–2, 224–6, 228–31, 236–7, 254, 268–9, 272–4
age of defendants, *see* juvenile crime 'wave'; sentences: mitigating factors: youth
agency, human 10–14, 43, 55, 123–4, 263–4
Ainsworth v D (A Child) (1992) 164, 182
alcohol, *see* drink-driving
Ambrosino, Mario 179
Armstrong, Jeremy, inquest 244–7
Association for Safe International Road Travel (ASIRT) 6
Australian Law Reform Commission 169
authority to drive 258

Barron v Western Australia (2010) 232
Blair v Semple (1989) 172–4, 218
Blurton, Margaret and Shane 180
Brake (road safety charity) 177, 249
Breen, Lauren 6, 68
Brown, Douglas 8, 29, 59
Buswell, Troy Raymond, Minister for Transport, Housing & Emergency Services 221

Callaghan v R (1952)
   at first instance 31–3
   civil versus criminal standard of negligence 34
   degree of negligence required equivalent to manslaughter 34, 36–8, 265
   difficulties of applying *Callaghan* 17, 34–8, 46, 129, 139
   grounds for appeal 33–4
   impact on Crown's approach 1952–1974: 30, 34, 38–9, 42–3, 72, 265–6
careless driving causing death (offence)
   and dangerous driving causing death 241, 243, 248, 254–5
   comparable offences in other jurisdictions 239–40, 246–7, 249–50
   inappropriate employ of 145–6, 148–9, 172–4, 193–4, 218, 241, 243–4, 247–50, 254–6, 271–3
   introduction of 239–43, 246–7
   opposition to 240–2, 247, 249–50
   penalty provisions 240, 242, 250–4
   test of 243–4, 247, 255–6
   to rectify 'lenient' penalties 240, 242–3, 247–8, 252–3, 255–6, 271–2
   Western Australian Police review (2018) 250–1
careless driving simpliciter 138–9, 239–40
causing death by careless or inconsiderate driving, UK 246–7, 249–50

INDEX

character references 55–6, 70–1, 90, 165
Charlotte's law 6, 256–61, 271, 274, *see also* dangerous driving causing death
Children's Court 41–2, 151–3, 178–81
Commonwealth Senate Select Committee of Inquiry into Road Safety 12
Cooter, Roger, and Luckin, Bill 8–9
Corbett, Claire 14, 22
coroners
   Hope, Alastair Neil 244–8
   Rodriguez, 'Pat' 32, 43
coronial
   advocacy regarding 'accidents' 43–4
   identification of bodies 68–9
   indictments not proceeded with 43
   inquests 43–4, 84, 149–50, 172
      Armstrong, Jeremy 244–7
   post-mortem reports 43, 66–8, 84
   see also coroners
Court, Sir Charles Walter Michael, Premier 151
Crawley v The Queen (1981) 169–72, 175–6
crime
   normative understandings of 13–14, 22, 56, 139–41, 264
   'real crime', *see* terminology
   vehicular homicide as 5–15, 22–3, 38, 48–9, 51–2, 54–9, 68, 70–2, 74, 109–10, 131, 138–41, 161–2, 165–7, 177, 181, 185, 192–4, 219–20, 222, 247–8, 263–5, 270, 272–4
Crime (Serious and Repeat Offenders) Sentencing Act 1992 (WA) 137, 177–82, 196–8, 269
Criminal Lawyers' Association of WA 140, 208–9, 214–18
Crown Law Department 19–20, 29–31
Cunningham, Sally, *see* Kyd, Sally
Curyer, Che 252–5
cyclists, *see* vulnerable road users

dangerous driving causing death (offence)
   0.15% deeming provision 102, 211–21, 232, 241, 269
   abolition of causation 208–21, 223, 269
   aggravating circumstances 137, 163, 180–1, 204, 214–15, 222–3, 225–6, 248, 256–60, 268–71, 273
   and manslaughter 146–9, 222
   as separate from the Criminal Code 19, 38, 130–1, 138–41, 160, 222, 270
   carelessness included in scope, contingent on context 144, 150–2, 163–4, 242, 248, 254–6, 266–7
   emphasis on fines 58, 90–1, 136–7, 139, 150–62, 166–7, 172–3, 192–4, 266–7
   inappropriate employ of 38, 144–6, 148–9, 153–5, 158–60, 172–4, 193–4, 196–8, 222, 224–5, 247–8, 254–6, 265–8, 271–4
   in other jurisdictions 131, 139, 141–2, 211–12, 214–16
   introduction of 8, 129–34, 141–4, 212–13, 266
   manner of the driving 133–6, 142–6, 154, 197–8, 202–4, 212–13, 217–18, 232, 240, 244, 247
   cannot be determined by fatal outcome 143–4, 203–4
   negligence not element of the offence 130–1, 133–4, 136, 141–2
   objective test 136, 142–4, 210–11, 217–18, 219, 265
   'ordinary' dangerous driving (post-2004) 196–7, 211–12, 223–4, 232–3, 235–8, 240, 254, 267, 269–73
   penalty provisions 136–9, 148, 196–98, 202, 211–12, 214–15, 223–5, 256, 258, 260–1, 269–70
   recklessness not element of the offence 142–4
   reversal of burden of proof 208–12, 215–17, 219–20
   scope of offence not utilised 148–51, 242, 248, 254–6
   summary judgment 133, 136–9, 156–8, 160, 172–4, 197, 202, 215, 223–5, 266–7, 269–71
dangerous driving simpliciter 133, 138–9, 214
Davis, Robert 10, 15, 22
Davison, Graeme 75–6
'death drivers' 172, 177, 202, 251–2
defences
   0.15% deeming provision 214, 216–17
   automatism and involuntariness 24, 134–5
   mechanical defect 134
   mistake of fact 24, 134–5

INDEX

other common informal defences 24, 52, 74–5, 84–6, 100–2, 113, 119, 120–4, 126, 147–8, 151, 194–5, 211
sudden emergency 24, 134–5
Department of Public Prosecutions 140, 216–17, 219, 257
Department of Transport 205, 221, 237
Devine v Western Australia (2010) 230–1
District Court, establishment and jurisdiction 42–3, 224–5, 267
disqualification, policy 49, 57–62, 163, 191, 205–6, 239, 258
drink-driving
0.5% offence 96
0.8% offence 96
0.15% offence 81, 83–4, 93–4, 102–3, 211–21, 232, 241, 269
admissibility of evidence 94, 102–7, 119–20, 141
alcotest 96–7
and masculinity 2, 3, 87–9, 130
appearing to drive normally 79, 94, 113–18, 143, 203–4, 206–7, 210–11, 217–19, 269
as normative, *see* driving culture
as socially acceptable 2, 16, 23, 26, 64–5, 73–7, 83–93, 106–7
blood alcohol testing 76, 93, 95–9
breath testing 76, 95, 97–9
disputing intoxication 81–2, 84–6, 97–100, 102–4, 106, 114–17
impact of alcohol on cognitive and motor skills 75–7, 212
not a breach of duty of persons in charge of dangerous things 72, 74, 78–9, 104, 106–7
offences in other jurisdictions 81, 94, 96
passengers' assumption of risk 80–1, 84
requiring eyewitness corroboration 82, 100–2, 117–18
refusal of tests 92, 95–7, 173–4, 188, 215, 218, 257
risk of crash involvement 22–3, 76–7, 94–5, 212
sobriety tests 54, 82–3, 85, 93, 111, 114, 218
to extent of incapability
post-1957 (0.15%) 81, 83–4, 93–5, 99, 102–3, 206–7, 211–15, 217, 219, 223, 229, 238
pre-1957, 81–2

driving culture
'bad drivers are other drivers' 21–2, 181–2
masculinity 1–4, 14, 16, 23, 26, 55, 87–8, 264, 272
normative 1–5, 7–9, 14–16, 23, 26, 73–4, 263–5
driving 'Other' 7, 181–2, 191–3, 222, 232, 248, 265, 269, 270
Dunbar, Nate 233–4

English v The Queen (1995) 164
European Federation of Road Traffic Victims (FEVR) 6
extraordinary licences 60–2, 194, 205–6, 237–8, 258, 268

failure to modify driving in accordance with circumstances 52, 65, 107, 109, 111, 113–20, 122–5, 127–8, 264–5
fatality statistics
as normalising 8–11, 177
by age and gender 9
global 9–10
Australia 8–9, 11, 39, 263
Western Australia 39, 49
fatigue and sleep 65–6, 75, 100–2, 118–19, 135, 192, 194–5, 235, 244–5, 252, 264
felony murder 180, 184, 186
First International Symposium on Accident and Traffic Medicine, Rome, 1963, 94
Fogarty, Antony 228, 260
Fox, Darrin 198–9, 202, 228

gender
female testimony, contempt of 65
imbalance on juries 26
male overrepresentation in fatality statistics 9
vehicular homicide as male crime 9–10, 26, 46, 55, 167, 265
see also driving culture: masculinity
Goiran, Nick (Nicholas Pierre), MP 240–2, 247
Grand Rapids Study 94–5

Harvey, Liza Mary, Minister for Police & Road Safety 239–43, 246–7
hit-and-run offences 20, 48, 70, 90–1, 104, 110–18, 153–4, 156, 159, 172–4, 183–4, 187–90, 198–9

445

INDEX

Hope, Alastair Neil, Coroner 244–8
Houghton, Leigh 180

intention 10–16, 19, 22–4, 48, 54–5, 73, 186, 220, 264
International Covenant on Civil and Political Rights 180

Jackson, Hal, President of Children's Court 179–80
Jess' law, *see Road Traffic Amendment (Dangerous Driving) Act 2004*
Jiminez v R (1992) 135
Johnson, Rob (Robert) Frank, MP 221, 240–1, 247
Johnston, Bill (William) Joseph, MP 240–1
juvenile crime 'wave' 178–82

Kay v The Queen (2004) 198–202
'killed/killing', *see* terminology
Kyd, Sally 14–15, 249–50
Kyd-Cunningham, Sally, *see* Kyd, Sally

Laporte v R [1970] 161–6, 176–7, 182–3, 188, 268
Law Reform Commission of Victoria (now Victorian Law Reform Commission) 8, 12, 131
Law Reform Commission of Western Australia 8, 34, 38–9, 129, 138–40, 146, 186, 216
Law Society of Western Australia 140–1, 208

manslaughter
 by criminal negligence
  acquittal rates (vehicular) pre-1945, 20, 29, 44
  Andrews v Director of Public Prosecutions [1937] 28–9
  Bateman test 27–9, 33
  conflation with recklessness 11, 27–9
  objective test 24, 26–8, 133, 136, 265
  within hierarchy of fault 11–12, 29
  diluting nomenclature of the conduct 139, 160–2, 222, 248, 266–8
  distinct from civil negligence 26–8
  duty of persons in charge of dangerous things 25–7, 29, 31, 33–5, 51, 63, 72, 79, 81, 107, 109–10, 122–3, 132, 142, 185, 189

estimate of charges laid, 1946–1974, 38, 44–6
penalty provisions 18, 19, 31, 35–8, 46, 53, 63, 137, 148, 224–5
recklessness not an element of the offence 27–9
see also Callaghan v R (1952)
intentional versus unintentional 24
McBride v R (1966) 142–4, 152, 213
McClurg, Andrew 66
McGinty, Jim (James) Andrew, Attorney General 202, 204, 207–11, 214, 224
McGowan, Mark, MP and Premier 6, 219, 256–7
McKenna v The Queen (1992) 164, 184–90, 195–6, 228
medical profession, lobbying 12–14, 23, 76–8, 87, 94–6
Meehan, Jess 203–7, 210–11
Meehan, Peter and Cheryl 205, 207–9
Mischin, Michael, Attorney General and Shadow Attorney General, 243, 260–1, 273
Moloney, Cathie 244, 247
multiple fatalities, approaches to 45, 60–1, 164, 167, 172–7, 190–1, 198–202, 234–6, 258–60, 269
multiple harms, *see* multiple fatalities, approaches to
murder 11–12, 24, 217, 275, *see also* felony murder

natural justice 62–3, 86–7, *see also* sentences: mitigating factors: death of friend/passenger
negligent driving causing death
 appeal to the High Court, *see Callaghan v R* (1952)
 comparable offences in other jurisdictions 18, 31, 38
 discrepancies in definition 30–1
 duty of persons in charge of dangerous things 25–7, 29–31, 33–5, 51, 63, 72, 81, 107, 109, 122–3
 guilty pleas 46, 90–1, 110, 118
 introduction of 7–8, 17–20, 24, 29–30, 46, 266
 number of charges laid 38, 43, 45
 penalty provisions 18, 24, 29–31, 35–8, 46, 53, 63, 137, 148
 repeal 38–9, 42, 129

INDEX

Numan, Gary, 'Cars' 5, 274

observed sequence of erratic conduct, requirement of 51–2, 72–3, 79, 107, 109, 111, 113–18, 128, 144, 163–4, 171, 203–4, 206–7, 210–11, 222, 243
O'Connell, Sean 172

passengers as uncooperative witnesses 65–6, 80, 100, 102, 218–19
Pearson, Alva Thomas, Dr 75, 84, 86
pedestrians, *see* vulnerable road users
Pemberton, Charlotte 6, 256, 271
Pemberton, Wayne and Jackie 6, 256–8, 271
Penny v Western Australia (2006) 228
Phillips v Carbone (No 2) (1992) 200
police
    abuse of by drivers 92
    crash investigations
        coronial criticisms of 244–7
        units responsible for 12, 43–4, 216–17, 245–6
    high-speed chases 178, 180–1, 184, 186–90, 192, 248, 269
    review, careless driving causing death (2018) 250–1
    submission to Standing Committee on Legislation (2004) 206–7
Porter, Charles Christian, Attorney General 221, 224–5
Prior, John 215–18
Punch v The Queen (1993) 182, 188–90, 195, 228

Quigley, John Robert, Attorney General, 234, 240–1, 247

Rally for Justice 178–82
'real crime', *see* terminology
reasonable driver 17, 25–8, 109–10, 136
    problems with benchmark 26, 52, 94, 265–6
recidivism 58–60, 70, 87, 91, 105, 140–1, 164–6, 168, 172–4, 180, 184, 186–9, 191–2, 198–9, 203–6, 232, 234–6, 268–9
recklessness
    as species of fault 11–12, 24, 26–9, 132–3
    inappropriate use of term 12, 27–29
    status in relation to intention 12

remission of sentences, policy 47–8, 198, 201–2
risk 3, 7–8, 13–14, 23–9, 51–2, 54, 74, 80–1, 128, 142, 222, 240, 255, 264, 266, 272
'road death' 10, 15, 160
RoadPeace 177
road safety
    as public health versus legal issue 13–14
    campaigns 2, 10–11, 20–3, 49, 76–7, 268
    criticisms of 13–14
    undermined by driving subculture 1–5, 13–14
'road toll' 4, 5, 9–11, 16, 20–2, 64, 66, 171, 177, 181, 265–6
Road Traffic Amendment (Dangerous Driving) Act 2004 (Jess' law) 94, 118, 203–4, 208, 223–4, 269
    failure to review (as condition of Bill's passage) 221, 238, 240
    see also dangerous driving causing death
Road Traffic Authority 130
Road Traffic Legislation Amendment Act 2016 239–242
Roberts, Michelle Hopkins, Minister for Police & Road Safety 6, 238, 251, 256–7, 259–60
Rodriguez, 'Pat', Coroner 32, 43
Royal Automobile Club of Western Australia (RAC) 12, 20, 76–7, 224–5
R v Coventry (1938) 142–3, 152
R v Evans [1963] 144
R v Guilfoyle [1973] 163–4, 173, 194–5
R v Stebbings (1990) 174–7, 194–5, 268–9
R v Wilkins (1988) 201

Sattler, Howard 178–9, 182
sentences
    careless driving causing death 249–53
    dangerous driving causing death 180–3, 248, 270
    aggravating circumstances 137, 180–1, 215, 222, 225–35, 248–9, 258–61, 267, 269–71, 273
    non-aggravating circumstances 141, 146, 149–60, 163–4, 166–7, 172–3, 192–4, 196–8, 224, 235–8, 254, 256–7
    discord between rhetoric and penalties imposed 46–9, 53–4, 58, 64–5, 110–18, 161–2, 166–7, 169, 271–4

INDEX

fines 49, 58, 61, 90–1, 118, 137, 150–62, 166–9, 172–4, 193–4, 224, 250–3, 266–8, 270, 272–3
manslaughter, 1946–1975, 28–49, 265–6, 328–50
maximum penalties imposed over time 47–8, 62, 148, 161–6, 174–7, 184, 186–91, 198–202, 228, 232, 260, 265, 268–9
mitigating factors
   death of friend/passenger 60–1, 63–5, 80–1, 151–2, 155, 192, 235–6, 254
   youth 52–8, 60–1, 65, 69–72, 90–1, 164–5, 167–9, 174–7, 182–6, 194–5, 265, 268–9
multiple fatalities 45, 60–1, 164, 167, 172–7, 190–1, 198–202, 234–6, 258–60, 269
negligent driving causing death 1946–1975, 45–9, 265, 267, 328–50
non-vehicular manslaughter 1946–1974, 47–8
other non-custodial penalties 49, 58, 60, 63, 65, 80, 82–3, 110–12, 155–9, 192–3
vehicle theft 49, 160, 197–8, 202
Sentencing Administration Act 1995 (WA) 198
Sentencing Advisory Council, Tasmania 6–7, 263
Sentencing Legislation Amendment and Repeal Act 2003 (WA) 198
Smith v The Queen [1976] 141–4, 150–2, 163–4, 211
stolen vehicles, *see* vehicle theft
Supreme Court jurisdiction and restricted access files xiii, 41

Tannin, George, SC 209, 213–14, 216–17, 219–20
Taylor, Joanna 252–4
Taylor, Jeanette and Ken 253
terminology
   'accidents' 1, 4–5, 10–13, 15–16, 22–6, 29, 44, 52, 54–5, 65, 70–4, 109, 119, 132, 150–1, 177, 220, 264–5, 272
   'killed/killing' 9–11, 15–16, 18, 69, 71–2
   'real crime' 7, 14, 140, 193, 264, 270

'road death' 10, 15, 160
'road toll' 4, 5, 9–11, 16, 20–2, 64, 66, 171, 177, 181, 265–6
see also agency, human
The Queen v S (No 2) (A CHILD) (1992) 164, 183–4, 186, 188–9
Tittums, Amiel James 258–60
Transport Accident Commission (Victoria) 2, 11

United Kingdom Crown Prosecution Service 62
United Kingdom House of Commons Transport Committee 250
United Nations Convention on the Rights of the Child 180
unlawful common purpose 145, 167–9

vehicle theft 49, 160, 197–8, 202
Victorian Law Reform Commission, *see* Law Reform Commission of Victoria
vulnerable road users 8–9, 53, 109–13, 127–8, 264
   cyclists 9, 55, 75, 79, 92, 109–13, 119, 123–8, 153–4, 187, 193, 203–5, 232
   pedestrians 9, 31–4, 53–5, 79, 90, 109–23, 127–8, 149–50, 153, 159, 218–19, 232, 244–6

Walsh, Mitchell William Donald, *see* Walsh-McDonald, Mitchell
Walsh-McDonald, Mitchell 203–7, 209, 217
Ward, Andrew, Senior Constable 1, 4–5, 7
Waters, Melissa Ann 233–4, 253–4, 271
Wells, Celia 29
Western Australia v Butler [2009] 226–30
Western Australia v Mitchell [2008] 226–8
Western Australian Bar Association 247
Wilson, Richard, Margaret and Neville 178–9
witnesses, *see* absence of eyewitness; drink-driving: requiring eyewitness corroboration; passengers as uncooperative witnesses
Wood v The Queen (2002) 194–5
World Health Organization 6, 9–10, 12–13

year and a day rule 134
Yeo, Stanley 12, 29

www.ingramcontent.com/pod-product-compliance
Lightning Source LLC
Chambersburg PA
CBHW021138160426
43194CB00007B/618